D0944065

I strove with none, for none was worth my strife.
Nature I loved and, next to nature, art.
I warmed my hands before the fire of life;
It sinks, and I am ready to depart.

WALTER SAVAGE LANDOR, 1850.

NEXT TO NATURE

LANDSCAPE PAINTINGS FROM
THE NATIONAL ACADEMY OF DESIGN

FOREWORD BY JOHN DOBKIN

INTRODUCTION BY BARBARA NOVAK

EDITED BY BARBARA NOVAK AND ANNETTE BLAUGRUND

HARPER & ROW, PUBLISHERS, NEW YORK
NATIONAL ACADEMY OF DESIGN, NEW YORK

This exhibition was organized by the National Academy of Design and the American Federation of the Arts. Both the exhibition and the publication have been made possible by grants from the National Endowment for the Arts and the New York State Council on the Arts.

CONTENTS

FOREWORD

The National Academy of Design, an honorary arts society of painters, sculptors, graphic artists, and architects, imposes only one obligation on its members. At the time of election an Associate must present to the National Academy a self-portrait or one executed by a colleague, and when the Associate becomes an Academician, he must present an example of his work.

This requirement, instituted in 1839, and in force today, has had the predictable result of creating, year after year, an ever-expanding collection of American art. This collection is a large one, consisting of more than 2,250 paintings, 600 sculptures, drawings, architects' portfolios, graphics. It is also very personal. Each work was selected by the artist, and the process of selection was always taken very seriously, according to correspondence in the Academy's archives.

NEXT TO NATURE is drawn solely from the Academy's collection of landscape paintings. The reasons for this are several. The collection, although rich, is not well known, and many of the paintings, although very important, have never been exhibited or published. Furthermore, the public is not fully aware of the role that the Academy has played in the instruction of artists and in the exhibition of their work. These paintings, therefore, supported by an extraordinary archive and nineteenth-century art library, offer a view of 150 years of the American landscape tradition, seen within the context of one of the great forces in American art, the National Academy of Design.

The exhibition has been organized by Barbara Novak, Professor of Art History at Barnard College and at the Department of Art History and Archaeology, Graduate School of Arts and Sciences, Columbia University, and her Columbia graduate seminar students, who met weekly at the Academy during the spring of 1980.

The students, under Miss Novak's direction, participated in each phase of the exhibition, from the preliminary culling to the preparation of the catalogue entries. The names of these students are listed below, and their initials appear as signatures to those entries for which they are responsible. Special thanks go to Annette Blaugrund who from the earliest stages assisted Barbara Novak in conducting the activities of the seminar, particularly in the organization and editing of the catalogue.

Kevin Avery	Kate Nearpass
Carey Bartram	Helen Raye
Annette Blaugrund	Janet Rosenthal
Cheryl Cibulka	Sally G. Shafto
Lewis Kachur	Susan M. Sivard
Kathie Manthorne	

Working alongside the Columbia scholars has been Barbara S. Krulik of the Academy staff, who unraveled many mysteries and unlocked many doors during the different phases of the exhibition.

Other participants deserving thanks and special mention are Noel Kunz, conservation consultant, Robert Fieux and Paul Himmelstein, conservators of the paintings, Steven Schoenfelder, designer, Elaine Andrews, copy editor, David Allison, photographer, and the American Federation of Arts, partners in the exhibition and the organizers of the tour.

John H. Dobkin
Director

Introduction

[The art historian] *knows* that his cultural equipment, such as it is, would not be in harmony with that of people in another land and of a different period. He tries, therefore, to make adjustments by learning as much as he possibly can of the circumstances under which the objects of his studies were created. Not only will he collect and verify all the available factual information as to medium, condition, age, authorship, destination, etc. but he will also compare the work with others of its class, and will examine such writings as reflect the aesthetic standards of its country and age, in order to achieve a more "objective" appraisal of its quality.

Erwin Panofsky, "Art History as a Humanistic Discipline."[1]

. . . the history of art is not secondarily but absolutely primarily a history of decoration. All artistic beholding is bound to certain decorative schemas or—to repeat the expression—the visible world is crystallized for the eye in certain forms. In each new crystal form, however, a new facet of the content of the world will come to light.

Heinrich Wölfflin, *Principles of Art History.*[2]

Unless he is an annalist or a chronicler the historian communicates a pattern which was invisible to his subjects when they lived it, and unknown to his contemporaries before he detected it.

George Kubler, *The Shape of Time.*[3]

Much of our art history has a peculiarly schizoid character. It is grounded either in Wölfflinian formalism or in iconography—the second stage of Panofsky's famous methodology. It would seem as if the basic issues of form and subject had been organized into two armies. Roaming over the surface of the picture plane, they send back different reports to headquarters. An easy parody of this situation, in which we have all at one time or another found ourselves, does not advance matters. Remedies are proposed. Panofsky's iconological third stage is invoked, but matters remain much the same. This is not the place to investigate why this is so, though it is an interesting issue in itself.

This exhibition and catalogue represent an attempt to take a body of paintings and documentation and see if the matter can be approached usefully on at least one occasion. Can the leap be made from formalism and iconography to that iconological synthesis where intuition is organized in the larger context that many of us, along with Panofsky, frequently call for? How difficult it is to do so! It demands that a stringent eye, an indefatigable mind, and a contextual humanism intersect at the point where an exhibition is generated and then carried through.

This exhibition of landscape paintings from the collection of the National Academy of Design, selected and organized by a group (with, admittedly, a "leader"), attempts to use each pole of the art historical dichotomy to maximum advantage. The paintings, taken along with their documentation, will, I hope, reconcile these extremes so unnaturally separated by our methodologies and push further into the arena of iconology. Choices have been made through group connoisseurship—a "group eye," relying heavily on formalist tools and making formalist judgments. Connoisseurship has been firmly grounded therefore in certain universals we believe will hold—consideration of the painter's reconciliation of the problems of painting: space and surface, line, color, form, texture, stroke or touch, light and dark, design or structure.

Such judgments encouraged a healthy self-consciousness about our tools for judging quality. Insofar as connoisseurship is a matter of ranking works, it makes of quality a somewhat limited entity. Connoisseurship is elitism at its best, and can perhaps be accused of neglecting social context. It may well be that our present conception of quality and connoisseurship, based largely on the formalist training many of us have received, is by definition locked into modernist assumptions, and just as vulnerable to criticism as anything else.

Is our conception of quality and connoisseurship a "period" one—coinciding with the rise and fall of modernism? Are our formalist judgments vulnerable because they are time-bound to modernist assumptions? Beyond this, how much do originality and invention really matter? A test case is, of course, the delayed masterpiece proposition. Can a remarkable painting by an artist continuing a style practiced at its peak twenty years earlier still be a great painting? Has that artist in George Kubler's astute insight, simply made "a bad entrance"?[4] Are our judgments of quality conditioned by our modernist impatience, by our preference for the newly invented solution? How, indeed, do we really define quality, and what is the genuine nature of connoisseurship? It seems to me that any ultimate definition of connoisseurship that does not encourage that elusive fluent congruity of formal judgment, iconographical erudition, and contextual grace is limited. This is a lot to ask for, but we should ask for it. At this point, of course, our systems dissolve into the insights, imagination, and strategies of the trained interpreter.

In the course of exercising our connoisseurship, it also became clear that formal judgments can only go so far. What are we to do with the painting that has no formal problems, in which perfect formal reconciliation has been achieved, but still lacks "something"? Is the art historian, using professional tools to make "objective" connoisseur's judgments, ready to admit that there is yet another factor that signals quality in art? Does this "unnameable something" have to do with the "person" behind the work, with the character, spirit, entire lifetime signaled by that work? And how is one to discuss it? Does this make us reexamine the degree to which our tools fail to find purchase on this problem? These questions arose during the seminar that resulted in this exhibition; they cannot be fully answered in this context.

Allied to the question of the displaced masterwork, and to iconology, is that aspect of revisionism that concerns itself with restoring the entire context of a period. As we ask more questions of our formal and iconographical tools, we are aware that a restoration of context is a preliminary to revising our aesthetic judgments by broadening their base. This has now become a common activity in a variety of art historical fields. The revisionist impulse is laudable. But its benefits and fallacies are much confused. In our exhibition, the revisionist question came down to the following: Were we to include paintings much admired in their own time, which our contemporary connoisseurship judged inferior in quality? For all our questions about the nature of that connoisseurship, it still seemed to us the best tool we have.

Was filling a historical gap sufficient reason for including a work that the "group eye" had rejected on qualitative grounds? As well as making us confront the organized fiction we agree to call history, this made us confront the nature of an exhibition. Historical didacticism is only one of several reasons for arranging works of art and hanging them on a wall. Since we had limited our universe to works in the collection of the Academy, we decided to dispense with the idea of historical revisionism where it was not supported by the quality of the work itself. Where our standards permitted, however, we tried to guide into the historical continuum works and artists deserving, in our opinion, of more notice than they have yet received. Thus we did, I suppose, take an implicit position: that the only element that can revise a period's *gestalt* is the introduction of newly perceived and discovered works of quality. The unedited cross-section of works of a given period is a necessary occasional exercise. It tests our opinions, to some degree challenges our assumptions, and often ends up confirming them. Sometimes we come to the conclusion that if some of the past is lost or ignored, there may well be reason for it. Yet despite this, perhaps in no field is more of the past being discovered, and more worthwhile discoveries being made, than in the field of American painting.

An exhibition, like any well-conceived venture, can have its parts very much of a piece with one another. To that extent, it can I suppose be itself a work of art. The great unifier is quality. Within this, certain groupings of forms will hang together better than others. This hanging is, again, dictated by the "rightness" of certain formal clusters. So formalism to a large extent controls quality, connoisseurship, even arrangement itself. This decorative principle, in a Wölfflinian sense, comes into play in the hanging process. Modes of hanging have, of course, their own fashions, which help us read the assumptions of those who arrange pictures in an exhibition. Our hanging will, I am sure, reveal the still prevailing formal bias of our own period.

II.

As in all art historical investigations, the paintings are, of course, our primary sources. From them, we can read a great deal about contemporary attitudes to nature and to art—using a mix of formalist tools and iconographic categorization that we ourselves can hardly disentangle. Categories are, of course, common to both formal and iconographic insights. Confronted with any body of data, the mind seems to need to organize, to define like and unlike, to compare and contrast. Applying this taxonomic urge to these landscape paintings, it is relatively easy to break down the pre-Civil War views into those that derive from Claude, a larger group of a less specific pastoral nature, some pragmatic "happened-upon" landscapes (the most imposing of which is Kensett's *Bash Bish Falls*), and a larger number of horizontal, often marine, views that sometimes fall into the category of luminism, with its connotations of the panoramic and the Dutch. This is a fairly standard cross-section of mid nineteenth-century categories, ranging from the more predictable "salon" type, through the freshly observed view, to the luminist contribution.

We do not, however, encounter as much "wilderness" here as expected. Most of these landscapes are, in some way, acculturated. Is this absent "wilder image" due to the artist's activity on what we could then, as now, refer to as the "New York Scene"? Many of these same artists painted wilderness at one time or another. But subtle processes of acculturation, perhaps even an inclination toward "cultivated" landscape, may have occurred through contact with the Academy, to which many of these paintings were offered as diploma pictures. From the record of this exhibition, however, it is very clear that when not painting in their New York studios, showing at the Academy, using the library, or serving as instructors, these artists traveled widely. The landscape sites depicted range from Bash Bish Falls, Cohasset, Marblehead, Long Island, Narragansett, North Conway, and the Sierras to Rome, Capri, Nemi, the Andes, Central America, and Bowditch Island, near Fiji. The geographical span covered by these works underscores the traveling impulse to partake of what both Whitman and Tuckerman defined as the "zest" of adventure.[5] Embodied here is the restless urge to conquer with the brush, the spirit of curiosity and exploration, the need to encounter God's virgin creation in nature, and the humbler, less grandiose intention simply to paint landscape with what Cole called a "loving eye."

In all these paintings, the evidence offered by that "loving eye" is underwritten by certain "givens"—the way nature was seen and approached in that earlier century when it still existed intact. For Cole even then: "The spirit of our society is to contrive but not to enjoy—toiling to product more toil—accumulating in order to aggrandize. The pleasures of the imagination, among which the love of scenery holds a conspicuous place, will alone temper the harshness of such a state; and, like the atmosphere that softens the most rugged forms of the landscape, cast a veil of tender beauty over the asperities of life."[6]

Cole's nature viewer, "cannot move from his dwelling without the salutation of beauty; even in the city the deep blue sky and the drifting clouds appeal to him."[7] Nature's spiritualizing and cultivating energy was recognized just as the cities were beginning to replace it. Those landscapes so intensely examined by a rapt public in illustrations of Academy exhibitions were capturing bits of a waning nature between the edges of their canvases and hanging them in the Academy with ecological haste. Though country dwellers were generally believed to be more in tune with landscape painting than city dwellers, these latter would be given their chance. The "loving eye" was the great equalizer. The viewer could respond to a nature that was spiritually endowed—that was, at the extreme, the Transcendentalist's God in nature, and at the very least, the product of a concept of providential design that remained unchallenged until the publication in 1859 of Darwin's *The Origin of the Species*.

The viewer could read the light in these pre-Civil War paintings as God's light, could fortify these ideas with readings in Emerson, who saw light as "the first of painters, as the reappearance of the original soul," and the sky as "the daily bread of the eyes."[8] He or she could add to this, as did the painters who so admired him, Ruskin's democratic observation that "the sky is for all; bright as it is, it is not 'too bright, nor good, for human nature's daily food'; it is fitted in all its functions for the perpetual comfort and exalting of the heart . . . almost human in its passions, almost spiritual in its tenderness, almost divine in its infinity, its appeal to what is immortal in us, is as distinct, as its ministry of chastisement or of blessing to what is mortal is essential."[9]

In these paintings, the loving eye could also discern other contemporary and philosophical preoccupations. It could draw close to Church's tangled tropical vegetation, as in *Scene on the Magdalene*, to discern in each separate, lovingly delineated leaf the artistic intention that prompted Tuckerman to write in *Book of the Artists* (1867) of Church's *Heart of the Andes* that he found here "a great lesson for our artists. They here see for themselves how essential to success it is that they should know how to do

what they aim at—to imitate nature in detail, as well as in general effects, to obtain a mastery of perspective, to elaborate correctly the flower and leaf, and at the same time, be equally expert in the management of distance and light."[10]

Such criticism implicitly called for a reconciliation of the Real and the Ideal that also occupied the early nineteenth century in Europe. It lent itself to endless permutations, all of which can be witnessed in the present exhibition. The dictum of detail and effect, of particulate realism suffused by general effects of light and atmosphere, was adhered to not only by some members of the Hudson River group, but by the luminist artists as well. Tuckerman's idea of "general effect" could perhaps be extended even to what he called the "manner and method of Nature."[11] This related to his colleague Jarves's "general principle," and to the great Humboldt's discussion in *Cosmos* about the distinction between "him whose task it is to collect the individual details of various observations, and study the mutual relations existing among them, and him to whom these relations are to be revealed, under the form of general results . . ."[12]

The scientific curiosity about a unified world that inspired Humboldt drew both Church and Darwin to South America. Darwin's experience set in motion those consequences that profoundly altered the nature of landscape painting, especially in America, after the publication of *Origin*. God in nature had fled; cities were replacing the trees and fields. What kind of landscape painting was possible?

Fortunately for the continued survival of landscape painting, the loss of God in nature coincided with a partial relinquishment of the American need for an indigenous artistic identity. European travel and contact brought Barbizon, Impressionism, Post-Impressionism, and modernism into American landscape history. God was replaced, in a sense, by "style," but a more limited Nature survived. Here we might talk, to some extent, of a *secular* rather than *divine* landscape.

Many of the paintings in this exhibition are, as noted earlier, diploma pictures. Thus considering these works involves us with the nature of the Academy itself, its similarity to and uniqueness from other such institutions in the western world, its special attitude to the landscape artist, and the implications of the situation of the landscape artist within the Academy.

A recent study of the Academy observes that through the 1860s landscapes and portraits were the most popular categories in the annual exhibitions and notes: "The large proportion of portraits and landscapes to figure subjects is evidence of the American departure from the accepted principles of the academic tradition. The divergence would be even more pronounced if one were to take into consideration the fact that many of the figure paintings were scenes of common life rather than subjects of loftier origin."[13]

As members of the Academy, the landscape artists were in a

unique position. They exhibited at and participated in the activities of an institution committed, as Academies traditionally were (and are), to the classic and humanist concern with the human form. As good Academicians, they attended the Antique and Life classes. Yet given the moral significance of nature in nineteenth-century America, it is not difficult to understand the smooth transfer of the didactic and moral purposes of the Academy to the category of landscape painting itself. Much of this can be read from the paintings. But our understanding of the works profits from the contextual background, the iconological framework fortuitously provided by the Academy archives.

III.

He who teaches innocent people to understand art without bothering about classical languages, boresome historical methods and dusty old documents, deprives naïveté of its charm without corjcting its errors.
Erwin Panofsky, "Art History as a Humanistic Discipline."[14]

In the collection of the Academy is a small, red leather-bound notebook that belonged to Samuel F.B. Morse, founder and first president of the Academy, entitled "Hints and Remarks on Painting and the Fine Arts generally & also more particularly with reference to a Series of Lectures on the Fine Arts," dated August, 1823.[15] This tiny document in Morse's hand is written in both pencil and pen, and somehow, the more ephemeral penciled passages have a special poignancy. When I opened the notebook to examine it, several loose scraps of paper fell to the floor. Recovering them, I saw that they were references to books and articles: "History of the several Italian Schools of Painting with Observations on the present state of the Art. Blackwoods Mag April. 1820, price 26/" and "An Inquiry into the Early Histy of Engraving on Copper and Wood with numerous facsimilies by W.J. Oaley F.S.A. 2 Vols. 8 #(?)8s" among others. They were addenda to a list of *Books to be consulted on the Arts*, which included references not only to Pliny, Quintilian, Plutarch, Plato, Aristotle, Cicero, but also "'Outlines of a Philosophy of the History of Man' by J.G. Herder. 4,t° (see Fuseli p. 5)," evidently recommended by Fuseli.[16]

The material itself is invaluable. From this page and its small addenda we learn a bit more about the elusive problems of schooling, study, and sources in early nineteenth-century America. The Italian references include others on "Italy & its inhabitants in 1816-17, Manners customs &c. Fine Arts &c, by James A. Galiffe of Geneva 2 Vols 8.00" and "Histy of the Italian Schools by T. James M.A. 9/6 8 vo."[17] They are of course a reminder of Morse's continued fascination with and visits to Italy. The classical references reinforce our knowledge of the importance of classical culture to our artists from the late eighteenth century on; they are

thoroughly appropriate to the aims of the Academy. But the reference to Herder at this early date, and even its conduit presumably via Fuseli, is still more fascinating. It touches on all the still unanswered questions about American artists' relations to German philosophy of this period. We have been aware for some time of the Transcendentalists' interest. Emerson borrowed Herder's *Outline of History of Men* (1800 ed.) from the Harvard College Library in 1829, and again, from the Boston Athenaeum in 1831.[18] Morse's note is one of the few certified expressions of interest on the part of the artists.

But my thoughts on holding these bits of paper went far beyond these realizations. I felt that I was making immediate contact with the afterthoughts of a great figure in history—who had become present to me by the simple act of tucking a bit of paper between the pages of a book more than a hundred and fifty years before. This casual immediacy is what is most valuable about the archival collections of the Academy. The materials deposited here make the artists—their minds and thoughts, their intellectual preoccupations, their social and political concourse on a day to day basis—real to us. The materials offer generous opportunities for research: registers containing nominations for membership, often with supporting voters listed by name and signature, with the local addresses of artist candidates listed in some years, with the names of those artists who were refused—as well as those accepted. A register of students in the Antique and Life classes tells us which artists were classmates in certain years.[19] A scrapbook of 1898-1902 includes rules for exhibitions, announcements of meetings, nomi-blanks, social announcements, exhibition tickets, student certificates (like our present IDs), season (family) tickets, stationery, annual dinner invitations, varnishing-day admission tickets, invitations to private viewings, and prizes, including one "For the best picture in the U.S. by a *woman*, without limitations of age."[20]

An 1852 "Schedule of Property belonging to the National Academy of Design," taken in August of that year, tells us which books were in the Academy library by that time.[21] Another document indicates which of these, along with a group of prints (including—naturally—works by Poussin and Claude) were purchased from J.G. Chapman in 1848.[22] A library register from 1862-1929 records which books the artists signed out, and for how long.[23] The Academy minutes have been carefully preserved, as have a full range of catalogues offering contemporary comment. They offer much more information than do the more recent anthologized listings of Academy exhibitions. The artist and exhibition files are filled with contemporary clippings.

The records are, unfortunately erratic. Perhaps an earlier library register will surface, or another nominations ledger, allowing us to fill in the data on some missing years.[24] But even the exploration of what is presently locatable resembles nothing so much as an archaeological dig. With each new chunk of material, bits and pieces of living history fall into place, and the strands of information add more lucidity to the hazed sketch we have of earlier periods.

We are left, for example, with a clear sense of the Academy as the focus of the New York art world, as the center of the "scene," so to speak, in the nineteenth century. We are even left with the realization that the present location of the New York art scene in the downtown area around SoHo had its nineteenth-century prototype: the students in the 1864 Life class listed addresses at 442 Broadway, 596 Broadway, 129 McDougal St., 224 Thompson St. Winslow Homer, whose large, firm signature is on this page, lists his address at N.Y. University, as does Eugene Benson, who signed his name directly beneath.[25] In the listing of 1843-44 for the Antique class, we find 66 Eldridge St., 141 and 389 Grand St., and M.J. Heed [sic](1844) at 82 Duane St.[26]

Heade was nominated but not elected by the Academy in 1868—interesting when we consider his close friendship with Church (a member of the Academy since 1848, an Academician in 1849) and his frequent residency at 15 Tenth Street. That address housed so many Academicians over the years that it must have been the political nexus of the artists' relationships.[27] This leads us to wonder whether Heade's horizontal luminist paintings were, indeed, acceptable to artists who were working more directly within the Hudson River mode. The Nominations Register for 1859, for example, lists the first-time nomination and election of "T.H. Hotchkiss, Landscape Pt.," who gives his address as "15 10th."[28] Thomas H. Hotchkiss, one of the finest landscape painters of the nineteenth century, is still virtually unknown, while Heade, of course, has become a major figure. Hotchkiss had been a protégé of Asher B. Durand, and shortly after his election to the Academy left for Europe, where he died of tuberculosis in 1869. While in America, Hotchkiss produced works that fell more readily into the Hudson River category, adapting a luminist structure for his later canvases probably out of the pragmatic experience of the flat Roman campagna.[29]

We still know little about Hotchkiss's biography and career. This new fragment of information about his brief residency at 15 Tenth Street in 1859 raises the possibility of his contact not only with Gifford, who was a very close friend, but with Shattuck, Church, Gignoux, Heade, Casilear, Haseltine, William Hart, Suydam, and Mignot, all of whom were in the Tenth Street Studio building at that time, and even possibly with Bierstadt and Whittredge, who arrived sometime in 1860.[30] So this one small reference opens up for Hotchkiss research a circle of artist contacts which can now be pursued. Hotchkiss must have been quite well known and well appreciated by the other artists to have been elected so quickly. Gifford was nominated several times for Academician before he was elected, and Jerome Thompson never managed to get past being an Associate.[31]

The Nominations Register also instructs us on which Europeans were valued enough to become Honorary Members. The nomi-nations for 1845 elected Charles E [sic] Eastlake, Painter London; Horace Vernet, Painter Paris; Paul Delaroche, Painter Paris. The following year, M. Le Vicomte de Kerckhove, President of the Archaeological Society of Belgium; M. Felix Bogaerts, Secretary of the A.A. of Belgium, and M.N. De Keyser, Treasurer of the A.A., as well as M. Chivalier De Kuyper, Sculptor to the King of Belgium, were elected. The Belgian contacts, especially, require some investigation, since to my knowledge most American scholars have been unaware of them.[32]

The Nominations Register for a few years from 1863 on lists individual sponsors' names for each candidate, so that we discover that Winslow Homer was sponsored for Associate on April 25, 1864, by Thomas Hicks, and by S.R. Gifford on May 10, 1865, for Academician.[33] To this picture of the artists forming a warm humanistic enclave within the Academy, and making choices that history has both accepted and disclaimed, we can add the image of the young Albert P. Ryder, historically reclusive, sitting in an unusually large Antique class in 1871-72, beside his longtime friend Julian A. Weir and about fifty-two others whose names, largely lost to history, included J.C. Beckwith, Maria R. Oakey (Mrs. Thomas Dewing), and H. [Helena] de Kay.[34]

We can also witness the artists taking favorite texts home from the Academy library. As early as 1848 the library had acquired from J.G. Chapman several perspective books: Thierenot's [sic Thenot's] Perspective, Arithmetical Perspective, and Jesuit's Perspective, which were probably useful to him in writing his own famous and much-used American Drawing Book (1847). The imposing volumes from the Chapman collection by Catlin on the American Indians, and by Stephens on travels in the Yucatán[36] would have fueled the strong adventure urges of those Academicians who listed themselves as landscape painters, including such figures as Church, Bierstadt, and Moran. Chapman owned, in addition, a volume of Düsseldorf Etchings, attesting to the early concern with German art.[37]

In the 1852 inventory, two volumes titled Dresden Gallery, 1836, and another listing of thirteen unbound numbers with the same title appear in the library.[38] The references to Dresden are even more provocative, for though scholars have long considered the matter of Düsseldorf contact and influence in the nineteenth century, they have rarely given sufficient credit to Dresden and the Friedrich circle, where the visual evidence, it seems to me, is even stronger for stylistic parallels than Düsseldorf.[39] So to know that by 1852 the Academicians and students could have been familiar in whatever way with Dresden is a considerable boost to those of us who feel the Dresden parallels deserve more scholarly attention.

The Dresden reference assumes even more significance in the light of recent interest in connections between American luminism and Russian nineteenth-century art,[40] for there is evidence that the Tsar's consul in Dresden during Friedrich's lifetime encouraged Russian patrons to acquire works by Friedrich. A group of Friedrich drawings in the Hermitage, and a painting by Friedrich recently acquired by the Hermitage from a private Russian collection testify to this taste for Friedrich in Russia.[41] Thus the idea of Friedrich as a key figure linking American luminist style (for which he is the closest European parallel) to the kind of luminist provincialism which has been noted in nineteenth-century Russian art becomes tenable. Indeed, since Friedrich's style shows so many parallels to American luminism, the idea of Friedrich as the European "disseminator" of attitudes similar to American luminism becomes even more tantalizing, though it would necessarily be coupled in Russia with the same provincial factors that link American luminism to other arts removed from the mainstream as far afield as South America and Australia in the nineteenth century.[42]

By 1852, the Academy library also contained, in addition to volumes on Constable and Turner, which would have been of special interest to the landscape painters, [43] a fairly large percentage of instruction books, fitting for an academy in which the school played such a large role. These included C.L. Eastlake, *Goethe's Theory of Colors*, London, 1840; J.D. Harding, *Elementary Art*, London 1844 and *Principles and Practices of Art*, London, 1845; C.W. Hackley, *Elementary Course of Geometry*, New York 1847; S. Prout, *Hints on Light and Shadow*, London, 1838; J. Burnett, *Painting in Four Parts*, London (undated); *Hints on Painting*, first part, New York, 1839, along with a duplicate copy; G. de Lairesse, *Art of Painting*, London, 1778; and *Principes du Dessin*, Amsterdam & Leipsick, 1746 (presented by J.F. Cooper). Theoretical books included H. Twining, *Elements of Picturesque*, London, 1844; Sir T.D. Lauder, Bart., *Sir Owendale* [sic Uvedale] *Price on the Picturesque*, London, 1842; John Burnett, *Sir Joshua Reynolds Discourses* with Notes and Plates, London, 1842; and L. Da Vinci, *Treatise of* [sic] *Painting*, Presented by J.F.E. Prud'homme, London, 1796.[44]

These last two are of special interest. For Samuel Morse had quoted Leonardo in his 1823 notebook: " 'When you have acquired the habit, and formed your hand to accuracy, *quickness of execution* will come of itself,' and again, 'Let him remember to acquire accuracy before he attempts quickness.' "[45] Morse opens his small book with an "Analysis" of Reynolds' *Discourses*, which begins, "His *first Discourse* treats of the advantages to be Derived from an Academy of Arts; offers hints for the consideration of the Professors & Visitors, recommends implicit obedience to the rules of Arts to the students, discourages premature facility, recommends diligence, and *that it should* be directed to its proper object," and then continues with a short, rather irritated criticism of Sir Joshua for not dealing sufficiently or adequately with "the Philosophy of the art," and for offering "observations . . . better adapted to the Student, than to the connoisseur." Morse hardly bothers to comment in any way after the fifth discourse, and stops

with the eighth. But then he opens a section on color in which he says, "Sir Joshua certainly underrates color, and it is surprising that one who loved it so well and practised it so long as he did, and one whose fame rests in so great measure on this excellence, should at least seem to place it so far below the first rank; it must arise from his not entering deeply into the philosophy of this part of his art, and so not perceiving its intellectual connections, or else he yields from courtesy to other excellences that which he knew he possessed himself in so great a Degree."[46]

Scholars have long known about the American painters' interest in Sir Joshua, dating back to West's relation to him, and Copley's advice to Henry Pelham in 1774 that he read the *Discourses*.[47] That Reynolds, both as artist and theorist, seems to have been of constant interest to American artists is indicated by the Library Register of the Academy from 1862 to 1929, in which the first entry indicates that Henry A. Loop took out Northcote's *Memoirs of Sir Joshua Reynolds* on November 10, and returned it on March 3, 1863.[48] On February 9, 1870, Samuel Colman took out "vol. one" of the works of Reynolds (probably from the three-volume set by E. Malone, London, 1793) and returned it on February 24, when he charged out volumes two and three, returning these on April 4 and charging out "Da Vinci on Painting."[49]

By far the most popular book in the Academy library seems to have been the Da Vinci. Inness took it out on April 8, 1868, R. Swain Gifford on March 12, 1869, David Johnson on January 5, 1872, and R. Swain Gifford again on January 12, returning to it once more on February 12, 1895.[50] The interest in Leonardo has not, to my knowledge, been known to scholars, or at the very least, has not been in any way stressed. What could they have gotten from him, and especially from the early edition that exists in the library?

Even the briefest sampling from this volume is instructive:

Chap. CLVII.—How to represent a Storm. To form a just idea of a storm, you must consider it attentively in its effects. When the wind blows violently over the sea or land, it removes and carries off with it every thing that is not firmly fixed to the general mass. The clouds must appear straggling and broken, carried according to the direction and the force of the wind, and blended with clouds of dust raised from the sandy shore. . . . Trees and grass must be bent to the ground, as if yielding to the course of the wind. . . . The high tremendous waves of the stormy sea will be covered with foaming froth; the most subtle parts of which, being raised by the wind, like a thick mist, mix with the air.

Chap. CCCI.—Of the Colour of Mountains. The darker the mountain is in itself, the bluer it will appear at a great distance. The highest part will be the darkest, as being more woody; because woods cover a great many shrubs, and other plants, which never receive any light. . . . Near the top of these mountains, where the air is thinner and purer, the darkness of the woods will make it appear of a deeper azure, than at the bottom, where the air is thicker.

Chap. CCVIII.—How to paint the distant Part of a Landscape. It is evident that the air is in some parts thicker and grosser than in others, particularly that nearest to the earth; and as it rises higher, it becomes thinner and more transparent. The objects which are high and large, from which you are at some distance, will be less apparent in the lower parts; because the visual ray which perceives them, passes through a long space of dense air; and it is easy to prove that the upper parts are seen by a line . . . so that a painter who has mountains to represent in a landscape, ought to observe, that from one hill to another, the tops will appear always clearer than the bases.

Chap. CCC.—Of the Colour of Objects remote from the Eye. The air tinges objects with its own colour more or less in proportion to the quantity of intervening air between it and the eye, so that a dark object at the distance of two miles (of a density of air equal to such distance), will be more tinged with its colour than if only one mile distant.

Chap. CCCXXXIV.—The Seasons are to be observed. In Autumn you will represent the objects according as it is more or less advanced. At the beginning of it the leaves of the oldest branches only begin to fade, more or less, however, according as the plant is situated in a fertile or barren country; . . . Endeavour to vary the colour of meadows, stones, trunks of trees, and all other objects, as much as possible, for Nature abounds in variety ad infinitum.

Chap. CCCXXXV.—The Difference of Climates to be observed. Near the sea-shore, and in southern parts, you will be careful not to represent the Winter season by the appearance of trees and fields, as you would do in places more inland, and in northern countries, except when these are covered with ever-greens, which shoot afresh all the year round.

Chap. CCCXXXII.—Of the Sun-beams passing through the openings of Clouds. The sun-beams which penetrate the openings interposed between clouds of various density and form, illuminate all the places over which they pass, and tinge with their own colour all the dark places that are behind: which dark places are only seen in the intervals between the rays.

Chap. CCCLXV.—That a Man ought not to trust himself, but ought to consult Nature. Whoever flatters himself that he can retain in his memory all the effects of Nature, is deceived, for our memory is not so capacious; therefore consult Nature for every thing.

This last entry, of course, says it all. For what Leonardo's advice offered to the landscape painters, and offered it even more pungently than the literal "how-to" advice, was the simple example of pragmatic observation. Leonardo, out of an arduous and relentless process of observation and pragmatic experience, arrived at observations about nature that are still pertinent today. The American landscapists could easily translate this into their own sensitivity to climate and seasons, to "on-the-spot" observation, to the landscape that transcends cliché through immediacy and spontaneity of experience.

It is abundantly evident, from these brief remarks, that the Academy archives and library offer extraordinary resources for the scholar of American art. Indeed, such scholars have been uniquely blessed by the conveniences of having primary textual material and documents close at hand. If American artists have often, especially in the late eighteenth and nineteenth centuries, felt deprived and distanced from the great masterpieces and traditions of Western Europe, American art historians who work in these great areas of scholarship have also been distanced—compelled to do "summer research" in the archives of England, France, Italy, Germany, and Greece and, with the exception of England, often compelled to cope with language problems when reading literature, philosophy, and theory in their fields of expertise.

Scholars of American art have few such problems, and no excuses, for ignoring the profound funds of corollary material that could lead them into what Panofsky has called "a history of cultural symptoms"; "The art historian will have to check what he thinks is the intrinsic meaning of the work, or group of works, to which he devotes his attention, against what he thinks is the intrinsic meaning of as many other documents of civilization historically related to that work or group of works, as he can master: of documents bearing witness to the political, poetical, religious, philosophical, and social tendencies of the personality, period or country under investigation."[51]

Barbara Novak

———————————

A special note of thanks is due to the dedicated group of Columbia University graduate students who worked so diligently to produce this catalogue. They have devoted time and energy far beyond the reasonable expectations for course work, and their commitment to original scholarship and to scholarly accuracy is evident in the product of their labors—truly a labor of love.

I am especially indebted to Annette Blaugrund, who co-edited this material with me and whose inspired tenacity brought this venture to its completion, to Barbara Krulik of the National Academy of Design, who covered the entire undertaking with the generous mantle of her cooperation, and to John Dobkin, whose open and imaginative approach to scholarship initiated this joint project.

B. N.

NOTES

1. Erwin Panofsky, "The History of Art as a Humanistic Discipline." In *Meaning in the Visual Arts* (Garden City, N.Y.: Doubleday Anchor, 1955) 17.
2. Heinrich Wölfflin, *Principles of Art History* (New York: Dover, 1932), 231.
3. George Kubler, *The Shape of Time* (New Haven: Yale University Press, 1965), 13.
4. *Ibid.*, 6-7.
5. See Walt Whitman, *Specimen Days* (1882; reprint Boston: David R. Godine, 1971), 89: "The element of danger adds zest to it all"; and Henry T. Tuckerman, *Book of the Artists*, (1867; reprint New York: James F. Carr, 1966), 389: "Adventure is an element in American artist-life which gives it singular zest and interest."
6. Thomas Cole, "Essay on American Scenery" (1835). In John McCoubrey, ed., *American Art 1700-1960, Sources and Documents in the History of Art Series* (Englewood Cliffs, N.J.: Prentice-Hall, 1965), 100-101.
7. *Ibid.*, 100.
8. Quoted in *Emerson: A Modern Anthology*, Alfred Kazin and Daniel Aaron eds. (Boston: Houghton Mifflin, 1958), 39 (from his journals, 1843).
9. John Ruskin, *Modern Painters*, vol. I (1843; reprint New York: John Wiley & Son, 1868), 202.
10. Tuckerman, *Book of the Artists*, 375. See also my discussion of general effect and detail in Barbara Novak, *Nature and Culture* (New York: Oxford University Press, 1980).
11. Tuckerman, *Book of the Artists*, 380.
12. Alexander von Humboldt, *Cosmos*, trans., E.C. Otté, 2 vols. (New York: Harper & Bros., 1850), 1:47.
13. Lois Marie Fink and Joshua C. Taylor, *Academy, The Academic Tradition in American Art*, An Exhibition Organized on the Occasion of the One Hundred and Fiftieth Anniversary of the National Academy of Design: 1825-1975 (Washington, D.C.: National Collection of Fine Arts, Smithsonian Institution Press, 1975), 40.
14. Panofsky, "The History of Art as a Humanistic Discipline," 19.
15. Samuel F.B. Morse Notebooks, 2 vols., vol. 1.*
16. *Ibid.*, 141. In volume 2, Morse records another list of Books to be Consulted which includes "Knight on taste, Barry's Lectures, Opie's Lectures, Reynolds' Lectures, Da Vinci on Painting, Stewart on the Mind, Mengs' Works, Alison on Taste, Hogarth's analysis of beauty, Burke on the Sublime & Beautiful, Fuseli's Lectures, Price on the Picturesque, P. Hoare on the Arts of Design." He also notes "See 67th No. Edin. review Aug 1820 for some excellent remarks on Painting."
17. Morse notebooks, vol. 1, insert.
18. See Stanley M. Vogel, *German Literary Influences on the American Transcendentalists* (New Haven: Yale University Press, 1955), 181, 177.
19. Register, "Schools of the National Academy of Design," 1 vol.*
20. Scrapbook 1898-1902, unpaged.*
21. *Schedule of Property Belonging to the National Academy*, Taken August 1st, 1852 (New York: Sackett & Co., 1852).* Pamphlet. Bound in "National Academy of Design Constitution and Schedule of the Property" (misc. pamphlets 1829-1903). In addition to books, the schedule of property lists furniture, costumes (wardrobe), books of records, prints and drawings, medals, paintings (including many oil portraits of members), and a large collection of statuary of classical subjects, including works by Canova, Thorwaldsen, and Gibson. Hereafter referred to as 1852 inventory. (Library inventories of 1888 and 1898 also exist.)
22. "Books, Prints, etc. bought of J.G. Chapman, 1848."* A still earlier document in the same folder is a "List of Properties, 1828" which consists of "Statues," "Masks," and "Torsos" of various Venuses, Dying Gladiators, and Adonises, etc.
23. Library Register.* The register includes the years from 1862 to 1897, breaks until 1906, and continues sporadically and briefly until 1929.
24. There are four Nominations Registers: "Nominations for Membership: 1840-1863"; "Nominations for Membership in the National Academy of Design, 1863-1887"; "Nominations for Associates, 1896-1900"; and "Nominations for Academicians, 1896-1900."*
25. Register, "Schools of the National Academy of Design."*
26. *Ibid.* Heade entered on January 15, 1844, listing himself as born Pennsylvania, Portrait Painter, age 24. Inness turns up in the same class earlier (October 28, 1843) and lists himself as age 19, "Pupil of Gignoux," with an address in the Granite Building. Casilear registered on November 6, 1843, with a residence at 191 Houston St.
27. I am grateful for information on the Tenth Street Studio to Annette Blaugrund, who offered a seminar paper (presently in progress as an article) on this subject, and whose dissertation on Tenth Street is also in progress under my supervision.
28. "Nominations for Membership," 1840-1863.*
29. See Barbara Novak O'Doherty, "Thomas H. Hotchkiss: An American in Italy," *Art Quarterly* 29, no. 1 (Spring 1966), 2-28.
30. Information Blaugrund. See also Bartlett Cowdrey, ed., 2 vols. *National Academy of Design Exhibition Record 1826-1860* (New York: New-York Historical Society, 1943).
31. See "Nominations for Membership, 1840-1863."* Gifford was elected Associate in 1850, not elected Academician in 1852, 1853, and elected Academician in 1854. Jerome Thompson was nominated but not elected Associate in 1850, elected in 1851, nominated but not elected Academician in 1852, 1855, and again in 1861.
32. *Ibid.*, A.A. here possibly represents the Annales Archiologique de Belgique listed in the 1852 inventory.
33. See "Nominations for Membership in the National Academy of Design, 1863-87."*
34. Register, "Schools of the National Academy of Design."*
35. Ms. "Books, Prints etc. bought of J.G. Chapman, 1848."* See also 1852 inventory,* and present National Academy of Design Library.
36. *Ibid.*
37. *Ibid.*
38. 1852 inventory.* In the inventory for 1888, the author of the two volumes on the Dresden Gallery is listed as F. Hanfstaengle. Thus far, we have been unable to locate these volumes in the present National Academy of Design Library.
39. See my comments in *Nature and Culture*, 255 ff.
40. See *American Light, The Luminist Movement 1850-1875* (Washington, D.C.: National Gallery of Art, 1980), essay by Theodore E. Stebbins, Jr. on "Luminism in Context: A New View." Though I have reservations about the term "international luminism," which requires careful consideration of important lags in dating and crucial formal differences in handling of light, structure, and surface as well as significant philosophical distinctions, the importance of Friedrich as a parallel is undeniable, as I have long argued. Count Raczynski's *Histoire de L'Arte Moderne en Allemagne* (Paris, 1841) in the National Academy of Design Library, which was included in the 1852 inventory (incorrectly dated 1836), contains a critique of Friedrich (vol. 3, 205).
41. I am grateful to Eugene Thaw, recently returned from the Soviet Union, for this information. Research remains to be done on the problem of nineteenth-century consular offices as bureaus of cultural disseminaton and conduits for international influence.
42. See my comments in *American Light*, "On Defining Luminism," 23-29.
43. 1852 inventory.* C.R. Leslie, *Life of Constable* (London, 1843) and Turner and Girtin, *River Scenery* (London, 1827).*
44. *Ibid.*
45. Library Register, vol. 1, 113.*
46. *Ibid.*
47. See *Copley-Pelham Letters* (Massachusetts Historical Society Collections, 1914) 241, 299.
48. Library Register, 1826-1929.*
49. *Ibid.*
50. *Ibid.* The volume presently in the library is *A Treatise on Painting by Leonardo da Vinci* (London: J. Taylor, 1802). The 1852 inventory lists a 1796 date, but this may be in error.
51. Erwin Panofsky, "Iconography and Iconology: An Introduction to the Study of Renaissance Art," *op. cit.*, 39.

*In Archives of National Academy of Design.

THE CATALOGUE

KEY TO ABBREVIATIONS

NA National Academician
ANA Associate of the National Academy
PNA President of the National Academy
HM Honorary Member

EDWARD LAMSON HENRY

(1841-1919)
ANA 1867; NA 1869

Born January 12 in Charleston, South Carolina. 1848 family moved to New York City. 1855 received first artistic training with landscape painter Walter Mason Oddie. 1858-1860 studied at Pennsylvania Academy of the Fine Arts. 1860 Grand Tour of Europe. Worked briefly with Charles Gleyre and Gustave Courbet; copied at Louvre. After return to New York in 1862, retained studio at Tenth Street Studio Building from 1863 to 1884. 1864 served in Union Army; made sketches subsequently used for Civil War paintings. Noted for meticulous renderings of places and situations such as railroad-station scenes. Interested in architecture, antiques, old costumes, and travel conveyances; hobby was photography. Used stereographic views to help recreate a pictorial history of American life. 1875 married. 1871, 1875, and 1885 went abroad again. Early 1880s till end of life summered in Cragsmoor, near Ellenville, New York; designed own home there. Spent winters in New York. Died May 11 in Ellenville.

REFERENCES: George C. Groce and David H. Wallace, *Dictionary of Artists in America 1564-1860* (New-York Historical Society, 1957). Elizabeth McCausland, *The Life and Work of Edward Lamson Henry, N.A. (1841-1919)* (Albany: The University of the State of New York, 1945). National Academy of Design Artists Biographical Files.

THE TENTH STREET STUDIO BUILDING

Edward Lamson Henry was primarily a genre painter who documented American life with great accuracy. His interest in architecture probably influenced his decision to depict the approach to the famous Tenth Street Studio Building as opposed to its studio interiors, which other artists of the period seemed to favor. Journalists too described the building, not because of its Neo-Greque façade or its Beaux-Arts plan but because it held under one roof a most distinguished group of painters, sculptors, architects, and writers. The significance of this little cityscape, as compared with Henry's more typical genre paintings—often crowded with figures and details—lies in its subject. It serves as a memento of the venerable institution at which sixteen artists represented in this exhibition maintained studios at some time during their respective careers.

Preserved on the back of this painting is a note specifying that it was done "from a lead pencil sketch from nature." The two figures, one with a painting under his arm, are identified as the artists "Wm. Beard and Wm. DeHaas [who] were passing at the time." The note continues: "The bad winter of '77 when there was very little business done & 'the prison van and funerals were most of the traffic through the street' as was said by the artists in the building at the time." In addition to capturing the mood of the scene through use of a somber palette, the artist has also detailed two types of carriages, a literal manifestation of his interest in travel conveyances.

Pasted alongside the note is a letter written by Henry from Cragsmoor on October 11, 1911, to George W. Maynard, then supervisor of the Academy's permanent collection. This letter further describes the painting and the manner in which it entered the Academy's collection:

Thank you so much for your letter in relation to the sketch of the "cor of 10th St and 5th Ave" made in 1877. I remember writing the letter offering it, but I do not recall ever having an answer, whether the Academy cared for it. However! I have it still and when I return early Nov. will get it Framed & send it or take it up. It isn't very much after all. Yet as so many of the older men lived and painted in that old "51" I thought it might help to recall the corner. The old sign on that corner as far back as I can remember it, was nailed on that old forlorn tree and when I made the sketch it had the Kite tail and the remnants of an old kite tangled in the branches, the end of the tail hanging down like a noose. A rainy dismal day, a little wet snow, & the prison van going down 10th St. to the courthouse—made a picture suited to that very dull season when few if any were paying Expenses. . . .

E.L. Henry (1911).

The singular characteristics of this first commercial studio building, constructed in 1857, were promulgated in *The Crayon* in January 1858:

THE ARTISTS BUILDING IN TENTH STREET—Here we have a building devoted entirely to the service of artists. This structure is an experiment, intended to provide studios for artists, accompanied with an exhibition-room, wherein the works of the occupants of the building can be visible at all suitable hours. There are about twenty-three studios (large and small) in the building, which occupies a space of ground one hundred square feet, besides a number of smaller rooms, etc., that can be used as required. The studios range in size from about fifteen feet by twenty feet to twenty feet by thirty feet. The exhibition-room is a prominent feature of the building, being fine in proportion, and beautifully lighted. The building is erected by James B. Johnston, Esq., and is a laudable enterprise; we would point to it as one of the evidences of an increasing estimation of Art in our midst. The front of the building is wholly constructed of brick; its ornamentation, such as window-mouldings, pilasters, cornices, etc., being developed in that material. The opportunity does not afford a chance to display the beauty of brick-work in all its fullness, but it indicates a use of brick which we hope will become more general. The architect is R.M. Hunt.[1]

THE OLD SIGN ON TENTH STREET, 1877
Oil on canvas, mounted on board, 11½ x 8¼″ (sight)
Signed lower left: *E.L. Henry, Feb. 1877*

Soon after the completion of the building, the studios were fully occupied. Painters appropriated the well-lit rooms, and writers, such as art critic Henry T. Tuckerman and novelist Theodore Winthrop, utilized the few rooms lacking in adequate light. Some artists even lived in and had meals provided for them by Mrs. Winter, the building's housekeeper. "Many of the studios have bedchambers attached: so the artist can live here and 'keep house' very cosily."[2]

Until 1865 the address of the Studio Building was 15 Tenth Street; in 1866, however, it was renumbered 51 West Tenth Street. An annex at 55 West Tenth Street was added about 1872. From its inception and throughout the 1860s and 1870s the building endured as a stronghold of Hudson River painters. These men worked together in an atmosphere of camaraderie, sharing ideas, observations, and techniques. Conviviality even extended as far as painting on one another's canvases.

Of the Tenth Street landscape painters in this exhibition, William Hart was one of the first to inhabit the building, and he proudly advertised his new address in the Calling Card section of *The Crayon*, December 1857.[3] Frederic Edwin Church, Sanford Robinson Gifford, and James Augustus Suydam came in 1858. They were joined by John William Casilear, William Stanley Haseltine, Louis Remy Mignot, and Aaron Draper Shattuck in 1859. Charles Temple Dix and (Thomas) Worthington Whittredge moved in the following year. To these illustrious names were added those of Albert Bierstadt in 1861, Edward Lamson Henry in 1863, Mauritz F.H. De Haas in 1865, the year Suydam died, and H.D. Kruseman Van Elten in 1867. All of these artists, except for Dix and Mignot, remained in the building at least until 1870, and most stayed longer. Casilear, De Haas, Church, Shattuck, Van Elten, and Whittredge spent approximately thirty years or more. E.L. Henry and Gifford exceeded twenty years, and Bierstadt, Hart, and Haseltine remained for over ten years.[4] At first their works were revered as paradigms of native American landscape painting; subsequently they were considered *retardataire*. The stability of the tenants in the building operated as a perpetual anchor to the past.

Side by side with the landscape painters were artists of great diversity. T.B. Aldrich in 1865 listed them according to floor, allowing us to envision relationships and speculate on possible influences:

On the ground floor are the studios of Whittredge, Bradford, Dana, Beard, Thompson, the sculptor, Le Clear, Guy, and Bierstadt. The second floor is appropriated by Church, McEntee, Leutze, Hays, Hart, and Gignoux. Mr. Tuckerman, the author, has a pleasant study and library on this floor. On the third story are Gifford, Hubbard, Suydam, Weir, Shattuck, Thorndike, Haseltine, DeHaas, Brown, Casilear, and Martin. Here they are all together,—historical, figure, portrait, landscape, marine, animal, fruit, and flower painters. It is not often that so many clever fellows are found living under one roof. A community of gifted men is unique, —a little colony of poets, for they *are* poets in their way, in the midst of all the turmoil and crime and harsh reality of the great city![5]
Aldrich, "Among the Studios" (1865).

Aldrich further describes some of the studios as having distinguishing features, characteristic of each occupant:

In Mr. Bierstadt's room, also, you will see at a glance the direction of his studies and wanderings. It is a perfect museum of Indian curiosities . . .

These traps Mr. Bierstadt brought with him in his trunks from the Rocky Mountains; but in his brain and his portfolios he brought more precious things;—those wild ravines, and snowy sierras, which he has bequeathed to us on canvas.

Mr. Church's love of the Tropics is plainly discernible in his studio as in his landscapes. Everywhere about the room we have sunny hints of the equator. Even the pot-plants at the casement threaten to turn into graceful date-palms and cocoanut-trees under the influence.[6]
Aldrich, "Among the Studios" (1865).

The inclusion of an exhibition space was unique. Prior to the construction of the Studio Building there were few galleries and museums. Artists often sold their paintings at auction. With the demise of the American Art-Union in 1852, the National Academy of Design (founded to provide exhibition facilities as well as a school of art) became the primary establishment in New York City at which artists could exhibit and dispose of their works. Studio Building exhibitions offered an alternative.[7] Invitations were issued and gala receptions were held to entice visitors to attend. It was on one of these occasions that E.L. Henry met his wife:[8]

A Reception was held at this fine temple of Art on the evening of the 18th January, attended with complete success. A liberal display of paintings in the well-lighted, handsome exhibition-room, by artists occupying studios in the building, furnished entertainment to a large company, also the studios in which the pictures were painted, most of these being thrown open to the inspection of visitors. The privilege of circulating through the building was much enjoyed; . . . Among the works exhibited were landscapes by Casilear, Gignoux, Gifford, Hubbard, W. Hart, Mignot, Boughton, Nichols, Heade, Hotchkiss, Suydam, and Thorndike; . . .[9]
The Crayon (1859).

In addition to joint exhibitions, tenants entertained dealers and prospective buyers in their rooms, and also held private exhibitions. For example, upon completion of *The Heart of the Andes* in 1859 (The Metropolitan Museum of Art), Church opened his studio to the public. Theodore Winthrop, his neighbor and friend, wrote an accompanying description which was available to the throngs of people who flocked to see this panoramic work.[10] By darkening the room and flanking the awesome tropical scene with potted palms, Church augmented the dramatic spectacle, for which he charged admission. The accurate representation of far-off places was inspired by the writing of the explorer and naturalist Alexander von Humboldt. He proclaimed that such subjects would motivate painters to combine "a profound appreciation of nature and . . . [an] inward process of mind."[11] His writings influenced Church and possibly Bierstadt, among others in the building. Bierstadt shared Church's taste for newly explored lands as well as for the panoramic format. He, however, devoted himself to the celebration of the "natural antiquity"[12] of the American West.

The exploration of exotic lands such as South America and the Arctic, as well as expeditions to the West, excited other Tenth Street men: Louis Remy Mignot, Martin Johnson Heade, and Horace Wolcott Robbins.[13] John La Farge, a peripatetic tenant from 1858 until his death in 1910, traveled to the South Pacific and the Orient. Whittredge and Gifford were two of the many artists in the building who painted the Roman campagna. Later they mined the western territories of the United States for scenery and adventure. Still other tenants were content with the more conventional Grand Tour of Europe. And some, like Aaron Draper

Shattuck, never traveled at all, but were almost certainly exposed to the sketches and reminiscences brought back by the voyagers.

In addition to providing a stimulating atmosphere, adequate work space, and an exhibition gallery, the building was also used for entertaining and teaching. Jervis McEntee, a long-term tenant (1859-91)—whose work, although not included in this exhibition, is represented in the Academy's collection—chronicled life in the Studio Building in his diary. His remarks bear witness to the communication that took place among the artists:

On Thursday I sent a note to each artist in the building inviting him to come and see for his free and frank criticism, my last picture, (not entirely completed) "Sea From Shore." Nearly every one came between 11 and 12 and it proved a pleasant occasion. I gave them each a good cigar and tried to make them feel that I should like their comments which I think they gave freely.[14]

McEntee's Diary (1873).

The artistic brotherhood continued outside the building as the men formed and joined art associations and social clubs:

In the evening I attended a private view of Kruseman Van Elten's pictures and studies which he is going to sell and from there Whittredge and I went to the Lotus Club, where we found Eastman Johnson and a number of the artists.[15]

McEntee's Diary (1875).

Many of the catalogue entries which follow attest to the camaraderie that persisted throughout the summers. In one another's company, the tenants visited the White Mountains, the Catskills, the Adirondacks, and the New England coast, where they gathered fresh, "on the spot" material for their winter's work. McEntee notes on August 26, 1872: "I joined Gifford and Whittredge in Hudson and the following morning (July 30) we left for Gloucester . . ."[16]

As with other painters of the period, the Tenth Street men were aware of the spate of nineteenth-century scientific literature dealing with meteorology, geology, optics, and color, as well as with the larger issue of evolution. In a letter of June 8, 1865, John Ferguson Weir, a tenant from 1861 to 1872, recalled a spontaneous meeting that occurred one evening on the front step of the Studio Building between himself, [Launt] Thompson, Whittredge, and Gifford:

. . . we sat for nearly an hour discussing the exceeding beauty of the moonlight and noting the curious forms of clouds as they drifted over the housetops. Talking of old times and right pleasant it was, until we all entered the Building and tumbled into bed.

And the next day:

This afternoon Gifford and [Richard W.] Hubbard and myself went up upon the housetops and had a pleasant time discussing the character of the sky. It was too dark to paint so we sat there talking for some time.[17]

Weir, Letter (1865).

The libraries of tenants such as Tuckerman, Church, Suydam, and Hunt comprised books on science, travel, religion, and philosophy, as well as art and architecture. Most likely these resources were available to the artists in the building, as was the comprehensive collection of books in the library of the National Academy of Design. Along with the writers, the artists produced articles and books on various subjects. William J. Stillman, land-scape student of Church and co-editor of *The Crayon*, wrote many books. His presence probably stimulated discussion of John Ruskin's ideas. Stillman, a tenant from 1858 to 1860, was only one of several artists in the building at that time who were proponents of Ruskinian verisimilitude to nature and reverence for nature as God.[18]

Influences within the building came of course from formal sources as well as conceptual ones. Places of training affected style and acquaintanceships. The homogeneity of the first generation, many of whom were products of the Düsseldorf School, was destroyed with the incursion of Munich-trained artists in the seventies, and also by the influx of men trained in the ateliers of Paris and its environs. New concepts infiltrated the building. The meticulous draftsmanship and precise attention to detail and finish of the Düsseldorfians was supplanted by the dramatic *chiaroscuro* and broad brushstroke of the Munich School and by moody landscapes with dissolved forms, prototypical of the Barbizon aesthetic. Artists who painted in the Barbizon mode were not altogether well received by older conservative painters, both in the Studio Building and at the Academy. For the most part, they found the new painting unappealing. McEntee, representative of his peers, records these attitudes:

On Wed. evening I attended a private view at Cottiers [?] of some pictures he brought over from Europe. They impressed me rather strangely as they were so different from my ideas of landscape. Corot I presume is very fine and satisfactory to those who are in sympathy but I confess his pictures are unsatisfactory to me. A Daubigny was simply black and most of the pictures were painted in cold grays and totally lacking in color. I think most of them affectations in art, at least so they seem to me who see nature and the sentiment of the landscape so differently.[19]

McEntee's Diary (1877).

Yet McEntee's later paintings evinced a hazed brushstroke. Others, such as Homer Dodge Martin (a tenant from 1865 to 1882), who began in the Hudson River tradition, gradually adopted some aspects of the increasingly popular Barbizon School. Eventually, and inevitably, some Tenth Street men embraced the tenets of Impressionism, using short, impastoed brushstrokes to display their interest in color and light.[20]

Pictures of the Hudson River School—as some people call the most honest, most American art we ever had—are excellent in composition, carefully, firmly painted, and full of artistic knowledge, but they are apt to lack the atmosphere, the harmony to be found in work that has been grounded in the fields and under the sky. Every day has its tone, and no amount of studio cleverness quite makes up for the lack of it.[21]

Charles M. Skinner, "Art Study Out-of-Doors" (1895).

Initially, association with the renowned originators of a distinctive American school of landscape painting made the building famous and desirable. William Merritt Chase, for one, was attracted by this prestigious affiliation. Nevertheless, a short time after he rented the gallery space in 1878 and converted it into the showplace of the Studio Building, he expressed an ambivalence to the old guard who persisted as anachronisms in the building.[22] E.L. Henry, in his waning years, poignantly phrased the sentiments of the older artists:

You younger men of today look upon the art of the early Hudson River School as old and antiquated. But you who are now on that end of the bench where I once sat, must move on and still again move on. Younger men will take your places. The art of this your day will change, too, for changes are in everything around us. You too will meet with harsh criticism by and by. . . . Remember this, and be kindly in your thoughts of those who have gone before you. Think of them not with ridicule of their way of painting the beautiful, but as the men who opened the way which you are walking in now.[23]

McCausland, *Life and Work of E.L. Henry* (1945).

Changes occurred "in everything around," but the Studio Building stood the test of time for almost one hundred years, and served a multiplicity of functions. In 1955 the building was demolished. Unfortunately, "no little old ladies threw themselves before the bulldozers"[24] to save this early Richard Morris Hunt structure that concealed within its walls the secrets of some of America's most illustrious artists. Today, twenty-five years later, only pictures such as E.L. Henry's *The Old Sign on Tenth Street* remain to commemorate the existence of the old Studio Building.

NOTES

1. *The Crayon* 5 (January 1858), 55. All page references in the notes of this essay and in those of all following entries are to the reprint (New York: AMS Press Inc., 1970).
2. Thomas Bailey Aldrich, "Among the Studios," *Our Young Folk* (Sept. 1865), 596.
3. *The Crayon* 4 (Dec. 1857), inside cover of the original edition (New York: Stillman and Durand, 1857).
4. Duration of tenancy has been compiled from various sources: Trow's and Wilson's New York City directories; New York business directories; National Academy of Design annual exhibition catalogues; miscellaneous biographies, art guides, and catalogues.
5. Aldrich, "Among the Studios," 596.
6. *Ibid.*, 597.
7. Prior to the Studio Building, and concurrently, the Dodsworth Building held exhibitions and receptions, but it was not totally an artist's building.
8. Elizabeth McCausland, *The Life and Work of Edward Lamson Henry, N.A. (1841-1919)* (Albany: The University of the State of New York, 1945), 320.
9. *The Crayon* 6 (Feb. 1859), 62.
10. Theodore Winthrop, *A Companion to The Heart of the Andes* (New York: D. Appleton, 1859). An order form for future line engravings, which would of course increase Church's income from this painting, was contained in this pamphlet.
11. Quoted in Barbara Novak, *Nature and Culture* (New York: Oxford University Press, 1980), 70, from Alexander von Humboldt, *Cosmos*, trans. E.C. Otté, 2 vols., (New York: Harper & Brothers, 1850), 2:94-95.
12. Novak, *Nature and Culture*, 145.
13. Mignot traveled with Church to Ecuador in 1857 and was at Tenth Street from 1859 to 1863-64. Heade was there from 1859 to 1860 and again from 1866 to 1879, at which time he occupied Church's studio in the latter's absence. He traveled to South America on his own. Robbins went to Jamaica with Church in 1865 and was a tenant from 1862 to 1868 and from 1882 to 1888. The National Academy of Design Collection includes one of his landscapes.
14. Garnett McCoy, ed., "Jervis McEntee's Diary," *Archives of the American Art Journal* 8 (July-Oct. 1968), 14.
15. *Ibid.*, 15.
16. *Ibid.*, 7.
17. Letter of June 9, 1865, to Mary Weir at West Point. Collection of Sterling Memorial Library, Yale University, Box 5, folder 133.
18. Stillman later became disenchanted with Ruskin. Charles Herbert Moore, who subsequently gave up landscape painting to teach at Harvard, was a tenant from 1859 to 1861 and contributed to *The New Path*, a periodical published in 1863 by the Society for the Advancement of Truth in Art. This group professed allegiance to Ruskinian principles—the selfless recording of nature—seen in the works of such other tenants as John William and John Henry Hill and Aaron Draper Shattuck. Such concerns as fidelity to nature can also be discerned in the study in this exhibition by Kruseman Van Elten. Since he first arrived at the Studio Building in 1867, however, his interest in natural detail may derive from other sources or earlier contact with these ideas in Europe.
19. McEntee Diary, March 3, 1877. I am grateful to Garnett McCoy who allowed me to read his transcript of this unpublished segment of McEntee's Diary. Archives of American Art, Smithsonian Institution, Washington, D.C.
20. For example, J. Alden Weir, a tenant from 1873 to 1874 and again from 1906 to 1919, during which time he served as president of the National Academy of Design (1915-1917). Two other Studio Building artists represented in the present exhibition, whose works demonstrate a shift in style, are Ralph A. Blakelock, a tenant in 1884, and Henry W. Parton, a tenant from 1881 to 1892.
21. Charles Skinner, "Art Study Out-of-Doors," *National Academy of Design Catalogue*, 1895, 32.
22. Nicolai Cikovsky, Jr., "William Merritt Chase's Tenth Street Studio," *Archives of American Art Journal*, 16 (1976) 2-14, discusses the importance of Chase's studio and his feelings about the men of the Hudson River School.
23. McCausland, *Life and Work of Edward Lamson Henry*, 24.
24. Mary Sayre Haverstock, "The Tenth Street Studio," *Art in America* (Sept.-Oct. 1966), 49.

Annette Blaugrund

JOHN JAMES AUDUBON

(1785-1851)
H.M. 1833

Born Jean Jacques Fougère Audubon, April 26, Les Cayes, Haiti. Youth spent in Nantes, France. At age seventeen possibly studied drawing with Jacques-Louis David, his only formal art training. 1803 to United States. Lived life of country gentleman at father's Mill Grove, Penn., estate. Dabbled in various business ventures, including mining, real estate, and slaves. 1808 to 1826 in Kentucky and Louisiana. Worked briefly as a taxidermist at Cincinnati museum in 1819, thereafter devoted himself to naturalist studies, hunting, and drawing. Supported himself at various times by painting portraits and teaching drawing, dancing, music, French, and fencing. Traveled throughout New York, Great Lakes area, and eastern United States. 1826 to 1829 in Edinburgh and England, arranging for publication of *Birds of America*. Briefly in Paris fall of 1828. 1829 returned to New Jersey and then New Orleans. 1830 back in Edinburgh, worked on *Ornithological Biography*. 1831-1832 traveled in Kentucky and Florida. 1832 to New Brunswick and Maine. Settled in Boston. Summer 1833 on Labrador journey. 1834-1836 in Europe. Returned to New York and then onto the southern United States in 1836. 1837 on expedition to Gulf of Mexico. 1837-1839 in England. 1839 settled in New York; began work on *The Viviparous Quadrupeds of North America*. 1842 established family residence in Washington Heights area of New York City. Subscription tour to Canada. Expedition on Upper Missouri River in 1843. Died January 27, New York City.

REFERENCES: Lucy B. Audubon, *The Life of John James Audubon* (New York: G.P. Putnam's, 1900). Maria R. Audubon with Elliott Coues, *Audubon and His Journals*, vols. 1,2, (New York: Scribner's, 1897). Howard Corning, ed., *The Letters of John James Audubon, 1826-40*, vols. 1,2 (Cambridge, Mass.: The Club of Odd Volumes, 1930). Alice Ford, *Audubon, By Himself* (Garden City: American Museum of Natural History, 1969). Ford, ed., *Audubon's Animals, The Quadrupeds of North America* (New York: Thomas Y. Crowell, 1951). Ford, *John James Audubon* (Norman: University of Oklahoma Press, 1964). Waldemar H. Fries, *The Double Elephant Folio: The Story of Audubon's Birds of America* (Chicago: The American Library Association, 1973). Francis H. Herrick, *Audubon the Naturalist*, vols. 1,2 (New York: D. Appleton & Co., 1917). *National Academy of Design Artists Biographical Files*.

Audubon's painting of *Black or Heath Grouse* is an instructive work through which to approach the naturalist as a nature painter and landscapist. Although no entry records document the arrival of the painting at the National Academy of Design, the provenance is not as problematic as it might initially appear. Audubon rarely signed his oils (his granddaughter notes that only one signed oil was in the possession of the artist's family), and this painting is likewise unsigned.[1] It is possible that it came into the Academy's possession at the time of the artist's election to honorary membership in 1833, although the contribution of a diploma painting was not necessary at that time. Audubon wrote to his wife, Lucy, on the eve of his departure on the Labrador journey of his appreciation of the gesture:

If God grants us success & a safe return, no man living will be able to compette [sic] with me in knowledge of the Birds of our Country, and I shall make it pay in Capital & Interest. I wish thou wouldst write a letter of thanks to the Academy of disign [sic] in my name for Honour they have done me—I fear that after we sail from this for Bay Chaleur, Labrador &c I shall have few or no opportunity to write to thee or anyone...[2]

The Audubon association with the Academy would later be continued. The naturalist's two sons, Victor Gifford and John Woodhouse, were elected Academician and Honorary Member respectively.[3]

The 1833 date suggested in the Academy records for the painting would seem to reflect the year of Audubon's election to the Academy and the acquisition of the painting rather than its execution. During much of 1833 Audubon was preparing for and later, recovering from, his extended sketching tour through eastern Canada. The artist was absorbed throughout the year with preparations for his volume of water birds for *Birds of America;* it is unlikely he would have had occasion to paint an oil of a species of bird commonly associated with forests or grassland.

A more plausible dating of the painting would place it earlier, from about 1826 to 1829. That it is titled *Study of Birds, Black Grouse or Heath Grouse*[4] reminds us that Audubon used oils, among other media, in his preparatory renderings for *Birds of America*. It is doubtful, however, that this painting is a study for a later engraving, since the species represented is not an American bird and is not represented in the Elephant Folio.[5] The black grouse occurs in northern and central Europe. The male is a deep black, about 20-21″ in height, with lyre-shaped tail feathers (hence its scientific name, *Lyrurus tetrix*); the female is browner, with black banding, and stands about 16 inches high.[6]

Audubon painted a large number of oils and watercolors of birds and animals while in Edinburgh and England from 1826 to 1829. Some of these were oil copies of earlier watercolors; others were new subjects showing European species. They were meant for sale to aid in obtaining further subscriptions for the Elephant Folio. In his European journals, Audubon mentions on several occasions

that he has been working on paintings of grouse.[7] Although he returned to Europe from 1834 to 1836, the large number of oil paintings executed during the earlier period and the interest in this species at this time support the earlier date.

The question of dating in Audubon's painting becomes critical in considering the naturalist as a landscape painter. As an animal painter in the tradition of George Stubbs and Edward Landseer (whom Audubon admired)[8], Audubon periodically used landscape painters to fill in the backgrounds of his pictures.[9] But as a landscapist, Audubon was without peer in his painstakingly acquired, intimate knowledge of American nature; few other artists could claim a similar familiarity with such far-ranging areas of the nation. Audubon's extended trips into the wilderness—hunting, living with the Indians, collecting specimens, and sketching—enforced an understanding of the American landscape which he could later draw on in setting in the backgrounds for his stuffed birds. Although he wrote to Victor about the trip to Labrador, saying, "I should have liked very much indeed to have had [a] good Landscape Painter with me in this Expedition, but my endeavors to procure one on whom I could rely for Industry were thwarted, and we will have to do the more work ourselves,"[10] Audubon for the most part preferred to paint his own landscapes his own landscapes and only hired assistants because of the sheer enormity of undertaking the production of *Birds of America*.[11]

Although the depiction of the birds, and later the quadrupeds, was of primary importance to Audubon, he occasionally painted pure landscape.[12] He paid great attention to rendering the details of setting for each of the species depicted. The landscape was usually the first section painted:

. . . it appears that after studying a particular bird, he chose the characteristic pose and action he preferred, and sketched in the outline of the bird as well as an appropriate floral or landscape background.
This background subject-matter seems to have been virtually, if not entirely, completed before the pencil outline of the bird was filled in. Then when Audubon saw a fine specimen with the best possible plumage, he shot it, took it with him and wired it up [to a board or backdrop], and completed his watercolor in one sitting in order to counteract the loss of brilliancy of the feathers after the bird had been shot.[13]

Shelley, *Magazine of Art* (1946).

Like the oversized figures in American naive portraiture, Audubon's grouse similarly dominate their settings, here appearing almost to topple out of the picture. The landscape setting, with carefully delineated foreground plant life, the red-streaked sky, and back-lit clouds, remains a subordinate element. The suggestion of recession into depth is reinforced by the inclusion, at middleground, of what appears to be a Classical temple, but might more likely refer to older rock formations such as occur at Stonehenge, a suitable detail for an English setting.

The Elephant Folio landscapes often became quite elaborate, including many varieties of plants, reeds, mosses, rocks and trees authentic to the habitat of the species. While the landscapes of *Birds of America* were engraved and colored by the Robert Havells, Audubon supplied sketches for many of the plates.[14] Audubon was conscious of the historical importance of *Birds* and spent years, initially by himself, and later, with Victor's assistance, overseeing the publication of the plates. He wrote in April 1833 to Havell:

The success of My Work depends much on your own exertions in the finishing of the Plates as accurately as you are able to do, and in seeing [*sic*]that the colours do their duty.—Knowing you as I do, I naturally expect your attention. . . . *Americans* are *excellent Judges* of Work particularly of such as are drawn from their country's soil—they are proud of every thing that is connected with America, and feel mortified when ever any thing is done that does not come up to their sanguine expectations.[15]

NOTES

1. Maria R. Audubon, *Audubon and His Journals*, notes by Elliott Coues, (New York: Scribner's, 1897), 1:66.
2. J.J. Audubon to Lucy B. Audubon, May 14, 1833, East Port, Maine. In *Letters of John James Audubon, 1826-40,* Howard Corning, ed. (Cambridge, Mass.: The Club of Odd Volumes, 1930), 1:221. Original in collection of Victor Morris Tyler, New Haven.
3. National Academy of Design Artists Biographical Files.
4. This is confused. The actual name for the bird depicted is black grouse. There is no such bird as the heath grouse (although there was an American heath hen, now extinct), and this designation probably reflected the bird's habitat in Europe, rather than suggesting a different species.
5. Species depicted in the Elephant Folio edition were Canada grouse (plate 176); dusky or longtailed grouse (plate 361); pinnated grouse (plate 186); rock grouse (plate 368); ruffed grouse (plate 41); sharptailed grouse (plate 382); and spotted grouse (plate 176). An eighth species, identified only by its scientific name, *Tetrao saliceti* (plate 191), is also included. John James Audubon, *The Birds of America* (London: R.A. Havell, 1835-38). Edition consulted at American Museum of Natural History, New York. The species depicted here does not appear in any of Audubon's published works and has not been included in the recent compilaton by Roger Tory Peterson, *The Art of Audubon: The Complete Birds and Mammals* (New York: New York Times Books/Quadrangle Press, 1979).
6. I am indebted to John Bull of the Ornithology Department, American Museum of Natural History, N.Y., for this information.
7. In the entry for August 9, 1828, Audubon reports on recent progress: ". . . I have been too busy with my plates, and in superintending the coloring of them, and with painting. I wished again to try painting in oil, and have now before me eight pictures begun . . ." Among those paintings was a copy of an earlier work depicting *Black Cocks or Grouse*, which he sold to a Mr. Gally for 100 pounds. "I copy it with his permission; if it is better than his, and I think it will be, he must exchange, for assuredly he should own the superior picture." On November 10 of the same year, Audubon noted that he had finished two pictures for the Duc d'Orléans: "that of the Grouse I regret much to part with, without a copy; however, I may at some future time group another still more naturally." (*Journals*, 299, 340). One version of *Black Cocks*, dated 1827, is in the Fogg Art Museum. A watercolor entitled *European Blackcocks*, formerly in the collection of Kennedy Galleries, New York, and now in private hands, was dated by Audubon 1828 (Inventory of American Painting, National Collection of Fine Arts, Smithsonian Institution, Washington, D.C.; Kennedy Galleries).
8. Audubon, *Journals*, passim.
9. Donald Shelley, "John James Audubon, Artist," *Magazine of Art* 39, no. 5 (May 1946), 173. Albert Ten Eyck Gardner and Stuart P. Feld, *American Paintings, A Catalogue of the Metropolitan Museum of Art* (New York: New York Graphic Society, 1967), 1:182. *Journals*, 65. Two of these landscapists were J.B. Kidd and the German-Swiss artist George Lehman. Lehman can be connected with some of the backgrounds of the South Carolina and Florida subjects from 1831 to 1832 and Kidd's services were called upon for a short period during 1831 to make oil copies of the original watercolors with accompanying background. Robert Havell, Jr. was also known to have painted oil versions after the engraved plates of *Birds of America*. Audubon also hired botanical painters, notably Joseph Mason and Maria Martin, to provide suitable foliate settings for the birds. Perhaps the two most important assistants to the naturalist were his sons, who assisted their father in all aspects of the business and later continued his work in finishing the *Quadrupeds* after his death. Both were artists in their own right.
10. East Port, Maine, May 31, 1833. In Corning, *Letters*, 234.
11. Wilfred Blunt, "The Original Water-Colour Paintings by John James Audubon for the Birds of America," *Burlington Magazine* 109 (June 1967), 372. Audubon's feeling for intimate landscape registers in his account of a pilgrimage to Niagara Falls:

[The Innkkeper] talked a good deal of the many artists who had visited the Falls that season, from different parts, and offered to assist me, by giving such accommodations as I might require to finish the drawings I had in contemplation. He left me, and as I looked about the room, I saw several views of the Falls, by which I was so disgusted, that I suddenly came to my better senses. "What," thought I, "have I come here to mimic nature in her grandest enterprise, and add *my* caricature of one of the wonders of the world to those which I here see? No. —I give up the vain attempt. I will look on these mighty cataracts and imprint them where they alone can be represented,—on my mind!" John James Audubon, *Delineations of American Scenery and Character*, Intro., Francis H. Herrick (London: Simpkin, Marshall, Hamilton, Kent and Co., 1926), 77.
12. Shelley, "John James Aububon," 171.
13. *Ibid.*, 175.
14. *Ibid.*, 174.
15. New York, April 20, 1833. Letter to Robert Havell, Esq. In Corning, *Letters*, 212-13. Original in collection of Harvard University.

CB

WILLIAM JAMES BENNETT

(1784-1844)
ANA 1827; NA 1828

Born and trained in England. Pupil of Richard Westall. Traveled throughout Mediterranean with British army. Exhibited at Royal Academy 1801-1803 and 1808; exhibited at other London galleries 1808-1825. In New York City by 1826. Made a number of sketching tours to various parts of the United States. At National Academy of Design exhibited landscapes and sea pieces, in addition to prints from his engravings, regularly 1827-1843. From the time of his arrival in the United States, executed aquatint engravings of American cities and street scenes of New York. Beginning in 1829, a series of engravings of Niagara Falls after paintings by Bennett issued by Henry J. Megarey. 1830 contributed to Asher B. Durand's series of engravings, *The American Landscape*. Served as Keeper of the National Academy of Design 1830-1839. Pictures included in collection of Philip Hone, among others. 1843 moved to Nyack, N.Y. Died New York City.

REFERENCES: Ronald Anthony DeSilva, "William James Bennett: Painter and Engraver" (unpublished Master's Thesis, University of Delaware, 1970). Algernon Graves, *A dictionary of artists who have exhibited works in the principal London exhibitions from 1760 to 1893* (Bath: Kingsmead Reprints, 1970).

Bennett seems to have achieved success almost immediately upon his arrival in New York. His watercolor landscapes were particularly well received, as a *New-York Mirror* review of one such work in the National Academy of Design exhibition of 1831 demonstrates:

The great reputation which Mr. Bennett has already obtained in this kind of painting will, we hope, prevent the visitor from passing over his pieces carelessly. This is one of superior merit. It shows like a reflection of the real scene in a camera obscura. It has everything of nature but sound and motion.[2]

In 1830 Bennett, along with Thomas Cole, Robert Weir, and Asher B. Durand, contributed pictures to Durand's enterprise *The American Landscape*, intended as a serial publication of engravings of native scenery. Although only one number was published (1830), it was an important early experiment in its effort to legitimize the American landscape as an appropriate subject for the artist's brush. The text, by William Cullen Bryant, included passages relating to Bennett's picture *Weehawken* that seem equally appropriate to this watercolor sketch:

Nothing can exceed the beauty of these walks about the close of May, when the verdure of the turf is as bright as the green of the rainbow; and

when the embowering shrubs are in flower, among which the dogwood and the viburnum, white as if loaded with snow, and the sassafras, with its faint yellow blossoms, are conspicuous; and the hum of innumerable bees over the heads of the well dressed throng passing to and fro, mingles with the buzz of voices and the murmurs of the shore. In the sunny nooks of this bank, long before the trees have put forth their leaves, and while the place is yet unprofaned by city feet, the earliest blossoms of the year are found—violets are in bloom before the vernal equinox—

They come before the swallow dares, and take
The winds of March with beauty.[3]

The unfinished state of this sketch affords us the opportunity of studying the artist's working method. It can be observed, for example, that Bennett carefully outlined the entire scene in pencil before adding the color, a procedure advocated by contemporary manuals on watercolor technique:

We will now, therefore, proceed to describe the usual way in which a water-colour painting is commenced. . .
The paper stretched. . ., having become thoroughly dry, a clear outline of the subject is to be made upon it, with a moderately hard pencil. This outline, although requiring to be carefully made, must be effected, if possible, without having recourse to India-rubber. . . No increase of power in the stroke indicating light and shade, no sparkling dots marking minute touches of foliage, should appear in the outline; all these interfere more or less with the tints and forms, which are to be produced entirely with the brush. . . .
It is customary to begin with a wash of some warm but broken colour applied all over the surface. . .[4]

Once the surface was covered with a wash, the artist was instructed to proceed with the clouds and sky, followed by the landscape and foliage, and then the foreground details. The last step—not yet completed in this picture by Bennett—was the addition of rustic figures, for as the manuals advised:

There are but few scenes in nature, how beautiful soever they may be, upon which the eye can rest with continued pleasure unless they exhibit some signs of animated life; consequently, few landscapes are complete without the introduction of figures—some objects in human form—whereby to enlist our sympathies in behalf of the scene before us. . .[5]
Barnard, *Landscape Painting in Water Colours* (1855).

Thus, Bennett's watercolor sketch offers us an important glimpse into the workings of his hand and mind, for as Goethe long ago reminded us: "Drawings are invaluable, not only because they give, in its purity, the mental intention of the artist, but because they bring immediately before us the mood of his mind at the moment of creation."[6]

UNTITLED (unfinished)
Watercolor and pencil on paper, 13¾ x 17½″
Signed lower right: *Bennett*
No record of acquisition[1]

NOTES

1. Although most sources give Bennett's year of birth as 1787 (see, for example, George C. Groce and David H. Wallace, *Dictionary of Artists in America 1564-1860* [New-York Historical Society, 1957], 45), DeSilva, pp. 6-7, argues convincingly for the year 1784. Although Cowdrey and others give the date of Bennett's election as a member of the Natonal Academy of Design as 1829 (see Mary Bartlett Cowdrey, *National Academy of Design Exhibition Record, 1826-1860* [New-York Historical Society, 1943], 1:30), DeSilva, p. 47, gives the correct date of 1828. See Ronald Anthony DeSilva, "William James Bennett: Painter and Engraver" (unpublished Master's Thesis, University of Delaware, 1970). In the "Schedule of Property belonging to the National Academy of Design. Taken August 1st, 1852," this work is listed as "Water Colored Drawing, Unfinished, J. Bennett." See *Constitution of the National Academy of Design, and Schedule of the Property* (New York: Sackett & Co., 1852), 28.

2. "The Fine Arts," *The New-York Mirror* 8, no. 44 (1831). In DeSilva, 62.

3. William Cullen Bryant, ed., *The American Landscape* (New York: Elam Bliss, 1830), 7. See Wayne Craven, "Asher B. Durand's Career as an Engraver," *The American Art Journal* 3 (Spring 1971), 52, for information on this enterprise.

4. George Barnard, *Theory and Practice of Landscape Painting in Water Colours* (London: William S. Orr and Co., 1855), 76-77. Although this book postdates Bennett's drawing, it reflects the technique of the first half of the century.

5. *Ibid.*, 150.

6. In Alfred Mansfield Brooks, "Fitz Lane's Drawings," *Essex Institute Historical Collections* 81 (January 1945), 83.

KM

SAMUEL F.B. MORSE

(1791-1872)
Founder, NA 1826; PNA 1826-1845, 1861-1862

Born April 27, Charlestown, Mass. 1810 graduated from Yale University; decided to become artist. 1811 to London with Washington Allston to study history painting with Benjamin West. 1815 returned to New York; painted portraits in New England and Charleston, S.C. 1823 settled in New York City. 1826 with other artists founded National Academy of Design; subsequently became first president. 1829-1832 to Europe; met Louis J.M. Daguerre and introduced daguerreotype to America. On return trip conceived idea of electromagnetic telegraph. 1832 appointed Professor of Literature of the Arts of Design at University of the City of New York (later New York University). Spent increasingly less time at painting because of public apathy to historical subjects. 1833 demonstrated his invention; 1838 developed Morse code; 1844 first long distance telegraphic communication. Involved in politics; ran for mayor 1836 and 1841. Late years embroiled in disputes over history and administration of telegraph. Philanthropist in old age. Died April 2, New York City.

REFERENCES: William Dunlap, *History of the Rise and Progress of the Arts of Design in the United States* (1834; New York: Dover Publications, 1969). George C. Groce and David H. Wallace, *Dictionary of Artists in America 1564-1860* (New-York Historical Society, 1957). *Morse Exhibition of Arts and Science* (Exhibition catalogue, National Academy of Design, Jan.-Feb., 1950).

The image of Samuel F.B. Morse as inventor of the electromagnetic telegraph and originator of the Morse code, is so firmly fixed in the minds of the general public that it annuls appreciation of Morse as an artist, as well as a writer, teacher, politician, and philanthropist. Disclosure of his other creative contributions invites recognition of the multiplicity of talents that rendered Morse a Renaissance man, sometimes referred to as the "American Leonardo."[1] In this vein, Morse can be placed in the lineage of such American artist-inventors as Charles Willson Peale, Robert Fulton, and William Sidney Mount.

Typical of his age, Morse sought training in England, studying history painting with his compatriot Washington Allston as well as with the American-born president of the Royal Academy, Benjamin West.[2] From them he learned the canons of academic preparation which he later espoused while president of the National Academy of Design. In the tradition of West and his predecessor Sir Joshua Reynolds, Morse dedicated himself to painting historical subjects of national and moral significance. Unfortunately, neither the American public nor its government fully shared this interest,

forcing the artist to devote himself to portraiture in order to support his family. As president of the Academy, he diverted his own lofty ambitions to the promulgation of academic methodology and to the elevation of taste in the young nation.

Notes made during the 1820s fill two little sketchbooks—one bound in red leather and the other in marbleized paper.[3] Among the sketches are entries that record such items as rules of painting and fragments of Sir Joshua's *Discourses*.[4] Morse's notations became the basis for a series of four lectures, "On the Affinity of Painting with the Other Fine Arts," which he delivered in various forms on several occasions.[5] In these lectures, Morse reiterated the academic mission—the systematic progression of the study of the part in relation to the whole:

All objects in Nature may be arbitrarily divided into a whole and parts, and each may change its relation[;] the whole may become part of a greater whole and a part become a whole in relation to smaller parts; we take a leaf from a tree we survey its general shape and its size and color, we proceed to examine its stalk and its fibers by itself it is a whole; but the single leaf taken from a tree of leaves is but a part of a greater whole; the tree again with its countless leaves belongs to a forest of trees; the forest to a wide extended landscape of forests, rivers, cities, mountains; these again to a world of landscapes, nor can we stop here, the world itself in the system of our Sun takes its station with the other worlds (merely as a part,) nor even here does the wonderful progression end.[6]

Morse, Lecture Two

In this exhibition, the finished drawing of a tree trunk is representative of the precise study of fragments that was deemed part of the academic procedure. The trunk, centered on the page, is delineated by hesitant marks which are often concealed by heavier, deeply incised lines. A modification of textures, in addition to the contrasts of light and dark is achieved by touches of white on the gray-green ground of the paper. Attention to such details as bark, knots, branch formations, and modeling of the tree marks this work as "not necessarily the mere copying of what is created, but . . . also that more lofty imitation the making of a work on the Creator's principles.[7]

A *picture* then is not merely a copy of any work of Nature, it is constructed on the *principles of nature*. While its parts are copies of natural objects, the whole work is an artificial arrangement of them similar to the construction of a *poem* or a *piece of Music*.[8]

Morse, Lecture Four

All the Fine Arts refer to Nature as the source whence they draw their materials, and the *Imitation* of Nature is always recommended to the student in any of these Arts.—But there are two kinds of Imitation; which

Attributed to Samuel F.B. Morse
TREE TRUNK, one of twelve drawings
Pencil on gray-green paper, heightened with white,
15 x 10¾″
Unsigned

should not be confounded, a copying exactly any object just as it is, with every beauty and defect, and an Imitation of the rules or methods according to which that object is constructed to serve a particular purpose.[9]

Morse, Lecture Two

Although Morse spent part of his term of office in Europe (1829-1832), letters in the Academy's archives attest to the energy he spent in guiding the newly formed institution through the vicissitudes of growth and change. In a congratulatory address to the students at the end of the first academic season in 1827, Morse reminded them that "... *Drawing* lies at the very foundation of all the Arts of Design; it is the language by which they all express their thoughts. ..."[10] Furthermore, he warned:

The pursuits of an Artist have their pleasures, indeed, and of the highest refinement, but they also have their pains, felt most keenly by those most susceptible of those pleasures. They are not arts acquired in a year, or in many years, and with ordinary industry; they require unremitting attention during a whole life. ...

Despite adversities, Morse encouraged the students and affirmed the Academy's purpose: to assist and instruct artists.

...go forward; all our experience is at your service freely; all we require in return is, that you extend the same privileges as freely to others; we have no secrets of trade; we know of none, but industry and perseverance.[11]

NOTES

1. Clipping in Morse file at the National Academy of Design entitled "Morse's invention in painting," *Art News* (Feb. 1950), 33.
2. Benjamin West befriended and taught many American artists who came to England. He was historical painter to King George III in addition to being president of the Royal Academy (1792-1820 with the exception of 1806). Sir Joshua Reynolds preceeded West as first president of the Royal Academy (1768-1792).
3. These are the same notebooks referred to by Barbara Novak in her introductory essay (see p. 12).
4. Reynolds delivered yearly lectures at the Royal Academy which were later published as *Discourses*; these summaries of seventeenth- and eighteenth-century art theory influenced West and Morse, as well as many other nineteenth-century artists.
5. According to William Dunlap, *History of the Rise and Progress of the Arts of Design in the United States* (1834; reprint New York: Dover Publications, 1969), 316: "Mr. Morse delivered a course of lectures on the fine arts before the New-York Athenaeum. ... This was the first course of lectures on the subject read in America. These lectures were repeated to the students and academicians of the National Academy of Design" [c. 1828]. Nicolai Cikovsky, Jr., who edited and transcribed "On the Affinity of Painting with the Other Fine Arts," from the original manuscripts in the Academy's archives, notes that the lectures were repeated in 1836 and 1840. See footnote no. 1, p. 41 of his unpublished transcript in the Academy's Morse file.
6. Cikovsky, Jr. transcript, Lecture Two, 69.
7. *Ibid.*, Lecture Two, 54.
8. *Ibid.*, Lecture Four, 156.
9. *Ibid.*, Lecture Two, 53.
10. Thomas Seir Cummings, *Historic Annals of the National Academy of Design* (Philadelphia: George W. Childs, 1865), 44. The "Arts of Design" comprised painting, sculpture, architecture, and engraving.
11. *Ibid.*, 45.

AB

THOMAS COLE

(1801-1848)

Born February 1, Bolton-le-Moor, Lancashire, England. During youth, apprenticed as an engraver. 1818 emigrated to United States; worked as wood engraver in Philadelphia. Early 1819 trip to Saint Eustatius, West Indies; then to Steubenville, Ohio. 1820 to 1823 learned basics of painting from an itinerant portrait painter named Stein. Painted first landscapes. 1823 to 1825 maintained studio in Philadelphia. Studied at Pennsylvania Academy of the Fine Arts. 1825 joined family in New York City; first painting excursion up the Hudson. Some of first Catskill landscapes allegedly bought by William Dunlap, Asher B. Durand, and John Trumbull. 1826 helped found National Academy of Design. Became titular "head" of Hudson River School. Around 1828 painted major works *The Garden of Eden* and *The Expulsion from the Garden*; exhibited them at the Academy. 1829-1832 traveled in England, France, and Italy. Fall 1832 returned to New York. 1833 patron, Luman Reed, commissioned the five-part allegory *The Course of Empire;* completed 1836. 1836 married, settled permanently in Catskill. Spring 1839 Samuel Ward commissioned major allegorical series *The Voyage of Life.* 1840 completed and exhibited *The Voyage of Life.* 1841 to 1842 made second trip to London, Paris, and Rome. Painted second set of *The Voyage of Life* in Rome. 1842 returned home. 1844 taught first, and most illustrious pupil, Frederic E. Church. 1846 began cycle of paintings *The Cross and the World.* Before completion of paintings, died February 8, Catskill, New York.

REFERENCES: Howard S. Merritt, *Thomas Cole* (Exhibition catalogue, Memorial Art Gallery of the University of Rochester, Rochester, N.Y., 1969). Louis Legrand Noble, *The Life and Works of Thomas Cole* (1853; Cambridge, Mass.: Harvard University Press, 1964).

In 1825, the young artists of the American Academy of Fine Arts could no longer tolerate the haughty attitude of that institution toward its students. Samuel F.B. Morse took up their cause, and in that year founded the New York Drawing Association, " 'for the Promotion of the Arts', and the Assistance of Students'—simply a union for improvement in drawing."[1] Thomas Cole belonged to Morse's group. It was not intended to be a rival institution to the American Academy, but conflicts arose. As a result, Morse instigated the formation of the National Academy of Design in 1826. Once again, Cole joined his friend Morse and became one of the founding members of the Academy. The impact of his vital presence as an inspiration and his leading role as "father" of the Hudson River School is profoundly felt in William Cullen Bryant's *Funeral Oration, Occasioned by the Death of Thomas Cole:*

He was one of the founders of the Academy whose members I address, as well as one of its most illustrious ornaments. During the entire space which has elapsed since the first of its exhibitions, nearly a quarter of a century, I am not sure that there was a single year in which his works did not appear on its walls; to have missed them would have made us feel that the collection was incomplete. . . . His departure has left a vacuity which amazes and alarms us. It is as if the voyager on the Hudson were to look toward the great range of the Catskills, at the foot of which Cole, with a reverential fondness, had fixed his abode, and were to see that the grandest of its summits had disappeared, had sunk into the plain from our sight.[2]

Bryant's equation of Cole with the Catskills seems especially appropriate when one reads Cole's own words about the mountains he loved. Louis Legrand Noble, his biographer, relates:

It was usually his habit at the close of the day, particularly in these choice haunts, to write some little description of the scenes and incidents of his rambles, or to embody in verse a thought or sentiment.[3]
Life and Works of Thomas Cole (1853).

An excerpt from one of these poems, "The Wild," could serve as an invitation to enter into his paintings:

> Friends of my heart, lovers of nature's works,
> Let me transport you to those wild, blue mountains
> That rear their summits near the Hudson's wave.
> Though not the loftiest that begirt the land,
> They yet sublimely rise, and on their heights
> Your souls may have a sweet foretaste of heaven,
> And traverse wide the boundless. . . .[4]
> *Life and Works of Thomas Cole* (1853).

Cole shared the view of his contemporaries, perhaps even more strongly than most, that "cultivating a taste for scenery" was not just stimulating, but also morally uplifting:

There is in the human mind an almost inseparable connection between the beautiful and the good, so that if we contemplate the one the other seems present; and an excellent author has said, "It is difficult to look at any objects with pleasure—unless where it arises from brutal and tumultuous emotions—without feeling that disposition of mind which tends towards kindness and benevolence; and surely, whatever creates such a disposition, by increasing our pleasures and enjoyments, cannot be too much cultivated."[5]
"Essay on American Scenery" (1835).

In his "Essay on American Scenery," Cole described the attractions of the mountains of the northeast:

LANDSCAPE SKETCH I
Pen and ink, 2 x 3″
Signed lower right border: *T.C.*

LANDSCAPE SKETCH II
Pen and ink, 3¼ x 8″
Signed lower right on rock: *T. Cole, 1841*

It is true that in the eastern part of this continent there are no mountains that vie in altitude with the snow-crowned Alps—that the Alleghanies [sic] and the Catskills are in no point higher than five thousand feet; but this is no inconsiderable height; Snowdon in Wales, and Ben-Nevis in Scotland, are not more lofty; and in New Hampshire, which has been called the Switzerland of the United States, the White Mountains almost pierce the region of perpetual snow. The Alleghanies [sic] are in general heavy in form; but the Catskills, although not broken into abrupt angles like the most picturesque mountains of Italy, have varied, undulating, and exceedingly beautiful outlines—they heave from the valley of the Hudson like the subsiding billows of the ocean after a storm.[6]

The tiny ink sketches could be of Mount Washington, or Ben-Nevis, or of scenes from Cole's imagination. Yet, though they are inexplicit, they contain all the elements he considered necessary—the mountains, the trees—and the water:

Like the eye in the human countenance, it is a most expressive feature: in the unrippled lake, which mirrors all surrounding objects, we have the expression of tranquillity and peace—in the rapid stream, the headlong cataract, that of turbulence and impetuosity.[7]

"Essay on American Scenery" (1835).

A bubbling waterfall animates the smaller drawing; the somewhat larger panoramic drawing reflects nature's more serene mood.

The Academy is fortunate to have at least these examples of Cole's work, for in the early days of the Academy no qualifying painting was required. Although the sketches lack the full-blown beauty of a painting, they have a candid quality that is valuable in its own right. They were apparently a gift from Cole to Samuel F.B. Morse and were pasted in a sketchbook of casual drawings by Morse and his friends. It is tempting to speculate about the origin of these drawings. Perhaps they were scraps preserved from meetings of the Sketch Club, to which both Cole and Morse belonged.

Founded in 1827, the club provided a congenial atmosphere for the mingling of artists, writers, and others interested in the fine arts.[8] Thomas S. Cummings, a fellow member, outlined its aims:

It was formed for the promotion of mutual intercourse and improvement in impromptu sketching. Drawing for ONE hour from a subject proposed by the *host*, whose property the drawings remained, was part of the programme *positive;* the poets and others frequently amusing themselves during *that* hour by passing round a subject, on which each, in turn, furnished four lines—no more, no less: and some truly amusing mongrels were the result.[9]

Historic Annals of the National Academy of Design (1865).

The first regular meeting took place at the rooms of Thomas Cole. It was a decided success. All the members exerted themselves to please, and everything was agreeable. . .[10]

C.C. Ingham, Letter. In *Historic Annals.* . . .

The club managed to survive for thirty-two years.[11] Whether or not Cole's drawings actually originated there cannot be determined. Nevertheless, looking at the sketches in Morse's sketchbook, one can readily conjure up visions of the paper-cluttered rooms and witty conversations that must have been the Sketch Club.

NOTES

1. Thomas S. Cummings, *Historical Annals of the National Academy of Design, New York Drawing Associations, Etc., With Occasional Dottings by the Wayside, From 1825 to the Present Time* (Philadelphia: George W. Childs, 1865), 21.
2. William Cullen Bryant, *A Funeral Oration, Occasioned by the Death of Thomas Cole, Delivered Before the National Academy of Design, New York, May 4, 1848* (New York: D. Appleton, 1848), 3.
3. Louis Legrand Noble, *The Life and Works of Thomas Cole* (1853; reprint Cambridge, Mass.: Harvard University Press, 1964), 39.
5. John W. McCoubrey, *American Art, 1700-1960, Sources and Documents* (Englewood Cliffs, N.J.: Prentice-Hall, 1965), 99.
6. *Ibid.,* 107.
7. *Ibid.,* 103.
8. James T. Callow, *Kindred Spirits* (Chapel Hill, N.C.: University of North Carolina Press, 1967), 13.
9. Cummings, *Historic Annals,* 111.
10. *Ibid.,* 110.
11. Callow, *Kindred Spirits,* 13.

HR

THOMAS DOUGHTY

(1793-1856)
HM 1827

Born July 19, in Philadelphia. 1814-1816 worked with brother as leather currier. 1816 first exhibited at Pennsylvania Academy of the Fine Arts (PAFA). Listed in city directory as painter. Minimal instruction in drawing, basically self-taught. 1818-1819 independent leather currier. 1820 became an artist; city directory listed as landscape painter. 1821 two commissioned views of Robert Gilmor's Baltimore estate. 1822 eight paintings shown at PAFA, and annually through 1829. Became friendly with local artists Thomas Sully and John Neagle around this time. 1824 elected Pennsylvania Academician. 1826 two landscapes in inaugural exhibition, National Academy of Design; Athenaeum Gallery, Boston, 1827. 1828 to Boston, exhibited many paintings at Athenaeum through 1839; only once at NAD from 1829 to 1838. 1830 returned to Philadelphia, published monthly "Cabinet of Natural History and American Sports" through 1832. Contributed lithographs of animals. 1832 back to Boston until 1837, taught art. 1833 held sale exhibition at Athenaeum to raise money. 1834 forty-three landscapes in group exhibition with friends Francis Alexander, Chester Harding, Alvan Fisher, at Harding's Gallery, Boston. 1837 to England; sees Sully and J.J. Audubon in London. Returned 1838, settled New York. Continued to travel widely in Northeast. 1839 first Hudson River scenes. 1844 to New Orleans; 1845 to London. 1846 in Paris, copied Jacob Ruisdael and others in Louvre. Returned to New York 1847. 1848-1850 severely ill, no dated paintings. 1850 last exhibitions at NAD and PAFA. Died New York City, July 24.

REFERENCES: Howard N. Doughty, *Biographical Sketch of Thomas Doughty* (unpublished ms., National Collection of Fine Arts, 1941). Frank H. Goodyear, Jr., *Thomas Doughty* (Exhibition catalogue, Pennsylvania Academy of the Fine Arts, Philadelphia, 1973).

Thomas Doughty is usually mentioned in the earliest discussions of the native landscape school:

"*Now*, all our refinement can be but during the interval of labor—as it were, the amusement of the woodman, as he lays down his axe, in the shade of the forest he is felling. . . . In landscape-painting, for which our country has such eminent advantages, we have artists competent to represent our scenes—the pictures of Doughty and Cole have a character decidedly American. The former infuses into his pictures all that is quiet and lovely, romantic and beautiful in nature.[1]
The Knickerbocker (1833).

The American school of landscape is decidedly and peculiarly original; fresh, bold, brilliant, and grand. Without wishing to institute invidious comparisons, we may mention Doughty, of Boston, as eminently combining these qualities in his various works. He must undoubtedly be considered the master and founder of a new school—no small honor in this imitative age. We allude chiefly to his pictures of American autumnal scenery. They are conceived and executed in the spirit of free, untramelled genius, deriving its inspiration from a gorgeous and unhackneyed species of scenery.[2]
The Knickerbocker (1839).

Doughty was thus acknowledged as the first American artist to devote himself exclusively to landscape. He was a "natural painter" from the first, eschewing Washington Allston's romanticism, Benjamin West's history painting, and Thomas Sully's portraiture for direct observation and transcription of nature.

The reputation he gained in Philadelphia and then Boston, however, was soon eclipsed by younger New York artists. Already in 1834 Dunlap gave the artist short shrift in his monumental *History*, granting, "Mr. Doughty has long stood in the first rank as a landscape painter—he was at one time the first and best in the country."[3] In 1837 the Athenaeum Gallery exchanged Doughty's *The Lake of the Mountains*, purchased in December, 1829, for his rival Thomas Cole's *Angel Appearing to the Shepherds*. A friendly critic considered Doughty preeminent only upon the death of Cole:

. . .the misty, the atmospheric, the nature-student, Doughty. . .boon-companion of the earth, the air, the sun, the rivers and the woods, our friend. Are we too extravagant? Look at the works of Reynolds; look into the lectures of Fuseli; the critical enthusiasm and beaming printed thoughts of the "Oxford Student," and accuse us not of "overstepping the modesty of nature". . .Doughty's distances are superb. It is not *paint* that we see before us. His blue does not look like ultra-marine and lake, but like mountain-land seen through the very atmosphere itself. His meetings of hills are softly blended, as if the breeze interlaced the lines, and the air quivered the branches of trees together.[4]
The Knickerbocker (1848).

This blending of lines and effacement of stroke was part of Doughty's development toward general effect over the precise detailing that characterizes his works of the 1820s. At the Pennsylvania Academy of the Fine Arts in 1829 and 1830, Doughty exhibited a copy of a landscape by Claude Lorrain, and began to introduce classical ruins and towers into his scenes. Increasingly his work became more Claudian, and began to be criticized for lack of fidelity to nature. Doughty's increased and repetitive production led one observer to question his motives:

LANDSCAPE, c. 1835-1837
Oil on canvas, 10 x 8″
Unsigned
Gift of James D. Smillie, NA

He commenced painting with the feeling that God made the world, and all things therein. . . . but . . . he married at a very early age, and soon found himself called upon for the support of a large family. He has painted too much—too hastily.[5]

Graham's Magazine (1854).

Yet in the 1830s he produced his most well-known paintings, and individual works like his *Landscape* shown here have their own charm. This was probably the picture exhibited in October, 1839, at the Apollo Association: #216 *Small Landscape*, purchased by J. Smillie. The engraver James Smillie passed the light-filled scene on to his son James David, who bequeathed it to the Academy. Apropos of the typical lone figure of a fisherman in the painting, one should note that Doughty, like A.B. Durand, enjoyed fishing, and also hunting. Doughty even illustrated Nathaniel P. Willis' light-hearted angling poem:

> Come! Take your baskets and away,
> We'll to the rock for trout today.
> Our hooks are good, our flies are new,
> Our flexile lines are strong and true.[6]

Willis in turn praised Doughty's illustrations of the author's *American Scenery:*

His forte lies in scenery of a softer and inland character—the lonely forest-brook, the misty wood-lake, the still river, the heart of the quiet wilderness. In painting these features of Nature, he has (in his peculiar style) no rivals among American painters. . . . He is a most sweet and accomplished artist; and when the time comes for America to be proud of her painters, Doughty will be remembered among the first.[7]

N.P. Willis, American Scenery (1840).

NOTES

1. J. Houston Mifflin, "The Fine Arts in America," *The Knickerbocker* 2 (July 1833), 34.
2. Thomas R. Hofland, "The Fine Arts in the United States," *The Knickerbocker* 14 (July 1839), 50.
3. William Dunlap, *A History of the Rise and Progress of the Arts of Design in the United States* (New York: Blom, 1965) 3:176.
4. Anonymous, "Doughty's Landscapes," *The Knickerbocker* 32 (October 1848), 362-63. Although the author is anonymous the preface introduces him as a "friend." Cole (1801-1848) is discussed in previous paragraphs. The "Oxford Student" is John Ruskin.
5. E. Anna Lewis, "Art and Artists of America," *Graham's Magazine* 45 (Philadelphia, Nov. 1854), 484.
6. Howard Doughty, *Biographical Sketch of Thomas Doughty* (unpublished ms., National Collection of Fine Arts, 1941), 36.
7. N.P. Willis, *American Scenery* (London: George Virtue, 1840), 2:37. Also quoted in Frank Goodyear, Jr., *Thomas Doughty* (Exhibition catalogue, Pennsylvania Academy of the Fine Arts, Philadelphia, 1973), 30.

LK

ASHER BROWN DURAND

(1796-1886)
FOUNDER, NA 1826

Born in Jefferson (now Maplewood), New Jersey, on August 21. Apprenticeship to engraver Peter Maverick 1812-1817; partnership with Maverick until 1820. Activities in portrait, gift book, and banknote engraving earned him great prominence over the next decade. By 1835, through the patronage of Luman Reed, began to turn attention to painting portraits and, more significantly, landscapes. Served as second president of National Academy of Design (1845-1861). Initial member of Sketch Club in 1827. In 1840-1841 traveled in Europe with John William Casilear, John Frederick Kensett, and Thomas Prichard Rossiter; visited England, Lowlands, France, Germany, Switzerland, and Italy. Sketching trips to White Mountains, Lake George, and area around his home in Catskill Clove with Christopher Pearse Cranch, Thomas Hiram Hotchkiss, Edward D. Nelson, and others, especially in 1850s. Became acknowledged leader of American landscapists upon Thomas Cole's death in 1848. Published "Letters on Landscape Painting" in *The Crayon* in 1855. Ceased to paint 1878. Died in Maplewood on September 17.

REFERENCES: *A.B. Durand 1796-1886* (Exhibition catalogue, Montclair Art Museum, N.J., 1971). Barbara Novak, *American Painting of the Nineteenth Century* (New York: Praeger, 1969).

Upon the exhibition of this pair of paintings at the National Academy of Design in 1840 a critic for *The New-York Mirror* remarked:

His "Morning," and "Evening", lately finished, and now exhibiting at the National Academy, are his greatest works. They abound in many beauties and some faults. In the first place, the idea is too much like Cole's "Departure" and "Return," to be original. He imitated very successfully the colouring of Cole, and tried, though without success, to use his pencil. The contrast between them is not sufficiently great, for it takes some time to decide which is "Morning" and which "Evening". . . . If Durand devotes his attention to landscape-painting alone, and studies nature more, he will eventually become a first-rate artist in this interesting branch.[1]

As suggested by this review, these paintings by Durand— among his earliest extensive attempts at landscape—are derivative of his close friend Thomas Cole's conceptions, particularly Cole's *Departure* and *Return*, 1837 (Corcoran Gallery of Art). Like Cole's pair, those of Durand represent two moments of the day: morning and evening, or sunrise and sunset.[2] In his juxtaposition of times of day with the stages of man's life— contrasting the youthful shepherd and his family in *Morning* with

the aged philosopher in *Evening*—Durand was probably also thinking of Cole's important series of four pictures, *The Voyage of Life*, 1840 (Munson-Williams-Proctor Institute, Utica, New York). During the same year that Durand was working on these paintings, Thomas Cole occupied one of the rooms of the National Academy of Design ". . .for the purpose of examining and completing, under that more favorable light, his series of the 'Voyage of Life.' "[3] Durand, doubtless, had visited Cole and had seen and discussed his pictures with him.

Morning and *Evening* take as their theme not only the passage of individual life but also the temporal course of human civilization. In *Morning* the classical statue and pagan temple connote an early period in history; in *Evening* the pagan temple has been replaced by a medieval cathedral, suggesting the progress of civilization. In this respect, Cole's five-painting series *Course of Empire*, 1836 (New-York Historical Society) was Durand's probable source of inspiration, with the column on the right of Durand's *Evening* retained as a visual footnote to its origin in Cole's *Course of Empire, Desolation*. At this early moment in Durand's career, then, he is producing a conflation of the Colean concepts of *Voyage of Life* and *Course of Empire* compressed into the two-painting format of the *Departure* and *Return*. Durand had a good deal of difficulty developing his personal landscape style, as he confided to Cole in a letter of February 19, 1840. Durand wrote of the problems he was experiencing with these pictures:

The truth is it is all owing to that unfortunate picture which you did not see when you were here and which I have often thought you never would see, but after more than 3 months hard labour from morning till night and no small portion of night in the bargain, I am at last induced to believe that I shall finish it such as it is—
Of a truth, untill [sic] now, I have been so jaded, disheartened, discouraged and in short *all the disagreeableness*, [?] for said space [?] of time that I could not take my pen to address you. I was determined to do nothing till I had accomplished in some shape what I had set out for in relation to that picture. Previous to the rect [receipt] of your kind letter. however, I had begun and nearly completed the match picture, which I accomplished in less than 4 weeks much more to my satisfaction which induced me to proceed forthwith in repainting the other—. . .[4]

Morning and *Evening*, painted just before Durand's departure for Europe, embody the American artist's veneration of Claude Lorrain and his expectations of the grand tradition of European painting. Having experienced the works of Claude largely through prints, Durand—when he confronted the pictures themselves in the great museums of Europe—underwent a change in attitude, as the reminiscences of John Durand reveal:

THE MORNING OF LIFE, 1840
Oil on canvas, 49½ x 84½"
Signed lower left: *A.B. Durand 1840*
Gift of Mrs. Frederick J. Betts, 1911

THE EVENING OF LIFE, 1840
Oil on canvas, 49⅜ x 84"
Signed lower left: *A.B. Durand 1840*
Gift of Mrs. Frederick J. Betts, 1911

It is evident that my father had "Claude on the brain," and was puzzled how to estimate the works of the creator—or, at least, populariser—of modern landscape art. Accustomed to regard Claude as a divinity, he found himself in the attitude of a disputer for the truth in relation to a recognised orthordox authority. There seems to have been a struggle in his mind as to which was right, nature or this "old master."[5]

Durand, *Life and Times of A.B. Durand* (1894).

Nowhere in Durand's *oeuvre*, then, can a more unqualified statement of his admiration for Claude be found than in these two pictures. In their dependence on the pictorial devices of the Claudian landscape formula, as well as in the choice of pairing a morning with an evening—almost half of Claude's works were done in pendants, usually in the combination of morning and evening, or sunrise and sunset—Durand's debt to the seventeenth-century master of the ideal landscape is in evidence.[6]

Durand's use of landscape pendants raises questions of how the paintings were actually meant to be displayed, as well as of their sources. It is known that the works were commissioned by Frederick Betts of Newburgh, New York, but the tantalizing question remains as to whether they may have been meant to hang side by side, on opposite walls, or perhaps one above the other.[7] One of the few explicit statements on the use of landscape pendants occurs in Gérard de Lairesse's *Art of Painting* (first published in Dutch as *Het Groot Schilderboek*, 1707). This book was no doubt consulted by the artists at the National Academy of Design, since an English translation of it was included in the Academy's library from early on. In this treatise, Book 6 (on landscape painting), Chapter 7, entitled "Of the placing and fellowing of Landscapes," Lairesse codified his attitude toward this problem, one that was certainly on Durand's mind. Lairesse criticizes the notion that landscape "fellows" are meant to be as close in conception as possible, describes their characteristics, and makes suggestions for their placement:

First, with respect to the several places where the pictures are to be hung; for I hope no one will argue, that a piece suits any place; and without a variety in the manner of a master, I cannot judge whether he be a true one, or how rich his thoughts are.

Secondly, Because the artist ought, in his ordonnances, to comply with the fancy of the proprietor, as far as reason and the rules of art and decorum permit. . . .

I think the word *fellows* sufficiently implies, that they are two pictures of equal size, alike framed, receiving the same light, whether they hang above or next each other, mostly alike filled with work, and the figures of equal magnitude, and lessening towards the point of sight. And as for the thoughts or design, the more different they are, the more agreeable; and the better shewing [sic] the richness of the master's fancy.[8]

Turning our attention from the format to the themes of the pictures, we find that in their preoccupation with the ideas of the continuity of life and the passage of time, these paintings suggest affinities with the poets and writers of previous generations. James Thomson's *Seasons* served a number of American artists in their search for literary allusions, and may well have been invoked here, for as John Durand recalls of his father:

His reading at this time consisted mainly of the English poets, of whom Goldsmith and Thomson were his favourites. Their works, presenting human life and character in haromony with his rustic experiences, suited his temperament . . . the descriptions of the seasons by Thomson, vividly presenting the life of the woods and the charm of lonely haunts, answered to the longings of his imagination. In after years, many of the subjects of

his landscapes were prompted by these poetic souvenirs.[9]

Durand, *Life and Times of A.B. Durand* (1894).

Thomson's descriptions of pastoral sunrises and sunsets, sketched in words, seem to match the mood and visual imagery in Durand's paintings.

In *Morning*:
. . .Young *Day* pours in a-pace,
And opens all the lawny Prospect wide.
The dripping Rock, the Mountain's misty Top
Swell on the Eye, and brighten with the Dawn . . .

In *Evening*:
Low walks the Sun, and broadens by degrees,
Just o'er the Verge of Day . . .
Tis all one Blush from East to West! And now
Behind the dusky Earth, He dips his Orb,
Now half immers'd, and now a golden Curve,
Gives one faint Glimmer, and then disappears . . .[10]

In Durand's utilization of the allegorical landscape to symbolize the ages of man and the progressive stages of civilization, the issue of American attitudes to the art of allegory is brought forward for consideration. In this aspect of his art, Durand shares ambitions not only with Cole, but also with Jasper F. Cropsey, and others of the Hudson River artists, who at times turned to this age-old mode of painting. The reasons for this bear further investigation.

Although early in his career Durand struggled with the problems of symbolic and moralistic themes in landscape painting, his own inclinations soon lead him to the execution of specific scenes in American nature. In 1855, in his "Letters on Landscape Painting," Durand himself was expressing his rejection of allegorical painting:

I appeal with due respect from the judgment of those who have yielded their noblest energies to the fascinations of the *picturesque*, giving preference to scenes in which man supplants his Creator, whether in the gorgeous city of domes and palaces, or in the mouldering ruins that testify of his "ever fading glory," beautiful indeed, and not without their moral, but do they not belong more to the service of the tourist and historian than to that of the *true* landscape artist?[11]

When in 1840 Durand painted *Morning* and *Evening*, however, he was still caught in the dilemma between the real and the ideal that characterizes so much of American painting, working his way through the styles of his predecessors to the formulation of his own personal idiom.

NOTES
1. *The New-York Mirror*, July 18, 1840. Quoted in Frederick A. Sweet, "Asher B. Durand, Pioneer American Landscape Painter," *Art Quarterly* 8 (1945), 154.
2. In *The New-York Mirror*, December 23, 1837, 203, for example, Cole's pictures are referred to as representing "Morning and Evening, or Sunrise and Sunset."
3. As pointed out by Barbara Novak, this information is to be found in Thomas S. Cummings, *Historic Annals of the National Academy of Design* (Philadelphia: George W. Childs, 1865), 164.
4. Thomas Cole Papers, Archives of American Art, Smithsonian Institution, N.Y., microfilm roll ALC 2. From Durand's comments it would be interesting to know which picture caused him the greater difficulty; one would presume that he started with *Morning*, although a final answer awaits the conservator's report.
5. John Durand, *The Life and Times of A.B. Durand* (New York: Charles Scribner's Sons, 1894), 158.*

6. See Marcel Röthlisberger, *Claude Lorrain. The Paintings* (New Haven: Yale University Press, 1961), 1:27-31, for section on pairs.

7. See Durand, 135, for information on paintings A.B. Durand executed for Betts. My own conclusion is that the paintings were to be hung side by side. The bridge at the left of *Morning* suggests entrance into the picture on that side. One would then travel not literally but figuratively along the path between the trees, with the tree form cut on the right of *Morning* and on the left of *Evening*, suggesting a sort of continuation. One's progress through the picture space would then be halted by the single column on the right of *Evening*. Durand intended the pictures to be seen separately but to be united in moral message and pictorial effect.

8. Gérard de Lairesse, *The Art of Painting* (London, 1778), 214-15 (first published in Dutch as *Het Groot Schilderboek*, 1707).* A copy of this book, inscribed "Frederick R. Spencer 1836" was donated by Spencer to the library of the National Academy of Design before 1852. See "Books, & c. contained in the Library of the National Academy of Design" in *Constitution of the National Academy of Design, and Schedule of the Property* (New York: Sackett & Co., 1852), 46. Röthlisberger, 27, note 38, states that "the only explicit theoretical statement on this question [ie, pairs] which I know occurs in Lairesse."

9. Durand, 38. Concerning Durand's use of Thomson's *Seasons* we know, for example, that his engraving *Musidora* is an illustraton of a passage in *Seasons* (*ibid.*, 75). Durand was described in a contemporary review as "a quiet, pastoral poet—a Thomson on canvas . . ." (*Daily Tribune*, May 20, 1852; quoted in *ibid.*, 218). William Sidney Mount also turned to Thomson for inspiration. See, for example, the entry on *Celadon and Amelia* (1829) in Alfred Frankenstein, *Painter of Rural America: William Sidney Mount* (Exhibition catalogue, The Suffolk Museum at Stony Brook, Long Island, 1968), 12.

10. In Elizabeth Wheeler Manwaring, *Italian Landscape in eighteenth century England; a study chiefly of the influence of Claude Lorrain and Salvator Rosa on English taste, 1700-1800* (New York: Russell & Russell, 1965), 102, 103.

11. "Letters on Landscape Painting," Letter III, *The Crayon* 1 (January 31, 1855). In Sweet, "Asher B. Durand," 154.

In Library of National Academy of Design.

KM

DANIEL HUNTINGTON

(1816-1906)
ANA 1839; NA 1840; PNA 1863-1869, 1877-1890

Born October 14, New York City. After one year at Yale, transferred to Hamilton College in Clinton, N.Y. There encouraged by portrait painter Charles Loring Elliott to become an artist. 1836 returned to New York to study under Samuel F.B. Morse, and later with portrait and genre painter Henry Inman. 1836 commission to draw Hudson views led to interest in landscape. Although major work was portraiture, also painted genre, still lifes, and allegories such as his well-known *Mercy's Dream* (1850). 1839 traveled to Europe, mainly in Italy. 1840 returned to New York. 1842 married and subsequently returned to Europe for three years. 1850 William Cullen Bryant and other friends organized a retrospective exhibition of Huntington's paintings, a tribute to his popularity. 1851-1858 went abroad again; last visit there 1882. Presidency at National Academy was longest in institution's history; vice-president of Metropolitan Museum of Art for thirty-three years concurrently. Prolific painter and draftsman. Died April 18 in New York City.

REFERENCES: Samuel Isham, *The History of American Painting* (1905; reprint New York: The Macmillan Co., 1927). *Memorial Exhibition of Works by the Late Daniel Huntington, N.A.*, Century Association, April, 1908. New York Public Library Artist's Clipping File. Henry T. Tuckerman, *Book of the Artists* (New York: G.P. Putnam's, 1867). H.T. Tuckerman, "Our Artists: The President of the Academy," *Putnam's Magazine* 11 (March 1867).

The editor of *Harper's Weekly* noted in 1867 that Huntington's "versatility is remarkable. His chief talent is for portraiture, but the imposing landscape in the present exhibition shows that he does not shrink from entering the lists with Kensett, Church, and Bierstadt."[1]

From West Campton, New Hampshire, on September 11, 1855, Daniel Huntington wrote the following letter to *The Crayon*:

Having heard of the merits of this place as a sketching ground, from Mr. Gerry and Mr. Williams of Boston, I have been passing some days here, and find it indeed a very agreeable and desirable place for landscape study. It is about seven miles north from Plymouth, on the road to the Franconia Mountains, and about seventeen from Centre Harbor, Plymouth being on the Concord and Montreal Railroad; it is a position very easily reached. I came by the way of Centre Harbor, passing Squam Lake, with its great variety of beautiful shores. The whole journey from the Harbor here is full of picturesque beauty. . . . The valley is narrower than that of the Saco, and is quite different in the character of its half-wooded hill-sides. These being partly cleared, and broken with full rich masses of forest, combine a great variety of lines to form half distances, very remarkable for their beauty. . . . Nearer to you and in another

direction are the Welch Mountains, whose outline is noble, with cliffs of a faint grey and fleshy color, which with the intermingled forests, deep gulleys, and ravines produce in the morning and evening light effects of light and shade, and delicate varieties of color, quite magical. This mountain, combining with the wooded half distances before described, and with the river, its rocks, and overhanging trees, furnish some most noble pictures. There is a brook, too, which empties here into the main river, with groups of white and yellow birches, willows, elms, and other graceful trees; with a foot bridge, a fordway, all of which afford rich materials for the portfolio. The hotel kept by Sandborn is also the post-office of the place, which really is not a village, but a succession of scattered farm houses, with a store, a saw mill, and a blacksmith shop, half a mile apart along the road. The house is very neat and comfortable, and the host and hostess are obliging. The charges for board are moderate. There is a drive from here up the valley of Mad River, which furnishes some new and bold mountain outlines.[2]

The Crayon (1855).

Subsequent critics noted:

M. Huntington was born a landscape painter, and it is to be regretted that the pictures he paints in this high department of Art are not more frequent, so as to reveal his fine perception of the beauties of external Nature. His landscapes seem to be more the pastime of leisure hours than of steady, laborious purpose. His feeling for Nature is broad and comprehensive, and certain details are often admirably expressed. The breezy aspect of the sea, and a recognition of the spirit and principles of light—a most important element of Art, characterize his works, . . .[3]

The Crayon (1858).

The 36th annual exhibition of the National Academy opened on the 20th ult . . . Huntington has two landscapes, *Shawangunk Mountain Scenery* and *Saco River Scenery*, the former with a particularly luminous sky, besides several portraits, . . .[4]

The Crayon (1861).

For prolific production of portraits, Huntington fairly vies with the men just described. Whether he or Elliott or Healy produced the greatest number, is probably an insoluble riddle; but Huntington, unlike the others, attempted every branch of painting, landscape, *genre*, allegory, and still-life. One of his first excursions was into the Catskills, and through his early life he was in sympathy with the Hudson River School, producing landscapes in their manner, including a huge Chocorua Peak.[5]

Samuel Isham, *History of American Painting* (1905).

In his chapter on Huntington, Henry T. Tuckerman briefly comments on the artist's landscape abilities:

Those who have seen the marine view painted by Huntington several years ago, at Newport, R.I., will not fail to accord him great skill and fine feeling in landscape, and he has lately finished a work of this kind more elaborate and characteristic than any picture of the same species he has ever attempted. It has occupied him at intervals for several years. The

LANDSCAPE (untitled)
Oil on canvas, 17¼ x 21″
Signed lower right: *D. Huntington*
Suydam Collection

subject is New Hampshire scenery, amid which he has passed many summers; Mount Chicora [*sic*] is prominent; each feature is a careful study from nature; a mountain that will be recognized at once by many—a lake, a cliff, groups of trees, and an effective foreground, with the gray mottled sky and subdued autumnal tints of early September. . . .[6]
Book of the Artists (1867).

Tuckerman concludes his essay on Huntington by observing that: "In a different era and country, as we have said, Huntington would have become preëminently a religious painter; but as is so often the case, portraiture soon chiefly occupied his pencil."[7]

Judging from the quality of Huntington's landscape sketches, and the painting in the present exhibition, one can only wonder why in that era and country, Huntington did not respond more frequently to his innate poetic feeling for nature and become a landscape painter.

NOTES
1. Anonymous, "American Artists," *Harper's Weekly* 11 (May 4, 1867), 274.
2. "Correspondence," *The Crayon* 2 (Oct. 1855), 215.
3. "Sketchings: Exhibition of the National Academy of Design," *The Crayon* 5 (May 1858), 147.
4. "Sketchings: National Academy of Design," *The Crayon* 8 (April 1861), 94.
5. Samuel Isham, *The History of American Painting* (1905; reprint New York: The Macmillan Co., 1927), 282,285.
6. Henry T. Tuckerman, *Book of the Artists* (New York: G.P. Putnam's 1867), 324.
7. *Ibid.*, 328.

SGS

SANFORD ROBINSON GIFFORD

(1823-1880)
ANA 1851; NA 1854

Born July 10, in Greenfield, N.Y. Son of prosperous foundry owner. 1842-1844 attended Brown University. Left Brown to study painting under John Rubens Smith in New York City. 1847 began exhibiting National Academy of Design. 1855-1857 first trip abroad; visited England, France, Holland, Germany, Austria, Switzerland, Italy. In Rome companion of Worthington Whittredge and Albert Bierstadt. 1858 took studio in Tenth Street Studio Building. 1861, 1863-1864 served in National Guard Regiment. 1868-1869 second trip abroad; visited Italy, Sicily, Greece, Turkey, Lebanon, Syria, and Jerusalem. 1870 to Colorado Rockies with Whittredge and John F. Kensett; toured California, Oregon, British Columbia, Alaska. In eastern United States traveled to Vermont, New Hampshire, Maine. Died August 29, in New York City. 1880-1881 memorial exhibition of Gifford's paintings at Metropolitan Museum of Art. 1881 Metropolitan Museum published *Memorial Catalogue* of Gifford's paintings.

REFERENCE: Nicolai Cikovsky, Jr., *Sanford Robinson Gifford* (Exhibition catalogue, University of Texas Art Museum, Austin, 1971).

Because of his family wealth, Gifford was one of the few American painters of his day not compelled to paint for a living. Yet his private fortunes were belied not only by an extraordinarily productive career[1] but by a reputation among his Academy colleagues for an extreme simplicity in manner and appearance.[2] His financial independence also permitted him to travel widely and at will. Indeed, Gifford seems to have earned something of a reputation also as an artist-explorer. His friend Worthington Whittredge described how Gifford found room and board one summer with "a family of plain country folk" residing in coveted isolation in Kauterskill Clove in the Catskills. Before long Gifford had brought along with him a host of painters from New York to share his secluded quarters, an arrangement that lasted several seasons. "But," as Whittredge recalls, "this experiment proved fatal in the end. Boarders came in flocks from the city and the place had to be abandoned and new quarters found further on."[3]

Whittredge's account hints at a paradoxical dilemma of the nineteenth-century American landscapist: the pictures he designed to celebrate the virgin majesty of American places often functioned as irresistible advertisements to city dwellers infected with the contemporary craze for picturesque travel. The painter's image subsequently became an historical document as the scene he had recorded was transformed—or often merely trampled upon—by the advance of civilization.

Gifford was already composing an elegy to a pristine past when he painted *Mount Mansfield, Vermont* in 1859, a scene he depicted many times.[4] In 1847 there barely existed a rude path up the mountainside. Yet, when the artist first arrived there eleven years later, he could take a coach to a hotel near the summit, which had been opened that year by settlers from a nearby village.[5] If there were any Indians remaining in the region in 1858 their presence could have been little more significant than their function in the foreground of Gifford's painting, as picturesque props.[6]

The inclusion of Indians as archaizing elements in American landscape art had a tradition extending back at least to the turn of the century.[7] And as Ila Weiss has pointed out in her dissertation on the artist,[8] only a few years before Gifford painted this work an anonymous editor in *The Crayon* was reminding his readers of the documentary and aesthetic value of using Indians in painting:

Soon the last red man will have faded from his native land, and those who come after us will trust to our scanty records for their knowledge of his habits and appearance. . . .

Setting aside all the Indian history of the West, how much there is that is romantic, peculiar, and picturesque in his struggles with civilization in our own section of the country. . . . As an accessory in landscape, the Indian may be used with great effect. He is at home in every scene of primitive country.[9]

The Crayon (1858).

The Indians in Gifford's picture are especially curious because they are the first he is known to have included in a landscape. One prefers to imagine his attitude toward them was as empathetic as it was historical, since in the summer of 1859, the year in which he painted this version of *Mount Mansfield*, he briefly lived with a tribe of Micmacs of Nova Scotia. Of this experience he wrote home to New York: "These Indians are a simple and friendly folk. We paddled about in their canoes, and in the evening had a pow-wow and smoked a pipe with them about the fire in a wigwam."[10]

Gifford might also have been aware of the regional lore surrounding Mount Mansfield itself when painting this picture. When white men first took stock of the range of hills comprising Vermont's loftiest elevation (the highest peak, 4,394 feet, occupies the center of the composition) they read into them the profile of a human face. Gifford's idyl seems to yearn vainly for the aboriginal epoch that revered the landmark as "Moze-o-de-be-Wadso": "the mountain shaped like the head of a moose."[11]

MOUNT MANSFIELD, VERMONT, 1859
Oil on canvas, 10½ x 20″
Signed lower left: *S.R. Gifford 1859*
Suydam Collection

NOTES

1. *A Memorial Catalogue of the Paintings of Sanford Robinson Gifford, N.A.,* intro., John F. Weir (New York: Metropolitan Museum of Art, 1881) lists 731 paintings executed during a career lasting thirty-three years.

2. For a description of Gifford's character see the address given by Worthington Whittredge in *Gifford Memorial Meeting of the Century,* New York, Century Rooms, Friday evening, November 19, 1880, 38-46.

3. *Ibid.,* 43-44.

4. The *Memorial Catalogue* of Gifford's paintings lists twenty-one depictions of Mount Mansfield or its vicinity: the first (no. 131), is a sketch dated August 1858, and the last (no. 469), was sold in 1868. The last dated *Mount Mansfield* (no. 285) was painted in 1863. The Academy's *Mount Mansfield,* signed and dated 1859, is probably no. 172 in the *Catalogue,* though it is wrongly listed as "undated." See the *Memorial Catalogue,* nos. 131-40, 163-64, 168, 172, 176, 201, 185, 327-29, and 469.

5. Walter Collins O'Kane, *Trails and Summits of the Green Mountains* (Boston: Houghton Mifflin, 1926), 232-34.

6. With the defeat of the French by the British in the French and Indian War of 1689-1763, the Indians who had sparsely inhabited Vermont were largely driven out. In the year of the treaty (1763), several tracts of land surrounding Mount Mansfield were incorporated into towns by colonial settlers. By the time Gifford arrived there in 1858, therefore, the region was well—if not densely—settled by whites, and Indians would have been an improbable sight. For a history of the Indian occupation of Vermont see Walter Hill Crockett, *Vermont,* vol. 1 (New York: Century History Co., 1921), 31-70. For a demographic description of the towns surrounding Mount Mansfield in 1840 see Zadock Thompson, *History of the State of Vermont* (Burlington: Smith & Co., 1883); see p. 109 for Mansfield; p. 166 for Stow; p. 175 for Underhill.

7. One notable landscape subject in American painting in which Indians were almost invariably included was Niagara Falls. John Vanderlyn had used them in one of his several views of the Falls painted 1801-1804 (Senate House Museum, Kingston, New York). John Trumbull included an Indian family in one of his two panoramas of Niagara Falls (New-York Historical Society), painted in 1808. Most notable in respect to Gifford's painting, however, are the two Indians in Thomas Cole's *Distant View of Niagara Falls* (Art Institute of Chicago), painted in 1829. As in the Gifford, both figures, one seated, one standing, are perched on a rocky platform in the lower center of the picture, directly beneath the subject. In Gifford's picture, however, the figures look not toward the subject, as they do in the Cole, but to the left, where the sun is setting. My account of the use of Indians in Niagara Falls iconography is derived from Ellwood C. Parry, *The Image of the Indian and the Black Man in American Art, 1590-1900* (New York: George Braziller, 1974), 53-58.

8. Ila J.S. Weiss, "Sanford Robinson Gifford" (Ph.D. dissertation, Columbia University, 1968), 180.

9. "The Indians in American Art," *The Crayon* 3 (June 1856), 28. In Weiss, 180.

10. Sanford R. Gifford, letter to *The Crayon,* July 26, 1859. In Weiss, 185-86.

11. O'Kane, 230-31.

KA

(Thomas) Worthington Whittredge

(1820-1910)
ANA 1860; NA 1862; PNA 1874-1877

Born May 22 near Springfield, Ohio. Began artistic training in Cincinnati as house and sign painter at age seventeen. Initially did portraits to support self, but within one year exhibited landscape paintings as well. With money from commissions of Cincinnati patrons traveled abroad in 1849. Visited Belgium and France; settled in Düsseldorf, befriended by Emmanuel Leutze. Work of this period reveals influence of Andreas Achenbach, Carl Friedrich Lessing, and Johann Schirmer, all members of Düsseldorf Academy. Summer 1856 sketching trip to Switzerland with Leutze and William Stanley Haseltine; subsequently joined by Albert Bierstadt with whom traveled to Italy. Spent next three years in Italy; supported self there by painting souvenir pictures for tourists. Began to omit first name when signing paintings. 1859 returned to United States and settled in Tenth Street Studio Building early 1860. 1866 first expedition to West with General John Pope. 1867 married. Three years later to West again (Colorado and Wyoming) accompanied by Sanford Gifford and John F. Kensett; returned a third time in 1871. Spent final years in Summit, N.J.; continued to paint and work on autobiography. Died there February 25.

REFERENCES: John I.H. Baur, ed., "The Autobiography of Worthington Whittredge, 1820-1910," *Brooklyn Museum Journal* 1 (1942). Anthony F. Janson, *The Paintings of Worthington Whittredge* (unpublished Ph.D. dissertation, Harvard Univ., 1975). Janson, "Worthington Whittredge: Two Early Landscapes," *Bulletin of the Detroit Institute of Arts* 65 (Winter 1977). Janson, "The Western Landscapes of Worthington Whittredge," *American Art Review* 3 (Nov.-Dec. 1976). Janson, "Worthington Whittredge: The Development of a Hudson River Painter, 1860-1868," *American Art Journal* 11 (April 1975).

In 1856, after spending six years studying in Düsseldorf, Whittredge decided to visit Italy. Leaving in July, he and his companions Leutze and Haseltine began their journey, traveling slowly up the Rhine into Switzerland. By September they were camped in Meyringen, where Whittredge made sketches of the Matterhorn. From these preliminary studies, the artist executed *Foot of the Matterhorn* in Rome early in 1857. Whittredge himself vividly described his response to the Swiss Alps:

We made the whole trip before it was cold weather and made many studies on the way. The first sight of the Alps made a deep impression on my mind, particularly the ruggedest parts of them. I had been accustomed to measure grandeur, at the most, by the little hills of Western Virginia; I had never thought it might be measured horizontally as on our great Western plains. In fact, I believe it is the accepted idea that all grandeur *must* be measured up and down. . . .

But I believe I was scarcely myself all the time I was in Switzerland, as well on this first visit as later when, to get away from the heat of Rome, I returned there for a month or two. I painted in Rome a few pictures of Swiss scenery, but Switzerland was not then and never had been the subject of many of my pictures and I can only account for this on the ground that it was altogether unsuitable for me. My thoughts ran more upon simple scenes and simple subjects, or it may be I never got into the way of measuring all grandeur in a perpendicular line, though I frequently returned to the quaint village of Brunnen which is one of the most picturesque and charming spots on the lake.[1]

John I.H. Baur, ed., "Autobiography of Worthington Whittredge"
(1942).

John Ruskin, in *Modern Painters*, in addition to extolling the sublimity of the Alps, also reiterated the difficulties that many artists encountered when trying to paint these awesome mountains:

. . . for Switzerland is quite beyond the power of any but first-rate men, and is exceedingly bad practice for a rising artist; but, let us express a hope that Alpine scenery will not continue to be neglected as it has been, by those who alone are capable of treating it.[2]

Whittredge was well aware of his own difficulties in dealing with the Alps, and perhaps in an effort to allay their terrifying grandeur, he treated the scene as literally as possible. Anthony Janson suggests that Whittredge probably undertook this painting because of his friendship with Albert Bierstadt, whose predilection for grandiose mountain scenes is well known. Indeed, Whittredge's execution echoes that of Bierstadt's early *Rhine Landscape* (location unknown).[3]

Notwithstanding Whittredge's own distaste for his Swiss pictures, they were well received by the public. In 1858, *The Crayon* reported:

Whitridge [sic], a landscape painter, who has resided many years at Düsseldorf, is now here. He delights in the green valleys of Switzerland and the glittering peaks of the Alps, which he renders with great force.[4]

NOTES
1. John I.H. Baur, ed., "The Autobiography of Worthington Whittredge, 1820-1910," *Brooklyn Museum Journal* 1 (1942), 31-32. (Original ms. in the Archives of American Art, Washington, D.C.)
2. John Ruskin, *Modern Painters* (London: J.M. Dent, n.d.), 2:19-20.
3. Anthony F. Janson, *The Paintings of Worthington Whittredge* (unpublished Ph.D. dissertation, Harvard University, 1975), 50-51.
4. "Foreign Correspondence," *The Crayon* 5 (June 1858), 170.

SGS

FOOT OF THE MATTERHORN, NEAR MEYRINGEN, c. 1857
Oil on canvas, mounted on masonite, 24¾ x 19⅝"
Signed lower right: *W.W.*

WILLIAM TROST RICHARDS

(1833-1905)
HM 1862; NA 1871

Born Philadelphia, November 14. 1846 entered Central High School of Philadelphia; left following year to work. 1850-1855 studied part-time with Paul Weber. Probably began work as designer of ornamental metalwork at Philadelphia firm: remained there full-time until 1853. 1854 acquired studio with Alexander Lawrie and traveled to New York. Met John F. Kensett, Frederic E. Church, Samuel Colman, and Jasper F. Cropsey. Summer 1855 traveled to Adirondacks. Left for Europe for a year. 1859 moved to Germantown, Pa., maintained Philadelphia studio. Summers of 1859, 1860, in Catskills and Atlantic City. 1863 elected member Society for the Advancement of Truth in Art; also elected Academician of Pennsylvania Academy of the Fine Arts. 1866 departed for Europe; returned 1867. Traveled on East coast during summers of 1868 through 1874. 1875 bought summer house in Newport. Subsequently spent most summers there, winters in Germantown. Winters of 1879 and 1880 in London, summers on Continent. 1881 purchased land in Newport to build Graycliff. 1884 exchanged Germantown house for Oldmixion farm. 1885-1888 most winters Cambridge, Mass. 1890 bought house in Newport for winter residence. 1891 sold Oldmixion; traveled to Europe. Spent remaining years traveling back and forth between Newport and Europe, spending time in England, Scotland, and Norway. 1904 summer at Lake Placid, N.Y. Died November 8 in Newport.

REFERENCES: *National Cyclopedia of American Biography* (New York: James E. White and Co., 1904). Harrison S. Morris, *Masterpieces of the Sea: William Trost Richards* (Philadelphia: J.B. Lippincott & Co., 1912). Linda S. Ferber, *William Trost Richards (1833-1905): American Landscape and Marine Painter* (Ph.D. dissertation, Columbia University. Reprint, Garland Series, 1980).

The ranges stood
Transfigured in the silver flood.
Their snows flashing cold and keen.
Dead white, save where some sharp ravine.
Took shadow, or the sombre green
Of hemlocks turned to pitchy black,
Against the whiteness at their back.[1]

John Greenleaf Whittier, "Snow-bound."

Among the stupendous mountain-landscapes of Switzerland, one is stricken with awe.[2]

Douglas William Freshfield, "Alpine Wanderings, I" (1876).

In their "wanderings" and "scrambles" in the Alps in the 1800s, English and American travelers were struck by the awesome sublimity of the high mountain peaks.[3] Richards, who had only experienced the ranges of the Adirondacks and the Catskills, was probably just as "stricken with awe" on his first trip to Switzerland in 1855 as those many adventurers who recorded their travels in periodicals of the day. He sought to record the drama of the scenery in a small pocket-sketchbook. Bad weather curtailed his sketching activities, but between storms he managed to complete a number of finished drawings and some "hasty sketches" that "capture a sense of [the] vast heights and depths" of the Alps.[4]

Richards returned to Switzerland with his family in the summer of 1867, visiting Lake Geneva first, then traveling east through the Bernese Alps that extend from Lake Geneva to Lake Lucerne. He drew constantly, probably eager to record all that he had missed on his first alpine trek. A large number of drawings exist from this trip, but as Linda Ferber notes, "few paintings of European subjects are recorded in the years following Richards' return [to the Unied States]."[5] This unfinished oil, dated c. 1870, may be one of the artist's aborted efforts.[6]

The canvas is interesting in that it shows Richards' working method. He painted in large areas of color, then completed the work a section at a time. The snow and ice-covered peaks and glacial gorge in the middle ground of this composition are more completely finished than the foreground slopes; delicately graded shadows are indicated, and cracks and ridges are denoted by thin lines of paint. By contrast, the dark slopes in the foreground are smudged and ill-defined, while the fir trees in the immediate foreground are painted in some detail

Had this painting been finished, the topography of the central glacial peaks probably would have been indicated in even greater detail. Some of the extant drawings from the trip are highly detailed: crevices, cracks, precipices are all delineated in extremely fine pencil lines.[7] The drawings recall the illustrations accompanying Ruskin's discussion "Of Mountain Beauty," published in 1856 in his fourth volume of *Modern Painters*.[8] As Ferber states, Richards was probably aware of Ruskin's writing and could have been familiar with his intructions regarding the rendering of complex mountain structures. In this painting his intent was probably "to seek out the underlying structure of the highly complex topography" rather than merely record a picturesque view.[9] In a similar manner in the next decade Richards would

SWISS MOUNTAIN LANDSCAPE (unfinished), c. 1870
Oil on canvas, 16 x 24″
Unsigned
Brewster Bequest

_____

carefully observe and record with geological accuracy the rock formations along the Newport coast, demonstrating his continuing fascination with the structure of nature as well as a reverence for its picturesque beauty.

It is possible that a sketchbook drawing in the Cooper-Hewitt Collection (no. 1953-179-58) may have been used as a study for this painting. The drawing, dated 1867, is of an unidentified subject, but the panoramic mountain scene it records is most likely a view of the Swiss Alps. The right half of the drawing shows ice-covered peaks and a triangular glacial gorge that are quite similar in formation to those represented in this Richards painting. Interestingly, too, while the top half of the drawing is carefully rendered in fine detail, the lower half, depicting the slopes extending to the horizon, is more sketchily indicated. The similarity of Richards' stylistic approach in the drawing and the painting, as well as the similarity of the mountain topography represented in both, suggests a possible link between the two.

The awesome mountains were not easy subjects to record. As Ferber notes, the panoramic alpine views were "difficult to draw because of [their] slope, scale, and complexity of surface." Detailed drawings like the one that may have been used as a study for this painting must have taken Richards considerable time to execute. Thus it is not surprising that he would consider buying photographs of the alpine views to supplement his drawings.[10] On his first trip to the Alps in 1855, he had written his sister Sallie, "I am deterred from sketching, because I can buy very cheaply photographs that are better so far as regards facts than any but the most elaborate sketches."[11] The one known sketchbook from Richards' second trip contains a list of expenses that includes the entry, "Bill at Interlaken—photographs & etc. 15.00."[12] Ferber speculates that Richards could well have purchased photographs of alpine views on his second trip through Switzerland. If so, it is conceivable that he consulted such photographs at the time he painted this scene.

One can only conjecture as to why this painting was left unfinished. Its incomplete state, however, does not lessen its impact, for it effectively conveys the grandeur of the snow-covered Alps bathed in bright sunlight:

The snow is an intense reflector of light . . . how bright that light is no one knows so well as he who has made the ascent of the snow peaks. It is at times blinding. The morning sun starts every facet glittering until the whole range becomes a blaze of splendor. . . . Nothing on the globe is comparable in intensity to the snow peaks under sunlight. The white crowning of the Alps is, indeed, their supreme glory.[13]

Van Dyke, "The High Alps" (1908).

The vast heights of the Alps must have elicited as much awe from Richards as the blinding intensity of their light. Steeped in nineteenth-century romanticism, Richards "divined a spiritual significance behind the appearance of reality."[14] He may well have considered the Alps—surely the highest mountains he had ever seen—a "link between heaven and earth," a particularly impressive symbol of God's presence in nature.[15] Van Dyke, writing shortly after Richards' death, noted:

Even at the present day when faiths and beliefs are less pronounced there is still a feeling with us that we are nearer God in the mountains than on flat lands. It is the land of the sky—the spirit land—something removed from the dross and dust of the material world . . .[16]

The Alps attracted other American landscapists of the nineteenth century, including the artists T. Worthington Whittredge and John W. Casilear (see pp. 42 and 48) who, like Richards, found the "stupendous mountain-landscapes" impressive images of God's handiwork in nature:

[the mountains are] the most transcendent of Nature's beauties. . . . Always they are majestic, always they are splendid. Where else on earth shall [one] see such aspiring grandeur of form, such purity of light, such clarity and simplicity of color! . . . they . . . are "everlasting" and "eternal."[17]

Van Dyke, "The High Alps" (1908).

Notes

K.N. and I wish to express our thanks to Linda S. Ferber for her generous loan of material and for her advice and suggestions regarding the Richards works shown in this exhibition.

1. John Greenleaf Whittier, "Snow-bound," quoted in Edward Whymper, "Scrambles Amongst the Alps in 1860-'69," *Lippincott's Magazine*, 8, no. 45, (September 1871), 231.
2. Douglas William Freshfield, "Alpine Wanderings, I," *Appleton's Journal* 15, no. 356, (January 15, 1876), 66.
3. According to the *Encyclopaedia Britannica* (Chicago: William Benson, 1973) 21, 671, railroads spread throughout Europe in the 1850s, providing easier access to the Alps. The second half of the century saw the systematic exploration of the mountains by individuals such as the Englishmen Edward Whymper and Douglas William Freshfield, who published accounts of their explorations in the 1870s (see notes 1 and 2 above.)
4. Linda S. Ferber, *William Trost Richards (1833-1905), American Landscape and Marine Painter* (Ph.D. dissertation, Columbia University, 1978, Reprint, Garland Series, New York, 1980), 75.
5. *Ibid.*, 195, 196, 198. Anne Whitney, a friend of Richards' who accompanied him on part of his trip through Switzerland, wrote from Interlaken in August of 1867 that "Mr. Richards sketches all the days, not withstanding the weather." (Anne Whitney, in a letter to an unknown correspondent, August 4, 1867).
6. William T. Brewster, in a note attached to this painting on its bequest to the National Academy of Design, entitled it *Swiss Mountain Landscape* and dated it c. 1870. Ferber agrees with this dating (conversation with Linda S. Ferber, April 22, 1980). The subject can be tentatively identified as the Swiss Alps upon comparison with extant drawings of the same executed by Richards on his trip to Switzerland in the summer of 1867. See following note.
7. See *Mountain Peaks* (no. 1953-179-58), *Scenes at Lauterbrunnen* (no. 1953-179-50), *Pflalten Stock, Meiringen* (no. 1953-179-53), drawings by William T. Richards in the Cooper-Hewitt Museum of Decorative Arts and Design, Smithsonian Institution, New York. The collection includes possibly 20 drawings from Richards' 1867 trip through Switzerland (some unidentified drawings are considered to be of Swiss subjects, but have not been positively identified).
8. See John Ruskin, *Modern Painters*, vol. 4, 1856 (New York: Merrill and Baker, 1886).
9. Ferber, *Richards*, (1980), 138, 196.
10. *Ibid.*, 196.
11. William Trost Richards' letter to his sister Sallie, 1855. Typescript of unlocated manuscript, quoted in Linda S. Ferber, *William Trost Richards, Landscape and Marine Painter, 1833-1905* (Exhibition catalogue, Brooklyn Museum, 1973), 42, note 69.
12. Ferber, *Richards* (1980), 196.
13. John C. Van Dyke, "The High Alps," *Scribner's Magazine* 43, no. 6 (June 1908), 684.
14. Ferber, *Richards* (1973), 32.
15. John Ruskin, *Modern Painters*, I, 1843, quoted in "On Divers Themes in Nature," edited and with introduction by Barbara Novak, from Kynaston McShine, ed., *The Natural Paradise: Painting in America, 1800-1950* (Exhibition catalogue, Museum of Modern Art, N.Y., 1976), 95.
16. Van Dyke, "The High Alps," 669.
17. *Ibid.*, 670.

CC

MRS. WILLIAM T. BREWSTER BEQUEST

With the exception of one painting, all the works by William Trost Richards in the National Academy of Design Collection were bequeathed to the museum by Anna Richards Brewster (Mrs. William T. Brewster), a daughter of the artist.[1] Born in Germantown, Pennsylvania, in 1870, Anna Mary Richards decided to follow her father's example and become a painter. She studied in Boston, New York, and Paris. She was awarded the Dodge Prize at the National Academy of Design in 1890 and became a member of the National Academy of Women Painters and Sculptors.[2] Sometimes she worked with her father "whom she wholly admired," and "instinctively followed the principles, few in number, on which he insisted . . . To them nature was inexhaustible and infinitely varied. He painted for over fifty years, she for some sixty."[3]

Upon her father's death in 1905, Anna Richards Brewster inherited one fifth of his estate.[4] In 1952, at the age of eighty-two, she and her husband sought to give their sizable collection—an estimated 250 works—of Richards' drawings, sketchbooks, watercolor and oil paintings, to the National Academy of Design.[5] Charles Downing Lay, archivist of the Academy, relayed their offer to the Academy's president, Lawrence Grant White, who subsequently brought the matter to the attention of the Academy Council. The Council's action is recorded in the minutes of its meeting of March 3, 1952:

Charles Downing Lay has written a letter to Mr. White concerning a gift Mr. William T. Brewster wishes to make to the National Academy of loose drawings, sketchbooks, and small paintings and a few very large paintings done by William T. Richards, an outstanding Academician of the second half of the 19th Century. A small group of examples was sent in for approval. The council was enthusiastic about the drawings and paintings shown and decided to accept the gift of small pieces with gratitude. As for the larger pieces, the President was instructed to write a letter, explaining the difficulties in providing space for those, and the necessity of looking at them before we can make a final decision.[6]

The Brewsters were pleased with the Council's action. On March 6, 1952, Brewster wrote President White, "My wife and I were happy . . . to know that the Academy cared for her father's pictures and would preserve them with care." He suggested that he and his wife send the Academy the smaller items after they had had a few weeks "to arrange and sort them and in some cases to identify the subjects."[7] He invited a representative from the Academy to view the larger works hanging in their home to decide whether they should be included in the bequest.

Action on the bequest was then delayed for several months because of the illness and subsequent death of Mrs. Brewster. Her husband continued work on the collection, which was found to include over 500 works—more than twice the originally estimated number. On September 25, 1952, Brewster could finally write to Charles Lay:

I now enclose the lists of William T. Richards' pictures and drawings, bequeathed by my late wife to the National Academy of Design. . . . There are six sheets of classified items, of which all are labelled. It has taken much of my spare time for the last six months to identify and label some two hundred items that could be labelled with sticker labels and some three hundred that had to be clipped on paper. . . .[8]

In a note important for future Richards scholars, Brewster commented on his method of dating and identifying the subject matter of the Richards material:

The classification is as close as we [Mr. and Mrs. Brewster] could make it, since only about ten percent of the items are signed or dated and we had to rely on the place of residence or of travel and the general quality and style to determine the year. Unless dated, therefore, everything is approximate. . . .[9]

Obviously the task of organizing and dating the Richards work had been formidable. "But," wrote Brewster,

it has been a very pleasant and profitable task; for he [Richards] was a marvellous [sic] man. Nobody ever drew better; his hand was so sure that he probably never needed a pencil eraser, an ink scratcher or and [sic] paint rag. Some of them are very beautiful and all interesting. Since it is my wife's gift and not mine, I may add that I think it a very splendid bequest, and in the hands of the National Academy of Design to be handled judiciously by that institution, may go somewhat to revive the memory and vogue of a great artist. And what energy! This is only about one-fifth of what was left at his death.[10]

The question of the monetary value of the works was raised. Charles Lay, in a letter to Brewster dated October 1, 1952, wrote:

As to Mr. Clark's [Brewster's lawyer, George W.M. Clark] suggestion that I look them [Richards' works] over and make some suggestion of their value, I could not attempt such a thing as I know nothing of values except as things are offered to me at a price; then I am quick to decide that it is or is not worth so much to me.
Richards' pictures are today unsaleable being out of fashion, but it is certain that work of such quality will always be valued and loved.[11]

At the October 6, 1952, Council meeting of the National Academy, "Eliot Clark moved, Frederick Whitaker seconded, and it was carried that the entire Brewster bequest be accepted as an outright gift.[12] The Council expressed pleasure at the acquisition but had to acknowledge that the acceptance of the *entire* bequest posed a problem. The matter was discussed at the December 1, 1952, Council meeting:

In reference to the huge number of works left us, the question came up whether it might not be advisable not to accept such gifts in the future, since our storage facilities are limited. The President explained we would have the right to dispose of the Brewster Bequest by assigning many of the works to Museums and other Collections.[13]

The following February the Council examined some of Richards' work in the Council room and, according to President White, "were greatly impressed by the beauty and high quality." They decided to display the works privately in the galleries the following summer in order to select those items to be retained in the permanent collection of the National Academy, to invite various museums to send representatives to select some of the works for their collections, and to contact by letter those museums at some distance from New York City, to offer them works. The Council sought Brewster's approval for this procedure and received it.[14]

Sixty-five public and private institutions, including such well-known museums as the Boston Athenaeum, the Smith College Museum, and the Brooklyn Museum, as well as other school, college, and municipal museums throughout the country, were contacted. Forty-seven institutions accepted the offer of the Richards works; eighteen declined.[15]

Only about fifty of Richards' works were selected for the

permanent collection of the Academy. These include paintings in oil or gouache: Richards' earliest known coastal painting—his *Coastal Scene* of 1862; an unfinished *Swiss Mountain Landscape*, c. 1870 (see p. 49); *Tintagel*, 1881; *Pennsylvania Cornfields*, c. 1880-1885; *Conanicut Shore with Breaking Wave*, 1890-95; and *Breaking Wave* of 1898 (see p. 133). The eleven watercolors in the collection include scenes of the New England coast (see pp. 146) and various other landscapes (see pp. 139-144). There are twelve small oil sketches, approximatly 3 by 6 inches, framed together in groups of six (see p. 135), and twelve other oil sketches, including *Whiteface Mountain, Lake Placid*, 1904 (see p. 137). The remainder of the Richards material consists of nine of the artist's sketchbooks containing drawings dating from c. 1865 to c. 1900. As previously mentioned, only a fraction of the material was dated by the artist; additional research is needed to verify the Brewsters' dating as well as their identification of subject matter.

NOTES

1. Richards' *Coast Scene* of 1863 (National Academy of Design no. 1067) belonged to James A. Suydam, whose collection is now part of the permanent National Academy of Design collection (See p. 59).

   The Richards' had eight children. Two died before Anna's birth in 1870, and a third died in 1880. Anna was the third daughter and sixth child.

2. Clara Erskine Clement, *Women in the Fine Arts* (New York: Hacker Art Books, 1974), 285, and Mantle Fielding, *Dictionary of American Painters, Sculptors, and Engravers* (1926; reprint New York: James F. Carr, 1965), 41.

3. William T. Brewster, foreword, *A Book of Sketches by Anna Richards Brewster* (Scarsdale (?), William T. Brewster, 1954), quoted in *William T. Richards and his Daughter Anna R. Brewster* (Exhibition catalogue, Butler Institute of American Art, Youngstown, Ohio, 1954).

4. Letter dated Dec. 2, 1952, from William T. Brewster to Lawrence Grant White.*

5. See letter dated March 4, 1952, from White to Brewster.* Both Brewsters were in agreement that the Richards paintings should go to the National Academy. They had "made similar wills in favor of each other" to ensure the bequest (see letter from Brewster to White, March 6, 1952). Mrs. Brewster died before her husband, and the gift was thus identified as the Mrs. William T. Brewster Bequest.

6. See National Academy of Design Council meeting minutes of March 3, 1952, Ralph Fabri, recording secretary.*

7. Letter dated March 6, 1952, from Brewster to White.*

8. Letter dated Sept. 25, 1952, from Brewster to Charles Downing Lay.*

9. *Ibid*. Brewster gave additional information regarding the dating of the Richards material in a letter of December 2, 1952, to White:

   Since I wrote you . . . about these pictures, my wife and I have been much occupied in sorting and labelling them. It has been largely a matter of guesswork, since Mr. Richards did not sign or date more than one in ten of his sketches, especially in his later years. Guesses were based on style, paper, the size of his sketch box and on what we knew of his whereabouts. In this 1st [*sic*] respect Harrison S. Morris's *Richards Masterpieces of the Sea* (Lippincott, 1912) was useful. . . .

   The only sets that I am quite sure of are the excellent Norway sketches, made in the summer of 1901, sketches of Lake Placid and Mantunuck, R.I. of 1904 and the beautiful sketches of Denby, Wales, probably his last out-of-door sketches, made in July, 1905, in company with his son Herbert, while my wife and I were on our honeymoon in Cornwall, where he later joined us. All these I can place personally.

   Less certain are such sets as the pictures of Cornwall, where he spent much time from 1878 to 1880,—though some may be as late as 1905,—and the small sketches in frieze framing, which, from the size of his box and the fact that he was in England and Italy in 1866-67 . . . [may be dated 1866-67. The Oldmixion sketches may be dated 1881-90 since Richards owned a farm in Oldmixion, Pa. during that period, and the Mt. Ranier sketches may be dated 1885, the year of Richards' visit to that site.] Much of the rest is conjecture, which might give employment to an expert in the Academy or an ardent young student of ways and means in art.

10. *Ibid*.

11. Letter dated Oct. 1, 1952, from Lay to Brewster.*

12. National Academy of Design Council meeting minutes of October 6, 1952, Ralph Fabri, recording secretary.*

13. National Academy of Design Council meeting minutes of December 1, 1951, Ralph Fabri, recording secretary.*

14. For quote, letter dated Feb. 9, 1952, from White to Brewster regarding National Academy of Design Council meeting of Feb. 2, 1953.* White contacted Brewster regarding the distribution procedure for the Richards works in a letter dated Feb. 9, 1953, to White.*

15. Lists of these museums and their responses.*

*Copy in National Academy of Design Files.

CC

JOHN WILLIAM CASILEAR

(1811-1893)
ANA 1833; NA 1851

Born June 25, New York. 1826 apprenticed to engraver Peter Maverick for four years. 1831 studied with Maverick pupil Asher B. Durand. 1832 established own banknote engraving business. 1840 departed for Europe with Durand, John F. Kensett, and Thomas P. Rossiter; in London to mid-August. To Continent with Durand, in Florence by October, Rome winter of 1840-1841. Spring 1841 in Amalfi, Sorrento, Naples; rejoined Kensett and Rossiter in Paris. To Rouen and Southampton 1841 with Kensett, back in Paris by February 1842. Summer along Rhone to Switzerland, return via Rhine. 1843 returned to New York with first oil sketches. 1847 engraved Daniel Huntington's *Sibyl*, published by American Art-Union. 1854 retired from engraving firm, opened studio. 1857-1858 to Paris, Savoy, Switzerland, England. On return settled at Studio Building. 1859 founding officer of New York Artists' Fund Society. Around 1881 possible trip to Rockies. Died Saratoga, N.Y., August 17.

REFERENCES: Casilear Papers, Archives of American Art. George C. Groce and David H. Wallace, *Dictionary of Artists in America 1564-1860* (New-York Historical Society, 1957). M. & M. *Karolik Collection of American Water Colors & Drawings 1800-1875*, vol. 1 (Boston: Museum of Fine Arts, 1962).

John Casilear's appreciation of the Alps can be seen in drawings done on his first European trip. As his close friend John Kensett recorded: "C. is in raptures with Swiss scenery—its grandeur and sublimity—and seems anxious to visit again the scenes that have so forcibly impressed his mind and called for the most unlimited admiration of boundless enthusiasm."[1]

Two years after Casilear had returned to New York, Kensett and Benjamin Champney traveled from Paris to Switzerland mostly on foot. Sketching in the valley of Meyringen, they met the influential Alexander Calame, whom Champney described as "the man who had done more to illustrate the grandeur and sublimity of Swiss scenery than any man before or since his time, and especially in the series of beautiful lithographs published by him."[2] Surely this assessment was shared not only by Kensett but also by Casilear.

Casilear revisited Switzerland on his second European trip, and returned to New York with sketches of Mont Blanc, the Jungfrau, and the Matterhorn. The mountain in this painting most resembles Mont Blanc as seen from Sallenches or Chamonix. Casilear reached Chamonix as early as July 12, 1857, the date of an inscribed drawing in the Karolik Collection (Museum of Fine

Arts, Boston). One guidebook describes Chamonix as

A large and important community, which displays almost the bustle of an English watering-place in the most retired, heretofore, of the Alpine valleys. Independently of the grand white mass of Mont Blanc and its accompanying aiguilles and glaciers, which are sublime, the mere valley . . . is not beautiful; it has even a desolate air about it.[3]
Murray, *Handbook for Travellers in Switzerland* (1854).

Among the many famous tourists at Chamonix in the nineteenth century was John Ruskin, who detailed and glorified Mont Blanc in the fourth volume of *Modern Painters*, which had appeared early in 1856.

The Alpine landscapes Casilear worked up in New York gained positive critical acclaim. Casilear exhibited *Composition, Scenery in Switzerland* at the National Academy of Design in 1859, and one critic wrote:

Some landscapes are beautiful again, and reveal a higher order of beauty because they are compositions, or creations. Of such are the works of Kensett . . . and Casilear. . . . Their pictures are more ideal in, asmuch as the forms and their arrangement are not controlled by an actual scene.[4]
The Crayon (1859).

This was followed by *Swiss Scenery*, his only entry of 1861:

Casilear's *Swiss Scenery*, a range of snow mountains reflecting the sunlight against a clear expanse of sky, affording one of those fine distances which he paints so successfully.[5]
The Crayon (1861).

Either of these may be the Academy's *Swiss Scene* or related works. The artist continued to produce generalized Alpine views, although he did not visit the site again.

Tuckerman pinpoints Casilear's graphic sensibility and singles out his Alpine mountainscapes:

J.W. Casilear, like Durand and Kensett, graduated from the engraver's discipline to the landscape-artist's more genial vocation . . . The rectitude of his character and the refined accuracy of his original profession are exhibited in his pictures. They are finished with great care, and the subjects chosen with fastidious taste; the habit of dealing strictly with form, gives a curious correctness to the details of his work; there is nothing dashing, daring, or off-hand; all is correct, delicate, and indicative of sincere feeling for truth, both executive and moral. . . . He excels in lake scenes and Alpine peaks.[6]
Tuckerman, *Book of the Artists* (1867).

The snowy peaks in *Swiss Scene* are a dramatic barrier to deeper space in the composition, a device echoed in Emily Dickinson's simile:

Swiss Scene, 1859
Oil on canvas, 18⅛ x 30⅛″
Signed lower right: *J.W.C. 1859*
Suydam Collection

Our lives are Swiss,
  So still, so cool,
Till, some odd afternoon,
The Alps neglect their curtains
  And we look farther on.
Italy stands the other side,
  While, like a guard between,
The solemn Alps,
  The siren Alps,
  Forever intervene![7]

      "Alpine Glow" (1896).

NOTES

1. Casilear Papers, Archives of American Art, Smithsonian Institution, N.Y., microfilm roll D177, frame 980.
2. Benjamin Champney, *Sixty Years' Memories of Art and Artists* (Woburn, Mass.: Wallace & Andrews, 1900), 66-67.
3. John Murray, *A Handbook for Travellers in Switzerland, and the Alps of Savoy and Piedmont*, 6th ed. (London: Clowes, 1854), 338.
4. "National Academy of Design," *The Crayon* 6 (June 1859), 191.
5. *Ibid.*, 8 (April 1861), 95.
6. Henry T. Tuckerman, *Book of the Artists* (New York: G.P. Putnam's 1867), 521.
7. "Alpine Glow," *Poems by Emily Dickinson* (Boston: Roberts, 1896), 55.

LK

LANDSCAPE
Oil on canvas, 12½ x 22″
Unsigned

The origin of this painting in the collection of the National Academy of Design is obscure.[1] Its attribution to the hand of John W. Casilear is based wholly on its style, which is consistent with the clear, silvery tonality and feathery brushwork found in many of Casilear's autograph works. The subject matter here, however, the "home in the wilderness" theme fairly popular in American landscape painting around the mid nineteenth century, is unusual within the more conventionally pastoral character of Casilear's known *oeuvre*. This factor, in combination with the overall freshness of the composition and a particular spontaneity of execution, may indicate that the picture was sketched directly from nature, a practice Casilear is known to have followed occasionally.[2] At the same time, it is tempting to imagine that when painting this picture, the artist was aware of Sanford R. Gifford's well-known *Twilight on Hunter Mountain*, painted in 1866 (The Lano Collection), which is similar in its choice and arrangement of motifs.

The image of the wilderness home in American art and literature has recently been examined by two scholars via the overriding symbols of the axe and the tree stump.[3] Nicolai Cikovsky, Jr. has indicated the peculiarly American character of wilderness home iconography by virtue of the presence of tree stumps, which lend it a raw and energetic aspect absent from European depictions of rustic dwellings lacking an accompanying stump motif.[4] And, as Barbara Novak first perceived, tree stump imagery is often fraught with conflicting cultural sentiments regarding the transformation of the landscape it implies.[5] The stumps and fallen logs in Gifford's *Twilight on Hunter Mountain*, for example— in Novak's words "like so many fallen soldiers on a battlefield"[6]—underscore the sense of gentle melancholy cast by the fading reddish light. The conquest of civilization depicted by Gifford savors somewhat of a Pyrrhic victory. It might well invoke Thoreau's petition to the farmers of Concord in 1858:

Pray, farmers, keep some old woods to match the old deeds. Keep them for history's sake, as specimens of what the township once was. Let us not be reduced to a mere paper evidence, to deeds kept in a chest or secretary, when not so much as the bark of the paper birch will be left for evidence, about its decayed stump.[7]

"Journal" (1858).

The Academy's picture, however, seems to bear little of the mournful overtone of Gifford's *Twilight* or Thoreau's supplication. Its straightforward vision is in keeping not only with Casilear's style, but with the prevailing sentiment of a growing nation that domesticating the wilderness was a necessary and creative, not destructive, process. Indeed, it was only from the comfortable vantage of civilization that Western man could come to romanticize the natural landscape and, in some measure, actually to see it. It is difficult to imagine the scenes represented either by Gifford or Casilear without their newly hacked clearings, which, in a way, replace the traditional motif of a lake that allows the eye to range into the mountainous background. However artificially produced, such openings provided the artist with another perspective before which to wield his pencil or brush. For American society in general, to clear the land was to fashion a literally enlightened context for its sustenance and thought.[8]

The reality of this concept is nowhere better illustrated than in the words of the frontier settler himself. In 1833 William Nowlin and his family were among the first white men to settle in Dearborn, Michigan (the name now almost synonymous with the Ford Motor Company). During the first years of their occupation, Nowlin and his father found the near infinite task of forest cutting as compelling as the farming that succeeded it. In the following series of excerpts from *The Bark-Covered House*, his privately printed recollections, Nowlin repeatedly links the progress of the clearing with the phenomena of light and vision, and not least, with the solace of human company:

Father brought his axe from [New] York State; it weighed seven pounds; he gave me a smaller one. He laid the trees right and left until we could see the sun from ten o'clock in the morning till between one and two in the afternoon, when it mostly disappeared back of Mr. Pardee's woods.

Father and I continued our chopping until we connected the two clearings. Then we commenced to see the sun in the morning and we thought it shone brighter than in [New] York State. . . . Perhaps it was because the deep gloom of the forest had shaded us so long and was now removed.

Father got our road laid out and districted for a mile and a half on the north and south section of the line. . . . After it was cut out I could get on top of a stump in the road, by the side of our place, and look north carefully among the stumps, for a minute, and if there was anyone coming, on the road, I could distinguish them from the stumps by seeing them move. In fact we thought we were almost getting out into the world.

Now finally I thought we had quite a clearing. I could stand by our house, and look to the west, and see Mr. Pardee's house and the smoke of his chimney. I could see Mr. Pardee and his sons when they came out in the morning and went to their work. I could look to the east and there joining ours, was the clearing and house of Mr. Asa Blare, and he could be seen. Then it began to seem as if others were living in Michigan, for we could see them. The light of civilization began to dawn on us. We had cleared up what was a few years before, the lair of the wolf and the hunting grounds of the red man.[9]

The Bark-Covered House (1876).

Having obliterated the forest, thus redeeming himself from his formerly benighted state, the author can then both ironically and fittingly devote an entire chapter of his memoir to the beauty and benefit of trees. If the trees in the foreground of Casilear's painting stand only formally representative of those removed and remaining beyond, a single huge oak left standing to mark Nowlin's property lends a moral perspective to those that have fallen before his axe, inspiring this paean of obvious biblical origin:

When I have been in the woods, hungry, trees furnished me food. When thirsty, they often supplied me with drink. When cold and almost freezing, trees have warmed and made me comfortable. Trees furnished most of the material for father's "bark-covered house," . . .

If trees have done so much for one, surely all humanity have derived great good from them. The earth itself is adorned and beautified by trees.[10]

NOTES

1. Following his election as an Academician in 1851, Casilear contributed one of his engravings of Daniel Huntington's *The Sibyl* as his diploma work. In a letter accompanying the engraving, addressed to James Shegogue, the Academy Secretary, Casilear expressed the hope of making "a further contribution of an oil picture" to the Academy's permanent collection. Conceivably this could be the promised picture, but if so, no record of its receipt was made, as was customarily done, in the minutes of the Academy's meetings. The present file card kept by the Academy on this picture, dating from the early 1950s, lists it as "attributed to John W. Casilear." Before this time, however, the records of the permanent collection are incomplete and contradictory. A *Catalogue of the Permanent Collection* published in 1911, for example, does not include any of the numerous paintings by unknown artists included in the collection. The present picture is probably one of the many anonymous "Landscapes" that are listed only in informal inventories of the collection dating from sometime between 1911 and 1950. There now appears to be no information concerning the acquisition of these paintings. See J.W. Casilear, letter to J.S. Shegogue, May 10, 1852, National Academy of Design Artists Biographical Files. A copy of the *Catalogue of the Permanent Collection, National Academy of Design* (New York, 1911) and miscellaneous inventories of the collection may be examined at the National Academy of Design.

2. Casilear evidently considered some of his plein-air oil sketches worthy of exhibition. In a letter to the American Art-Union in 1850, the artist describes one of his entries into the Union's annual show as "painted on the spot." He further characterized two other entries as "sketched partly from nature." See J.W. Casilear, letter to the American Art-Union, February 20, 1850, in Daria Rigney, "John William Casilear," ms., Independent Research Paper, Columbia University, 1979, 13.

3. See Barbara Novak, "The Double-Edged Axe," *Art in America* 64, no. 1 (Jan.-Feb. 1976), 45-50; and Nicolai Cikovsky, Jr., "The Ravages of the Axe: The Meaning of the Tree Stump in Nineteenth-Century American Art," *Art Bulletin* 61, no. 4 (Dec. 1979), 611-26.

4. Cikovsky, Jr., 622-23.

5. Novak, 47-50.

6. *Ibid.*, 48.

7. Henry David Thoreau, "Journal," November 8, 1858. In *Selected Works of Thoreau*, Walter Harding ed., (Boston: Houghton-Mifflin, 1975), 34.

8. In his article, "Ravages of the Axe," Cikovsky draws attention to the presence of tree stumps in nineteenth-century images of American schools and colleges. As the author notes, the stump in such images is an "attribute of civilization" appropriate to the notion of education—a grass-roots symbol, as it were, of intellectual enlightenment. See pp. 618-19.

9. William Nowlin, *The Bark Covered House* (1876; reprint Chicago: The Lakeside Press, 1937), 28, 50, 132, 170. Page 170 is quoted in part in Cikovsky, Jr., p. 626.

10. *Ibid.*, 186. The author has adapted the words of Christ on the Mount of Olives as he forecast the Last Judgment (Matthew 25:34-36, 40): "Then the King [the Son of Man] will say to those at his right hand, 'Come, O blessed of my Father, inherit the kingdom prepared for you from the foundation of the world; for I was hungry and you gave me food, I was thirsty and you gave me drink, I was a stranger and you welcomed me, I was naked and you clothed me, . . . Truly, I say to you, as you did it to one of the least of my brethren, you did it to me' " (Revised Standard Version).

KA

JAMES AUGUSTUS SUYDAM

(1819-1865)
HM 1858; NA 1861

Born in New York City on March 27. Attended New York University. Began study of medicine, but soon abandoned it because of interest in architecture. 1842 to 1845 traveled throughout Europe, including Italy, Austria, Turkey, Russia, and Paris. In Florence, 1843, met artist Miner K. Kellogg, with whom he began instruction in art. From 1845 to 1854 presumably in business with his brother John in New York City. 1847 to 1851 with Kellogg back in New York, both occupied in drawing from nature. About 1852 began friendship with New York artists, particularly John F. Kensett, Sanford Robinson Gifford, and Worthington Whittredge. 1856 début at National Academy of Design. Continued to exhibit there and at Boston Athenaeum. In 1858 invited on Baltimore and Ohio Railroad excursion for artists, began to maintain studio in Tenth Street Building. Painted subjects include traditional repertoire of views along the Hudson, in White Mountains, on Long Island, at Lake George. By 1859 turned attention to New England shore, which was to become favorite sketching ground. Formed collection that included contemporary European works and figure paintings and landscapes by American artist friends. Died at North Conway, N.H., on September 15.

REFERENCES: John I.H. Baur, "A Tonal Realist: James Suydam," *The Art Quarterly* 13 (Summer 1950). Sanford Gifford, Ms. Memoir of James A. Suydam, 1865, National Academy of Design Artists Biographical Files. Henry T. Tuckerman, *Book of the Artists* (New York: G.P. Putnam's, 1867).

Paradise Rocks, painted in the year of the artist's death, represents the culmination of the interests and attitudes of his all-too-short career. Daniel Huntington characterized Suydam's artistic spirit:

His passion for art was deep, and he studied the quiet aspects of nature with a determination and perseverance worthy of all reverence. When seated at his studies in the fields he would linger till twilight darkened the canvass [sic]. He loved to study along the meadows and salt-marshes of Long Island, to catch glimpses of the distant sea, and fishing boats gliding through bays and inlets. Low reaches of sandy beach, the sea rolling gently in, and softly breaking with a lulling sound pleased him better than savage cliffs and the roar of breakers. When rallied on his choice of quiet subjects he replied "I must paint what I feel."[1]
Huntington, Memoir of James A. Suydam (1865).

Described by his friend Sanford Robinson Gifford as a "thoroughly educated and accomplished man," Suydam accompanied his artistic endeavors with the study of science, literature, and history. As a result of this careful investigation of man and his

universe, Suydam's is a more conceptual art in which his ideas and pursuits can be seen to be reflected.[2] In his choice of Paradise Rocks as the subject of this painting, as well as in the manner in which he rendered the rocks, questions are raised as to the way in which the artist perceived the landscape.

We do know that Suydam aggrandized this natural structure. According to a scientist examining the geomorphology of American landscape painting:

James Suydam, modifying the scale of men and livestock, saw *Paradise Rocks* as an extraordinary form which some simple calculation shows to be about 400% greater in height in his painting than their actual height of some ten meters.[3]
Shepard, "Paintings of the New England Landscape" (1957).

Furthermore, not only were the rocks increased in height, but also their surfaces had become cleaner, more angular, and more architectural, suggesting that these natural sculptures were the New World's answer to the cathedrals and ancient ruins of Europe.

In this case, however, the site had specific significance in the history of Newport, Rhode Island, for Bishop George Berkeley was known to have chosen these rocks as his place of contemplation, as evidenced by an 1852 guidebook of Newport:

One hundred and twenty-four years ago, the wanderer near . . . [Paradise Rocks] might have noted, sitting beneath the superincumbent mass, a man of grave yet pleasant aspect, reading or committing his thoughts to paper: this was the celebrated Dean Berkeley, who, it is said, here wrote the greater part of his "Minute Philosopher," a work, which it has been said, will stand an imperishable monument from age to age of the intelligence, refinement and piety of its author. Here would he repair from his dwelling in the immediate neighborhood, and amid nature's fairest scenery, lift his thoughts to Nature's God.[4]
Dix, *Handbook of Newport, and Rhode Island* (1852).

Suydam, no doubt cognizant of the local legend, would have been attracted to this locality as a traditional one of contemplation. It may be possible, however, to draw more specific connections between Suydam's painting and the writings of Bishop Berkeley.

In *Alciphron or the Minute Philosopher* (1732), the product of his stay at Newport, Berkeley included in Dialogue IV a discussion of "The Truth of Theism (Natural Theology)—that God exists and can be known." Here he argued that there is "in natural productions and effects a visible unity of counsel and design," that from the corporeal world we may infer the existence of a Divine Creator. This idea of God, proved by reference to Divine Design, became common currency in the nineteenth century, mainly through the influence of William Paley, whose writings were included in

PARADISE ROCKS, 1865
Oil on canvas, 25⅛ x 45⅛″
Signed lower right center: *J.A. Suydam / 1865*
Suydam Collection

Suydam's library. It is not impossible then to suggest that part of the intention behind this painting—the ennobling of Paradise Rocks as an expression of God's handiwork—shares something with the philosophy of Berkeley's *Alciphron:*

The soul of man actuates but a small body, an insignificant particle, in respect of the great masses of nature, the elements, and heavenly bodies, and system of the world. And the wisdom that appears in those motions which are the effect of human reason is incomparably less than that which discovers itself in the structure and use of organized natural bodies, animal or vegetable. A man with his hand can make no machine so admirable as the hand itself; nor can any of those motions by which we trace out human reason approach the skill and contrivance of those wonderful motions of the heart, and brain, and other vital parts, which do not depend on the will of man.[5]

The era in which Suydam was painting—from 1856 to 1865—witnessed one of the most important revolutions in the history of man: the publication and gradual acceptance of Darwin's *Origin of Species* (1859). Men clung desperately to their traditional views of the world's creation, for their religious beliefs were shaken to the core; artists took solace in nature, testimony to the existence of God.

Also important to a comprehension of *Paradise Rocks* is the fact that it represents Suydam's turning from the traditional subject matter of the first generation Hudson River School—the Adirondacks, Lake George, and the White Mountains—to the rendering of the New England coast, a subject that would become extremely popular in the post-Civil War period. No doubt following the lead of his close friend Kensett, Suydam came to regard the quiet shores of Massachusetts and Rhode Island as the supreme subject for his brush. It is tempting to suppose that for Suydam the coast was important not only for reasons of its inherent beauty but also as a place of particular geological significance. This idea was articulated by Robert Chambers in his *Vestiges of the Natural History of Creation* (1844), a copy of which Suydam owned:

As the diluvium and erratic blocks clearly suppose one last long submersion of the surface, (*last,* geologically speaking,) there is another set of appearances which as manifestly shew [*sic*] the steps by which the land was made afterwards to reappear. These consist of *terraces,* which have been detected near, and at some distance inland from, the coast lines of Scandinavia, Britain, America, and other regions; being evidently ancient beaches, or platforms, on which the margin of the sea at one time rested. They have been observed at different heights above the present sea-level, from twenty to above twelve hundred feet; and in many places they are seen rising above each other in succession, to the number of three, four, and even more. . . The irresistible inference from the phenomena is, that the highest was first the coast line; then an elevation took place, and the second highest became so, the first being now raised into the air and thrown inland. Then, upon another elevation, the sea began to form, at its new point of contact with the land, the third highest beach, and so on down to the platform nearest to the present sea-beach . . . we have in these platforms indubitable monuments of the last rise of the land from the sea, and the concluding great event of the geological history.[6]

NOTES

1. Daniel Huntington, Ms. Memoir of James A. Suydam, 1865, National Academy of Design Artists Biographical Files.
2. Sanford Robinson Gifford, Ms. Memoir of James A. Suydam, 1865, National Academy of Design Artists Biographical Files. For contents of Suydam's library see *Catalogue of a Choice Private Library being in the Collection of the Late Jas. A. Suydam. To be sold at auction Nov. 22 & 23 1865* (New York: Bangs, Merwin & Co., 1865).
3. Paul Shepard, Jr., "Paintings of the New England Landscape. A Scientist looks at their Geomorphology," *College Art Journal* 17 (Fall 1957), 32.
4. John Ross Dix, *A Hand-book of Newport, and Rhode Island* (Newport, R.I.: C.E. Hammett, Jr., 1852), 80.
5. George Berkeley, *Alciphron or the Minute Philosopher,* T.E. Jessop, ed., *The Works of George Berkeley Bishop of Cloyne* (London: Thomas Nelson and Sons, 1950), 3:146. For reference to Suydam's ownership of Paley's work, see *Catalogue of a Choice Private Library . . .* no. 361.
6. Robert Chambers, *Vestiges of the Natural History of Creation* (London: John Churchill, 1844), 140-42. For reference to *Vestiges* and its *Sequel* in Suydam's library, see *Catalogue of a Choice Private Library . . .* nos. 4 and 5.

SUYDAM COLLECTION

James Augustus Suydam, upon his death in 1865, bequeathed his collection of ninety-two paintings to the National Academy of Design. As a man of substantial means, Suydam was able to purchase works of art from his American artist friends and from contemporary European painters. A landscape painter himself, he had a particular love for landscape painting; his taste is reflected in a number of the finest works in this exhibition, including Frederic Church's *Scene on the Magdalene* (1854), John Frederick Kensett's *Mountain Stream: Bash Bish Falls* (1855), and Jasper F. Cropsey's *Coast Scene* (1855). Suydam also procured works from a number of promising figure painters, among them Eugene Benson, J.G. Brown, and William P. W. Dana. His choices of European works are consistent wih the trends of his day, for he purchased pictures by Edouard Frère, Andreas Achenbach, Emile Lambinet, and other foreign artists then popular in America.[1]

As a bachelor and a man with a serious commitment to the progress of the arts in America, Suydam was also able to leave to the Academy the sum of 50,000 dollars, which under the terms of his will was to be used to establish a permanent fund, "the income of which shall be appropriated by the Council in such manner as they in their discretion shall deem most desirable to the purposes of instruction in the Arts of Design." The Suydam Fund provided a solid foundation for the conduct and development of the Academy's school during the succeeding years.

As a tribute to this artist and patron, the Academy named the first medal offered as a prize in its school in his honor. These medals are awarded annually in the Life class.[2] Among the distinguished recipients was Marsden Hartley, who was awarded the Suydam Silver Medal for still-life drawing in 1902.[3]

NOTES

1. The collection originally numbered ninety-two paintings; some works are presently unlocated. Paintings and studies from Suydam's own hand are also included in this collection. Information compiled from acquisition records of the National Academy of Design and from undated roster "National Academy of Design. Catalogue of the Suydam Collection (Bequeathed to the Academy by the late Jas. A. Suydam, N.A.)" in the Academy's Archives.
2. Information from Suydam's National Academy of Design Artists Biographical Files, and from Eliot Clark, *History of the National Academy of Design 1825-1853* (New York: Columbia University Press, 1954), 90, 94.
3. For reference to Hartley's receipt of the Suydam Medal, see Barbara Haskell. *Marsden Hartley* (New York: Whitney Museum of American Art, 1980), 185.

KM

ELIHU VEDDER

(1836-1923)
ANA 1864; NA 1865

Born in New York City, February 26. Spent childhood in Schenectady, N.Y., and in Cuba. Art instruction from Thompkins H. Matteson in Sherbourne, N.Y., and François-Edouard Picot in Paris, where Vedder went in 1856. From Paris traveled to Florence and studied with Raffaello Bonaiuti. Returned via Cuba to America in 1860. 1861-1865 did magazine illustrations in New York City and Boston to support his painting. Began allegorical paintings as well as landscape. In 1865 settled permanently in Italy, although made several trips to America. Illustrations for *The Rubaiyát of Omar Khayyám* published in 1884. Famous in later life for mural decorations such as those in Walker Art Building at Bowdoin College in 1892 and the Library of Congress in 1896. Traveled extensively in Italy, France, and up the Nile 1888-1889. Published autobiography, *The Digressions of "V.,"* in 1910. Died Rome, January 29.

REFERENCES: *Perceptions and Evocations: The Art of Elihu Vedder,* Introduction by Regina Soria (Exhibition catalogue, The National Collection of Fine Arts, Washington, D.C., 1979). Regina Soria, *Elihu Vedder: American Visionary Artist in Rome (1836-1923)* (Rutherford, N.J.: Fairleigh Dickinson Press, 1970).

Regina Soria lists a possible eight paintings of Cohasset, Massachusetts, in 1864, titling the two here *Cohasset—Boys and Sea Weed Barrels* and *Cohasset—Boy Packing Sea Weed Barrels*.[2] Vedder exhibited a painting of Cohasset, perhaps one of these, in the Fortieth Annual Exhibition of the National Academy of Design in 1865 (no. 278).

These small works, painted on the spot two days apart, elicited much less critical attention than such imaginative paintings as Vedder's *Lair of the Sea Serpent,* also done in 1864. According to Vedder, not even the beach in the latter work was painted from nature. When two friends suggested they knew where he painted it, he replied, "As a matter of fact, I did not paint it there, but like the talented little boy, 'drew it all out of my own head with a common lead pencil.' "[3]

Vedder spent many months from 1863 to 1865 with William Morris Hunt and John La Farge painting and sketching in the region around Boston. But he was not passionately drawn to the New England coast. On seeing signs reading "No trespassing allowed" at the shoreline, he expressed surprise, "for our shoreline is not so very picturesque that the best part should be preëmpted in this way."[4] In these paintings, however, he seems to echo Walt Whitman (who, like Vedder, frequented Pfaff's, a favorite New York meeting place of artists and writers in the early 1860s). Whitman's affection for life by the sea is voiced in "A Song of Joys":

> O to have been brought up on bays, lagoons, creeks, or
> along the coast,
> To continue and be employ'd there all my life,
> The briny and damp smell, the shore, the salt weeds exposed
> at low water,
> The work of fishermen, the work of the eel-fisher and clam-fisher.[5]

Although Vedder settled permanently in Italy in 1865, his reason for the move may have been different from that of some of the American artists hastening there. Having heard Emerson's remark that "Nature being the same on the banks of the Kennebec as on the banks of the Tiber—why go to Europe?" he told Emerson that although "Nature is the same everywhere,"[6] America was "Patagonia" when it came to being able to see paintings. The picturesque presence of humanity in the European landscape also appealed to him. As an art student, he went sketching around Sherbourne, New York, and ". . . sought for lofty granite peaks catching the last rays of the sun; for hills convent-crowned, or castles on abrupt cliffs frowning down on peaceful abbeys below, reflected in the tranquil stream. . . ." Instead he found that "The rocks were of a disintegrating slate, hills rounded, and covered wth monotonous green, no convents, no castles, no abbeys. . . . It was all my own fault. I was looking for things with a tinge of romance in them."[7]

Rather than romantic imagery, the Cohasset paintings show Vedder's response to ordinary American scenes in a manner similar to Winslow Homer's work at this time. Homer and Vedder were elected Associates and Academicians at the National Academy of Design in the same years, and Homer, like Vedder, was introduced to Japanese prints by John La Farge in the early 1860s. Both were friends of La Farge, and he may have had some influence on their choice of everyday subject matter.[8] La Farge described his pictorial aims at this time:

. . . I wished to apply principles of light and color of which I had learned a little. I wished my studies from nature to indicate something of this, to be free from *recipes,* as far as possible, and to indicate very carefully, in every part, the exact time of day and circumstances of light.

His scenes would be . . .

thoroughly commonplace, as we see it all the time, and yet we know it to

COHASSET, 1864
Oil on wood panel, 4 x 7½"
Signed lower right: *July 17/64*[1]
Gift of the American Academy of Arts and Letters, 1955

BOYS AND BARRELS, COHASSET, 1864
Oil on wood panel, 4 x 6½"
Signed lower right: *V. July 19/64*
Gift of the American Academy of Arts and Letters, 1955

be beautiful, like most of "out-of-doors." I modelled these surfaces of plain and sky upon certain theories of the opposition of horizontals and perpendiculars in respect to color and I carried this general programme into as many small points of detail as possible.[9]

Cortissoz, *John La Farge* (1911).

Vedder picks out some small details—the pebbles on the sand, the barrel slats, the ladder and the planks. But the low hills of the dunes, the barrel cylinders, and the figures are simply silhouetted against La Farge's "surfaces," the sand and the blue sky.

Joshua Taylor offers an explanation for the size of the paintings, beyond the fact that it was easier to carry a tiny panel when painting from nature:

There is a special charm in a small painting . . . since it demands a close scrutiny that effectively cuts off all awareness of the surroundings. The viewer is invited to push in, to become part of the tiny universe within the frame.[10]

Perceptions and Evocations:
The Art of Elihu Vedder (1979).

NOTES

1. There are inscriptions on the reverse of these two paintings as well as on the two Vedder pastels included in the exhibition—*Huts, Viareggio* and *Orvieto*—that do not seem to have been written in Vedder's hand; notes on the back of the oil panels indicating that they were done when Vedder was "17-18" or "24 years old" are, of course, incorrect.
2. Regina Soria, *Elihu Vedder: American Visionary Artist in Rome (1836-1923)* (Rutherford, N.J.: Fairleigh Dickinson University Press, 1970), 285, cat. nos. 44 and 45.
3. Elihu Vedder, *The Digressions of "V."* (Boston: Houghton Mifflin, 1910), 264.
4. *Ibid.*
5. Walt Whitman, "A Song of Joys," *Leaves of Grass* (1855; Philadelphia: Rees Welsh, 1882), 143.
6. Vedder, *Digressions*, 233.
7. *Ibid.*, 94.
8. Soria, *Elihu Vedder*, 43.
9. Royal Cortissoz, *John La Farge, A Memoir and a Study* (Boston: Houghton Mifflin, 1911), 112-13, 130.
10. Joshua Taylor, "Perceptions and Digressions." In *Perceptions and Evocations: The Art of Elihu Vedder* (Exhibition catalogue, The National Collection of Fine Arts, Washington, D.C., 1979), 96.

SMS

WILLIAM HART

(1823-1894)
ANA 1854; NA 1858

Born Paisley, Scotland, March 31. Emigrated to America, settling in Albany, 1831. Apprenticed to a carriagemaker; decorating panels. Began painting portraits about 1840. Shortly after 1840, left Albany and traveled as itinerant portrait painter to Virginia and Michigan, where he spent three years. Returned to Albany around 1845. Concentrated on landscape art. 1848 entered first work at National Academy of Design. Through generosity of a patron in Albany, went to Scotland in 1849. Studied and sketched for three years. 1852 returned to Albany opened studio. By 1854 studio in New York City. 1858-1870 Studio Building at Tenth Street. 1865 first president of Brooklyn Academy of Design. Lectured on American painting. 1870-1873 president of American Water-Color Society, of which he was a founding member. Exhibited frequently in New York, Boston, Philadelphia, Washington, D.C., Baltimore. Brother James McDougal Hart also landscapist and Academician. Spent later years at Mt. Vernon, N.Y. Died there on June 17.

REFERENCES: "American Painters—William Hart," *The Art Journal* (1875). National Academy of Design Artists Biographical Files. Catalogues of annual exhibitions, National Academy of Design, 1848-1890. George C. Groce and David H. Wallace, *Dictionary of Artists in America, 1564-1860* (New-York Historical Society, 1957). George W. Sheldon, *American Painters* (New York: D. Appleton & Co., 1879).

In *Book of the Artists* (1867), Henry Tuckerman called William Hart a "familiar and cherished name"[1] among American landscape painters. An anonymous writer in *The Art Journal* (1875) considered him "one of the recognised leaders of the American School of landscape-art."[2] *Landscape—Sunset on Long Island*, which predates these comments, is a product of the years shortly after his return from study in Europe:

Mr. Hart remained three years abroad, and devoted his whole attention to out-door study. He returned to Albany in 1852 . . . greatly benefitted by his study. His portfolio was filled with sketches taken in the Scottish Highlands and elsewhere on the British Islands, which were admirable in their character, and gave an influence to his pencil which was of lasting value. In 1853 William Hart settled in New York. He had for some time previous sent an occasional picture to the National Academy of Design, but now became a constant contributor, and his works attracted great attention, particularly among artists and connoisseurs. They were at once recognised as works of genius. He had studied Art guided by no academic rules, and under no master; hence his style was new and fresh, and, as the result of earnest study, at once appealed to popular favor.[3]

Art Journal (1875).

Sunset on Long Island offers tranquility at the end of the day; the calm water reflects the red and orange glow on the horizon. The straightness of the horizon line and the mirror-perfect reflections of the trees call to mind the expressive and compositional devices of the luminists. Yet Hart also reflects the Hudson River School in his attitudes toward painting. Portions of his lecture "The Field and the Easel," recall Asher B. Durand's famous instructions to young artists:

I would urge on any young student in landscape painting, the importance of painting direct from Nature as soon as he shall have acquired the first rudiments of Art. If he is imbued with the true spirit to appreciate and enjoy the contemplation of her loveliness, he will approach her with veneration, and find in the conscientious study of her beauties all the great first principles of Art. Let him scrupulously accept *whatever* she presents him, until he shall, in a degree, have become intimate with her infinity, and then he may approach her on more familiar terms, even venturing to choose and reject some portions of her unbounded wealth; but never let him profane her sacredness by a wilful departure from truth. . . .[4]

Durand, "Letters on Landscape Painting" (1855).

Tuckerman's synopsis of Hart's lecture indicates that Hart shared Durand's respect for the "truth" in nature, but insisted still more on "feeling":

. . . Hart's subject was "The Field and the Easel," . . . His object would be to take his hearers on a tour through the fields, and thence back to the studio, laden with the spoils of the campaign. . . . Having gone forth into the broad sunshine and the fields, his first question would be what subject he should select for his pencil. And here he would caution the student against the selection of any particular scene merely because "it looked like a picture." If he did, the chances were it would be tame; and, however true he might be in the delineation of nature, he would incur the criticism of having imitated some ideal picture manufactured for the occasion. . . . Try, if possible, to embody a sentiment or idea of your own, and one in unison with your own feelings . . . there should always be an idea, either preceding or succeeding the subject, and that idea should always be his own—an idea or sentiment in which he was interested, and which should be wrought out with his pencil in such a manner as to interpret his own thought and soul, and not in imitation of another man's. . . . The student was cautioned not to alter or modify the scene at the expense of nature and truth. . . .

Returning from the field to the studio, the student's purpose must now be earnest. He must now seek to contract, intensify, and subject the sentiment to the picture. . . . Care should be taken not to follow too closely a favorite artist. . . . Above all, let your pictures tell something that you feel. If you feel nothing, keep silent until you do feel something, and do not attempt to tell what you think you ought to feel, or what you imagine somebody else feels.[5]

Tuckerman, *Book of the Artists* (1867).

LANDSCAPE—SUNSET ON LONG ISLAND, c.1856
Oil on canvas, 12 x 22″
Signed lower left: *Wm Hart*
Suydam Collection

Tuckerman also pointed out the affinity between Hart's painting and the poetry of William Cullen Bryant. A more recent writer states that Hart used the poem "After a Tempest" as the basis for his painting *After the Storm*.[6] Bryant's friendship with Cole and Durand is well known, and it seems logical that Hart too would find an affinity with the poet's writings. The opening lines from Bryant's "An Evening Revery" (1842) might be used to describe the mood set by *Sunset on Long Island*:

> The summer day is closed—the sun is set:
> Well they have done their office, those bright hours,
> The latest of whose train goes softly out
> In the red west. The green blade of the ground
> Has risen, and herds have cropped it; the young twig
> Has spread its plaited tissues to the sun . . .[7]

NOTES
1. Henry T. Tuckerman, *Book of the Artists* (1867; reprint New York: James F. Carr, 1966), 546.
2. "American Painters—William Hart," *The Art Journal* (1875), 246. National Academy of Design Artists Biographical Files.
3. *Ibid.*, 246.
4. Asher B. Durand, "Letters on Landscape Painting," Letter I, *The Crayon* 1, no. 1 (January 3, 1855), 2.
5. Tuckerman, *Book of the Artists*, 549-51.
6. Bertha Monica Stearns, "19th Century Writers in the Art World," *Art in America* 40, no. 1 (1952), 33.
7. William Cullen Bryant, "An Evening Revery," *The Poetical Works of William Cullen Bryant*, (1842; reprint Roslyn Edition, New York: Appleton, 1910), 194.

JR

LOUIS REMY MIGNOT

(1831-1870)
ANA 1859; NA 1860

Born Charleston, South Carolina. 1851 traveled to Holland and became pupil of Andreas Schelfhout at the Hague. Presumably in New York City in 1853; returned to Europe 1854-1855. By 1856 back in the United States and opened a studio in N.Y.C. Exhibited at the National Academy of Design 1853 and 1856-1861.[2] On several occasions in 1850s collaborated with other painters to produce joint works, Mignot supplying the landscape background and Julius Gollmann, John W. Ehninger, Eastman Johnson, and Thomas P. Rossiter supplying the figures. 1857 accompanied Frederic E. Church on trip to Ecuador. 1858 moved into Tenth Street Studio Building. 1859 one of six New York landscapists to participate in Ehninger's *Autograph Etchings by American Artists, produced by new a application of Photographic Art. . . .* Because of Southern sympathies, unable to remain in New York on outbreak of Civil War; sailed for England 1862. Just prior to departure sold collection of paintings. 1863-1870 exhibited at Royal Academy in London; among landscapes exhibited were Ecuadorian subjects and English views. 1868 and 1869 trips to Switzerland resulted in number of Swiss scenes. 1870 visited France. Died Brighton, England, September 22.

REFERENCES: *Catalogue of the Mignot Pictures with Sketch of the Artist's Life by Tom Taylor, Esq., and Opinions of the Press* (London and Brighton, 1876). Mary Bartlett Cowdrey, *National Academy of Design Exhibition Record, 1826-1860* (New-York Historical Society, 1943). *Dictionary of American Biography* (New York: Charles Scribner's Sons, 1943). Algernon Graves, *The Royal Academy of Arts* (Bath: Kingsmead Reprints, 1970).

Louis Remy Mignot was recognized from the outset of his career as an artist of outstanding promise and abilities. The early work here, along with three others in the National Academy of Design exhibition in 1857, earned him the praise of *The Crayon* reviewer:

Mr. Mignot shows in all his works a fine perception of Nature and great fidelity, and he is, moreover, endowed with original powers that are adequate for the attainment of great excellence.[3]

Unfortunately, Mignot was also an artist who managed so to elude art historians that as late as 1977 it could still be stated ". . . our knowledge of the range of his production is skeletal."[4] Since a firmly attributed body of works has yet to be associated with Mignot's name, this painting—purchased by his friend James

A. Suydam the year it was painted and bequeathed to the Academy in 1865—is an important addition to our understanding of his *oeuvre*.[5]

On the basis of contemporary exhibition records and sales catalogues it is possible to distinguish several basic categories among Mignot's pictures: his student works, predominantly Dutch-inspired scenes; the North American subjects, particularly New York State; views of South America; and English and Swiss landscapes, produced after his move to England.[6] The Academy's picture marks an important turning point in the artist's career, for it was in the summer of 1857, probably soon after its completion, that Frederic E. Church and—as Church records in his diary—his "companion, the noted artist, Mignot . . ." set sail for Ecuador.[7] Mignot's South American scenes were perhaps the best-appreciated of his work in his own lifetime, and probably the most well known today. Yet it was the North American landscapes, such as this one, that first won him acclaim as an artist in this country and were still highly lauded in British reviews even after his death. Mignot's English patron, Thomas Taylor, recalled that soon after the artist's arrival in New York he ". . . won distinction among his contemporaries by his subjects from the river and mountain scenery of New York State."[8] Thus, the *Sources of the Susquehanna* represents an important phase of Mignot's art.

The Susquehanna, the longest river in the Eastern United States, rises in Otsego Lake, central New York. It runs a twisted course through that state and also flows through areas of Pennsylvania before emptying into the Chesapeake Bay.[9] It was the Otsego County area, and the source of the river, that held the greatest fascination for Mignot and served as the subject for a number of sketches and finished works. In 1857 *The Crayon* noted the high degree of quality the artist had achieved in the canvases he had painted there during the past year; the sketches for this picture could well have been among them.

Among Mr. Mignot's studies from Nature is one of a hemlock tree, of remarkable [sic] truthful rendering. Mr. Mignot's studies are large, and of peculiar aim. He has been particularly successful in the expression of foliage, preserving in an assemblage of trees, detail without confusion as well as truthful play of light. Mr. M.'s studies have been confined to various localities in Otsego County.[10]

The Crayon (1857).

Along with Mignot's aptitude for expressive treatment of foliage, praised in *The Crayon*, he was also thought to excel as a sky

Sources of the Susquehanna, 1857[1]
Oil on canvas, 24 x 36″
Signed lower right: *Mignot 1857*
Suydam Collection

painter. This picture of the Susquehanna appears to be a scene of summer gloaming; Mignot's fondness for twilight, and his skill in painting a sky characteristic of that time of day, was noted by a British reviewer in 1876:

His skies are very remarkable. Sunsets would seem to have been his delight; and no wonder, for his facility for representing upon canvas the delicate and beautiful tints produced by the rays of declining light illuminating the fringy edges of clouds, is perfectly marvellous.[11]

Catalogue of Mignot Pictures. . . .

It was above all as a colorist, and as a delineator of native scenery, that he was particularly appreciated in America. Henry T. Tuckerman described *The Source of the Susquehanna* as:

A grand production. This is a powerful, deeply *American* landscape. Others may paint what may be termed cosmopolitan scenes, but here the artist has dipped his brush in the "colors of America," stern and rough-hewn as her face is, and hard as a sculpture in bronze, but none the less true to nature, —with its evergreens which are hardly ever quite green, its deep brown streams, and its skies blurred and blotted, as it were, with lumps of cloud edged with fire.[12]

Book of the Artists (1867).

Perhaps it is not inappropriate to conclude with Bayard Taylor's recollection of his own steamboat ride on the Susquehanna. Taylor, as a good friend of Church, was probably acquainted with Mignot. Just as important, Mignot and Taylor were kindred spirits in their incessant quest for new lands. Taylor, one of the most accomplished mid nineteenth-century travel writers, roamed the globe in search of material for his readers. And Mignot, as London's *Morning Post* put it, was ". . . one of the most enterprising of travellers, his enthusiasm for his art as well as his innate spirit of adventure alluring him to the most remote regions in search of the picturesque and beautiful."[13] Probably unknowingly, the writer and artist shared in a youthful exploration of the Susquehanna:

The first fifteen miles led through a lovely region of farms and villages—a country of richer and more garden-like beauty than any which can be seen this side of England. The semi-tropical summer of Southern Pennsylvania and Virginia had just fairly opened in its prodigal splendor. Hedge-rows of black and white thorn lined the road; fields were covered, as with a purple mist, by the blossoms of the clover; and the tall tulip-trees sparkled with meteoric showers of golden stars. June, in this latitude, is as gorgeous as the Indian Isles. As the hills, however, begin to subside towards Chesapeake Bay, the scenery changes. The soil becomes more thin and sandy; the pine and the rough-barked persimmons supplant the oak and elm; thickets of paw-paw—our northern banana—and *chincapin* (a shrub variety of the chestnut) appear in the warm hollows, and barren tracts covered with a kind of scrub oak, called "black-jack," along the Eastern Shore, thrust themselves between the cultivated farms. Mason and Dixon's line seems here to mark the boundary between different zones of vegetation. The last northern elm waves its arms to the first southern cypress.[14]

Taylor, At Home and Abroad (1859).

NOTES

1. Although the National Academy of Design Artists Biographical Files list this painting only as "Landscape," its presence in Suydam's collection and its date of 1857 allow us to identify it as the painting exhibited by Mignot at the Academy in 1857 (no. 526) with this title and cited as being in Suydam's ownership at that time. See Mary Bartlett Cowdrey, *National Academy of Design Exhibition Record, 1826-1860* (New-York Historical Society, 1943), 2:24. We know from *The Crayon* (see note 10) Mignot was working mainly in Otsego County, the location of the Susquehanna's source, early in 1857, a fact that further supports the identification.

2. *Dictionary of American Biography* (New York: Charles Scribner's Sons, 1943), 12:609-10, states that Mignot was in Europe from 1851 to 1855, but the Academy catalogue for the 1853 exhibition included three of his works and listed a New York City address for him. See Cowdrey, 2:24. This leads to the assumption that he came to the U.S. that year and then returned to Europe, for he exhibited no works at the Academy in 1854 or 1855.

3. "National Academy of Design," *The Crayon* 4 (July 1857), 222.

4. Graham Hood, entry on Mignot, "American paintings acquired during the last decade," *Bulletin of the Detroit Institute of Arts* 55 (1977), 95.

5. Evidence that Suydam and Mignot were friends can be found in Suydam's letter to John Frederick Kensett, in which Mignot is referred to as a mutual friend. Letter dated August 7, 1861, John Frederick Kensett Papers, Archives of American Art, Smithsonian Institution N.Y. For date of purchase of painting see note 1.

6. Cowdrey, *Exhibition Record*; Algernon Graves, *The Royal Academy of Arts* (Bath: Kingsmead Reprints, 1970), 3:240. *Catalogue of the Mignot Pictures with Sketch of the Artist's Life by Tom Taylor, Esq., and Opinions of the Press* (London and Brighton, 1876); *Catalogue of a choice collection of paintings, and studies from nature painted by Louis R. Mignot . . . to be sold at auction . . . on the evening of Monday, June 2d, 1862, at the gallery of J. Snedicor* (New York: Bloom & Smith, Steam printers, 1862).

7. Frederic E. Church, diary entry, Riobamba, July 9, 1857. In David C. Huntington, "Landscapes and Diaries: The South American Trips of F.E. Church," *The Brooklyn Museum Annual* 5 (1963-1964), 88. See p. 75 and p. 86 for itinerary of the trip.

8. *Catalogue of the Mignot Pictures*, 2. See *ibid.*, 5, for Taylor's reference to himself as one of Mignot's patrons. On preference for South American views, see *ibid.*, "Opinions of the Press" (unnumbered page).

9. For a summary of information on the Susquehanna River, see *Encyclopedia Britannica* (Chicago: Encyclopedia Britannica, Inc., 1973), 21:461.

10. "Domestic Art Gossip," *The Crayon* 4 (Feb. 1857), 55. For information on other pictures of Otsego County see the illustration of *Three Mile Point, Otsego Lake* by J. Gollmann and L.R. Mignot in the *Journal of the Warburg and Courtauld Institutes* 13 (1950), 33 (present location of the picture is unknown; it is dated "about 1850"). Another work listed in the *Catalogue of the Mignot Pictures* (p. 23, no. 64) is *Autumn on the Susquehanna, North America* (n.d.).

11. "Opinions of the Press," *Catalogue of the Mignot Pictures*, 20. As some of the pages of the catalogue appear to be missing in the copy available to me, it is not clear whether this is from *The Morning Post*, July 1876, cited on a previous page, or from another periodical.

12. Henry T. Tuckerman *Book of the Artists* (New York: G.P. Putnam's, 1867), 564. Tuckerman is quoting from an unidentified source; the work he refers to may be another version of the same painting and not necessarily that in the Suydam Collection.

13. *Catalogue of the Mignot Pictures*, unnumbered page. The connection between Taylor and Mignot must await further research.

14. Bayard Taylor, *At Home and Abroad* (1859; New York: G.P. Putnam's, 1886), 15-16.

KM

SAMUEL COLMAN

(1832-1920)
ANA 1854; NA 1862

Born March 4, Portland, Maine, son of a successful publisher in New York City. Around 1850 possibly studied with Asher B. Durand. 1851 first exhibited at National Academy of Design. By 1856 maintained summer studio at Jackson, near North Conway, N.H. Shared studio with Academy colleagues Durand, Aaron D. Shattuck, Daniel Huntington, William Sidney Mount, Sanford R. Gifford, and Richard Hubbard. 1860 traveled to France, Italy, Spain, Morocco; returned late 1861. 1866 with William Hart and others founded American Society of Painters in Watercolor and served as its first president. Society held its first exhibition in December 1867 at the National Academy of Design. Around 1870 traveled to American West. 1871-1875 toured Italy, France, Holland, Algeria, Morocco, Egypt. 1877 with George Inness, Thomas Moran, and others formed Society of American Artists. 1878 joined New York Etching Club; also became associate of Tiffany and Company as an interior decorator. 1883 built home in Newport, R.I., and decorated interiors of other homes there. Left Tiffany in 1890. From 1880s through early 1900s traveled extensively in West, Mexico, and Canada. 1912 wrote *Nature's Harmonic Unity.* 1920 co-authored *Proportional Form.* Died March 26, New York City.

REFERENCES: Wayne Craven, "Samuel Colman (1832-1920): Rediscovered Painter of Far-Away Places," *American Art Journal* 3 (May 1976). Charles B. Ferguson, *Aaron Draper Shattuck, N.A.—A Retrospective Exhibition* (Exhibition catalogue, New Britain Museum of American Art, New Britain, Conn., 1970).

When Samuel Colman died in 1920 at the age of eighty-eight, he was only the second oldest member of the National Academy of Design. The oldest was his brother-in-law and exact contemporary, Aaron D. Shattuck (elected 1861, a year before Colman), who survived him by eight years. By 1920 both men had long outlived the taste for the Hudson River School style they had practiced. In fact, neither any longer practiced painting professionally: Shattuck had ceased altogether in the 1880s, turning to the breeding of pigs and the crafting of violins. After 1878 Colman was devoting so much of his energy to interior design with Tiffany and Company that, although he continued to paint and etch at least into the late 1890s,[1] he could, only a year before the 1913 Armory Show, arrive at this conclusion:

The time cannot be far distant . . . when it will be universally recognized that the highest plane of work for the sculptor, painter, and architect will be that in which each collaborates with the other, all engaged simultaneously upon and engrossed in one great whole, and all alike endowed with a scientific knowledge of the laws of Nature. Then the easel picture, which should be of secondary importance and not the first as we now make it, will take its proper place in our art history.[2]
Nature's Harmonic Unity (1912).

Notwithstanding his own altered tastes, Colman was, like Shattuck, a dedicated and highly respected painter in the golden age of American landscape painting, and in their early period the two artists were closely associated. Shattuck was one of several painters from the Academy who shared Colman's summer studio near North Conway in 1856, and in that summer met Colman's sister, Marian, his future wife. In 1864 Colman, Shattuck, and Jervis McEntee together held an auction of their works, all of which were sold. In referring to the exhibition Henry T. Tuckerman aptly characterized the differences between the styles of the former two by observing that "Shattuck imparts a rural feeling so genial and genuine that we seem transported to the very spot he represents; while Colman has a touch of sentiment, a mellow tact and beauty, which charms us with idyllic suggestions."[3]

Some notion of Colman's more refined spirit is also conveyed in this excerpt from a letter he wrote to his sister from North Conway in the summer spent with Shattuck and the other Hudson River School painters:

I had some blessed thoughts come to me when I was high up on the hills that strengthened my faith in God. Sunshine, Rain, and Hail storms have made a wreath of beauty and terror[,] a wreath of poetry and truth I shall not soon forget[,] encircling future hours with a sunshine more than their own[.][4]
Letter to "Mela" [Pamela] (1856).

Through his extensive travel abroad, beginning in 1860, Colman also developed a distinctly cosmopolitan sensibility contrasting with Shattuck's parochial loyalties. His entries at the annual Academy exhibitions through the 1890s, as well as the vast collection of exotic artifacts he amassed, amply reflect his fascination with foreign locales.[5] Indeed, his early reputation and even perhaps his very election as an Academician in 1862 seem to have been based on the novelty of his scenes of Spain, a country of exotic reputation which had received little if any treatment by earlier American painters.

Eight of Colman's eleven entries at the Academy shows of 1862 to 1866 were of Spanish subjects.[6] In 1863, for example, his large *Gibraltar* (Knoedler Galleries, New York) invited favorable comparisons with views of the same subject by J.M.W. Turner and Andreas Achenbach.[7] However, his equally ambitious *Hill of the*

LANDSCAPE—GENESEE VALLEY, NEW YORK, c. 1862
Oil on canvas, mounted on masonite, 15 x 24"
Signed lower right: *S. Colman*
Diploma painting

Alhambra, Granada, Spain (Metropolitan Museum of Art), which he exhibited in 1865 along with his diploma painting, *Landscape, Genesee Valley*, was less charitably received. While acknowledging that Colman's fellow Academicians admired the work, the critic of the *New York Evening Post* advised the artist not to "repeat on so large a scale a truth that could have been told on a canvas twelve by fourteen." The critic also perhaps alluded to *Genesee Valley* and Colman's more modestly scaled pre-European works when he allowed that the artist "has painted some exquisite and delightful little pictures."[8]

Between his European trips of 1860 and 1871 Colman painted, besides his Spanish subjects, mostly scenes of New York and its vicinity. The influence of Turner prevailed in his large harbor views of this period, but smaller pictures like *Genesee Valley* demonstrate that he was also affected by the French Barbizon painters, whose works he could have seen in Paris in 1860. Colman was certainly also looking at the work of his fellow Academician-to-be George Inness. At Colman's death, his collection included two landscapes by Inness, one of which was inscribed in Colman's hand on the reverse: "I saw this picture in Inness' studio in 1854."[9] Whether or not he actually acquired the picture at that time, Colman was evidently impressed by Inness's Barbizon-like style some years before it found popular acceptance. The mild bucolic sentiment conveyed in works like Inness's *Delaware Water Gap* 1861, (Metropolitan Museum of Art) must surely have appealed to the delicacy of Colman's nature. Indeed, the present picture seems a much simplified adaptation (in reverse) of Inness's composition to Colman's subject. As subject matter, too, the Genesee River, seen here, has much in common with the Delaware. Both are narrow, meandering waterways bounded by low hills or pasture lands which lend themselves to pastoral rather than sublime interpretation.

Because of the agricultural use to which it was put during the last century, the Genesee region of western New York in the 1860s would have appeared to Colman much as it had to the English traveler Emanuel Howitt in 1819, who described the "fine prairie" about the Genesee as "resembling more than anything we have yet seen an English park, a few white oaks standing at intervals, and cattle grazing under them, . . ."[10]

At around the same time, Frances Wright, an Englishwoman, was staying at the estate of James Wadsworth on the Genesee River. In her account of her visit she offered an idyllic characterization of the countryside, to which she added a somewhat naive, if touching, editorial on farm life in America versus that in England. It is one which appears verified by Colman's amiable vista:

The [Wadsworth] house stands pleasantly on the gentle declivity of a hill, commanding a fine prospect of the Genesee flats (beautiful prairie land bordering the river,) and the rising grounds, covered with dark forests, bounding them. Some scattered groups of young locust trees spread their checquered shade upon the lawn; down which . . . the eye glances, first

over a champaign country, speckled with flocks and herds, and golden harvests; and then over primeval woods, where the Indian chases the wild deer . . .

Sometimes . . . I cannot help contrasting the condition of the American with that of the English farmer; no tithes, no grinding axes, no bribes received or offered by electioneering candidates or their agents; no anxious fears as to the destiny of his children, and their future establishment in life. Plenty at the board; good horses in the stable; an open door, a friendly welcome, light spirits, and easy toil; such is what you find with the American farmer.[11]
Views of Society and Manners in America, by an Englishwoman, (1821).

NOTES
1. Colman last exhibited at the National Academy of Design in 1896. His entries in the fortieth and fiftieth anniversary exhibitions (1906 and 1916) of the American Watercolor Society seem to have been mere gestures by the former president of the Society to oblige the occasions, and not representations of himself as an active painter. Moreover, a drawing by Colman, dated 1904 and showing mountainous scenery juxtaposed with a geometricized rendering of a flower identical in character with the diagrams in his theoretical treatises *Nature's Harmonic Unity* (1912) and *Proportional Form* (1920), suggests that the formulation of these volumes preoccupied the artist for at least the last sixteen years of his life. See the drawing in the collection of the Cooper-Hewitt Museum, reproduced on microfilm in the Archives of American Art, Smithsonian Institution, N.Y., roll NCUD 11, frames 1939-35-99.
2. Samuel Colman, *Nature's Harmonic Unity* (New York: G.P. Putnam's 1912), 2.
3. Henry T. Tuckerman, *Book of the Artists* (New York: G.P. Putnam, 1867), 561.
4. Samuel Colman, Letter to "Mela" (his sister Pamela), August 21, 1856, Archives of American Art, Smithsonian Institution, N.Y., microfilm roll 832, frame 1021.
5. Besides his Spanish scenes, Colman's contributions to the Academy shows included, in 1876, *On the Scheldt, Holland* (no. 227) and *Venetian Fishing Boats* (no. 363); in 1877, *Morning at Lake Annercy, Savoy* (no. 272) and *A Sunny Afternoon in the Port of Algiers* (no. 342); and in 1875, *Marfil, Mexico* (no. 326). Colman also exhibited various scenes of the American West. See Maria Naylor, *The National Academy of Design Exhibition Record, 1861-1900* (New York: Kennedy Galleries, 1973), 177-79. For a catalogue of Colman's collection of Oriental prints, ceramics, tapestries, etc., see Anderson Galleries, "The Art Collections of the late Samuel Colman, N.A." (sale no. 2162, New York, April 16, 1927), Archives of American Art, Smithsonian Institution, N.Y., microfilm roll N99, frames 320ff.
6. See Naylor, 177.
7. The comparisons are made in a review from an unspecified source quoted in Tuckerman, 559-60.
8. "Sordello," "National Academy of Design: Fortieth Annual Exhibition," *New York Evening Post*, May 22, 1865, 1.
9. The picture was entitled *On the Esopus River, Catskill Mountains* (present location unknown). See Anderson Galleries, Archives of American Art, Smithsonian Institution, N.Y., microfilm roll N99, frame 329. For an illustration, see LeRoy Ireland, *The Works of George Inness* (Austin, Tex.: University of Texas Press, 1965), 26, no. 102.
10. Emmanuel Howitt, *Selections from Letters Written during a Tour through the United States in the Summer and Autumn of 1819* (Nottingham, 1820). In Myrtle M. Handy and Blake McKelvey, "British Travelers to the Genesee Country," *The Rochester Historical Society Publications*, 18 (Rochester, 1940), 27.
11. Frances Wright, *Views of Society and Manners in America, by an Englishwoman* (New York, 1821). In *ibid.*, 24-25.

KA

ALBERT FITCH BELLOWS

(1829-1883)
ANA 1859; NA 1861

Born November 29, Milford, Mass. At age sixteen moved to Boston and entered architectural office of A.B. Young; later worked with Boston architect John D. Towle. Principal of New England School of Design, Boston, 1850-1856. Resigned and studied first in Paris and then in Antwerp at Royal Academy, where his main interest was genre. 1858 elected honorary member of Royal Society of Painters in Belgium. Upon return to United States, moved to New York. 1865 started painting in watercolor. 1867-1868 returned to Europe: spent sixteen months in England, where he met leading watercolorists. 1868 elected honorary member of Royal Belgian Society of Painters in Water Colors. After return to United States, lived in Boston until great fire of 1872, in which his studio and much of his work were destroyed. Returned to New York and settled in studio on Fourth Avenue and Twenty-Fifth Street. Early member of American Society of Painters in Water Color, which published his book, *Water Color Painting: Some Facts and Authorities in Relation to its Durability* (1868). At end of his career devoted much time to etching. Member of the New York Etching Club, the Philadelphia Society of Etchers and the Royal Society of Painters-Etchers and Engravers, London. One of early contributors to American Art-Union, and a member of Century Association for almost twenty years. Exhibited at National Academy of Design 1857-1883, Dudley Gallery in London in 1869, Philadelphia Centennial in 1876, and Paris Exposition of 1878. Died at Auburndale, Mass., November 24.

REFERENCES: Samuel G.W. Benjamin, *Our American Artists*. (Boston: D. Lothrop and Co., 1879). *Dictionary of American Biography*, (New York: Charles Scribner's Sons, 1928-1936). Henry French, *Art and Artists in Connecticut*, (Boston, 1879). *M & M Karolik Collection of American Water Colors and Drawings, 1800-1875*, (Boston: Museum of Fine Arts, 1962). Walter Montgomery, ed., *American Art and American Art Collections* . . . (Boston: E.W. Walker and Co., 1889). George William Sheldon, *Hours with Art and Artists* (New York: D. Appleton and Co, 1882). Henry T. Tuckerman *Book of the Artists*, (New York: G.P. Putnam's, 1867).

Upon his first return from Europe, Albert Fitch Bellows settled in New York. From 1857 to 1860 *The Crayon* commented on the rising career of this artist:

Mr. A.F. Bellows, formerly of Boston, occupies a studio in Dodsworth's Building. Mr. Bellows devoted himself to figure and portraiture. Of pictures by him in the former department we would mention *No Place Like Home* and the *Footstep*, both expressive of true feeling and adequate artistic power. We have too few painters among us who find material in the world of human associations for the employment of their thought. We are, accordingly, glad to chronicle the advent of one more artist whose feeling leads him to study and portray incidents that interest us through any marked degree of sympathy with our kind.[1]

The Crayon (1857).

The artists in Dodsworth's Building have made ample preparation the past summer for a busy winter campaign. . . . Bellows has been procuring material in Vermont, among the Green Mountains, not far from the village of Bellows Falls. His sketches represent picturesque old houses and mills, demonstrating the fact that picturesque buildings do exist in some regions; he also shows us transcripts of beautiful passages of brook scenery, many fine old ash trees, and mountain background.[2]

The Crayon (1858).

The most important items in relation to art-productions in New York are what has been done in the way of studies from nature, during the past summer. . . . Bellows found material for his pencil in the wilds of Maine. Most of his studies consist of pencil drawings, which are little gems of composition and effect. Whatever he describes to us with his pencil, whether an old rickety house or mill, an old fence or gateway, a shady nook, a flashing vista among the trees, is presented with true picturesque feeling.[3]

The Crayon (1859).

The 35th annual exhibition of the National Academy of Design opened on the 12th ult. . . . Bellows is represented by "Forest Life—a Penobscot Encampment," and the "Haymakers' Ford," two fine compositions; the figures, particularly the group in the latter, are skillfully introduced. In this picture if the reflections in the perfectly calm water were better defined, its effect would be improved.[4]

The Crayon (1860).

Shortly after the death of A.F. Bellows, the *Art-Union* made the following tribute to him:

The life of Mr. Bellows was a rich, beautiful harmony. Into it there entered nothing sensational, nothing spasmodic. It was simple, quiet, beautiful. He won his way gradually to the front rank of the American artists, and maintained his position there by the conscientious work which was characteristic of him. His paintings were not obtrusive, never aggressive, but reflected the quiet, tender, sympathetic nature of the man, and were lovable as he was lovable.[5]

The Art Union (1889).

Bellows unabashedly appealed to the nineteenth-century taste for sentimentality:

Bellow's art was in perfect sympathy with the country life of both Old and New England, and his paintings of quiet rural scenes in those favored portions of the earth are full of charm and beauty. He has represented one phase, in particular, of the New England landscape with marked success, and no one at all familiar with the originals of his pictures can fail to bear witness to the fidelity of the copy. There is the roomy old

LANDSCAPE, c. 1861
Oil on canvas, 14 x 23¼″
Signed lower left: *A.F. Bellows*

farmhouse with its great dooryard elm bending graceful branches protectingly over the gambrel roof; there the village meeting-house, whose slender white spine has pointed heavenwards for so many changing years, and there the country road runs, flecked with sun and shade, from which one sees, with Whittier,

> Old summer pictures of the quiet hills
> And human life, as quiet, at their feet.[6]

Walter Montgomery, ed.,
American Art and American Art Collections (1889).

NOTES
1. "Sketchings: Domestic Art Gossip," *The Crayon* 4 (Feb. 1857), 54.
2. "Domestic Art Gossip," *The Crayon* 5 (Nov. 1858), 328.
3. "Domestic Art Gossip," *The Crayon* 6 (Dec. 1859), 379.
4. "Sketchings: National Academy of Design, first notice," *The Crayon* 7 (May 1860), 139-40.
5. *The Art Union* (Jan. 1889), 16.
6. Walter Montgomery, ed., *American Art and American Art Collections*, (Boston: E.W. Walker & Co., 1889) 2:923.

SGS

(HENDRICK DIRK) KRUSEMAN VAN ELTEN

(1829-1904)
ANA 1871; NA 1883

Born Alkmaar, Holland, November 14. Pupil for five years of C. Lieste in Haarlem. After traveling through Germany, Switzerland, and the Tyrol, continued art training in Brussels and later moved to Amsterdam. 1861 became member of Royal Academy in Amsterdam; 1862 member Royal Academy in Rotterdam. 1865 settled in New York City. Studio in Tenth Street Studio building. 1870 and 1873 returned to Europe. Member of American Society of Painters in Water Colors. Published eighty original etchings of Dutch and American landscapes, and twelve original lithographs. Returned to Europe 1898. Died Paris, July 12.

REFERENCES: American Art Association, Gibbs sale, Feb. 24-26, 1904 (New York Public Library Artists File). *American Art Review* 1 (1880). *Un centaine de Peintres*, vols. 7, 8 (Philadelphia, n.d.). Catalogue, posthumous sale of works by Kruseman Van Elten (American Art Gallery, N.Y., April 27-28, 1905).

The fifty-fourth exhibition of the Academy of Design opened April [1879], with about six hundred paintings."[1] One of the artists whose paintings were on exhibition that year was Kruseman Van Elten, whose works, a contemporary reviewer said, showed "the result of new and good thought . . . 'New Milford, Connecticut' [no. 241] has a very brilliant treatment of a distant meadow and village, where the lights on the buildings and upon the trees sparkle in their contrasts with the heavy shadow which cuts them crisply."[2] Crispness and sparkle are qualities that apply to other works by Van Elten, including the close-up sketch of growing plants in the present exhibition, which serves as a small indicator of contemporary interest in botanical representation.

By 1879, Van Elten had become a well-established occupant of the Tenth Street Studio Building where he rented space two years after his arrival in the United States. He remained there for thirty-one years, working side-by-side with members of the Hudson River School as well as renowned portrait and genre painters. Little is known of his interpersonal relationships with other artists. He married and had at least one child, a daughter who also became an artist.[3]

Although most of the advocates of Ruskinian philosophy had left the building by the time Van Elten arrived, the meticulous handling and exactitude seen in his nature study, with its profusion of leaves, precisely rendered, demonstrates an affinity for these ideas. The larger, more generalized landscape, though of unspecified locale, recalls William Cullen Bryant's mood in his poem "A Scene on the Banks of the Hudson":

Cool shades and dews are round my way,
And silence of the early day;
Mid the dark rocks that watch his bed,
Glitters the mighty Hudson spread,
Unrippled, save by drops that fall
From shrubs that fringe his mountain wall;
And o'er the clear still water swells
The music of the Sabbath bells.

All, save this little nook of land,
Circled with trees, on which I stand;
All, save that line of hills which lie
Suspended in the mimic sky—
Seems a blue void, above, below,
Through which the white clouds come and go;
And from the green world's farthest steep
I gaze into the airy deep.

Loveliest of lovely things are they,
On earth, that soonest pass away.
The rose that lives its little hour
Is prized beyond the sculptured flower.
Even love, long tried and cherished long,
Becomes more tender and more strong
At thought of the insatiate grave
From which its yearnings cannot save.

River! in this still hour thou hast
Too much of heaven on earth to last;
Nor long may thy still water lie,
An image of the glorious sky.
Thy fate and mine are not repose,
And ere another evening close,
Thou to thy tides shalt turn again.
And I to seek the crowd of men.[4]

Van Elten's style ranged from meticulously rendered vignettes of nature to more broadly handled non-specific scenes. A contemporary critic commented:

To the earnest student of landscape-Art Mr. Van Elten's pictures furnish an agreeable surprise; their originality of treatment raises them above the common Art level, and their boldness and vigour of colouring are not reflected in the works of any of his contemporaries. In his pictures Van Elten rarely composes; he selects his studies with the idea of making pictures, and hence, when finished, they are perfect and truthful portraits of the scenes they purport to represent. Such studies, Mr. Van Elten very justly claims, are not only useful to himself in their original form, but can be understood by Art-students generally; they do not represent an artist's impressions solely, but actual views from Nature. His studies are also as truthful in regard to local colour as they are in their topographical features. With all of this conscientious vigour shown in Van Elten's studies and pictures, they also embody much of that other element, so delightful in landscape Art, which is known as sentiment. . . .[5]

The Art Journal (1877).

LANDSCAPE, c. 1880
Oil on canvas, 15¼ x 22¾″
Unsigned

LANDSCAPE STUDY
Oil on canvas, mounted on masonite, 10 x 15″
Signed lower left: *K. van Elten*

NOTES
1. "The Academy Exhibition," *The Art Journal* 5 (1879), 158.
2. *Ibid.*, 160.
3. Ulrich Theime and Felix Becker, *Allgemeines Lexikon der Bildenden Künstler
   . . .* (Leipzig: Veb. E.A. Seemann, 1907-). See entry on Elisabeth Kruseman
   Van Elten.
4. William Cullen Bryant, "A scene on the Banks of the Hudson," *The Poetical
   Works of William Cullen Bryant*, Household ed. (New York, D. Appleton &
   Co., 1897).
5. Anonymous, "Kruseman Van Elten," New Series, *The Art Journal* (1877), 341.

SGS

AARON DRAPER SHATTUCK

(1832-1928)
ANA 1858; NA 1861

Born March 9, Francestown, N.H. By age twelve showed talent for drawing. Studied portrait painting with Alexander Ransom in Boston 1851. 1852 enrolled in Antique and Life classes at National Academy of Design in New York. Also continued lessons with Ransom, who had moved to New York. 1855 first exhibited at Academy: *Portrait of a Lady*, owned by Ransom. 1859 rented studio at 15 Tenth Street, which he retained until 1896. 1856-1868, exhibited regularly at Boston Athenaeum. 1860 married Marian Colman (sister of Samuel Colman, Jr.). Beginning early 1860s exhibited frequently at Brooklyn Art Association and Maryland Historical Society. In 1864 Shattuck, Colman, and Jervis McEntee exhibited and sold at H.H. Leeds & Co., Auctioneers, N.Y.C. 1870 moved to farm in Granby, Conn. Painted his only two large works (4' x 6') during this period: *White Hills in October* (1868) and *Sunday Morning in New England* (1873). 1876 three of Shattuck's paintings chosen for Philadelphia Centennial Exhibition. 1883 invented and patented his successful stretcher key. Suffered serious illness in 1888 and gave up painting. Busied himself with making violins and farming. Died July 30, Granby, Conn.

REFERENCES: National Academy of Design Artists Biographical Files. Conversation with Katherine S. and Eugene D. Emigh, New Britain, Conn., April 5, 1980 (Mrs. Emigh is A.D. Shattuck's granddaughter). *Aaron Draper Shattuck, NA 1861: A Retrospective Exhibition* (1970; reprint Exhibition catalogue, New Britain Museum of American Art, New Britain, Conn., 1975).

Unlike most of his contemporaries, Aaron Draper Shattuck never traveled far beyond the borders of New England and New York. In addition to the environs of Granby, Connecticut, one of his favorite spots was the area around the popular North Conway, New Hampshire. Shattuck is sometimes numbered among "The White Mountain School" artists, a group made up of most of the second-generation Hudson River School painters, including John F. Kensett, Benjamin Champney, and Samuel Colman, among others.[1] According to his account book, Shattuck spent the first of many summers painting in New Hampshire in 1854, and in 1856, "spent 30 days with Samuel Colman, and paid him in full for same."[2] Colman's studio was in Jackson, New Hampshire; Daniel Huntington, Asher B. Durand, and William Sidney Mount were some of the other artists who shared Colman's studio in the summer of 1856.[3]

Benjamin Champney, whose home was in nearby North Conway, described it:

North Conway is one of the most charming places in the world to me. I have seen valleys both in this country and in Europe, but I do not recall one where more beauty is centred than there. The valley is broad, the mountains are high, but not too high or near to shut out the sunlight. The meadows or intervales are bright and fresh, broken with fields of grain and corn, giving an air of fruitfulness and abundance. Elms and maples are scattered here and there in picturesque groups, breaking the monotony of broad spaces [4]

Art and Artists (1900).

An article entitled "American Country Life" remarked on the American public's attraction to such places as North Conway:

The remarkable development of American life reveals itself attractively as we contemplate the annual summer migration from the cities to the seaside and to the country. This desire to seek relief from toil amidst the beauties of nature dates from the dawn of time. The first abode of mankind was a garden. The nations of antiquity cherished an intense love for rural life. The ruins of the villas of the grandees of Greece and Italy, and of the watering places to which the noble old Romans resorted, speak of this natural taste.[5]

The Crayon (1858).

The residents of North Conway were so accustomed to the yearly influx of artists that a slowdown that summer prompted a letter to *The Crayon* questioning

What has become of all the artists? Time was when you could not take a stroll or a drive about the mountains without seeing their white umbrellas. I remember to have counted seven artists one fine day making sketches of Mount Washington from North Conway. Not one has been seen here this season. . . . The painters have not exhausted the beauties of Conway; nor is Conway the only beautiful section of the mountains. Vast unexplored regions yet await the adventurous pencil—wild ravines, beautiful cascades, new combinations of mountain form, great gulfs full of mystery and grandeur—not to be successfully rendered at the first attempt.[6]

However, the correspondent added that upon returning from a walk, ". . . we heard that SHATTUCK had just passed into the mountains from Gorham, with a young artist, BROWN, of Portland, and that they intend sketching here for a season."[7]

A letter from Shattuck of that same year indicates his own continued enthusiasm for the White Mountain region:

At Shelburne, which lies a few miles upstream, there is a fine view of the White Mountains, one of the finest I know. Mr. Nichols the artist was there and I spent two days sketching with him. I ran upon him one day by the river with his white umbrella spread over him.[8]

Letter (August 1858).

Shattuck's paintings of pastoral subjects were popular with collectors and critics alike in the latter half of the nineteenth

THE FORD, 1856
Oil on canvas, 16¼ x 24¼"
Signed lower right center: *A.D. Shattuck 1856*

century. His work found ready buyers, and he frequently bypassed exhibitions, selling works on the basis of drawings or small oil sketches he would enlarge to the size desired by his patrons.[9] Like many of his contemporaries, Shattuck strove to render the conditions of nature as precisely as possible. During his later years he kept a daily journal of weather conditions.[10] The notes on his drawings reveal his preoccupation with exact color and lighting conditions. A drawing of the Farmington River, for instance, is annotated:

Very rich and strong Golden light shining through strong olive shadows. Gray log. Gray and russet foreground with broken purplish gravel overrun with blackberry vines[.] A great variety of quiet colour in broad mass.[11]
Collection of Katherine S. and Eugene D. Emigh.

Shattuck's truth to nature and sensitivity to color earned him attention from the very beginning of his career. *The Ford* was exhibited at the thirty-first annual exhibition of the National Academy of Design in 1856. *The Crayon* noted:

Mr. Shattuck's studies . . . are excellent and promising. A small picture by him, No. 174, is replete with picturesque feeling, a little too facilely executed for a young man, who should spend his energy in trying to do things well rather than easily.[12]

The *New York Daily Times* was more positive:

When, in our first article, we spoke of the promise that we found in this Exhibition, we alluded to those few pictures, mostly by young and little-known men, in which the truth we have here only lamely hinted seems to have been clearly sought. The pictures of Mr. COLMAN, Mr. SHATTUCK, Mr. SUYDAM, the little "Paestum" of Mr. CROPSEY, . . . these things give us hope.[13]

Frank Leslie's Illustrated Newspaper was so enthusiastic about the painting that it was given a lengthy review accompanied by an illustration. After expressing dismay at the "color blindness" evidenced in most of the academic works, the reviewer went on to say that "a new era" was dawning, and some young landscape artists were beginning to "look at the sun at its coming." Of *The Ford*, in particular, the critic wrote:

We have selected this charming little picture for illustration, believing it to be one of the most promising in the exhibition. The combination of objects is most agreeable, while the simplicity and unpretending character of the whole has a quiet, soothing influence of the mind. To Mr. Shattuck and his young confreres in art we look for the future excellence of our Academy exhibitions. If he will only close his eyes to all examples of the past, and resolutely carry out his present purpose of going alone to nature for studies, and then cultivate his mind by the examination of the principles of the best masters, we can place no limit to his improvement. The middle ground of the picture is quite perfect, full of color, and cleverly handled. The "color blindness" of example, we fear, has caused him to make the sky too cold, and the beautiful dark nook on the right is *hard* for the want of *warmth*—red has been mistaken for black or green.[14]
(April 12, 1856).

Shattuck's paintings reflect his intimate relationship with nature. He was equally familiar with the ways of the city. His granddaughter Katherine S. Emigh, recalls his urbane manners. Unlike his wife, Marian, who was "like one of the kids," Aaron Shattuck was kind but aloof. According to Mrs. Emigh, "He was like a storybook character." The patriarchal head of a family of six children and twenty-two grandchildren, he would remain in the library when they gathered in the main room of the Granby farmstead. If the children wished to speak with him, they had to seek him out. Yet he was always genial; sometimes he would walk through the room where the family was gathered and survey the scene "with a twinkle in his eye." Shattuck's neighbors remembered him as a well-dressed gentleman who would stand, waiting for the stagecoach, with his black cape thrown back, a black, silk top hat on his head and a gold-topped cane in his hand. His elegance put off his country neighbors who "didn't take kindly to his city ways."[15]

Although perhaps not popular with the rural townsfolk, Shattuck mingled with some of the best-known celebrities of his day. Mark Twain, P.T. Barnum, and Tom Thumb attended his wedding,[16] and the poet Thomas Bailey Aldrich was his best man. In New York, he frequented Pfaff's beer cellar, the favorite meeting place for the "Bohemians" of the day.[17] On Broadway just above Bleeker Street, Pfaff's attracted well-known artists, dancers, actors, and writers. Walt Whitman, one of Pfaff's regulars, described the place:

I used to go to Pfaff's nearly every night. It used to be a pleasant place to go in the evening after taking a bath and finishing the work of the day.

When it began to grow dark Pfaff would politely invite everybody who happened to be sitting in the cave he had under the sidewalk to some other part of the restaurant. There was a long table extending the length of this cave; and as soon as the Bohemians put in an appearance Henry Clapp would take a seat at the head of this table. I think there was as good talk around that table as took place anywhere in the world.[18]

In Francis Wolle, *University of Colorado Studies* (1944).

Shattuck found Whitman different and vulgar; he preferred the company of Thomas Bailey Aldrich. Like Shattuck, Aldrich was born in New Hampshire. In his poem, "A Touch of Nature," he conveys the predicament of a nature-loving city dweller:

> When first the crocus thrusts its point of gold
> Up through the still snow-drifted garden mould,
> And folded green things in dim woods unclose
> Their crinkled spears, a sudden tremor goes
> Into my veins and makes me kith and kin
> To every wild-born thing that thrills and blows.
> Sitting beside this crumbling sea-coal fire,
> Here in the city's ceaseless roar and din,
> Far from the brambly paths I used to know,
> Far from the rustling brooks that slip and shine
> Where the Neponset alders take their glow,
> I share the tremulous sense of bud and brier
> And inarticulate ardors of the vine.[19]
> *Works of Thomas Bailey Aldrich* (1915).

NOTES
1. *Aaron Draper Shattuck, NA 1861: A Retrospective Exhibition* (1970; reprint Exhibition catalogue, New Britain Museum of American Art, New Britain, Conn., 1975), unpaginated.
2. Nettie Adams, "A.D. Shattuck, Artist, Granby, Connecticut," *The Lure of the Litchfield Hills*, 27, no. 13 (1967), 33, National Academy of Design Artists Biographical Files.
3. *Ibid.*
4. Benjamin Champney, *Sixty Years' Memories of Art and Artists* (Woburn, Mass., Wallace and Andrews, 1900), 154-55.
5. "American Country Life," *The Crayon* 5 (1858), 279.
6. "Country Correspondence," *The Crayon* 5 (1858), 300-301.
7. *Ibid.*
8. Xeroxed portion of a letter written by A.D. Shattuck, August 1858. Collection of Katherine S. and Eugene D. Emigh, New Britain, Conn.
9. In conversation with Katherine S. and Eugene D. Emigh, New Britain, Conn., April 5, 1980.
10. *Shattuck*, Exhibition catalogue.
11. Aaron Draper Shattuck, *Farmington River*, collection of Katherine S. and Eugene D. Emigh, New Britain, Conn.
12. Review of the National Academy of Design exhibition, *The Crayon* 3 (1856), 118.
13. "National Academy of Design—Thirty-first Annual Exhibition," *New York Daily Times*, April 4, 1856, 2. (National Academy of Design Clippings Files).
14. "Academy of Design—Landscape Department," *Frank Leslie's Illustrated Newspaper*, April 12, 1856, 281-82. (National Academy of Design Clippings Files).
15. Conversation with K.S. and E.D. Emigh.
16. *Ibid.*
17. Francis Wolle, "Fitz-James O'Brien: A Literary Bohemian of the Eighteen-Fifties," *University of Colorado Studies, Series B, Studies in Humanities* 2, no. 2 (Boulder: University of Colorado, 1944), 1.
18. *Ibid.* 125.
19. Thomas Bailey Aldrich, *The Works of Thomas Bailey Aldrich* (1873; reprint New York: Jefferson Press, 1915), 2:119.

HR

GEORGE INNESS

(1825-1894)
ANA 1853; NA 1868

Born May 1, at Newburgh, N.Y. Raised in New York City and Newark, N.J. First studied painting under itinerant artist John Jesse Barker. Worked a year in a New York engraver's shop; studied a month under French emigré painter Régis François Gignoux. 1844 first exhibited at National Academy of Design. About 1851 first trip to Europe, primarily Italy. Late 1853 second trip to Europe, to Paris, where son, George, Jr., was born in 1854. Late 1854 returned, lived in Brooklyn. 1860 to farm in Medfield, Mass. 1864 to Eagleswood, N.J. 1870 third trip to Europe; stayed mostly in and around Rome, then briefly in Paris. Returned 1875. 1878 made home in Montclair, N.J. Travels in United States included excursions to Florida, California, Niagara Falls, New Hampshire, Virginia, Nantucket. Died August 3, at Bridge-of-Allan, Scotland. Funeral at National Academy of Design.

REFERENCES: *Dictionary of American Biography* (New York: Charles Scribner's Sons, 1931). Nicolai Cikovsky, Jr., *George Inness* (New York: Praeger, 1971).

When Inness painted his *Landscape* in 1860, his art already represented a distinct alternative to that of his associates at the Academy. Whereas the second generation Hudson River School painters promoted in their art a more literal reverence for local identity in American scenery, Inness almost from the first made nature the aspirant to art. He would have agreed with the painters of the Hudson River School only on the matter of a Divine presence in natural creation. Yet, since he stressed that man is created in God's image,[1] it followed that nature was as much at his disposal as it was at the Almighty's. Accordingly, Inness preferred, as he expressed it in 1878, "the civilized landscape" to the primordial Eden popularized by his contemporaries:

The highest art is where has been most perfectly breathed the sentiment of humanity. Rivers, streams, the rippling brook, the hill-side, the sky, clouds—all things that we see—can convey that sentiment if we are in the love of God and the desire of truth. Some persons suppose that landscape has no power of communicating human sentiment. But this is a great mistake. The civilized landscape peculiarly can; and therefore I love it more and think it more worthy of reproduction than that which is savage and untamed. It is more significant. Every act of man, every thing of labor, effort, suffering, want, anxiety, necessity, love, marks itself wherever it has been.[2]

Inness, "A Painter on Painting."

Landscape was painted at an important juncture in Inness's development.[3] After six years of absorbing into his art elements of the French Barbizon style, which he admired during his stay in Paris in 1854, he gained a technical assurance not previously displayed. *Landscape* shows clear evidence of the artist's confidence, as well as his debt to the French school, in particular to the work of Theodore Rousseau. It was also shortly after 1860, when for reasons of health he moved to a farm in Medfield, Massachusetts, that Inness's painting began to show an interest in content revived from his pre-European period. In the 1860s titles like *The Light Triumphant* and *Peace and Plenty* appeared beneath his canvases as indications of his religious and allegorical intentions.

The change in Inness's art was probably inspired in part by the noted clergyman Henry Ward Beecher who, by 1860, was a collector of Inness's work and who bestowed the title *The Light Triumphant* on his picture.[4] Beecher shared with Inness not simply a deep affection for nature as God's handiwork but the belief that nature existed also as an outward manifestation of man's intellect and emotion. In 1857 Beecher asserted:

The roots of Nature are in the human mind. The life and meaning of the outward world is not in itself, but in us. . . . He will see the most without who has the most within; and he who only sees with his bodily organs sees but the surface. He who paints or describes with the senses alone is but a surface artist.[5]

Beecher, "Hours of Exaltation."

In his emphasis on interpretation over documentation—really a kind of emulation of God's intervention in nature—Inness was again aided by the example of the Barbizon painters. The freer, more direct technique they had formulated enabled him to accommodate the swiftly changing attitudes both of outward nature and of his own. The anecdotes are legion of his mercurial working methods, of over-painting canvases five or six times in his efforts to capture desired effects. George Inness, Jr. describes how at Medfield his father would begin a seascape that might quickly be transformed into a pastoral, then a winter scene.[6] The son records Inness's own words in respect to his struggles with a picture:

Sometimes . . . it is hard to find out just where the thing [picture] is wrong; it doesn't seem to hitch. It may be in the sky or in the patch of light across the foreground; and then you will find out that it isn't that at all, but the fault lies in the composition, and those trees in the right are out of place and mar the breadth and grandeur of the picture. . . . It has been the curse of my life, this changing and trying to carry a thing nearer to perfection. After all, we are limited to paint. Maybe, after we get to heaven, we shall find some other medium with which to express our thoughts on canvas.[7]

Inness, Jr., *George Inness* (1917).

What is to the painter a "curse," however, is to the preacher, unencumbered by the painter's medium, a blessing. In his solitary musings on his farm in Lenox, Massachusetts, in 1854, Beecher not only anticipates the mutable nature of Inness's art but supplies its ultimate justification:

Ah! mighty worker is the head! These farmers that use the foot and the hand, are much to be pitied. I can change my structures every day, without expense. I can enlarge that gem of a lake that lies yonder, twinkling and rippling in the sunlight. I can pile up rocks where they ought to have been found, for landscape effect, and clothe them with the very vines that ought to grow over them. I can transplant every tree that I meet in my rides, and put it near my house without the drooping of a leaf.

But of what use is all this fanciful using of the head? It is a mere waste of precious time!

But, if it gives great delight, if it keeps the soul awake, sweet thoughts alive and sordid thoughts dead, if it brings one out of conceit with hard economies, and penurious reality, and stingy self-conceit, if it be like a bath to the soul, in which it washes away the grime of human contacts, and the sweat and dust of life among selfish, sordid men; if it makes the thoughts more supple to climb along the ways where spiritual fruits do grow; and especially, if it introduces the soul to a fuller conviction of the Great Unseen, and teaches it to esteem the visible as less real than things which no eye can see, or hands handle, it will have answered a purpose which is in vain sought among stupid conventionalities.[8]

Beecher, "Dream-Culture."

NOTES

1. In 1877, for instance, Inness wrote to his daughter:

Every individual man or woman born into this world is an offshoot of that Infinite Mind or Spirit which we call God. God creates in us sensation, and through it we are made conscious of the world we live in. A world which we eventually find to be a continually changing state, but a state which forms the basis of all our knowledges. This state is continually changing because our spirits individualized here, or born, created as distinct from the Infinite, gradually recede from natural surroundings into what each one eventually becomes, viz., the embodiment of his or her own love or desires.

Here, Inness seems to characterize, in effect, the subjective nature of his art, one expressive both of nature's and the artist's actual condition of flux. See Inness's letter in George Inness, Jr., *The Life, Art and Letters of George Inness* (New York: The Century, 1917), 199-200.

2. "A Painter on Painting," *Harper's New Monthly Magazine* 56 (1878), 469.

3. My characterization of Inness's painting around 1860, from the standpoints both of form and content, follows that of Nicolai Cikovsky, Jr., *George Inness* (New York: Praeger, 1971), 28-38.

4. *Ibid.*, 35-36.

5. Henry Ward Beecher, "Hours of Exaltation" (dated Matteawan, New York, August 17, 1857), *Eyes and Ears* (Boston: Ticknor and Fields, 1862), 35. Beecher's words are partially quoted in Cikovsky, Jr., 35.

6. Inness, Jr., 46.

7. George Inness addressing the collector Thomas B. Clarke. In Inness, Jr., 192. Clarke began to collect Inness's work and to act as his agent about 1878 (see Cikovsky, Jr., p. 40). Since George Inness, Jr. does not date his father's remarks to Clarke, they could have been made at almost anytime between 1878 and 1894, the year of Inness's death.

8. Henry Ward Beecher, "Dream-Culture" (dated Lenox, Massachusetts, August 10, 1854), *Star Papers; or Experiences of Art and Nature* (New York: J.C. Derby, 1855), 268-69.

KA

LANDSCAPE, 1860
Oil on paper, mounted on wood panel, 16¼ x 24″
Signed lower right: *G. Inness 1860*
Diploma Painting

ALEXANDER HELWIG WYANT

(1836-1892)
ANA 1868; NA 1869

Born January 11, Evans Creek, Ohio. Spent youth in nearby Defiance. Apprenticed to harnessmaker, but demonstrated early talent for drawing. May also have worked as sign painter during this period. 1857 to Cincinnati, saw exhibition of George Inness's paintings. 1858 to New York to meet Inness. Through Inness introduced to Cincinnati patron Nicholas Longworth. Studied a year at National Academy of Design. 1861-1863 in Cincinnati, painting photographs and portraits, some landscape work. Returned to New York by 1863. Studied at Academy and first exhibited there in 1864. 1865 to Karlsruhe, Germany; studied with Norwegian painter Hans-Fredrik Gude. 1866 to England and Ireland. By 1867 settled in New York. Began to exhibit at Academy and Boston Athenaeum, frequently painting also in watercolor. Early member of American Society of Painters in Water Colors. 1873 joined government expedition to Southwest. Hardships of trip caused stroke and loss of use of right hand. During 1870s at YMCA building in New York. Taught himself to paint with left hand. 1878 joined Society of American Artists. 1880 married pupil and watercolorist Arabelle Locke. Settled Keene Valley in Adirondacks. Occasionally worked at 23 Street studio, N.Y.C. Became a semi-invalid latter portion of his life. 1889 to Arkville, Catskill. Died New York City, November 29.

REFERENCES: John D. Champlin and Charles C. Perkins, *Cyclopedia of Painters and Paintings* (New York: Scribner's, 1886). Eliot Clark, *Alexander Wyant* (New York: Frederic Fairchild Sherman, 1916). Eliot Clark, *Sixty Paintings by Alexander H. Wyant* (New York: Frederic Fairchild Sherman, 1920). National Academy of Design Artists Biographical Files. Maria Naylor, ed., *The National Academy of Design Exhibition Record, 1861-1890*, vol. 2 (New York: Kennedy Galleries, 1973). New York Public Library Clipping File. Mabel Munson Swan, *The Athenaeum Gallery, 1827-1873* (Boston: The Boston Athenaeum, 1940).

I can, in this country [Germany] see things clearing up which I only grasped after in America. I always knew there was much to learn without knowing what it was. Now I begin to understand what must be learnt[.] It is much like science . . . you will be surprised to learn that this training of the mind is only intended to teach one to study nature in the right manner. To be sure there are many learned artists here in Germany, but their learning is to their pictures, what dry pedantry is in a haranguer, to Church's or Kensett's infinite suggestion & detail, or H.W. Beecher's burning eloquence.[1]

Wyant, Letter to Thomas Mells Turlay (Jan. 26, 1866).

The greatest imagination, wrought up to fever heat, prevails not generally here, but may be found among the young men occasionally, but the business of an art school is to smother that quality first. & then of the physical man to make a machine. I am thankful[?] to have breathed the air of art which moans & whistles around this old-old country . . . This feeling which becomes a part of religion was before only a fancy—vague, undefined & irreverential.[2]

Wyant, Letter (1866).

Wyant's 1866 letters from Germany to his friend and patron Thomas Mells Turlay, written just prior to his trip to England and Ireland, document a critical moment in his early career.[3] Having fulfilled his desire to study landscape painting in Germany, by March of 1866, Wyant's matured critical facility and increased self-confidence as an artist, added to his personal unhappiness and loneliness at Karlsruhe, caused him to cut short his visit.[4] He declined Hans-Fredrik Gude's invitation to stay another season and set out for London and the National Gallery's collection of Constables, en route to America.[5] As he wrote in February of that year: "I am looking out for the time when I shall go back to America, with great interest, as I shall try to paint a picture within the year which follows that. So with sanguine hopes . . ."[6]

Wyant is largely recalled today, in Peter Bermingham's phrase, as an American painter working in the Barbizon mood.[7] Critics closer to his time referred to Wyant as "the poet of the Adirondack mountains."[8]

Wyant is a sweet and tender artist talking in whispers . . . On a canvas of this size many objects may be introduced, but Wyant has kept it all in reserve and in tender tints of gray and green. It is a noble example of the artist's poetical painting.[9]

James William Pattison, *Fine Arts Journal* (1914).

Wyant's renderings of wooded groves and rolling vales attest to his devotion to the *paysage intime*. While he turned increasingly toward intimist views, smaller scale, and broader application of paint after his 1873 stroke (reflecting his greater physical limitations and increasing introspection), throughout his career he had chosen to portray quiet, unpopulated nature. This was part of the "religious feeling" he referred to in his letter of February 6, 1866, and which remained the basis for Wyant's personal approach to painting nature. Although a clear demarcation exists between his earlier Hudson River style and the later, mistier Barbizon mode, there is much in this work, (dated in the late 1860s)[10] that may be viewed as archetypal Wyant.

For Wyant the study of nature could evoke feelings akin to religion, but his letters indicate that an element of science was also involved.[11] Some kind of meteorological awareness is also suggested in titles of works shown at the National Academy of Design: *A Changeful Day, Driving Mist, The Coming Storm,*

ON THE OLD KENMARE ROAD NEAR KILLARNEY, c. 1869
Oil on canvas, mounted on masonite, 9 x 14½″
Signed lower left: *A.H. Wyant*
Diploma painting

Drifting Clouds, Summer Grays, and *Sunset After Storm.*[12]

He wrote from Karlsruhe: "I make a few sketches of skies when they please me,"[13] and has been quoted as having stated "the sky is the key to a picture."[14] These are sentiments that echo Constable's famous October 23, 1821, letter to John Fisher: "I have done a great deal of skying" and his claim that "it will be difficult to name a class of landscape in which the sky is not the key-note, the standard of scale, and the chief organ of sentiment . . ."[15]

Additional evidence of Wyant's scientific inclinations and professional investigations—in this instance, an interest in color theory—can be inferred from the February, 1869, notation in the National Academy's Library Register, when "A.H. Wyant" signed out a copy of Eastlake's translation of Goethe's *Farbenlehre* (Theory of Colors) for a month.[16] The Irish countryside may have dictated the green-blue-gray tonality Wyant favored in *Old Kenmare Road Near Killarney,* but it is tempting to consider whether the artist may have had in mind certain of Goethe's writings:

If yellow and blue, which we consider as the most fundamental and simple colors, are united as they first appear, in that first state of their action, the color which we call green is the result. The eye experiences a distinctly grateful impression from this color . . . The beholder has neither the wish nor the power to imagine a state beyond it. Hence for rooms to live in constantly, the green color is most generally selected.[17]
                                        Goethe's Theory of Colors (1840).

Certainly, by the time of an 1880 interview, Wyant seems to have absorbed Goethe's suggestions:

I shall key up the purples and the blues, making the purples more red, and the blues more green, so that they shall harmonize with the brightened yellows . . .

If I had here some pictures that I painted a long time ago, you would see that they do not contain the right proportions of red and green, or, red, blue and yellow . . .

Now the gray of a picture should be chock-full of primaries—of red, yellow, and blue, or of violet-gray and greenish-gray—if the result is to be delicious and satisfying.[18]
                                        Harper's Weekly (1880).

In the larger context of Wyant's *oeuvre,* meteorological issues and color theory remain tools with which he can better state his response to the landscape. He would almost certainly have agreed with Charles Lock Eastlake, who in his Preface to the first edition of the *Theory of Colors* wrote:

Let the eye be closed, let the sense of hearing be excited, and from the lightest breath to the wildest din, from the simplest sound to the highest harmony, from the most vehement and impassioned cry to the gentlest word of reason, still it is Nature that speaks and manifests her presence, her power, her pervading life and the vastness of her relations; so that a blind man to whom the infinite visible is denied, can still comprehend an infinite vitality . . .[19]

NOTES

1. Alexander Wyant, Letter to Thomas Mells Turlay, Jan. 26, 1866. Wyant-Turlay Correspondence, Archives of American Art, Smithsonian Institution, N.Y., microfilm roll N/70-48, frames 662-87).
2. *Ibid.* Feb. 6, 1866.
3. *Ibid.*
4. *Ibid.* Wyant wrote on February 3, 1866: "I begin to despise the place with all my heart," and a few days later (Feb. 6): "I go nowhere & am of course lonely until I settle my mind upon some friendly subject, or paint–or write. I shall probably marry the first American girl I see,—that is if she'll have me."
5. *Ibid.* Also, Eliot Clark, *Alexander Wyant* (New York: Frederic Fairchild Sherman, 1916). One periodical wrote that Wyant studied "Turner, and the elder Linnel [*sic*]" as well as Constable, while in London, and "with ever-increasing delight." "American Painters—Alexander H. Wyant, N.A.," *Art Journal* (December 1876), 353.
6. Wyant-Turlay Correspondence, Feb. 6, 1866.
7. Peter Bermingham, *American Art in the Barbizon Mood* (Exhibition catalogue, National Collection of Fine Arts, Smithsonian Institution, Washington, D.C., 1975).
8. W. Stanton Howard, "A Landscape by Wyant," *Harper's* (April 1905), New York Public Library Clipping File.
9. James William Pattison, "Loan Exhibition of American Pictures," *Fine Arts Journal* (February 1914), 89.
10. The dating of Wyant's Irish landscapes varies widely. Most are dated in the late 1860s and early 1870s after the 1866 trip. Examples are *Pat O'Donohue's Farm, Kerry,* c. 1870 (New Britain Institute); *View in County Kerry, Ireland,* c. 1870 (Metropolitan Museum of Art); *Scene in County Kerry, Ireland,* c. 1873 (Smith College Museum of Art); and *Irish Landscape,* before 1870 (no location given). *Road to Ireland* (Boston, Museum of Fine Arts) is presently dated to 1866, but with the exception of the Cleveland Museum of Art's Irish landscape, dated by Wyant to the Ireland tour, most examples appear to have been executed after the artist's return to America. (See *American Paintings in the Museum of Fine Arts, Boston,* vols. 1 and 2 [Boston: New York Graphic Society, 1969]; American Paintings Department, Metropolitan Museum of Art; Frick Art Reference Library Study Photograph File; Inventory of American Painting, National Collection of Fine Arts, Smithsonian Institution, Washington, D.C.).
11. Wyant-Turlay Correspondence, Jan. 26, 1866.
12. Maria Naylor, ed., *National Academy of Design Exhibition Record, 1861-90,* (New York: Kennedy Galleries, 1973), 2:1067-69. Eliot Clark, *Sixty Paintings by Alexander H. Wyant* (New York: Frederic Fairchild Sherman, 1920), passim.
13. Wyant-Turlay Correspondence, Jan. 26, 1866.
14. Frances Stover, "Some Favorite Older Paintings Back at Layton," *Milwaukee Wisconsin Journal* (July 20, 1952). National Academy of Design Artists Biographical Files.
15. Cited in Barbara Novak, "The Meteorological Vision: Clouds," *Art in America* 68, no. 2 (February 1980), 103, from *Nature and Culture* (New York: Oxford University Press, 1980).
16. National Academy of Design Library Register.
17. Charles Lock Eastlake, trans., *Goethe's Theory of Colors* (London: John Murray, 1840), 316.*
18. "Alexander H. Wyant," *Harper's Weekly* (October 23, 1880), 677.
19. Eastlake, *Goethe's Theory of Colors,* xviii.
*In Library of National Academy of Design.

CB

THOMAS HICKS

(1823-1890)
ANA 1841; NA 1851

Born October 18, Newtown, Penn. At fifteen apprenticed as coach painter to father's cousin Edward Hicks (famous primitive painter of *Peaceable Kingdoms*). Instructed in painting by Edward. Painted Edward's portrait after one year of training. 1837 studied at Pennsylvania Academy of the Fine Arts. 1838 continued studies at National Academy of Design. 1845-1849 traveled throughout Europe, studying in London, Florence, and Rome. Completed training in studio of Thomas Couture, Paris. 1849 returned to New York. Quickly achieved success as portrait painter. Best remembered for portraits of famous people, including Abraham Lincoln and William Cullen Bryant. 1873-1885 served as president of Artists' Fund. Died October 8, Trenton Falls, N.Y.

REFERENCES: George C. Groce and David H. Wallace, *Dictionary of Artists in America 1564-1860* (New-York Historical Society, 1957). George A. Hicks, "Thomas Hicks," *Readings Before the Society* (Doylestown, Penn.: Bucks County Historical Society, 1910). *A Century and a Half of American Art* (Exhibition catalogue, National Academy of Design, N.Y., 1975).°

Thomas Hicks is remembered primarily as a portrait painter. Recognition of his skill as a portraitist, however, should not preclude acknowledgment of his talent as a landscapist.[1]

Italian Landscape reveals a sensibility more akin to the romantic spirit of Cole than to the luminist mode of some of Hicks' closer contemporaries. Hicks incorporates the volatile Italian spirit into his painting by portraying the Roman campagna during the onset of a sudden storm. Tense anticipation of the impending gale is underscored by his restless brushstroke. The threatening gray clouds sweeping in from the right contrast sharply with the sun-warmed rocks in the foreground, creating a theatrical effect. A glimpse of Roman ruins in the background and a scarlet-clad peasant boy standing atop the rocks add a more conventionally picturesque quality to a scene which manages to remain fresh and unexpected.

By making an artistic pilgrimage to Italy, Hicks participated in a long tradition. Benjamin West was the first American artist to travel to Italy (1760-1763); John Singleton Copley followed soon after and complained of Americans' lack of interest in art. American art patronage increased considerably between Copley's day and that of Hicks'. By the mid nineteenth century, William Curtis could write from Staten Island to Christopher Pearse Cranch in Rome, "Undoubtedly, there is a greater general respect for art and artists here. It is quite 'the thing' to know them and to have

them." But he added, "I should think an artist would prefer to live in Rome . . ." even though, "one who would succeed there would also succeed here."[2] America had a bountiful supply of scenery that Americans came to appreciate more and more. In 1855 Asher B. Durand advised young artists: "Go not abroad then in search of material for the exercise of your pencil, while the virgin charms of our native land have claims on your deepest affections."[3]

Nonetheless, the primeval attraction of America's "virgin charms" could not stop the craving for the more cultivated beauty of a long-established culture. Reports in *The Crayon* fluctuated from year to year regarding the number of sales made by American artists abroad. One artist lamented a dismal winter season in 1857:

The only commissions I had for this winter have been countermanded. There is little new here. A few more American artists have come to town. Very many of us have nothing to do. Only one work of painting or sculpture has been sold this winter.[4]

Letter, Rome, *The Crayon* (1858).

Still, the artists continued to go, seeking, perhaps, the artistic heritage that young America lacked. Possibly also the mild climate of Italy and the convivial life drew them:

Was there not always a meeting, a junketting, an excursion in order—some church-feast, some curiosity of colour and sound, not to be missed, some new "find" in some admirable scene of excavation, some Cervara *rendezvous* of fraternising artists, costumed, polyglot, theatrical, farcical, delightful; something new finished, reported of, in somebody's, poor fellow's, clever chap's studio . . . ?[5]

Henry James, *William Wetmore Story and His Friends* (1903).

There were veritable colonies of American artists in Rome at mid-century. Jasper F. Cropsey, John F. Kensett, and the genre painter James E. Freeman were among those with whom Hicks socialized. A sense of the jovial society they shared may be gleaned from a passage in the journal of Christopher Pearse Cranch: "One evening at Tom Hicks's room, I truly enjoyed myself . . . By great good luck there were four of us who sang Moore's 'Melodies.' We had also glees and solos, and the evening passed away delightfully."[6] Benjamin Champney, another American artist in Rome, also recalled Hicks' congenial nature:

. . . Kensett and myself were very short of means, and it came at last to the point that we had not the wherewithal to buy a cheap breakfast. . . . Kensett had already borrowed of his friend Rossiter, and felt delicate about asking for more. Hicks had a studio in the same house with me,

ITALIAN LANDSCAPE, c. 1848
Oil on paper, mounted on
composition board lamination,
15 x 21″
Signed bottom center: *T. Hicks*
Suydam Collection

and he was a new arrival in Rome—with a pocket full of money. Kensett said he would go to Hicks and tell him of my predicament, and say he thought it would be a great boon if he would even offer to lend me ten dollars. Hicks was a generous, loyal fellow, and came to me at once with the money. Then Kensett and I divided it. This was a reprieve, and we at once visited the well-known Café Grequo [sic] to breakfast on a cup of weak coffee and two little rolls.[7]

Art and Artists (1900).

The Café Greco, where Champney and Kensett breakfasted, was a time-honored meeting place for expatriate artists of all nationalities. Years later, Freeman described it in his memoirs:

This place was resorted to, not because of its superior appointments and fare, for it was decidedly one of the smallest, darkest, and untidiest of restaurants; its central position and superior coffee were its chief attractions . . . The interior consisted of three insignificant rooms; the largest and nearest the entrance had a low-arched ceiling, pretentiously painted with nondescript allegory, in which hideous and grotesque animals were strangely mixed with mythological monstrosities, and driven into Stygian confusion by dense clouds of tobacco-smoke. . . . Added to this were the commingling of a dozen languages and dialects, and a variety of costumes, physiognomy, and gesticulation peculiar to Russians, Poles, Hungarians, Danes, Swedes, Spaniards, French, Dutch, English, and other mixed races and eccentric characters.[8]

Gatherings From an Artist's Portfolio (1877).

The combination of Italy's picturesque environment and her flamboyant people blended history and life into a bewitching present in which fantasies became almost real. An interchange between Freeman and Nathaniel Hawthorne sums up the magical qualities Italy held for the artists. Hawthorne and former President Franklin Pierce once called on Freeman when the painter was working on a picture of Christ. The author was so taken with the representation that he inquired about the model:

"I should like to see him," he said.

"And so should I, too," I replied. "I went to find him the other day, to engage him for more sittings, when his family informed me that he had enlisted as a soldier and left the city."

It would be difficult to describe the peculiar smile on Hawthorne's face as he said: "So Christ has gone to war! Is it true," he asked, "that there are also models who sit for pictures of the Eternal Father?"

I replied in the affirmative: "Two or three old men, with long white beards, who are generally to be seen sitting on the steps of the Piazza di Spagna."

"Let us go," said he to Mr. Pierce, "and see the gods."[9]

NOTES

1. Hicks painted landscapes along with John F. Kensett, James A. Suydam, Louis R. Mignot, and others who were commissioned by the Baltimore and Ohio Railroad Company to advertise the beauties of the vistas to be seen along the train route between Baltimore and Wheeling, Virginia. *The Crayon* 5 (1858), 208.

2. Leonora Cranch Scott, *The Life and Letters of Christopher Pearse Cranch* (Boston: Houghton, Mifflin, 1917), 242.

3. Asher B. Durand, "On Landscape Painting—Letter II," *The Crayon* 1 (1855), 34.

4. "Extract from a Private Letter," Rome, December 16, 1857, *The Crayon* 5 (1858), 83.

5. Henry James, *William Wettmore Story and His Friends* (Boston: Houghton, Mifflin, 1903), 1:347.

6. Scott, *Christopher Pearse Cranch*, 124.

7. Benjamin Champney, *Sixty Years' Memories of Art and Artists* (Woburn, Mass.: Wallace and Andrews, 1900), 73.

8. James E. Freeman, *Gatherings from an Artist's Portfolio* (New York D. Appleton, 1877), 1:11-12.*

9. *Ibid.*, 208.

*In Library of National Academy of Design.

HR

JULES ÉMILE SAINTIN

(1829-1894)
ANA 1859; NA 1861

Born August 14, at Lemé, in Aisne, France. Entered École des Beaux-Arts in September 1845. Teachers included Michel Martin Drölling, François Édouard Picot, and Achille Jean-Baptiste Leboucher, history, genre, and portrait painters, themselves pupils of Jacques-Louis David and Antoine Jean Gros. Exhibited at Paris Salon at age nineteen. By 1856 working in New York City, exhibiting frequently over next seven years at National Academy of Design, and beginning in 1860, at Boston Athenaeum. Returned to settle in Paris 1863, apparently journeying to Rome the following year. Regularly represented at annual Salons until death, receiving number of medals, including Chevalier of the Legion of Honor. *Oeuvre* largely comprised of portrait and genre paintings; produced sizeable body of work in pastel, including many portraits of actors and actresses of Comédie Française. Member of jury to select French entries for Philadelphia Centennial. Represented in 1878 Paris International Exhibition and in 1893 at World's Columbian Exposition in Chicago. Died Paris, July 14.

REFERENCES: Émile Bellier De La Chavignerie and Louis Auvray, *Dictionnaire Général Des Artistes De L'École Française*, vol. 2 (Paris: Librairie Renouard, 1885). John D. Champlin, Jr. and Charles C. Perkins, *Cyclopedia of Painters and Paintings*, vols. 3, 4 (New York: Scribner's, 1886). *Explication des ouvrages de peinture, sculpture, architecture, gravure et lithographie des artistes vivants, exposés au Grand Palais des Champs-Elysées* (Paris: Ministère de L'Instruction publique; after 1880, Société des artistes français, 1854-1883). Ernest Glaeser, ed., *Biographie nationale des contemporains* (Paris: Glaesser et cie, 1878). National Academy of Design Artists Biographical Files. Obituary, *The New York Times* (July 16, 1894). *Salon de 1888, Catalogue Illustré* (Paris, 1888). Edward Strahan, ed., *The Chefs-D'Oeuvre D'Art of the International Exhibition* (Philadelphia, 1878). Henri Sylvestre, Jr., *The Marvels in Art of the Fin de Siècle*, vols. 1, 2 (Philadelphia: The Gebbie Publishing Co., 1893).

In Rome, therefore, the mind, by the contrasting feebleness of the present government, its ragged magnificence, and futile claims to dominion, is irresistibly thrown back to the great past, which looms up so vast in the horizon of history. The Past lives while the Present swoons. . . . It is difficult to sleep quietly where every stone has a tongue, and the very air is peopled with the shapes of olden life, sincere and strong, in its contrasting lights of vice and virtue. There is too much vitality of association for sensitive nerves. This, joined to an atmospherical torpor, arising from poisonous exhalations, as well as the constant mental conflict between reality and vision . . . produces an intellectual excitement in many minds unfavorable to health . . . Extremes meet in Rome. To some it is a renewal of the lease of life; while to others, every breath they inhale savors of death. Two classes alone of strangers can enjoy Rome. Artists who live only in their ideal world, or visitors who turn Rome into a watering place.[1]

James Jackson Jarves, *Italian Sights and papal principles, seen through American spectacles* (1856).

Saintin's *View Near Rome* would seem to be atypical of his career as an artist. As a native Frenchman who worked briefly in New York City before returning to spend the rest of his life in Paris, the Rome journey during 1864 represents a brief interlude in a career spanning some fifty years and may well have been the artist's single visit to Italy. As a portrait and genre painter, who produced works with such titles as *Woman Carried Off By Indians* (exhibited at the 1864 Salon), *Heartfelt Mourning* (1868), *Will He Return?* (1878), and *The Indiscreet Soubrette* (1878), landscape was outside of Saintin's usual realm.[2]

Given the artist's predilection for the charming and the colorful, one might have expected him to paint scenes of Roman street life as more likely subject matter for picture souvenirs of the trip to Italy. Saintin was also certainly aware of the artistic and iconographic tradition that Rome represented (and which, for both Continental and American painter-pilgrims, was, by 1864, becoming passé), for both Picot and Drölling, his earliest masters, had traveled to Italy as recipients of the Prix-de-Rome.[3] In any event, on this occasion Saintin felt the impulse while visiting the Eternal City to turn his hand to landscape.

The environs of Rome depicted here may have appealed to Saintin as it had to an earlier visitor:

In this delightful spot we find shade and privacy, or sunshine and society, as we may feel inclined. Today it was intensely hot; and we found the cool sequestered walks and alleys of cypress and ilex, perfectly delicious. I spread my shawl upon a green bank carpeted with violets, and lounged in most luxurious indolence. I had a book with me, but felt no inclination to read. The soft air, the trickling and murmuring of innumerable fountains, the urns, the temples, the statues—the localities of the scene—all dispose the mind to a kind of vague but delightful reverie to which we "find no end, in wandering mazes lost."[4]

Anna Jameson, *Diary of an Ennuyée* (1826).

It is equally evident that *View Near Rome* is unlike many of the Roman landscapes painted by American artists traveling abroad. Instead, Saintin offers a restrained and almost coolly topographical composition. In place of picturesque ruins, the blocky forms of the villa architecture and the "landscaped" gardens are the protagonists. In this, Saintin's rendition of the Italian campagna can be allied with the Roman landscapes of his compatriot Camille Corot, whose studies of the landscape (such as *Italian Landscape* and *Lake Albano and Castel Gandolfo*, both c. 1825, Metropolitan Museum of Art), manifest a similiar architectonic approach. Saintin's painting can also be related to the established Italian *veduta* or view-painting tradition.

Nonetheless, Saintin's American experience and his work at the

VIEW NEAR ROME, 1864
Oil on canvas, mounted on masonite, 8 x 12¾"
Signed lower left center: *J.E. Saintin—Rome 1864*
Artist's Bequest

National Academy of Design provide the underpinning for *View Near Rome* and must be considered an important watershed for his artistic development. It would appear a curious sort of reverse pilgrimage, a trip to the New World, yet it provided Saintin with more than the Wild West subject matter which found an appreciative audience abroad.[5]

Of nearly eighty paintings exhibited by Saintin at the Academy during his New York years, the large majority were portraits and genre paintings. At most, ten can be considered possible landscapes; of these, three, painted between 1859 and 1860, were Hudson River views. He also seems to have known John Frederick Kensett, for he exhibited a portrait of that artist in 1862 at the Academy, and the year before, Saintin's painting *An Interesting Lecture*, owned by Kensett, was shown there.[6]

Afterwards, in Paris, Saintin focused on genre works and portraits, and landscape became little more than a backdrop for the central figures. Yet his New York years appear to have held greater significance than might be expected of a visit of six years. At his death, it was discovered that Saintin had left the entire contents of his studio and all of his American paintings to the Academy—an enormous mass of material that the modest insti-

tution was unable to accept. As a result, the bequest was sold in Paris, and at this time, the small *View Near Rome* entered the Academy's collection as a testament to Saintin's Academy years.[7]

NOTES
1. James Jackson Jarves, *Italian Sights and papal principles, seen through American spectacles* (New York: Harper & Brothers, 1856), 358-59.
2. For a listing of Saintin's paintings exhibited at the Salon, see *Explication des ouvrages de peinture, sculpture, architecture, gravure et lithographie des artistes vivants, exposés au Grand Palais des Champs-Élysées* (Paris: Ministère de L'Instruction publique, France, 1848-88; Société des artistes français; 1881-1894.)
3. Ulrich Thieme and Felix Becker. *Allgemeines Lexikon der Bildenden Künstler* (Leipzig: Veb. E.A. Seemann, 1866-).
4. Mrs. Anna Brownell (Murphy) Jameson, *The Diary of An Ennuyée* (1826; reprint Boston: Ticknor and Fields, 1857), 256.
5. *Explication des ouvrages . . . 1863-1865.*
6. Mary Bartlett Cowdrey, ed., *National Academy of Design Exhibition Record, 1826-1860* (New-York Historical Society, 1943), 109-10. Maria Naylor, ed., *National Academy of Design Exhibition Record, 1861-1900* (New York: Kennedy Galleries, 1973) 819-20.
7. J.C. Nicoll Correspondence, 1894-95, National Academy of Design Artists Biographical Files.

CB

JASPER FRANCIS CROPSEY

(1823-1900)
ANA 1844; NA 1851

Born Rossville on Staten Island, New York, February 18. While apprenticed 1837-1842 to architect Joseph Trench, took watercolor lessons from Edward Maury. After apprenticeship turned to painting and exhibited first picture at the National Academy of Design in 1843. In 1847 traveled to Europe, staying primarily in Italy. Returned to America in 1849. Traveled and sketched in New England, Canada, and Michigan. Taught in New York City, sharing studio space with Thomas Hicks. Continued to work many drawings done in Italy and England into finished paintings. To Europe again in 1856, painting numerous American scenes there, which were much in demand. Illustrated collections of poetry by Edgar Allan Poe and Thomas Moore. On return to United States in 1863 renewed interest in architecture. Completed his twenty nine-room mansion, Aladdin, in Warwick, New York, in 1869. Designed platforms and stations for Sixth Avenue elevated subway in New York. Forced to sell Aladdin in 1884 due to financial circumstances. Following year purchased home at Hastings-on-Hudson, New York, which now houses his archives. Continued painting scenes of the Hudson, primarily autumn landscapes. In later years worked more in watercolor. Died Hastings-on-Hudson, June 22.

REFERENCES: Kenneth W. Maddox, *An Unprejudiced Eye: The Drawings of Jasper F. Cropsey* (Exhibition catalogue, The Hudson River Museum, New York, 1979). William S. Talbot, *Jasper F. Cropsey 1823-1900* (New York: Garland Publishing, Inc., 1977).

On the eve of his departure for Europe in the Spring of 1847, Jasper Francis Cropsey exhibited two Staten Island landscapes at the National Academy of Design. One reviewer praised his directness and then launched a general appeal:

Mr. Cropsey is one of the few among our landscape painters who go directly to nature for their materials. For one so young in his art, his attainments are extraordinary. . . . We wish it were in our power to impress it upon the minds of our landscape painters, particularly, that they have a high and sacred mission to perform. . . . The axe of civilization is busy with our old forests, and artisan ingenuity is fast sweeping away the relics of our national infancy. What were once the wild and picturesque haunts of the Red Man, and where the wild deer roamed in freedom, are becoming the abodes of commerce and the seats of manufactures. . . . Yankee enterprise has little sympathy with the picturesque, and it behooves our artists to rescue from its grasp the little that is left, before it is for ever too late.[1]

Literary World (1847).

Already the youngest Associate at the Academy, Cropsey was nominated as Academician with these landscapes, but no one was elected that year. He was renominated and elected in 1851, at the same time as another returnee from Rome, Thomas Hicks.

Meanwhile, Cropsey married Maria Cooley in 1847, and the couple set sail for a prolonged honeymoon and Grand Tour of Europe. After three months in England and Scotland, they departed for Italy in mid-September. Upon their arrival in Rome, Maria wrote to her sister, "From my window is seen the Piazza del Popolo."[2] Cropsey used Thomas Cole's former Roman studio, and even sketched the same motifs as his predecessor.[3] The couple stayed in Italy for a year and a half, apparently undismayed by the 1848 Revolution. Cropsey wrote to Cole early in 1848 that despite the political turmoil, "Rome and its environs stand with a sentiment apparently more beautiful and enduring than ever."[4]

The Cropseys spent the summer of 1848 in the campagna outside Rome, mostly near the Christopher P. Cranchs at Sorrento. Cranch kept a diary of those months in "peaceful retreat" from the armed conflict in Naples.[5] Cranch records that he and Cropsey went on sketching outings to Amalfi on July 5, and Capri on July 18, when they were joined by William Wetmore Story.[6] In August the three visited the ruins at Paestum. Cranch describes their delight at the

picturesquely broken columns, with flowers and briers growing in and around, and sometimes over fallen capitals. . . . And over all brooded such a silence and solitude. Nothing stood between us and the Past . . .[7]

Life and Letters of Christopher Pearse Cranch (1917).

This description also applies to the *Lake of Nemi*, the result of a similar excursion the following month to a site previously sketched by Kensett and Hicks in the summer of 1846.[8] The lake view was popular with artists from the late eighteenth century on, as John R. Cozens' comparable watercolor of 1782 indicates. In 1846 also, Karl Lindemann-Frommel produced a more prosaic version from the same viewpoint as Cropsey.[9] Four Cropsey pencil drawings from Nemi are inscribed and dated *Sept. 1848*,[10] but none can be considered studies for this painting. Rather, it seems Cropsey made a drawing on paperboard at the site, then made an oil sketch over it.

The sustained interest in architecture that Cropsey manifests in his pencil drawings carries over to the sketch, where the structures surrounding the lake are very precisely rendered. The cubic mass of the buildings at the right contrasts with the overgrown fore-

LAKE OF NEMI, 1848
Oil on paperboard, 15⅜ x 22¼"
Signed lower right: *J. F. Cropsey 1848*
Inscribed in pencil across top: "*with much breadth
and quick . . . from palazzo the —th of* (illegible)
Suydam Collection

ground. A lone, hooded figure walks below the cypress tree. This is probably the vista above the village of Nemi recommended in a popular guidebook:

From the hills above, the traveller enjoys one of those scenes which cannot be described: the eye wanders over the vast plains of the Campagna from the Circaean promontory to Porto d'Anzo . . . and from thence to the mouth of the Tiber, comprehending within this range the scene of half the Aeneid, and of some of the grandest events in the history of Rome.[11]

John Murray, *Handbook* (1843).

Thus situated in the historic Alban Hills southeast of Rome:

This beautiful little lake occupies, like that of Albano, the well-defined crater of an extinct volcano. . . . It is five miles in circumference and rather more than 100 feet higher than the surface of the lake of Albano. . . . The village of Nemi, with a population of 1100 souls, is beautifully placed on the margin of the lake immediately opposite to Genzano.[12]

Murray, *Handbook*.

It is the buildings of Genzano that are visible in the center, across the "unrippled lake," "the earth's eye," which calmly mirrors the gathering gray cumulus clouds above.[13]

Tuckerman records a similar painting also done in late 1848: "Another picture, painted the same winter, of Lake Nemi, was afterwards presented to the Academy, and by the Academy sold to the Art-Union, to cover a deficiency in their funds."[14] In 1852 the Art-Union sold *View near Nemi, Italy*, a 40 by 27-inch painting which has not yet been traced.[15] Meanwhile the Academy received *Lake of Nemi* in the Suydam bequest of 1865.

In the spring of 1856, Cropsey sold the contents of his studio before traveling to London. His receipt book lists payment from "Mr. Jam. A. Suydam for studies, lot of 7," most likely including *Lake of Nemi*. Suydam also purchased a "Set of Ruskin books, Stones of Venice, etc."[16] Before selling the books, Cropsey seems to have heeded Ruskin's criticism of Turner's Italian landscapes:

The chief reason of these failures I imagine to be the effort of [Turner] to put joyousness and brilliancy of effect upon scenes eminently pensive, to substitute radiance for serenity of light, and to force the freedom and breadth of line which he learned to love on English downs and Highland moors, out of a country dotted by campaniles and square convents, bristled with cypresses, partitioned by walls, and gone up and down by steps.[17]

John Ruskin, *Modern Painters* (1843).

NOTES

1. *Literary World* 1 (May 15, 1847), 347-48.
2. Maria Cropsey to Jane Cooley, October 13, 1847. Typescript in the Print Room, Museum of Fine Arts, Boston. I am grateful to Kenneth Maddox for making his copies of the letters available to me. The Cropseys were welcomed into the American colony in Rome, for the letter already mentions Christopher P. Cranch, Thomas Crawford, Thomas Hicks, and the arrival of Margaret Fuller.
3. See *Italian Campagna* (1848, Reinhardt Collection). In John Wilmerding, *American Light* (Exhibition catalogue, Washington: National Gallery of Art, 1980), 122. Cropsey's enthusiasm was probably sparked by Cole's Italian scenes shown in his retrospective at the National Academy during the winter of 1843. Cropsey subsequently painted imaginary Italian landscapes in 1844 and 1846.
4. Letter from Cropsey to Cole, March 16, 1848, Cole Papers, Archives of American Art, Smithsonian Institution, N.Y., microfilm roll D10, frame 1166. Apparently Cropsey had not received his regular correspondent John Falconer's letter of February 24, 1848, telling of the death of Cole.
5. Leonora Cranch Scott, *The Life and Letters of Christopher Pearse Cranch* (New York: Houghton Mifflin, 1917), 144.
6. *Ibid.*, 145-146. For Story's memoirs of the same period, see Henry James, *William Wetmore Story* (Boston: Houghton Mifflin, 1903), 1:Ch. 3. Cropsey is mentioned on p. 123.
7. *Ibid.*, 147.
8. John K. Howat, *John Frederick Kensett* (New York: American Federation of the Arts, 1968), n.p. In 1849 the American Art-Union sold a Kensett *View on Lake Nemi*. Sanford R. Gifford's larger, more atmospheric version of 1856-57 (Toledo Museum of Art) is from the same viewpoint as Cropsey's. See also Ila Weiss, *Sanford Robinson Gifford* (Ph.D. dissertation, Columbia University, 1968), 145.
9. Illustration in Guido Ucelli, *Le Navi di Nemi* (Rome: Libreria dello Stato, 1940), fig. 24, p. 35. According to Thieme-Becker, Lindemann-Frommel was in Rome contemporaneously with Cropsey from 1845 to 1849. See also Leo Montecchi, *Nemi* (Rome: Luciano Morpurgo, 1929), plate XIX, for the Cozens.
10. Kenneth W. Maddox, *An Unprejudiced Eye: The Drawings of Jasper F. Cropsey* (Exhibition catalogue, Hudson River Museum, Yonkers, N.Y. 1979), fig. 14: *Old Gateway at Nemi. Trees at Nemi* (Karolik Collection, Boston, Museum of Fine Arts). William S. Talbot, *Jasper F. Cropsey 1823-1900* (Ph.D. dissertation, New York University, 1972. Reprint Garland Series, 1977), cat. no. 37 refers to *View of the Town of Nemi* and *Mill at Nemi*. The latter is the only drawing specifying the day—Sept. 8, 1848.
11. *Handbook for Traveller's in Central Italy* (London: John Murray, 1843), 507. In a letter to her parents from Florence on April 18, 1849, Maria mentions "Murray's guide book." She also relates that during the rainy weather in Florence, "Frank" worked in Cranch's studio.
12. *Ibid.*, 506-07.
13. On Diverse Themes from Nature," edited and introduced by Barbara Novak. In Kynaston McShine, ed., *The Natural Paradise: Painting in America, 1800-1950* (Exhibition catalogue, Museum of Modern Art, N.Y., 1976), 102. For Cropsey's interest in clouds, see his essay "Up among the Clouds," *The Crayon* 2 (Aug. 8, 1885), 79.
14. Henry T. Tuckerman, *Book of the Artists* (New York: G.P. Putnam's, 1867), 535.
15. Talbot, *Cropsey*, cat. no. 37.
16. Cropsey Papers, Archives of American Art, Smithsonian Institution, N.Y., microfilm roll 336.
17. John Ruskin, *Modern Painters* (1843; reprint New York: Dutton, 1935), 1:123.

LK

WILLIAM STANLEY HASELTINE

(1835-1900)
ANA 1860; NA 1861

Born June 11, Philadelphia, Penn. Mother amateur landscape painter, two brothers also artists. At age fifteen studied locally with Paul Weber, a German-trained painter. 1850 entered University of Pennsylvania. Transferred to Harvard two years later, graduating in 1854. 1855-1857 in Düsseldorf; summers on sketching tours with Worthington Whittredge, Albert Bierstadt, and Emmanuel Leutze. To Italy in 1857. Returned to United States mid-1858; opened studio at 15 Tenth Street. Exhibited frequently during these years at National Academy of Design, Salmagundi, and Century clubs in New York, Pennsylvania Academy of the Fine Arts, and the Boston Athenaeum. Exempted from service in Civil War because of chronic eye ailment. 1866 to Paris; established a studio there. Friendships with Antoine-Auguste-Ernest Hébert, Adolphe William Bouguereau, and Jean-Léon Gérôme. Studied at Barbizon. Moved permanently to Rome 1870. Four years later, settled into apartment at Palazzo Altieri, Haseltine family residence for next twenty-five years and meeting place for visiting and expatriate writers and artists. Founding member of American Academy in Rome and benefactor of city's Episcopal Church. Traveled extensively throughout Europe, returning infrequently to United States. Several trips to America toward end of life; returned to New England and toured the West, especially California, Yellowstone Park, and Alaska. Died Rome, February 3.

REFERENCES: John D. Champlin and Charles C. Perkins, *Cyclopedia of Painters and Paintings*, vol. 2 (New York: Scribner's, 1886). George C. Groce and David H. Wallace, *Dictionary of Artists in America, 1564-1860* (New-York Historical Society, 1957). National Academy of Design Artists Biographical Files. New York Public Library Clipping File. Helen Haseltine Plowden, *William Stanley Haseltine: Sea and Landscape Painter* (London: F. Muller, Ltd., 1947). Anna Wells Rutledge, ed., *The Pennsylvania Academy of the Fine Arts, 1807-1870. . .* (Philadelphia: American Philosophical Society, 1955). Mabel Munson Swan, *The Athenaeum Gallery, 1827-1873* (Boston: The Boston Athenaeum, 1940). Henry T. Tuckerman, *Book of the Artists* (New York: G. P. Putnam's, 1867).

William Stanley Haseltine gives ample evidence of his Düsseldorf studies, whereof the correct drawing and patient elaboration are more desirable than the color—although herein he has often notably excelled. Few of our artists have been more conscientious in the delineation of rocks; their form, superficial traits, and precise tone are given with remarkable accuracy. His pencil identifies coast scenery with emphatic beauty . . . Italy and America are, as it were, embodied in the authentic tints of these rock-portraits set in the deep blue crystalline of the sea . . . there is a history to the imagination in every brown angle-projecting slab, worn, broken, ocean-mined and sun-painted ledge of the brown and picturesquely-heaped rocks, at whose feet the clear, green waters plash: they speak to the eye of science of a volcanic birth and the antiquity of man, and their surroundings, distinctly and, as it were, personally, appeal to the lover of nature for recognition or reminiscence.[1]

Tuckerman, *Book of the Artists* (1867).

They agreed it was the earthly paradise, and they passed the mornings strolling through the perfumed alleys of classic villas, and the evenings floating in the moonlight in a circle of outlined mountains, to the music of silver-trickling oars. One day, in the afternoon, the two young men took a long stroll together. They followed the winding footway . . . past the gates of villas and the walls of vineyards, through little hamlets propped on a dozen arches, and bathing their feet and their pendant tatters in the gray-green ripple; past frescoed walls and crumbling campaniles and grassy village piazzas, and the mouth of soft ravines that wound upward, through belts of swinging vine and vaporous olive and splendid chestnut, to high ledges where white chapels gleamed amid the paler boskage, and bare cliff-surfaces, with their sun-cracked lips, drank in the azure light. It all was confoundingly picturesque; it was the Italy that we know from the steel engravings in the old keep-sakes and annuals, from the vignettes on music-sheets and the drop-curtains at theatres; an Italy that we can never confess to ourselves—in spite of our own changes and of Italy's—that we have ceased to believe in. . . . Rowland had never known anything so divinely soothing as the dreamy softness of that early autumn afternoon. The iridescent mountains shut him in; the little waves, beneath him, fretted the white pebbles at the laziest intervals; the festooned vines above him swayed just visibly in the all but motionless air.

Roderick lay observing it all with his arms thrown back and his hands under his head. "This suits me," he said; "I could be happy here and forget everything. Why not stay here forever?"[2]

Henry James, *Roderick Hudson* (1875).

Capri was a favorite sketching site for Haseltine, as it was for other American artists abroad. Indeed, this site may have been specifically popular with artists, for at least one similar view by a European painter visiting Italy exists, attesting, incidentally, to Haseltine's faithful rendering.[3]

Haseltine's love of nature, evidenced also in such favored pursuits as trout fishing, gardening, and astronomy,[4] and his love for his adopted home, Italy, perhaps found its fullest expression in excursions into the campagna and along the coast. As Haseltine's daughter, Helen H. Plowden, wrote:

. . .he would start out for the Campagna in one of those post-chaises that used to bring the country-folk back and forth between the Roman gates and the hill-towns, and then, armed with his sketching equipment, tramp the hills for hours until he had found his subject.[5]

Haseltine was not just seeking new motifs in these plein air sorties. His daughter suggests he may have viewed such excursions as a retreat from the pressures of Rome, which for the indepen-

dently wealthy Haseltine were not the usual artist's concerns but rather the fatigue brought on by his extensive social life.[6] Helen Plowden recalls the family's annual exodus each summer into the campagna as eagerly anticipated expeditions planned around Mrs. Haseltine's amateur love of archaeology and the artist's dedicated connoisseurship of local wines.[7]

Haseltine's initial trip to Italy was part of the Grand Tour, his return and permanent exile in Italy after 1870, when Rome was no longer the artists' mecca, represents a different sort of quest. Although his daughter suggests that he sought greater varieties of landscape to paint ("he had gone to Rome solely for inspiration for his work"),[8] Haseltine also enjoyed an exceedingly comfortable and social existence. He was a noted collector (including tapestries, Pre-Raphaelite works, and sixteenth-century Italian mural paintings),[9] a patron of other artists in the city, and characterized always as a gentleman. Plowden notes that he felt stifled by family responsibilities and expectations in Philadelphia, and believed that his talent could not develop in America. In Plowden's words, "he wanted to live his own life, be his own ancestor,"[10] and perhaps the older civilization of Rome ironically offered the American Haseltine a chance to start anew.

Like so many of his countrymen, Haseltine appears to have been caught up in the mythic allure of Italy. Among the cherished books in the Palazzo Altieri library was an edition of Samuel Rogers' prose poem *Italy* (illustrated with engravings after works by Turner), a classic in expatriate literature, and as familiar to every traveler on the Grand Tour as Byron's *Childe Harold*.[11] Rogers' rapturous cry:

> I am in Rome! Oft as the morning-ray
> Visits these eyes, waking at once I cry,
> Whence this excess of joy? What has befallen me?
> And from within a thrilling voice replies,
> Thou art in Rome![12]
>
> *Italy* (1823-1828).

may indeed have expressed feelings similar to those of Haseltine. It seems evident that the particularly dreamlike quality of expatriate life in Rome, which has been characterized as "the much-talked-of Rome sickness,"[13] that air of being forever rootless, a visitor, living a life always gay and vital and full of new faces, exerted a considerable pull on Haseltine, drawing him back to live out his life in the Eternal City.[14] As the steadfast heroine, Mary, in Henry James' *Roderick Hudson*, explains it:

"I used to think," she answered, "that if any trouble came to me I would bear it like a stoic. But that was at home, where things don't speak to us of enjoyment as they do here. Here it is such a mixture; one doesn't know what to choose, what to believe. Beauty stands there—beauty such as this night and this place, and all this sad, strange summer, have been so full of—and it penetrates to one's soul and lodges there, and keeps saying that man was not made to suffer, but to enjoy. This place has undermined my stoicism, but—shall I tell you? I feel as if I were saying something sinful—I love it!"[15]

THE HASELTINE ESTATE

In 1961, Helen Haseltine Plowden, Haseltine's daughter and biographer, asked Vernon C. Porter, then Director of the National Academy of Design, to act as "executor" for the many oils, watercolors, and drawings by Haseltine in her collection and to assist her in placing these works in museums throughout the United States. Mrs. Plowden, whose book *William Stanley Haseltine: Sea and Landscape Painter* (London, 1947, copy in NAD Library) remains today the definitive biography of the artist, had organized a number of exhibitions of her father's work in this country, most notably at the Doll and Richards Gallery in Boston and the Macbeth Gallery and Cooper Union in New York. A longtime resident of London, she wished to see Haseltine's paintings returned to his native country.

The Haseltine Estate file at the Academy contains letters detailing Porter's efforts to carefully place more than ninety works by Haseltine in collections across the United States. The file is an important index to the location of these works, especially for less documented materials such as drawings and studies, and thus is an irreplaceable archive for American scholars.

NOTES

1. Henry T. Tuckerman, *Book of the Artists* (New York: G.P. Putnam's, 1867), 556-57.
2. Henry James, *Roderick Hudson* (1875 Boston: J.R. Osgood & Co., 1876), 423-24.
3. *View on the Coast of Capri*, by Jean-Achille Bénouville (n.d., Collection of Hazlitt, Gooden and Fox, London). This is an undated work, but probably done before 1870, when Bénouville left Rome. He had lived in Rome since 1845, having won the Prix-de-Rome for historical landscape painting. Haseltine could have met the artist on either of his two journeys to Rome. Reproduced in Hazlitt, Gooden and Fox, *The Lure of Rome: Some Northern Artists in Italy in the Nineteenth century* (Exhibition catalogue, Hazlitt, Gooden and Fox, London 1979), plate no. 39.
4. Helen Haseltine Plowden, *William Stanley Haseltine: Sea and Landscape Painter* (London: F. Muller, Ltd., 1947), 83, 104, 155, 157.
5. *Ibid.*, 63.
6. *Ibid.*, 63-64, 121-22.
7. *Ibid.*, 126, 129.
8. *Ibid.*, 67.
9. *Ibid.*, 110, 198.
10. *Ibid.*, 72.
11. *Ibid.*, 110. Other favorites in the Haseltine library included Washington Irving, William M. Thackeray, Charles Dickens, and Jane Austen, as well as William Cullen Bryant's *Picturesque America* (with Haseltine's *Indian Rock, Nahant* illustrated) and Turner's *Views of England*.
12. Samuel Rogers, *Italy, A Poem* (1823-28; reprint London: Routledge, 1890), 168.
13. Van Wyck Brooks, *The Dream of Arcadia: American Writers and Artists in Italy, 1760-1915* (New York: E.P. Dutton, 1958), 105.
14. As Plowden describes it (p. 67):
    By coming to Rome, Haseltine had followed the deep-rooted tradition of landscape-painters of all ages; he had gone to Rome solely for inspiration for his work, but the solitude and tragic grandeur of the Campagna, with its ruins abandoned to decay and yearly clothed in the fresh verdure of spring, had laid tender, compelling hands on him; just as with so many of the other artists—German, Dutch, French, English and American—he was to leave Rome resolved to pursue his calling at home, but the touch of those invisible hands were to draw him back again and again, until they forced him to yield and remain in Rome for the rest of his life.
15. James, *Roderick Hudson*, 416.

CB

CAPRI, 1858
Ink, gray wash and graphite on paper, 18⅛ x 23⅛″
Unsigned
Inscribed in ink lower left: *Capri,*
Inscribed in pencil lower right: *highest light in foreground*
Gift of Helen Haseltine Plowden

The Capri drawing of 1858 provides a counterpoint to the large oil by Haseltine in this exhibition, *Sunrise at Capri*, dated between 1880 and 1900. *Sunrise* represents Haseltine's late work: a brighter palette, a more painterly stroke, and an interest in the effects of light, arising out of his work at Barbizon, his study of Joseph M. W. Turner and Claude Monet, and especially his exposure to the Italian landscape.[1] This drawing, done during the artist's first trip to Italy in the company of his Düsseldorf sketching partners Whittredge, Bierstadt, and Leutze, is characterized by the faithful rendering of natural detail which informed Haseltine's earliest work and defines a context for the later oil.

Haseltine can accurately be described as a painter of coast scenes, for a large part of his *oeuvre* is devoted to depicting such areas, either in the United States or Italy, which were favored by the artist for their rich combination of light and air, sea and rocks. Haseltine was known in America for his carefully delineated coast scenes, in particular for his many paintings of the Nahant seashore in Massachusetts; he once said he received so many commissions for views of the New England coast that he feared he would never have time to paint anything else.[2] The coast at Capri seems to have held special appeal for Haseltine, however, and numerous paintings and drawings of the motif in private and public collections in this country and abroad attest to the artist's continued fascination with this site.[3] Haseltine's drawings have considerable graphic merit as landscape renderings and not simply as possible studies for later oils. His diverse production ranged from very finely drawn pencil sketches to broadly executed oil studies to sensitive watercolors and washes.[4]

Capri, as a youthful work, offers an introduction to Haseltine's draftsmanship. The composition is highly schematized and deliberate in its approach to planar definition (the blocked-out masses of the three rocky foreground areas, the ruled coast line, and the tight parallelism of the offshore rock outcroppings reinforce by their fixedness the recession into depth). By contrast, the soft clouds, the daubed-in foreground foliage, and a rather modern approach to the uncovered surface area seem more spontaneous. A villa on the mountaintop at the far left is a small concession to the picturesque.

Haseltine was a prolific sketcher, often rising before dawn to journey out to his favorite sites.[5] He seems to have delighted in the varieties of landscape, translating onto his sketch pad not only plant life and rocks but also peasants working and fishing, and local architecture and ruins. He jotted notations on his drawings for later study or painting, as he has noted here, lower right, "highest light in foreground." Though Capri may have been intended as a study for a later painting, perhaps the subject's appeal for Haseltine lay also in the topographical lessons it offered. Haseltine sought the landscape as a source of unending information—his favorite hours were spent out of doors. His singleminded devotion to his work did not go unremarked by his fellow artists. As an unidentified friend wrote:

It embarrasses me to go out sketching with Haseltine; he is usually halfway through a sketch before I have *even started* mine, and, whereas I find myself obliged to interrupt my work for numberless reasons, such as the sun beating down on my head, or shining in my eyes, or because a bee is bothering, or a child is stepping into my paint-box, or because I am hungry, he, on the other hand, works straight on and never notices anything or anybody until it is time to go home.[6]

NOTES

1. Helen Haseltine Plowden, *William Stanley Haseltine: Sea and Landscape Painter* (London: F. Muller Ltd., 1947).
2. *Ibid.*, 83.
3. Many of these paintings are listed in the Inventory of American Paintings, National Collection of Fine Arts, Smithsonian Institution, Washington, D.C., The Haseltine Estate file at the National Academy of Design identifies the locations of a number of drawings of the subject in the U.S.
4. In particular, see the collection of Haseltine drawings at the Cooper-Hewitt Museum, Drawings and Prints Department, N.Y.
5. Plowden, 63-64, 89, 123, 150.
6. *Ibid.*, 154-55.

CB

ELIHU VEDDER

(1836-1923)
ANA 1864; NA 1865

Vedder explored Umbria and Tuscany thoroughly on his frequent sketching trips in Italy. Augustus Hare described Viareggio, on the west coast of Tuscany, in his 1876 guidebook *Cities of Northern and Central Italy* as "a dull sea place, but it has exquisite views of the mountains."[1] These can be seen in the background of Vedder's Viareggio drawing. Regina Soria lists four drawings of Viareggio that Vedder did in 1911, excluding this one.[2] But Vedder had begun visiting Viareggio much earlier, spending summers there with his family in the early 1880s. As well as the distant mountains, the thatched huts and haystacks of this coastal region fascinated him. Of *Thatched Huts, Viareggio*, a work sold in 1907 to J.W. Ellsworth, Vedder noted:

These huts of Viareggio, owing to the dampness of their location, get to be of a velvety blackness from the mingling of black and green moss; bright green vines grow over them, with orange-colored gourds, and the evening sun through the trees flecks them with orange gold.[3]

Digressions of "V." (1910).

Vedder probably passed through Orvieto several times on his visits to the "poor little forgotten towns, off the track of travel."[4] This walled town in Umbria, built high upon a steep tablerock, is north of Rome, not far from Perugia, where he and his family spent many summers. Vedder's friend William Davies described the road to Orvieto from Bagnorea in his *Pilgrimage of the Tiber* (1873):

The country was very peaceful and quiet—the very ideal of the "Golden Age," when everybody was occupied in rural pursuits, and the simplest form of agricultural practice was the traditional heritage from father to son. Shepherds, leaning upon their staves beneath the shade of the brown olive, watched their flocks all day. . . . In spite of the primitiveness of agricultural operations, the country did not appear to be wanting in wealth, judging from the not infrequent villas and large houses surrounded by groves and orchards which were scattered at intervals on our way; looking, it is true, as if uninhabited; for never a living soul was seen about them. . . .[5]

Vedder does not seem to have found a more populated spot when he sketched the sunlit wall surrounding crooked olive trees in 1897. He would often roam around the countryside, and although he loved exploring, he remembered the mishaps he endured when sketching near an interested audience:

The landscapes required long walks over hill and dale, and when perspiring, getting at once to work so as not to lose some effect, perhaps catching it and a cold at the same time. Sometimes working surrounded by a grinning crowd and hearing their unflattering comments, or perchance attended by a solitary boy with a bad cold in his head, munching an apple. . . .[6]

Digressions of "V." (1910).

Despite his complaints, he enjoyed doing landscapes. He did claim, however, that

I loved landscape, but was eternally urged to paint the figure; thus my landscape was spoiled by the time devoted to figure; and the figure suffered by my constant flirting with landscape. . . .
It is strange how, when I paint landscapes, I don't seem to care for the figures: that is, I feel as if I ought to put them in, but don't most of the time.[7]

Soria points out that his family, at the beginning of his career, felt if Vedder did not succeed as an artist

. . . it would be his own fault for indulging himself in painting landscapes when portraits, according to Dr. Vedder [his father], or original compositions, according to Carrie [his wife], shown to the right people, would bring him all the money he wanted.[8]

Some critics, however, preferred his landscapes. One, in the November 1880 issue of *Scribner's*, wrote that Vedder ". . . is most powerful, most unconscious, most himself, in purely landscape work, or those pictures which have landscape for a chief part of the composition."[9]

As John C. Van Dyke has noted, Vedder's pastels were not well-known:

Another phase of his art that is little known is the wonderful use he could make in landscape of wax colored pencils. He would carry a few in his pocket and some colored paper. The smaller pictures the artist would do standing with a few strokes; only for the larger a folding stool was taken, but he never used an eraser or changed a stroke. . . . [He] only used this medium in his old age—when he could not resist working, and oil painting was too tiring.[10]

Like these pictures the pastels were often done on dark gray paper, with subdued cool colors predominating. One reason for Vedder's use of gray paper may have been his discovery, apparent in his paintings, that colors stand out better against "gloomy skies, grey days," and that "the traditionally sunny sky of Italy tends to blur outlines and fuse all colors in a luminous haze."[11] Working on the gray paper enhanced the warmth of the flecks of yellow and orange.

Upon her death, Vedder's daughter Anita bequeathed his paintings and drawings to the American Academy of Arts and Letters, to which he had been elected in 1908. The AAAL in turn distributed the works to fifty or more American museums in 1955. Other Vedder pastels given to the National Academy of Design include two drawings done in 1889 on his trip up the Nile, and one undated work titled *Big Coal-Shed*, done at Badia Prataglia, near Arezzo.

HUTS, VIAREGGIO, 1911
Pastel on dark gray paper, 6¼ x 8¾″
Signed lower right: *V. Sep 1911*
Inscribed lower left: *Viareggio*
Gift of the American Academy of Arts and Letters, 1955

ORVIETO, 1897
Pastel on dark gray paper, 6½ x 12¾″
Signed lower right: *V.*
Signed upper right: *V. Orvieto May 19th/97*
Gift of the American Academy of Arts and Letters, 1955

NOTES

1. Augustus J.C. Hare, *Cities of Northern and Central Italy* (London: Daldy, Isbister & Co., 1876), 1:73.
2. Regina Soria, *Elihu Vedder: American Visionary Artist in Rome (1836-1923)* (Rutherford, N.J.: Fairleigh Dickinson University Press, 1970), 383.
3. Elihu Vedder, *The Digressions of "V."* (Boston: Houghton Mifflin, 1910), 500.
4. *Ibid.*, 441.
5. William Davies, *The Pilgrimage of the Tiber from its Mouth to its Source: with some account of its Tributaries*, (London: Sampson Low, Marston, Low & Searle, 1873), 236-37.
6. Vedder, *Digressions of "V."*, 506.
7. *Ibid.*, 139, 156.
8. Soria, *Elihu Vedder*, 57.
9. "Elihu Vedder," *Scribner's Magazine* (November 1880), 115. In National Academy of Design Artists Biographical Files.
10. John C. Van Dyke, *Catalogue Exhibition of the Works of Elihu Vedder* (Exhibition catalogue, American Academy of Arts and Letters, New York, 1937), 23.
11. Soria, *Elihu Vedder*, 99.

SMS

ALFRED THOMAS AGATE

(1812-1846)
ANA 1832; HM 1840[1]

Born Sparta, New York, February 14. Received art instruction from elder brother, Frederick, and from Thomas S. Cummings, miniaturist and author of *Historic Annals of the National Academy of Design*. Worked in New York City. Exhibited portraits and miniatures at the National Academy of Design 1831-1839. In 1838 joined Scientific Corps of the United States Exploring Expedition, his name appearing on the ship's roster as "portrait and botanical artist." Upon return assisted in preparing illustrations of expedition survey for publication. Died Washington, D.C., January 5.

REFERENCES: Mary Bartlett Cowdrey, *National Academy of Design Exhibition Record, 1826-1860* (New-York Historical Society, 1943). *Dictionary of American Biography* (New York: Charles Scribner's Sons, 1943). *M. and M. Karolik Collection of American Water Colors and Drawings 1800-1875* (Boston: Museum of Fine Arts, 1962).

In 1838, after fifteen years of delays and planning, the United States Exploring Expedition set off on its four-year journey around the globe under the command of Charles Wilkes. Among the staff were Alfred T. Agate, natural history draftsman Joseph Drayton, artist and zoologist Titian Ramsay Peale, geologist James Dwight Dana, and others. Nathaniel Hawthorne had applied for the post of official historian and Asa Gray had been appointed botanist but neither actually accompanied the voyage, the objects of which were to explore the Pacific and Antarctic oceans, to examine the almost unknown northwest coast of North America, and to increase scientific knowledge. This painting, as well as the drawings by Agate also included in the exhibition, were made during the expedition and used afterwards as the basis of the engraved illustrations that accompanied the written report. That Agate successfully carried out his task was affirmed by Wilkes:

To Messrs. Drayton and Agate, the Artists of the Expedition, I feel it due to make known how constantly and faithfully they have performed their duties. The illustrations of these volumes will bear ample testimony to the amount of their labors, and the accuracy with which they have been executed.[3]

The five-volume account of their experiences by Wilkes, *Narrative of the United States Exploring Expedition* (1845), became one of the most widely read travel books of the decade. In it the commander told of discovering Fakaafo (the native name, which

appears on present-day maps), or Bowditch Island, which the explorers happened upon on the night of January 28, 1841:

This proved to be a new discovery, as it was not to be found on any chart. The island, which I have named Bowditch, agreeably to the wish of Captain Hudson, was of coral formation, and its shape that of a triangle, with the apex to the south.[4]

Following his usual practice, the author provided navigational facts as well as a vivid account of island life, including an enumeration of the temple, statue, and other particulars in Agate's painting:

The whole islet was covered with a grove of cocoa-nut trees, under whose shade about sixty houses were scattered, only a few yards from each other. . .

The most remarkable building was that which they said was their "tui-tokelau" (house of their god). This stood in the centre, and was of an oblong shape, fifty by thirty-five feet, and about twenty feet in height. . . . All the sides were open, excepting a small railing, about fifteen inches high, around the foundation, which allowed the free passage of the air through. It was one of the most beautiful and pleasant spots, and is well represented . . . by Mr. Agate. . . .

The edifice contained but little furniture. Around the eaves a row of mother-of-pearl shells was suspended, giving the appearance of a scolloped curtain. The whole was covered with mats. . . . Their gods, or idols,—tui-tokelau,—were placed on the outside, near by. The largest of these was fourteen feet high and eighteen inches in diameter. This was covered or enveloped in mats, and over all a narrow one was passed, shawl-fashion, and tied in a knot in front, with the ends hanging down. The smaller idol was of stone, and four feet high, but only partially covered with mats. About ten feet in front of the idols was one of the hewn tables, which was hollowed out: it was four feet long by three broad, and the same in height.[5]

In addition to recording the geography, geology, and botany of the lands visited, Agate assisted the sciences of ethnology and anthropology by producing accurate delineations of indigenous peoples. He drew portraits in which native physiognomy could be studied and often annotated his landscapes with figures, providing information on local habits. The behavior of the figures at the left of this picture, for example—a member of the crew smoking his pipe as three natives recoil in varying gestures of fear—finds its explanation in the Wilkes *Narrative:*

There was no sign of places for cooking, nor any appearance of fire, and it is believed that all their provisions are eaten raw. What strengthened this opinion, was the alarm the natives felt when they saw the sparks emanating from the flint and steel, and the emission of smoke from the mouths of those who were smoking cigars.[6]

Although scientific objectivity was the prevailing attitude of

COCOANUT GROVE AND TEMPLE:
FAKAAFO (BOWDITCH ISLAND), 1841[2]
Oil on canvas, mounted on support, 10 x 14"
Unsigned
Gift of James S. Smillie, 1902

the Wilkes Expedition, Americans in the 1840s conceived of the South Pacific islands as places of mystery mixed with horror. As Melville wrote in his pioneering South Sea novel *Typee* (1846):

The Marquesas! What strange visions of outlandish things does the very name spirit up! Naked houris—cannibal banquets—groves of cocoa-nut—coral reefs—tatooed [sic] chiefs—and bamboo temples; sunny valleys planted with bread-fruit-trees—carved canoes dancing on the flashing blue waters—savage woodlands guarded by horrible idols—*heathenish rites and human sacrifices*.[7]

Later in the century the notion of Polynesia as a place of sensual escape appealed to French artist Paul Gauguin as well as to the American painter John La Farge who, in the company of Henry Adams, also traveled there in 1890. La Farge left us his impressions of one of the Samoan islands not far from Fakaafo:

For a thousand years, probably two thousand, perhaps three—for an indefinite period—these people of this smallest island have lived here and modified nature, while its agencies have as steadily and gently covered again their work. So that everything is natural, and everywhere one is vaguely conscious of man. Hence, of any place that I have seen, this is the nearest to the idyllic pastoral; it is not so beautiful as it is complete.[8]

La Farge, *Reminiscences of the South Seas* (1916).

Along with the wonder of a new place, the traveler to the South Seas also experienced the sensation of journeying back in time, of witnessing an earlier and more primitive stage of man's development. The explorers who accompanied Wilkes would, no doubt, have shared La Farge's sentiment:

As Polynesia has faded away, the sadness of all past things comes upon me—that summer is gone—those hours and those islands which spotted great blue spaces of time and place will be merely memories for autumn. . .
Good-bye to brown skins and skies and seas of impossible azure. Good-bye to life in [the] presence of the remotest past.[9]

NOTES

1. National Academy of Design records give the erroneous year of birth as 1818; for the correct date of 1812 see *Dictionary of American Biography* (New York: Charles Scribner's Sons. 1943), 1:122. Although Agate was made an Associate of the Academy in 1832, his status was changed to Honorary Member in 1840, probably due to his absence from New York while on the Wilkes Expedition.

2. National Academy of Design records list the title of the painting as *Cocoanut Grove and Temple; Fiji Island.* However, in Charles Wilkes, *Narrative of the United States Exploring Expedition* (Philadelphia: Lea & Blanchard, 1845), 5: opposite p. 14, an illustration of this picture with the title *Cocoanut Grove at Fakaafo or Bowditch I.* appears. I have listed the latter as the corrected location and dated it 1841 on the basis of the expedition's arrival there in January 1841. This picture must have enjoyed wide currency, for it appeared in J.G. Heck, *Iconographic Encyclopedia of Science, Literature, and Art*, trans. and edited by Spencer F. Baird [original text in German] (New York: Rudolph Garrigue, 1851), 1: plate 56.* Nowhere on the illustration, however, is Agate's authorship acknowledged.

3. *Dictionary of American Biography*, 1:122. See Robert Silverberg, *Stormy Voyager: The Story of Charles Wilkes* (Philadelphia: J.B. Lippincott Co., 1968), 35-37, for information on the staff.

4. Wilkes, *Narrative*, 5:10. See Silverberg, 180, for popularity of the *Narrative*.

5. Wilkes, *Narrative*, 14-15.

6. *Ibid.*, 18.

7. Herman Melville, *Typee* (1846; reprint New York: Lancer Books, Inc., 1968), 8.

8. John La Farge, *Reminiscences of the South Seas* (Garden City, N.Y.: Double-day, Page & Company, 1916), 169.

9. *Ibid.*, 478-80.

*In Library of National Academy of Design.

KM

By May 1840 the Charles Wilkes Expedition had arrived at the Fiji Islands, a beautiful coral group covered with palm trees and surrounded by blue lagoons. They were so lovely Wilkes could scarcely believe ". . . they were the abode of a savage, ferocious, and treacherous race of cannibals."[2] The explorations of these various islands included Muthuata, where Agate and other members of the Scientific Corps observed the burial practices and skeletons of the island:

Mr. Hale succeeded in getting permission to disinter some skeletons on the island of Muthuata, which lies immediately off the town. This island not only protects the harbour from the north wind, but adds much to its beauty by its high and luxuriant appearance. It is a little over a mile in length. It appears to have been for a long time a burial-place for both chiefs and common people. The graves are scattered in groups along the shore, those of the chiefs being apart from the rest, and distinguished by having small houses built over them, from two to six feet high. The fronts of these houses were of a kind of lattice-work, formed of braided sennit. . .
The graves of the common people (kai-si) had merely stones laid over them. On the natives who accompanied Messrs. Hale and Agate being told that they had permission to take a skeleton, which they call "kalou mate," they showed no reluctance whatever to assist, and took them to a grave where they said two Ambau men were buried. . .[3]

Wilkes, *Narrative of the United States Exploring Expedition* (1845).

Fifty years later John La Farge and Henry Adams also visited the Fiji Islands, where missionaries had made some progress in Christianizing the natives. Despite the efforts of the missionaries and the passage of time, however, the people remained somehow unchanged, and Henry Adams—in one of his rare comments on the art forms of Polynesia—was able to admire the same Fijian houses that had been delineated by Agate. Adams compared them to a Samoan house, which he fittingly described as "turtle-back on posts," and said he was ". . . surprised to find the Fijian native house quite the finest yet seen . . . the decoration shows taste, and the dignity of it is really something pretty effective."[4]

The South Sea islands lured Adams and La Farge far from home, as they had Herman Melville, Wilkes, Agate, Titian R. Peale, and others on the expedition. Each, however, in his own way, experienced a strange and unsettling feeling—almost one of disappointment—in the face of reality, as if the charm of the islands had been a white man's illusion. D. H. Lawrence, perhaps, explained it best:

Without doubt the Pacific Ocean is aeons older than the Atlantic or the Indian Oceans. When we say older, we mean it has not come to any modern consciousness. Strange convulsions have convulsed the Atlantic and Mediterranean peoples into phase after phase of consciousness, while the Pacific and the Pacific peoples have slept. . . .
The Maoris, the Tongans, the Marquesans, the Fijians, the Polynesians. holy God, how long have they been turning over in the same sleep, with varying dreams? . . . The scientists say the South Sea Islanders belong to the Stone Age. It seems absurd to class people according to their implements. And yet there is something in it. The heart of the Pacific is still the Stone Age; in spite of steamers. The heart of the Pacific seems like a vast vacuum, in which, mirage-like, continues the life of myriads of ages back. It is a phantom-persistence of human beings who should have died, by our chronology, in the Stone Age. It is a phantom, illusion-like trick of reality: the glamorous South Seas.[5]

Lawrence, *Studies in Classic American Literature* (1923).

NOTES

1. The title of the drawing is taken from Charles Wilkes, *Narrative of the United States Exploring Expedition* (Philadelphia: Lea & Blanchard, 1845), 3, in which

100

TOMBS AT MUTHUATA ISLAND, FEEJEE, 1840[1]
Pencil and brown wash on paper, 4 ½ x 7″
Signed lower left: *A.T. Agate*
Gift of James D. Smillie, 1902

this drawing is included as an engraved illustration, opposite p. 231.

2. Robert Silverberg, *Stormy Voyager: The Story of Charles Wilkes* (Philadelphia: J.B. Lippincott Co., 1968), 119.
3. Wilkes, *Narrative*, 3:230-31.
4. Ernst Scheyer, *The Circle of Henry Adams: Art & Artists* (Detroit: Wayne State University Press, 1970), 86.
5. D.H. Lawrence, *Studies in Classic American Literature* (New York: The Viking Press, 1972), 132-33. See also Wilkes, who throughout his *Narrative* constantly expressed disappointment at the lands visited.

KM

Oregon, the Wilkes Expedition's next goal, was a vast and almost unknown region encompassing the present states of Oregon, Washington, and Idaho. When Wilkes and his men arrived, it was uninhabited except for the fur traders and Indians along the coast and some scattered farming settlements in the interior. Since the United States Government had no clear idea of the geography, and much less of the economic value of the area, Wilkes was assigned the tasks of obtaining detailed maps of the territory and of assessing its worth. As always, however, in addition to his official duties, Wilkes wrote of his fascination with the local customs, while Agate made sketches with his pencil.

During the time of their stay, Mr. Agate made many sketches. One of these is of a burying-place, which I have thought worth inserting, as exhibiting one of the peculiar features of a race which is now fast disappearing. The mode of burial seems to vary with almost every tribe: some place the dead above ground, while others bury their departed friends, surrounding the spot with a variety of utensils that had been used by the deceased.
The graves are covered with boards, in order to prevent the wolves from disinterring the bodies. The emblem of a squaw's grave is generally a cammass-root digger, made of a deer's horns, and fastened on the end of a stick.[2]
Wilkes, *Narrative of the United States Exploring Expedition* (1845).

The Lewis and Clark Expedition, journeying westward from the Rocky Mountains in the years 1805 and 1806, traversed land that the Wilkes Expediton would later visit. Lewis and Clark too were impressed by the majestic trees as well as the unusual burial practices that prompted Agate's drawing.

The country is covered with a thick growth of timber . . . At one o'clock we reached the Cathlamah village, where we halted for about two hours, and purchased some wappatoo and a dog for the invalids. This village we have already described as situated opposite the Seal islands; on one of these the Indians have placed their dead in canoes, raised on scaffolds above . . . the tide. These people seem to be more fond of carving in wood than their neighbors, and have various specimens of their taste about the houses. The broad pieces supporting the roof, and the board through which doors are cut, are the objects [totem poles] on which they chiefly display their ingenuity, and are ornamented with curious figures, sometimes representing persons in a sitting posture supporting a burden.[3]
Coues, *Lewis and Clark* (1893).

The year 1846 was a decisive one in the western movement and in the settling of Oregon and California. Among the travelers on the Oregon Trail that year was Francis Parkman who, although he never reached the west coast, kept journals of his experiences in the wilderness. As scholars have suggested, much of the emphasis in Parkman's account falls upon the relationship of the plainsman to weather and landscape, a fact that underlies Parkman's kinship with Agate and the other men of the Wilkes Expedition.

In Agate's rendering of this burial place, the emphasis is not on funereal accouterments; rather, the tall pine tree is the central fact of the drawing, reflecting again the concern with the Indian's relation to his natural surroundings. A passage in Parkman, describing his observations of his Indian friend seated among the bushes, shares something of the mood of Agate's drawing:

. . . I saw him seated alone, immovable as a statue, among the rocks and trees. His face was turned upward, and his eyes seemed riveted on a pine-tree springing from a cleft in the precipice above. The crest of the pine was swaying to and fro in the wind, and its long limbs waved slowly up and down, as if the tree had life. Looking for a while at the old man, I was satisfied that he was engaged in an act of worship, or prayer, or communion of some kind with a supernatural being. I longed to penetrate his thoughts, but I could do nothing more than conjecture and speculate . . . To him all nature is instinct with mystic influence. Among those mountains not a wild beast was prowling, a bird singing, or a leaf fluttering, that might not tend to direct his destiny, or give warning of what was in store for him; and he watches the world of nature around him as the astrologer watches the stars. So closely is he linked with it that his guardian spirit, no unsubstantial creation of the fancy, is usually embodied in the form of some living thing,—a bear, a wolf, an eagle, or a serpent; and Mene-Seela, as he gazed intently on the old pine-tree, might believe it to inshrine [*sic*] the fancied guide and protector of his life.[4]
Parkman, *Oregon Trail* (1849).

NOTES
1. The title I have given here, *Indian Burial Place, Oregon*, appears below the vignette drawing in Charles Wilkes, *Narrative of the United States Exploring Expedition* (Philadelphia: Lea & Blanchard, 1845), 5:219. It is listed in the National Academy of Design records simply as "Brush and Trees—Woodland Scene." A more highly finished wash drawing made from this preliminary pencil sketch is also in the National Academy of Design collection.
2. Wilkes, *Narrative*., 5: 219.
3. Elliott Coues, ed., *History of the Expedition under the Command of Lewis and Clark* (New York: Francis P. Harper, 1893), 3:905-06.
4. Francis Parkman, *The Oregon Trail*, E.N. Feltskog, ed. (1849; reprint Madison: The University of Wisconsin Press, 1969), 286-87. See also editor's introduction, particularly pp. 13a-18a, for Parkman's route; see p. 40a for mention of the relation of man to landscape in Parkman.

KM

On the last leg of its journey home, the Wilkes Expedition arrived at the Philippine Islands in January 1842. Titian Ramsay Peale, the artist-naturalist on the voyage, recorded the "pleasant week on shore" around Manila. A passage in Peale's journal recalls Agate's drawing, which was probably sketched as they investigated the island together:

Made an excursion to Maraguina, which is 8 or 10 miles from Manilla. The country was very beautiful, abounding in highly cultivated farms where the Natives produce rice, maize, sugar, etc. They are generally surrounded with bamboo groves with the stems of which the houses are built, fences made, and indeed almost every article, even floors & water buckets, etc. We crossed a river in our carriages on a raft of it guided by a single rattan at least 100 yds long. Buffalos are the only animals used in preparing the ground and in Carrying burthens. . .
Maraguino [*sic*] has about 10,000 inhabitants, all of whom are Christians, though few speak the Spanish language. The houses are mostly built of Bamboo, & Mat trees and are all elevated 6-8 feet from the ground on posts, are kept very clean, the people appearing very contented and happy. Chinese intermixture is observable every where. They are easily told by the oblique eye.[1]

Peale, *Journal* (1842).

INDIAN BURIAL PLACE, OREGON, 1841[1]
Pencil on paper, 8¾ x 7⅜"
Signed lower right: *Agate, del, Aug. 1841*
Gift of James D. Smillie, 1902

_____

NATIVE HOUSE NEAR MANILA, 1842
Watercolor on paper, 6⅝ x 8¼"
Signed lower left: *A.T. Agate, del.*
Inscription below: *Native house near Manila/Luzonia 6*
Gift of James D. Smillie, 1902

Agate's drawings of the expedition raise questions as to their mode of execution, under circumstances when only a few precious hours were spent on shore exploring while months of tedium passed aboard ship. Again, the journal of Peale—who, along with the geologist James Dwight Dana, chose to do his own drawings independently of the official artists on the staff—gives us some insight into the picture-making process employed on the voyage. Of their landing at Madeira, September 1838, Peale reports:

...the scenery was of the most stupendous and beautiful, and consequently could approximately be described by the pencil only ... Eye sketches of complicated mountain scenery are nearly always too inaccurate to be useful. I therefore solicited the company of Lt Perry and returned on a second occasion to the summit of the Coural mountains, armed with a camera lucida & table, etc.[2]

Like the scientists, the artists Agate and Joseph Drayton also used the camera lucida, an instrument for projecting a distant image upon paper as an aid to precise draftsmanship. It appears that they made one or more sketches on the spot, completing the compositions when they were again afloat, for in a diary entry for August 1, 1839, Peale writes: "The sea sufficiently smooth for Mr. Agate and myself to be occupied in finishing up some of our paintings & Sketches."[3]

The overriding concern with the accurate depiction of landscape topography that would lead to the use of such a device— natural in the production of what are essentially scientific illustrations—suggests the possibility of parallels in the practices of our American landscape painters around mid-century. As the nineteenth century progressed, artists strove to express the geological and botanical facts of a given landscape. In that sense the practices of an artist-explorer like Alfred Agate established an important precedent in the forging of the alliance between science and art.

NOTES

1. Jessie Poesch, *Titian Ramsay Peale and his Journals of the Wilkes Expedition* (Philadelphia: The American Philosophical Society, 1961), 200-01. This drawing appears as an illustration in Charles Wilkes, *Narrative of the United States Exploring Expedition* (Philadelphia: Lea & Blanchard, 1845), 5, opposite p. 292.

2. Poesch, *Peale Journals*, 128. For the drawings by Dana and Peale, see *ibid.*, 68-69.

3. *Ibid.*, 149. Wilkes *Narrative*, 4:171, and elsewhere, mentions the utilization of the camera lucida by Agate and Drayton.

KM

FREDERICK CATHERWOOD

(1799-1854)
HM 1837

Born February 27, London. Apprenticed to Michael Meredith, architect, 1815-1820. 1820 began to attend free art classes at the Royal Academy, where Sir John Soame lectured on architecture and introduced him to Piranesi. 1821-1825 traveled to Rome, Sicily, Greece, and up the Nile. 1825-1828 again in London, practicing architecture. In 1828 with Robert Hay's expedition in Egypt to investigate and diagram ruined sites. In London 1835, trained by Robert Burford as a panoramist; worked with Burford on Panorama of Jerusalem, followed by murals of Thebes, Karnak, and ruins of Baalbek. Met John Lloyd Stephens in 1836. Went that year to New York; formed a partnership with architect Frederick Diaper. Completed his own Rotunda for panoramas at Broadway and Mercer Street, the first and last permanent one in New York. Showed frequently at National Academy of Design 1839-1845. 1839 accompanied Stephens on expedition to Central America to search out and study ruins of lost civilizations. Illustrated Stephens' account of the trip, *Incidents of Travel in Central America, Chiapas, and Yucatán* (1841). To Yucatán in 1841 with Stephens; illustrated Stephens' *Incidents of Travel in Yucatán* (1843).[1] 1844 published in London *Views of Ancient Monuments in Central America, Chiapas, and Yucatán*, 25 folio, hand-colored lithographs with text. Surveyed first railroad in South America. 1850 moved to California, 1852 to London. On return from London to New York in 1854, drowned when S.S. *Arctic* sank on September 27.

REFERENCE: Victor Wolfgang Von Hagen, *Frederick Catherwood Arch[t]* (New York: Oxford University Press, 1950).

On October 3, 1839, John Lloyd Stephens and Frederick Catherwood departed from New York for Central America, where they planned to explore the ruins of lost civilizations and preserve "some memorials of their present state."[2] Stephens was sent by President Martin Van Buren on a diplomatic assignment but was at liberty to travel on completion of his duties. He chose Catherwood to accompany him, as Catherwood was an ". . . experienced traveller and personal friend, who had passed more than ten years of his life in diligently studying the antiquities of the Old World; and who was familiar with the remains of ancient architectural greatness. . . ."[3]

Upon arriving in Guatemala, then a state in the Central American Federation, the two men found themselves in the midst of a civil war, and were warned against traveling. Nevertheless, Stephens and Catherwood pressed on with their journey. Stephens extensively described the political climate of Central America in *Incidents of Travel in Central America, Chiapas, and Yucatán*, in which he also gave details on the itinerary of their travels: "a journey of nearly three thousand miles in the interior of Central America. . . including visits to eight ruined cities. . . ."[4]

Their immediate party, when traveling together, "consisted of five mules: two for Mr. Catherwood and myself, one for Augustin [their servant] and two for luggage; besides which, we had four Indian carriers."[5] Years later, Aldous Huxley praised Catherwood for surmounting one of many hardships the expedition must have faced:

It was in Guatemala, while trying to do a little sketching among the almost unbelievably picturesque ruins of Antigua, that I first became interested in Frederick Catherwood. . . . My concern with Catherwood as a person was aroused by the insects. To the would-be landscape painter, even in salubrious Antigua, these are a very severe trial. I bore with them for a couple of hours, then packed up my paints, discomfited and full of new admiration for the man who had made the illustrations to Stephens' *Incidents of Travel*. From dawn till dusk, day after day and for weeks at a stretch, this martyr to archaeology had exposed himself to all the winged and crawling malice of tropical nature.[6]

In April 1840, enroute from Guatemala City to Yucatán, the two men stopped at Quezaltenango, 150 miles west of Guatemala City. Called "The Palace-of-the-Quetzal," the city is named after the quetzal bird. From their approach to the city, Stephens found the sight impressive:

Two leagues beyond [the "River of Blood"] we came in sight of Quezaltenango, standing at the foot of a great range of mountains, surmounted by a rent volcano constantly emitting smoke, and before it a mountain ridge of lava, which, if it had taken its course toward the city, would have buried it like Herculaneum and Pompeii.[7]

Stephens' written description of the city matches Catherwood's drawing:

The streets were handsomely paved, and the houses picturesque in architecture; the cabildo had two stories and a corridor. The Cathedral, with its facade richly decorated, was grand and imposing. The plaza was paved with stone, having a fine fountain in the centre, and commanding a magnificent view of the volcano and mountains around. It was the day before Good Friday; the streets and plaza were crowded with people in their best attire.[8]

Catherwood chose to make a pencil drawing, from which he later did a pen and wash drawing of this scene. Although most of the

CITY OF QUEZALTENANGO, CENTRAL AMERICA, c. 1840
Sepia ink and wash on paper, 5 x 7½″
Unsigned

PLAZA AT QUEZALTENANGO, 1840
Pencil on paper, 11 x 17¼″
Signed lower right: *Plaza at Quezaltenango, F. Catherwood,*
1840
Estate of James D. Smillie

final engravings in *Incidents of Travel in Central America* were of Mayan temples and steles, the view of this beautiful city, with its seven towering churches, and the mountains beyond impressed both Catherwood and Stephens deeply enough to be included. As Stephens noted:

There was no place we had visited, except ruined cities, so unique and interesting, and which deserved to be so thoroughly explored, as Quezaltenango. A month, at least, might be satisfactorily and profitably employed in examining the many curious objects in the country around. For botanical research it is the richest region in Central America. But we had no time even for rest.[9]

It was not only the scenery, however, that made an impression on Catherwood and Stephens. Both religious and political events occupied them during their stay. The ceremonies of Holy Week began the evening of their arrival. After attending a service in the cathedral, Catherwood and Stephens went out to the street to watch the crowd forming into a procession:

In turning the corner of the street at which we stood, a dark Mestitzo, with a scowl of fanaticism on his face, spoke to Mr. Catherwood, "Take off your spectacles and follow the cross."[10]

Catherwood seems to accentuate the religious fervor of the inhabitants by placing the vanishing point of the drawing near a central cross on one of the churches. Elaborate ceremonies and processions continued throughout the next few days but apparently few whites took part. The revolutionary turmoil had terrified most of them, driving them into hiding. Shortly before Stephens and Catherwood arrived, eighteen leading members of the municipality had been taken into the plaza and shot. Stephens wrote that "the stones and the wall of the house were still red with their blood."[11]

The expedition continued on its way in a few days, traveling until the end of July when the two men were forced to return to New York because of Catherwood's constant fever. Stephens immediately began writing his book, and Catherwood was given complete charge of its illustration. He chose six well-known New York engravers to engrave his drawings. Von Hagen notes that

"Catherwood had to see that the engravings closely followed his own sepia and watercolor drawings. . . . Unfortunately, the engravings were hurriedly done and Catherwood's original designs suffered greatly."[12]

In spite of the clumsiness of the engravings compared to the original drawings, the eighty illustrations were highly praised. William H. Prescott, then working on his *Conquest of Mexico*, wrote in a letter to Fanny Calderón de la Barca:

Too much praise cannot be given to Mr. Catherwood's drawings. . . . They carry with them a perfect assurance of his fidelity, in this, how different from his predecessors, who have never failed by some overfinish or by their touches for effect to throw an air of improbability, or at best, uncertainty, over the whole.[13]
Von Hagen, *Frederick Catherwood Arch!* (1950).

Unfortunately, few of Catherwood's original watercolors and pencil drawings remain. Most of them were destroyed when his Rotunda burned on July 31, 1842.[14]

_____

NOTES
1. In National Academy of Design Library, purchased from John G. Chapman in 1848.
2. Frederick Catherwood, Introduction to *Views of Ancient Monuments in Central America, Chiapas, and Yucatán*, reprinted in Victor Wolfgang Von Hagen, *Frederick Catherwood Arch!*, (New York: Oxford University Press, 1950), 120.
3. John Lloyd Stephens, *Incidents of Travel in Central America, Chiapas, and Yucatán* (New York: Harper & Brothers, 1841), 1:10.
4. *Ibid.*, iii.
5. *Ibid.*, 40.
6. Aldous Huxley, Introduction to Von Hagen, *Frederick Catherwood Arch!*, xv.
7. *Ibid.*, 202.
8. *Ibid.*, 204.
9. *Ibid.*, 219-20.
10. *Ibid.*, 211.
11. *Ibid.*, 208.
12. Von Hagen, *Frederick Catherwood Arch!*, 73.
13. In *ibid.*, 74.
14. *Ibid.*, 84.

SMS

FREDERIC EDWIN CHURCH

(1826-1900)
ANA 1848; NA 1849

Born May 4, Hartford, Conn. Trained there by Benjamin A. Coe and Alexander H. Emmons. Studied with Thomas Cole, Catskill, N.Y. 1844-1846. First exhibited two landscapes at National Academy of Design 1845. Moved to Art-Union Building, N.Y.C. 1847-1848. William James Stillman, later co-editor of *Crayon*, was first pupil 1848-1849, Jervis McEntee second pupil 1850-1851. First trip to Mt. Desert Island, Maine, 1850. 1853 first trip to Colombia and Ecuador with Cyrus W. Field. 1856 to Niagara Falls. Returned to Ecuador 1857 with Louis Remy Mignot. Famous paintings developed from these journeys: *Niagara* (1857), *The Heart of the Andes* (1859), and *Cotopaxi* (1862). 1859 sailed to Newfoundland and Labrador with Louis Noble. Painted recently rediscovered *The Icebergs* 1861. 1865 to Jamaica with Horace Walcott Robbins, Jr. Extensive European and Middle Eastern tour with family 1867-1869. 1870 began construction of Olana, villa of oriental design, Hudson, N.Y. Inflammatory rheumatism 1876 or 1877, painting activity declines. Subsequent summers divided between Olana and Maine; winters in Mexico. Died April 7, in New York City.

REFERENCES: *Frederic Edwin Church* (Exhibition catalogue, National Collection of Fine Arts, Washington, D.C., 1966). David C. Huntington, *The Landscapes of Frederic Edwin Church* (New York: Braziller, 1966).   LK

Frederic Church first exhibited *Scene on the Magdalene* in the Academy's 1855 annual exhibition under the title *La Magdalena*. At that time it was already in the collection of James A. Suydam, and in 1865 it was acquired by the Academy as part of the Suydam Bequest.[1] As a tropical subject, *Scene on the Magdalene*—and three other South American landscapes Church exhibited with it in 1855—represented a dramatic break from the artist's traditional New England subjects. Only a year earlier, for example, his entries in the annual exhibition were *A Country Home* and *A New England Lake*.[2] A contemporary writer reviewed the change favorably:

Church shows, this year, that his genius is not confined to painting northern scenes. We have a most brilliant triumph from him. These South-American pictures of his are noble achievements. The golden hues, the painted flowers, the rich fruit, the luxuriant foliage of the tropics, have been seized by him and placed lovingly on his canvas.[3]
The Knickerbocker (1855).

Another reviewer commented more specifically on the painting illustrated here:

The sun, and southern nature, the warm, vapory atmosphere, and the careful details of tropical vegetation, are displayed here equally in *The Cordilleras . . . and La Magdalena. . . .* Mr. Church has skillfully animated them with characteristic details, aquatic birds in flocks, crocodiles on the water, trailing plants entangled in inextricable knots, and so forth. Certain details of early vegetation are perhaps exaggerated in dimension. . . . [but] this is only a detail, of which the possible inexactitude disappears among the fine qualities which distinguish the works of Mr. Church.[4]
The New-York Daily Tribune (1855).

In 1853, at age twenty-seven, Frederic Church traveled to New Granada, South America (now Colombia), with his friend Cyrus Field. In Barranquilla, at the mouth of the Magdalena River, they boarded "*El Vapor*"—the steamboat that carried them up the river to Conejo—and from Conejo continued "en una canoa" to Honda.[5] While at Honda, Church wrote to his mother about their trip on the river:

We left Barranquilla on the 10th [of May, 1853] and made one of the quickest trips up the river that has ever been made but the steamer does not come so far as Honda. Conejo a place some ten leagues below here is usually the terminus and passengers and freight are carried to Honda in champans (large native boats) or canoes. Our trip up from Barranquilla was exceedingly interesting and although the shores were flat nearly the whole distance yet the wonderful richness of vegetation and the many novelties made our journey anything but tedious.[6]

Any sketches made specifically as preparation for the painting were probably done between May 10 and May 23, during their trip up the river. (The painting itself was probably completed after Church's return to his New York studio, where he could synthesize elements from various sketches into the finished composition.)[7] According to his journal, written in enthusiastic if informal Spanish, Church sketched passing scenery while aboard the boat: "Esquiciaba con plomachos [*sic*] diferentes objetos del Vapor." [With lead pencils I was sketching different objects from the steamboat.][8]

Perhaps the painting represents scenery the artist sketched on or around May 13, when he sighted some of the few mountains visible along the river cruise: "El jornado [*sic*] hoy estaba aun [*sic*] de mas [*sic*] interés que ayer, porque estambamos [*sic*] perspectivas de algunos altos Montes." [The journey today was even of more interest than yesterday, because there were perspectives of some high Mountains.][9] Church also made frequent reference to tropical foliage such as that in the painting: "Hoy el exuberancia [*sic*] del vegetacion [*sic*] ha deleytandome [*sic*] mas [*sic*] que en qualquier [*sic*] tiempo antes." [Today the luxuriance of the vegetation has delighted me more than at any time before.][10]

The "vegetacion exúberante y verde,"[11] which particularly appealed to him, is evident in *Scene on the Magdalene*, as well as

SCENE ON THE MAGDALENE, 1854
Oil on canvas, mounted on board, 28¼ x 42″
Signed lower left: *F. Church 1854*
Suydam Collection

in various sketches. At the Cooper-Hewitt Museum there are drawings that may have been done as studies for this painting or others. One page of sketches depicts an alligator and a tree, the latter labeled a "Monstrous Tree" and resembling the drooping foliage at the left side of *Scene on the Magdalene*.[12] Such lush, tropical plant life interested the gardener and botanist in him, as well as the artist:

It will be necessary to have a large hothouse if all the seeds which I have got are planted although a large part of them I have picked without knowing whether the flowers are desirable or not, having made it a principle to gather any dry seeds or pods that I saw. I have seen many very beautiful flowers where [sic] were not in seed and the natives never take the trouble to cultivate the wild flowers.[13]

Church's decision to travel and paint in South America was part of the natural development of a mid nineteenth-century mind, combining as it did interests in exploration and travel, in natural history and science, and in romantic and exotic imagery. During this American era of Manifest Destiny, it seemed appropriate that "In the pursuit of his art [Church had] visited every zone and clime."[14] Or as William Cullen Bryant expressed this desire for the new and unusual, "Art sighs to carry her conquests into new realms."[15]

Church's interest in the scientific writing of such figures as Alexander von Humboldt, Charles Lyell, and John Tyndall has been documented. He owned Humboldt's famous *Cosmos: A Sketch of a Physical Description of the Universe*, and was especially inspired by that noted scientist.[16] Church also had an 1852 edition of Humboldt's *Personal Narrative of Travels to the Equinoctial Regions of the New Continent*. Portions of Humboldt's narrative seem to have taken visual form in Church's painting:

[We have] seen much of crocodiles during six months, on the Orinoco, the Rio Apure, and the Magdalena, . . .

. . . we perceived two canoes sailing along the coast. . . . These canoes, like all those in use among the natives, were constructed of the single trunk of a tree. In each canoe there were . . . Indians, naked to the waist, . . . They had the appearance of great muscular strength, and the colour of their skin was something between brown and copper-colour.

The plain was covered with the tufts of Cassia, Caper, and those arborescent mimosas, which, like the pine of Italy, spread their branches in the form of an umbrella. The pinnated leaves of the palms were conspicuous on the azure sky, . . . The sun was ascending rapidly toward the zenith. A dazzling light was spread through the air, along the whitish hills . . . and over a sea ever calm, the shores of which were peopled with alcatraz [a large brown pelican], egrets, and flamingoes. The splendour of the day, the vivid colouring of the vegetable world, the forms of the plants, the varied plumage of the birds, everything was stamped with the grand character of nature in the equinoctial regions.[17]

Charles Darwin was also influenced by Humboldt's writings; Darwin's own *Journal of Researches*, which Church owned, could have added to the artist's desire to visit the tropics. In 1832, while exploring South America aboard the H.M.S. *Beagle*, Darwin wrote that

. . . when at sea, . . . the beauty of the sky and brilliancy of the ocean together make a picture. But when on shore, and wandering in the sublime forests, surrounded by views more gorgeous than even Claude ever imagined, I enjoy a delight which none but those who have experienced it can understand. If it is to be done, it must be by studying Humboldt.[18]

This intricate cross-fertilization of art and science is characteristic of the mid nineteenth century, and Church may have identified his own explorations with those of Humboldt—"his scientific prototype"[19]—and Darwin. S.G.W. Benjamin, writing in 1880, drew similar parallels with other famous explorers:

Yes! What "Childe Harold" did for the scenery of the Old World, the art of Church has done for that of the New. The vastness and the glory of this continent were yet unrevealed to us. With the enthusiasm of a Raleigh or a Balboa he has explored land and sea, combining the characteristics of the explorer and the artist.[20]

This view of "artist as explorer" is typical of the attitude of the time, weaving together a love of science, of the exotic and unusual, and of nature as God's creation. Theodore Winthrop, a friend and traveling companion of Church's, exemplified this sensibility:

Why paint the tropics? Every passionate soul longs to be with Nature in her fervor underneath the palms. . . . Rosy summer dwells fair and winning beyond our northern wastes, where winter has been and will be, and we sigh for days of basking in perpetual sunshine. . . . For some years past, Mr. Church has been helping us to a complete knowledge of the exciting and yet indolent beauty of the tropics. . . . He has painted the dreamy haste of the Magdalena, the cataract of Tequendama . . . Men of science have sighed over their bewilderment in tropic zones, where every novelty of vegetation is a phenomenon. . . . But Art should sing paeans, when it discovers the poetry of form and color entangled among those labyrinths, and hasten to be its interpreter to the world. Mr. Church has attempted to fulfil this duty . . . Men are better and nobler when they are uplifted by such sublime visions, and the human sympathies stirred by such revelations of the divine cannot die . . .[21]

Winthrop, *Companion to the Heart of the Andes* (1859).

In *Scene on the Magdalene*, Church has combined a tropical, South American subject with a mode of representation some consider more indigenous to the art of North America. In organizing the painting in relatively flat planes of foliage, plateaus beyond, and distant mountains—with each section nearly parallel to the picture plane—Church has utilized the measured progression of a classic organization of space found in American luminist paintings.[22] The water, marked off in parallel, horizontal bands, reinforces this orderly recession into space. In addition, the atmospheric, luminous glow of the sky again brings to mind the luminist painters, just as it evokes spiritual associations of "God in nature" beaming down on the scientifically detailed plants and animals below.

The scientific and didactic aspects of Church's South American paintings were recognized at the time, and were often considered highly appropriate:

Mr. Church's pictures stand alone not merely as works of art but as matters of fact. They bring before us scenes which none but the most enduring traveller and the boldest explorer may hope to see with his own eyes; and, setting altogether aside their value as works of the highest art, they are of inestimable worth if regarded only from an educational point of view.[23]

London Morning Post (1865).

Church undertakes to give on canvas an epitome of tropical scenery—delineating the vegetation, and effectively the mountainous perspective, and atmospheric gradations. Such a purpose is quite legitimate; it is a scientific landscape, such as Humboldt earnestly suggested from his experience of this very region.[24]

New-York Evening Post (1864).

110

Depending upon the taste of the viewer for realistic detail and for reorganizing or "composing" nature, Church's paintings received mixed reviews. One writer found them "cold, unimpassioned, without any dramatic talent, little or no imagination." Another wrote, "They are faithful and beautiful, but they are not so rich as they might be in the poetry, the aroma, of art."[25] Many critics reacted more favorably; "Fidelity to Nature is one great secret of success in Mr. Church's paintings. He also possesses the power of interpreting his subjects, so that the most superficial observer is able to comprehend their artistic motive . . ."[26] Each critic felt perfection was to be found in a different proportion of individual detail to overall unity, of scientific fact to dramatic or romantic interpretation, of the real to the ideal. In 1856 an unidentified author in the *New-York-Daily Times* seems to have summarized it as well as any:

Every landscape has its own sentiment . . . the painter is great or little, as he can seize this sentiment and imprison it in his lines and colors. And it would seem clear enough that he can attain this end only by working as Nature works. . . . A painter who shirks the detail, and thinks he can without it give us the soul, slanders; a painter who gives us the detail with studious care, and is satisfied with that for an end—slanders, and as fatally as the first.[27]

NOTES

1. Card catalogue of paintings, National Academy of Design, New York, New York.
2. Mary Bartlett Cowdrey, ed., *National Academy of Design Exhibition Record, 1826-1860*, (New York: J.J. Little & Ives, 1943), 1: 81.
3. "Editor's Table. Exhibition of the National Academy of Design," *The Knickerbocker*, May 1855, 532.*
4. "Exhibition of the National Academy of Design," *The New-York Daily Tribune*, May 7, 1855, 6-7.*
5. David Carew Huntington, *Frederic Edwin Church, 1826-1900: Painter of the Adamic New World Myth* (Ph.D. dissertation, Yale University, 1960), 41.
6. Letter from Frederic Church to Mrs. Joseph Church, Hartford, Conn., from Honda, Colombia, May 25, 1853. Carson Collection, Downs Library, Henry Francis du Pont Winterthur Museum, No. 57 X 18.34. Photocopy available at Olana State Historic Site, Office of Parks and Recreation, Taconic Region, Hudson, N.Y.
7. George Sheldon was among those who commented on this technique: "Where landscapes are the stateliest and the most radiant, there Mr. Church's brush is eager to be at work; but it is most eager when the artist has selected from a wide range of objects, fair, bright and grand, those which are especially fair, bright, and grand, and made of them a single composition." (*American Painters*, New York: D. Appleton, 1879), 11.
8. Frederic Church, personal journal of travels in Colombia and Ecuador in 1853, entry marked "Rio Magdalena, Miércoles 11 Mayo" (Wednesday, May 11),

collection of the Olana State Historic Site, Hudson, New York. Translations given here are the author's, with greatly appreciated assistance from Bertha Spooner Willsie.
9. *Ibid.*, entry marked "Rio Magdalena, Viernes 13 de Mayo" (Friday, May 13).
10. *Ibid.*, entry marked "Lúnes 16 de Mayo" (Monday, May 16).
11. *Ibid.*, entry marked "Mompox, Jueves 12 de Mayo" (Thursday, May 12).
12. 8 ½ x 11" page of pencil sketches from Church's 1853 trip to Colombia, Cooper-Hewitt Museum, New York, no. 1917.4.132. I wish to thank Lewis Kachur for bringing this sketch to my attention.
13. Letter from Frederic Church to Mrs. Joseph Church, Hartford, Conn., from Bogotá, Colombia, July 7, 1853. Carson Collection, Downs Library, Henry Francis du Pont Winterthur Museum, no. 57 X 18.36. Photocopy available at Olana State Historic Site, Office of Parks and Recreation, Taconic Region, Hudson, N.Y.
14. "American Painters—Frederic Edwin Church, N.A.," *The Art Journal* (March 1878), 65.
15. William Cullen Bryant, *Picturesque America* (New York: D. Appleton, 1872), 1:iii.
16. Albert Ten Eyck Gardner, "Scientific Sources of the Full-Length Landscape: 1850," *Metropolitan Museum of Art Bulletin* (October 1945) 63-65.* Library card catalogue, Olana State Historic Site, Office of Parks and Recreation, Taconic Region, Hudson, N.Y.
17. Alexander von Humboldt, *Personal Narrative of Travels to the Equinoctial Regions of America, During the Years 1799-1804*, trans. Thomasina Ross, 3 vols. (London: Henry G. Bohn; vols. 1 and 2, 1852; vol. 3, 1853), vol. 1: 143, 144, 147, vol. 3: 179, 180. The library at Olana includes volumes 1 and 3, quoted here.
18. Charles Darwin to W.D. Fox, May 1832, from Botofogo Bay, near Rio de Janeiro. In Francis Darwin, ed., *The Life and Letters of Charles Darwin*, 3rd ed. (London: John Murray, 1887), 1:234.
19. "Church's Cotopaxi," *The New-York Times*, March 17, 1863, 4. "Mr. Church is steadily vindicating his claim to be considered as the artistic Humboldt of the new world. His untiring pencil, like the pen of his scientific prototype, gathers force from the magnitude and grace [and] from the amazing contrasts of the scenes which it depicts."
20. S.G.W. Benjamin, *Art in America, A Critical and Historical Sketch* (New York: Harper & Bros., 1880), 81.
21. Theodore Winthrop, *A Companion to the Heart of the Andes* (New York: D. Appleton, 1859), 10, 11, 43.
22. Barbara Novak, *American Painting of the Nineteenth Century* (1969; reprint New York: Harper and Row, 1979), 105.
23. "Mr. Church's American Landscapes," *The London Morning Post*, July 21, 1865.
24. Untitled review. *The New-York Evening Post*, April 12, 1864, 2.
25. Unidentified article in the New York Public Library Clipping File. Sheldon, *American Painters*, 11.
26. "Mr. Church's New Painting," *The Art Journal* 1 (new series, 1875), 179.
27. "National Academy of Design, Thirty-first Annual Exhibition," *New-York Daily Times*, April 4, 1856, 2.

*Copy in National Academy of Design Clipping and Artists Biographical Files.

KN

SCENE AMONG THE ANDES, 1854
Oil on canvas, 15⅞ x 24"
Signed lower center: *F. Church 1854*
Suydam Collection

When Frederic Edwin Church journeyed to South America with financier Cyrus W. Field in mid-1853, he was already an important young landscape painter and a member of the National Academy. In 1851, Church had traveled with Cyrus and Mary Field to the Natural Bridge in Virginia, Mammouth Cave in Kentucky, and along the Mississippi River from Cairo, Illinois, to Saint Paul, Minnesota. Not surprisingly, Church "found the river disappointingly serene" and went off to view thunderous Niagara Falls.[1]

After Field retired in 1853, the two mapped out an itinerary of mines and natural wonders, ambitiously intending to travel as far south as Valparaiso, Chile.[2] Sailing from New York, Church and Field reached Barranquilla, New Granada (now Colombia), on May 2, 1853. They spent most of the following five months moving south through New Granada, including an arduous seven-week journey on muleback along the Cordilleras mountain chain from Bogotá to Quito. The party crossed the border into Ecuador

on August 25, and Church soon wrote enthusiastically in his journal:

After a disagreeable journey . . . we finally came to the edge of an eminence which overlooks the valley of Chota. And a view of such unparalleled magnificence presented itself that I must pronounce it one of the great wonders of Nature. I made a couple of feeble sketches this evening in recollection of the scene. My ideal of the Cordilleras is realized.[3]

Though Church made numerous oil sketches on paperboard from local motifs, this entry indicates that he worked from memory as well. Once back in his New York studio, the artist would combine on canvas both his studies from nature and his recollections of the scene. As Tuckerman noted, "He has looked on the mountains, skies, and valleys of South America with his firm, clear New England vision—has seen everything, wisely chosen, aptly combined, and effectively reproduced his materials."[4] *Scene Among the Andes* is not necessarily the valley of the above journal entry, as it may also reflect his more general impressions of Colombia:

Beyond these giant cliffs sweeps one of the loveliest valleys that can be imagined . . . both delighting and confounding the artist with its picturesque confusion. . . . Forests, scattered trees, meadows, furrows in the hillsides and thatched cottages serve still further to add to the variety . . . the valley gradually determines itself into mountains which are piled up most gradually one above the other until the whole are lost in one huge range. . . .[5]

Travel notes (1853).

The pair pushed farther into Ecuador, first to the volcano Cotopaxi, then to the slightly higher Mount Chimborazo, at 20,561 feet the highest peak they saw. Church made some drawings and oil sketches of these, but was partially frustrated by adverse weather. They climbed partway up Chimborazo in the early morning of September 19, then began their descent from the Andes to the port of Guayaquil. Even had Church wished to linger, Field was anxious to return in time to attend a large family dinner in honor of his parents' fiftieth anniversary.[6] Thus they boarded a steamer for Panama on October 1. When the boat stopped over in Aspinwall (now Colón), a local journalist recorded the three volcanoes and two mines they had seen, plus general impressions of the Edenic continent:

They say that the scenery in some parts of the Andes is grand and beautiful beyond description . . . that gold in large quantities can be obtained in Antioquia; and from the beds of many small streams that run down the Andes . . . and that they have been so much pleased with their journey that they intend to return to the land of beautiful flowers and birds, and to the continent for which the Almighty has done so much and man so little.[7]

Aspinwall newspaper (1853).

The two men arrived in New York on October 29. Besides the products Field had shipped home earlier, he returned with a live jaguar and twenty-four parrakeets.[8] Church also returned with specimens, plus important oil sketches and dozens of drawings, many now preserved at the Cooper-Hewitt Museum, New York. The oils are primarily of mountains, including Cotopaxi, Chimborazo, Sangay, and Cayambe. The sketchbook drawings are more various, and aside from landscapes, include many types of plants and foliage, townscapes, and an occasional exotic animal. Although common artistic practice, this sketching and drawing corresponds with the German naturalist Alexander von Humboldt's advice:

Coloured sketches, taken directly from nature, are the only means by which the artist, on his return, may reproduce the character of distant regions in more elaborately finished pictures; and this object will be the more fully attained, where the painter has, at the same time, drawn or painted directly from nature a large number of separate studies of the foliage of trees; of leafy, flowering, or fruit-bearing stems; of prostrate trunks . . . and the soil of the forest. The possession of such correctly drawn and well proportioned sketches will enable the artist to dispense with all the deceptive aid of hothouse forms, and so-called botanical delineations.[9]

Cosmos (1849).

Sparked by the researches of Humboldt earlier in the century, Church himself made this connection known to his contemporaries. Thus Tuckerman recorded that in Church "the descriptions of tropical scenery by Humboldt find their pictorial counterpart."[10]

In *Cosmos*, Humboldt's enthusiasm for the Andes even caused him to downplay the higher Himalayas:

But although the mountains of India greatly surpass the Cordilleras of South America, by their astonishing elevation, . . . they cannot, from their geographical position, present the same inexhaustible variety of phenomena by which the latter are characterised. . . . The chain of the Himalaya is also wanting in the imposing phenomena of volcanoes, which in the Andes . . . often reveal to the inhabitants, under the most terrific forms, the existence of the forces pervading the interior of our planet.[11]

Thus, Cotopaxi, the world's highest active volcano, not only represented the fiery sublime but also betokened Nature's forces. Similarly, equatorial botanical life signified both the exotic and the Edenic garden, unspoiled proof of heavenly purpose, as Humboldt makes clear:

The regions of the torrid zone not only give rise to the most powerful impressions by their organic richness and their abundant fertility, but they likewise afford the inestimable advantage of revealing to man . . . the invariability of the laws that regulate the course of the heavenly bodies, reflected, as it were, in terrestrial phenomena.[12]

As the wayside shrines in both *The Andes of Ecuador* (1855) and *Heart of the Andes* (1859) further suggest, Church, like many of his contemporaries, saw landscape as the bearer of higher spiritual and moral associations. Landscape art was "an expression of the majesty and beauty of the divine in nature."[13]

The sketches from the journey served as Church's guideposts for the South American paintings he produced in New York over the following four years, one of the earliest being *Scene Among the Andes*. In this painting the spreading valley scene is hushed, recalling Church's earlier views of New England. With a *repoussoir* left foreground, and mountains rising beyond a vast middleground, *Scene Among the Andes* has the same compositional formula as *Scene in the Catskill Mountains*, 1852, (Walker Art Center, Minneapolis) or *Mt. Ktaadn*, 1853, (Yale University). Indeed, at times Church analogized between equatorial and native vistas, "The scenery of the Cauca, coming down the mount shows magnificently . . . and in some places might resemble New England were it not for the Tropical foliage."[14]

In this painting Church does depict some specific tropical foliage in the foreground, most notably the large stalk of the "century plant," or amaryllis, in the middle. He later gave an oil sketch of this to William Cullen Bryant.[15] On the far left, a tree with hanging vines is quite close to one in Church's sketchbook, which was accompanied by the notation: "This tree grows in many beautiful forms, often resembling the Elm, with a multiplicity of branches which are more irregular than the Elm. Branches at top Vandyke brown."[16]

The artist was often praised for his "near-looking" detail: "Church is finishing a South American view, remarkable for the fullness and minuteness of the foreground, which is filled with portraiture of the tropical flora."[17] The mountain at the far right, on the other hand, cannot be identified from the existing studies. As Winthrop said of the snow peak in *Heart of the Andes*, "This mountain is a type, not a portrait."[18]

Coloristically, the painting is restrained, and only the notes of blue and red in the peasant and llama stand out. Perhaps tokens of the mode of travel from Bogotá, they are bathed in the sunlight breaking through the trees. Stylistically, *Scene Among the Andes* relates more to Church's earlier quietism than to the quite different major works which followed. After 1856, increasing public acclaim spurred him to a more declamatory, theatrical style, aflame with brighter, synthetic paints.[19]

Church first showed three Colombian scenes and a generalized *Cordilleras* at the National Academy annual exhibition of 1855. One observer found these "the chief attraction" of the show:

They are most lovely and beautiful: warm, rich, hazy air, copious masses of brilliant, many-colored equatorial foliage, with outlying festoons and draperies of tangled vine-growth. . . . He seems to deal quite as well with this new field of subjects; is as strong, real, and true in depicting the still sunny inland lake and the tropical wilderness as in the Mt. Desert region.[20]

Diary of George Templeton Strong (1855).

Yet the mixed critical reaction was less than Church would have wished. *The Knickerbocker* praised his "aerial distance, and skies, and foreground," yet objected, " 'Tacquedama [*sic*] Falls' is not quite up to the mark. He should not paint falling water—for he cannot. It is weak and feathery."[21] Fortunately, Church challenged rather than followed the last bit of advice. In fact his fame was not secured until he retrenched with native scenery, turning from *The Falls of Tequendama* to the falls of *Niagara* (1856-57). This and an even more ambitious South American "machine" *Heart of the Andes* (1859) toured the country and fully established a national reputation that is only now being revived.

NOTES

1. Samuel Carter III, *Cyrus Field: Man of Two Worlds* (New York: G.P. Putnam's, 1968), 68-69.
2. Isabella Field Judson, *Cyrus W. Field* (New York: Harper Brothers, 1896), 53.
3. *Journal*, August 26, 1853, at Olana, State Historic Site, Office of Parks and Recreation, Taconic Region, Hudson, New York.
4. Henry T. Tuckerman, *Book of the Artists* (1867; reprint New York: James F. Carr, 1966), 375.
5. Miscellaneous travel notes in South American Journal, Colombia, 1853 (unpaginated) at Olana State Historic Site Office of Parks and Recreation, Taconic Region, Hudson, N.Y.
6. Judson, *Cyrus W. Field*, 55-57.
7. *Ibid.*, 54-55.
8. *Ibid.*, 56.
9. Alexander von Humboldt, *Cosmos* (London: Henry G. Bohn, 1849), 2:452-53.
10. Tuckerman, *Book of the Artists*, 372. See also p. 370 and Theodore Winthrop, *A Companion to Heart of the Andes* (New York: Appleton, 1859), 4.
11. Humboldt, *Cosmos*, (London: Henry G. Bohn, 1848), 1:8-9.
12. *Ibid.*, 13.
13. Charles Dudley Warner, *Frederic Edwin Church* (Exhibition catalogue, Metropolitan Museum of Art, N.Y., 1900), introduction.
14. Letter to Elizabeth Church from Cartago, New Granada, July 23, 1853. Carson Collection, Downes Library, Henry Francis DuPont Winterthur Museum, Delaware.
15. A. Hyatt Mayor and Mark Davis, *American Art at the Century* (New York: The Century Association, 1977), ill. p. 9.
16. "Trees," Cooper-Hewitt Museum, 1917.4.878. Reproduced in David C. Huntington, *The Landscapes of Frederic Edwin Church* (New York: Braziller, 1966), plate 26.
17. *The Crayon* 1, no. 9 (Feb. 28, 1855), 140.
18. Winthrop, *Heart of the Andes*, 16.
19. E.P. Richardson, *Painting in America* (New York: Crowell, 1956), 219.
20. Allan Nevins and Milton Halsey Thomas, eds., *the Diary of George Templeton Strong*, (New York: Macmillan, 1952), 2: entry of Sunday, March 18, 1855.
21. "Editor's Table. Exhibition of the National Academy of Design," *the Knickerbocker* 45 (May 1855), 532.

LK

ALBERT BIERSTADT

(1830-1892)
HM 1858; NA 1860

Born January 7, at Solingen, near Düsseldorf, Germany. 1832 emigrated to New Bedford, Mass. 1853 to Düsseldorf to study painting under Karl Friedrich Lessing and Andreas Achenbach. Spent a winter in Rome before returning to New Bedford in 1857. 1858 began exhibiting at National Academy of Design. 1859 first traveled to American West with expedition of Colonel Frederick W. Lander; toured Nebraska, Wyoming, Utah. Returned late 1859, taking studio in Tenth Street Studio Building. 1863 second trip west to Nebraska, Colorado, Utah, California, Oregon. 1865-1866 built house and studio at Irvington-on-Hudson, N.Y. 1867-1869 in Europe, visiting England, France, Germany, Austria, Switzerland, Italy, Spain. Returned 1869. Other European trips in 1878, 1883, 1884, 1887, and 1891. 1871-1873 in California, Washington, Vancouver, Yellowstone Park. 1882 Irvington-on-Hudson estate destroyed by fire. 1886 visited Wisconsin and vicinity. 1889 traveled to Canadian Rockies and Alaska. 1893-1896 took out several patents for improvements on railway cars. 1895 suffered bankruptcy. Died February 18 in New York City.

REFERENCES: *Dictionary of American Biography* (New York: Charles Scribner's Sons, 1931). Gordon Hendricks, *Albert Bierstadt* (New York: Harry N. Abrams, 1974).

On the Sweetwater near the Devil's Gate resulted from Bierstadt's first journey to the American West in the spring and summer of 1859. The artist traveled under the protection of Colonel Frederick W. Lander, who was leading an expedition to improve the Overland Trail through the Rocky Mountains.[1] Bierstadt not only made numerous sketches during the trip but, with the assistance of photographer S.F. Frost of Boston, made a number of stereographs, most of which were of Indians and emigrants.[2]

Bierstadt did not range very far on this first excursion, going only to the Wasatch Mountains of present-day Wyoming and Utah. The sketches derived from this trip, however, resulted in one of his greatest popular successes, *The Rocky Mountains* (1863), a large panoramic painting now in the collection of the Metropolitan Museum of Art.[3] Bierstadt wrote home to New York his first impressions of the Rockies:

As you approach them, the lower hills present themselves more or less clothed with a great variety of trees, among which may be found the cotton-wood, lining the river banks, the aspen, and several species of the fir and the pine, some of them being very beautiful. And such a charming grouping of rocks, so fine in color—more so than I ever saw. Artists would be delighted with them—were it not for the tormenting swarms of mosquitoes. In the valleys, silver streams abound, with mossy rocks and an abundance of that finny tribe that we all delight so much to catch, the trout. We see many spots in the scenery that remind us of our New Hampshire and Catskill hills, but when we look up and measure the mighty perpendicular cliffs that rise hundreds of feet aloft, all capped with snow, we then realize that we are among a different class of mountains; and especially when we see the antelope stop to look at us, and still more the Indian, his pursuer, who often stands dismayed to see a white man sketching alone in the midst of his hunting grounds.[4]

Letter to *The Crayon* (1859).

Bierstadt was still more than a hundred miles east of the Rockies when he painted this scene. Although the picture is dated 1860, it was probably at least begun the year before, since the artist inscribed the words "sketched 1859" on the reverse of the panel.[5] The Sweetwater River of Wyoming, seen in the foreground, was part of the Overland Trail leading to the South Pass of the Rockies; the Devil's Gate, which is possibly a part of the long ridge in the background of the picture, is a high granite chasm through which the river flows. In the 1850s the United States government had installed a stockade near the Gate for the protection of emigrants whose predecessors at that point had suffered from Indian attacks.[6] Since the mid-1840s a horde of various idealists had moved through this site: on one extreme were the Mormons in search of a new Israel, on the other were the Forty-Niners and Pike's-Peakers in pursuit of easy mammon. In the middle were prospective farmers seeking fertile lands in California and Oregon. Though he probably did not intend to, Bierstadt has here recorded a kind of threshold beyond which countless hopes were projected. The glittering river winding towards the silvery edged cloud pillar in the background draws the spectator's eyes to the horizon as irresistibly as the notion of the West lured the emigrants (and the artist) more than a century ago.

"The true point of view in the history of this nation is not the Atlantic coast, it is the great West." Thus claimed the historian Frederick J. Turner in 1893, prefacing his contention by observing that "this fluidity of American life, this expansion westward with its new opportunities, its continuous touch with the simplicity of primitive society, furnish the forces dominating American character."[7]

However one may question the cultural pervasiveness of Turner's landmark thesis, he was accurate at least insofar as the spatial possibilities of the young Republic could influence not only its artists but its most characteristic writers. Walt Whitman, for

ON THE SWEETWATER NEAR THE DEVIL'S GATE, 1859-60
Oil on millboard, 12 x 18″
Signed lower right: *A Bierstadt. 60*
Inscribed in artist's hand on reverse:
on the Sweetwater near the Devil's Gate/
sketched 1859 / Nebraska / price $100, with Frame

example, who did not visit the West until 1879, could exhort in 1856:

Allons! Whoever you are, come travel with me!
Traveling with me, you find what never tires.

The earth never tires!
The earth is rude, silent, incomprehensible at first—
    nature is rude and incomprehensible at first,
Be not discouraged—keep on—there are divine things,
    well enveloped,
I swear to you there are divine things more beautiful
    than words can tell!

Allons! We must not stop here!
However sweet these laid-up stores, however convenient
    this dwelling, we cannot remain here!
However sheltered this port, however calm these waters,
    we must not anchor here!
However welcome the hospitality that surrounds us, we
    are permitted to receive it but a little while.

Allons! The inducements shall be great to you . . .[8]

"Poem of the Road" [later "Song of the Open Road"].

Even Henry David Thoreau, the Walden recluse, could confess:

I turn round and round irresolute sometimes for a quarter of an hour, until I decide, for a thousandth time, that I will walk into the southwest or west. Eastward I go only by force; but westward I go free. . . . I should not lay so much stress on this fact, if I did not believe that this is the prevailing tendency of my countrymen. I must walk toward Oregon, and not toward Europe. And that way the nation is moving, and I may say that mankind progresses from east to west. . . .

Every sunset which I witness inspires me with the desire to go to a West as distant and as fair as that into which the sun goes down. He appears to migrate westward daily, and tempt us to follow him. He is the Great Western Pioneer whom the nations follow. We dream all night of those mountain-ridges in the horizon, though they may be of vapor only, which were last gilded by his rays.[9]

"Walking" (1862).

As Whitman admits, however, and as Bierstadt suggests with the storm encroaching upon his peaceful scene, "nature is rude and incomprehensible at first." The western ideal held up by painters, poets, prophets, politicians, and entrepreneurs obscured a crueler Darwinian struggle along the western passage. In the year Whitman published his "Poem of the Road," a group of Mormons, pulling their wagons by hand because they could not afford horses, were overtaken by a blizzard near the Devil's Gate. A few found shelter at the stockade, but when the storm passed, the children of those who had perished were found on the plains gnawing at the barks of trees for lack of other sustenance.[10]

More grim was the report of the *Harper's Weekly* correspondent accompanying the Lander expedition of 1859 (Bierstadt supplied the illustrations for his article), telling of the plight of one of the many luckless Pike's-Peakers:

I conversed with a returning emigrant who saw and spoke to the insane survivor of these brothers by the name of Blew, from Whiteside County, Illinois, who had eaten the dead bodies of his brethren, and was found by the Indians in a dying state, and by them carried to the nearest passing train.[11]

The reporter claimed to have seen along the way "five thousand desponding and disappointed men returning to the States," yet he hastened to add that "this number is small compared to those who have passed on toward California."[12] American history, too, has shown that in the settlement of the West, heroic ideals prevailed over every real impediment, even as the history of art has acknowledged Bierstadt, with all the rhetorical excesses of his large pictures, as the "Painter of the American West."[13] Likewise the poet Whitman, when in 1879 he finally stood "amid all this grim yet joyous elemental abandon" of the Colorado Rockies, confirmed his own declamatory mode in concluding: "I have found the law of my own poems."[14]

NOTES

1. See the account of the Lander expedition in Gordon Hendricks, *Albert Bierstadt* (New York: Harry N. Abrams, 1974), 63-90, and in Gordon Hendricks, "The First Three Western Journeys of Albert Bierstadt," *Art Bulletin* 46 (Sept. 1964), 334-39.

2. Bierstadt's brothers, Charles and Edward, issued a catalogue of stereo views in 1860, fifty-one of which were made by Bierstadt and Frost on the 1859 journey. Only four of these, judging from their titles, were pure landscapes, but two of them, nos. 64 and 75, were of the Devil's Gate, the site near which the present picture was painted. See Hendricks, *Albert Bierstadt*, 63, 68, 76, 80, 87. For a listing of the stereographs advertised by Bierstadt's brothers, see Joseph Snell, "Some Rare Western Photographs by Albert Bierstadt Now in the Historical Society Collections," *The Kansas Historical Quarterly* 24 (Spring 1958), 4-5.

3. See an illustration of one of the 1859 sketches used in *The Rocky Mountains* in Hendricks, *Albert Bierstadt*, 149, fig. 106.

4. Albert Bierstadt, Letter to *The Crayon*, July 10, 1859, *The Crayon* 6 (Sept. 1859), 259.

5. The fact that the picture is painted on a panel, the edges of which are crudely cut, seems to indicate that it was done while Bierstadt was traveling in 1859. The date "60" inscribed on the front suggests that the artist worked the picture into a more finished state the following year. Evidently he also had intended to sell the painting before turning it over to the Academy on his election to full membership. The word "Nebraska," inscribed on the reverse, refers to the Nebraska Territory, a tract encompassing the area of several modern states, among them Wyoming, where the present picture was sketched.

6. Writer's Program, Work Projects Administration, *Wyoming; a Guide to Its History, Highways, and People* (New York: Oxford University Press, 1941), 387-88. See also Virginia Cole Trenholm *Footprints on the Frontier* (Douglas, Wy.: published privately, 1945), 58.

7. Frederick Jackson Turner, "The Significance of the Frontier in American History" (1894; reprint Ann Arbor, Mich.: University Microfilms, 1966), 200.

8. Walt Whitman, "Poem of the Road" (later called "Song of the Open Road"), *Leaves of Grass* (Brooklyn, N.Y.: privately published, 1856), 231-32.

9. Henry David Thoreau, "Walking" (1862). In *Excursions, Poems, and Familiar Letters of Henry D. Thoreau* (Boston: Houghton-Mifflin, 1929), 217-18, 219.

10. Mae Urbanek, *Wyoming Wonderland* (Denver: Sage Books, 1964), 38.

11. Anonymous, "The Pike's Peak Gold Mines" (dated South Fork of the Platte, June 1859), *Harper's Weekly* (August 13, 1859), 516.

12. *Ibid.*

13. This is the subtitle of Gordon Hendricks' book cited in note 1.

14. Walt Whitman, "An Egotistical 'Find'" (1879). From *Specimen Days*, in *Complete Prose Works* (Boston: Small, Maynard, 1907), 136.

KA

THOMAS MORAN

(1837-1926)
ANA 1881; NA 1884

Born January 12, Bolton, Lancashire, England. 1844 emigrated to America; later settled in Philadelphia. Apprenticed to a wood engraver 1853-1856. Began sharing studio with brother, Edward, 1856. First painted in watercolor. By 1860 also using oil. Met and received advice from marine painter James Hamilton. 1862 returned to England for short stay. Copied Turner's oils at National Gallery, London. 1866 again in England. On to Paris and Italy by early 1867. 1871 joined United States Geological Expedition under F. V. Hayden to Yellowstone region. 1873 with Major John Wesley Powell's expedition to Rockies and Grand Canyon of the Colorado River. 1874 second trip with Hayden to Mountain of the Holy Cross, Colorado. Later created one of his most famous paintings from views of this natural phenomenon. Sketched extensively on all expeditions. *Grand Canyon of the Yellowstone* and *Chasm of the Colorado* purchased for Capitol. Contributions to exploration and representation of West commemorated by Mount Moran in Teton Range, Wyoming, and Moran Point, Arizona. Lived in Philadelphia until 1872, then Newark, N.J. 1881 moved family to New York City; studio in Booth's Building on Twenty-third St. First visited East Hampton, L.I., summer of 1878. Began spending summers there in 1880. 1884 built East Hampton studio. Traveled frequently throughout his life, including England and Mexico in the 1880s, and Venice in 1886, 1890. Also visited Florida in 1887 and the West many times through the 1920s. Moved to Santa Barbara, California, in 1916. Died there August 26.

REFERENCES: National Academy of Design Artists Biographical Files. Eliot Clark, *History of the National Academy of Design, 1825-1953* (New York: Columbia University Press, 1954). George C. Groce and David H. Wallace, *Dictionary of Artists in America 1564-1860* (New-York Historical Society, 1957). *Dictionary of American Biography* (New York: Scribner's, 1928-1934). Thurman Wilkins, *Thomas Moran, Artist of the Mountains* (Norman: University of Oklahoma Press, 1966).

Moran enjoyed a long and highly productive career as painter, engraver, and watercolorist. His panoramas of the American West, and later his canvases of Venice, executed with Turneresque coloring and atmosphere, brought him great acclaim. Images of the Long Island landscape and its sunsets elicited the critics' praises as well. Moran gave *Three Mile Harbor, Long Island* to the Academy as his Diploma picture after his election as an Academician in 1884.[1] Along with *Sassafrass Hill, Appaquogue, Five Mile River,* and the sand dunes of Amagansett, Three Mile Harbor was one of Moran's favorite spots for sketching during the summers.[2] Thurman Wilkins writes that *Three Mile Harbor* is representative of the period around 1880 when Moran turned to ". . . smaller canvases, in a quieter, more poetic mood."[3]

This "quieter" mood is also to be found in the Academy's etching *Long Island Marshes* (see no. 120). Moran wrote "Three Mile Harbor" on the plate itself; the words appear in reverse just to the right of the road in the foreground.[4] Moran took up etching with renewed interest in 1878 (having ignored the medium for almost twenty years). During the summer of 1880 Moran made etchings of the scenery near East Hampton, its marshes and the sea.[5] *Long Island Marshes* displays the fine draftsmanship and "fluent lines" that Alfred Trumble praised in the catalogue of Moran's "Complete Etched Works" shown at the Klackner Gallery in 1889.[6]

One of Moran's etchings, *The Breaking Wave* (1880), also drew praise from John Ruskin, whom he met while in London in 1882: "the finest drawing of water in motion that has come out of America!"[7] Later, Ruskin recommended that Moran paint works in the "quiet" mood which would characterize *Three Mile Harbor*:

—and I *do* wish with all my whole heart you would give up—for a whole all that flaring and glaring and splashing and roaring triumph— and *paint*, not etch—some quiet things like that little tree landscape absolutely from nature.[8]

Ruskin, Letter to Moran (1882).

Still earlier, Tucherman had noted:

This young artist when abroad paid particular attention to the pictures of Turner, and has since his return to this country been assiduous in his study of nature, in all her manifestations.[9]

Tuckerman, *Book of the Artists* (1867).

Moran's skill at close observation is evident in *Three Mile Harbor*. The painting also shows the artist's sensitivity to the harmonies of color and mood in the painterly handling of the thick banks of clouds. These qualities are intimately related to those which Moran praised in Turner's own canvases:

Turner is a great artist, but he is not understood, because both painters and the public look upon his pictures as transcriptions of Nature. He certainly did not so regard them. All that he asked of a scene was simply how good a medium it was for making a picture; he cared nothing for the scene itself. Literally speaking, his landscapes are false; but they contain his impressions of Nature, and so many natural characteristics as were necessary adequately to convey that impression to others. . . . I think that one of his best pictures is the *Crossing the Brook*, in the London National Gallery; it is simple, quiet, grey in colour; the harmonies of its greys are

THREE MILE HARBOR, LONG ISLAND, *1884*
Oil on wood panel, 20 x 30″
Signed lower right: *T Moran* (T superimposed on M) *1884*
Diploma painting

LONG ISLAND MARSHES
Etching, 3½ x 7¾″
Signed lower left: *TM* (T superimposed on M)
Inscribed in plate lower center: *Three Mile Harbor* in
reverse

wonderful. It is, perhaps, the most suggestive of Claude of all his canvases. His aim is parallel with the greatest poets who deal not with literalism or naturalism, and whose excellence cannot be tested by such a standard. . . . He generalises Nature always; and so intense was his admiration for colour that everything else was subservient to that. He would falsify the colour of any object in his picture in order to produce what he considered to be an harmonious whole. In other words, he sacrificed the literal truth of the parts to the higher truth of the whole. And he was right.[10]

Moran, quoted in *The Art Journal* (1879).

While Moran might praise Turner's ability to capture a vision of "the higher truth of the whole," he still retained the basic tenet calling for study from nature itself which Tuckerman and Ruskin had voiced earlier. After more than forty years of experience as a painter, Moran reiterated this idea:

In art, as in any profession, knowledge is power. Twist this into any form you may, but it remains a truth, and the foundation-stone of all true art. It will always be the same, and this will always show itself in the pictures of the artist, no matter how humble, or how pretentious.

Just how far the artist shall go with his knowledge is left to him. He must typify his own personality. This covers all—taste, opinions, everything. The man must exhibit himself in his pictures. This is the theory of art, and also of judgement. . . . Knowledge in art cannot be excluded. Knowledge in art is the power behind the hand-work. Eyesight is nothing unless backed by brains.

In condensed form, this is my theory of art. . . . I have to have knowledge. I must know the geology. I must know the rocks and the trees and the atmosphere and the mountain torrents and the birds that fly in the blue ether above me. Whatever of arbitrary forms that grow out of this intimacy with nature becomes a part of the work, and is legitimate in

after work, because my knowledge of the topic leads me to take liberties. This is the strength of all artists.[11]

Interview with Moran (1903).

NOTES

1. Eliot Clark, *History of the National Academy of Design, 1825-1953* (New York: Columbia University Press, 1954), 121. Moran had exhibited a picture at the Annual Academy Exhibition of 1882 under the title *Three Mile Harbor, Long Island.* cat. no. 555, National Academy of Design Annual Exhibition Catalogue of 1882, 30. (According to the catalogue the painting was for sale; no measurements were given). It may be that the picture shown in 1882 was reworked by Moran then signed, and dated 1884 at the lower right, and given to the Academy as his diploma painting. Recent conservation reports indicate that some portions of *Three Mile Harbor* had been repainted by the artist over an old layer of varnish.
2. Thurman Wilkins, *Thomas Moran, Artist of the Mountains* (Norman: University of Oklahoma Press, 1966), 180-81.
3. *Ibid.*, 183.
4. Thomas Moran, *Long Island Marshes,* n.d., etching, 3¾ x 7¾″ monogram at lower left.
5. Wilkins, *Thomas Moran,* 135.
6. Alfred Trumble, *The Complete Etched Works of Thomas Moran, N.A. and M. Nimmo Moran, S.P.E.* (Exhibition catalogue, C. Klackner's Gallery, March 4-16, 1889), 5.
7. John Ruskin to Moran, quoted in Wilkins, *Thomas Moran,* 162-63.
8. Ruskin to Moran, letter of December 27, 1882, Typescript, C6, Moran Papers, Gilcrease Institute, in Wilkins, *Thomas Moran,* 163, note 18.
9. Henry T. Tuckerman, *Book of the Artists* (1867; reprint New York: James F. Carr, 1966), 568.
10. "Thomas Moran and J.R. Meeker," *The Art Journal* 5 (1879), 42-43.
11. Thomas Moran, "Knowledge is a Prime Requisite in Art," *Brush and Pencil,* 12, no. 2 (April 1903), 14.

JR

JOHN FREDERICK KENSETT

(1816-1872)
ANA 1848; NA 1849

Born March 22, Cheshire, Conn.; son of English immigrant engraver. Around 1828 apprenticed in shop of father and uncle in New Haven. 1829 may have worked with John W. Casilear in New York engraving shop for a short period. 1829-1839 worked as an engraver in New Haven, New York City, and Albany. 1840 sailed for England with Casilear, Asher B. Durand, and Thomas P. Rossiter. Between 1840 and 1845 traveled between England and France; met Thomas Cole in Paris in 1842. Summer of 1845 took walking tour with Benjamin Champney along Rhine through Switzerland. 1846-1847 sketched in Roman campagna and vicinity with Thomas P. Hicks. Toured Italy in 1847; returned to New York in autumn. 1848 established studio in New York University Building. 1850 elected to Council of National Academy of Design and member of Sketch Club. 1854 traveled to Mississippi River region. Throughout the 1850s and 1860s traveled in Britain, Europe, and western United States. 1859 appointed member of commission to decorate U.S. Capitol. 1870 member of first Board of Trustees, Metropolitan Museum of Art; with Sanford R. Gifford and Worthington Whittredge journeyed west to Colorado and Rockies. During his career, he also summered and sketched variously in Newport, R.I., throughout New York State, the Berkshires, the Green Mountains, the White Mountains, Maine, Ohio, New Jersey, Maryland, West Virginia. Died December 14, New York City.

REFERENCE: John K. Howat, *John Frederick Kensett* (Exhibition catalogue, American Federation of the Arts, N.Y., 1968). KA

Of all the falls Kensett depicted—Rydal, Niagara, Catskill, and Trenton—that of Bash Bish in South Egremont, Massachusetts, occurs most frequently in his *oeuvre*. He did at least five versions of this theme, and in 1855 executed two very similar compositions. One was sold to his friend James Suydam, and through the Suydam Bequest entered the collection of the National Academy of Design in 1865. The other was purchased for 300 dollars by New York governor Hamilton Fish in 1855. Concerning the latter version (Museum of Fine Arts, Boston), a critic for *The Crayon* observed in 1855:

We learn that Kensett has just completed a landscape for the Hon. Hamilton Fish. It is a view of part of the Bashbish Fall in Berkshire county, Massachusetts, near the New York State line; one of the wildest and most beautiful cascades in the country.[1]

In four of the five known versions of this site, Kensett represents

the lower falls at Bash Bish and crops the falls in essentially the same way, creating a tectonic composition by depicting first the pool, the falls, the two massive boulders above, then the bridge, foliage, and sky. In his fifth version (Yale Art Gallery) Kensett depicts not the lower falls but the upper, more monumental cascade, which a contemporary writer describes as

. . . a series of cascades in Mount Washington leading into a steep gorge and a series of cataracts. Two are seventy feet high, the third more than fifty feet. Below the falls, the stream runs out its violent descent along the floor of the long valley, with the south wall of the gorge rising in a great sweep into the sky.[2]

Richard V. Happel, *The Berkshire Eagle* (1980).

An Indian legend exists about Bash Bish Falls:

Legend tells that once upon a time an Algonquin village stood near the great falls, from which comes the story of the Spirit Squaw. It seems that the son of Black Thunder, chief of the tribe, wed a foundling known as White Swan. Alas, it became apparent that she never could bear him a child to succeed him as chief of the tribe. The solution was to bring a second squaw into the teepee. As may be imagined, this arrangement caused White Swan to brood, even though the love between her and her mate never wavered.

In her distraction, White Swan often wandered among the crags above the falls. There was a tradition that an evil witch lived in the eerie cavern below the falling water. The legend relates that the Indian squaw believed she heard a voice from the bosom of the falls, inviting her to find solace in the swirling water.

Breaking free of the spell, she would walk slowly back to the teepee, her thoughts far afield. Her health failed; her face became luminous, unearthly. Then one day, she rushed crying from the wigwam. Pursued by her mate, she fled to the falls. There he heard her call, "Mother, mother, I am here. Take me in your arms . . . I want rest."

Before her mate's eyes there appeared a glistening, ghostly, white-robed form of a woman from the falls—the witch of the cascade. The maid he loved, the foundling baby from nowhere, was the child of the water witch. He cried out to White Swan just as two ghostly arms reached out from the bosom of the falls and gathered her in. Her frantic mate plunged into the falls and his lifeless body later was found among the rocks. White Swan never was found, but many visitors to the falls claim they have seen her face formed in the swirling water at the falls' base, ever looking up toward the spot where her Indian lover plunged in. . . .[3]

Happel, *Berkshire Eagle* (1980).

In 1850, Kensett wrote: "We are in search of the picturesque but have not yet found it."[4] Clearly, the artist found Bash Bish appealing on some level. If the falls qualified for his definition of the "picturesque," they also probably answered scientific questions that artists at that moment were probing in their paintings.

Of all the studies which relate to the material universe, there is none, perhaps, which appeals so powerfully to our senses or which comes into

MOUNTAIN STREAM: BASH BISH FALLS, 1855
Oil on Canvas, 36 x 29″
Signed lower right: *JFK 55*
Suydam Collection

such close and immediate contact with our wants and enjoyments, as that of geology. In our hourly walks, whether on business or for pleasure, we tread with heedless step upon the apparently uninteresting objects which it embraces. . . .[5]

The North British Review (1850).

Kensett's intense preoccupation with the rocks at Bash Bish has been noted by recent scientists:

Once out of the rustic, domestic, alluvial-lacustrine bottoms the traveler entered the wilderness—with its accumulated connotations from the time of Lord Shaftsbury to the contemporary views of W.F. Cooper [sic] and William C. Bryant. Often as not, the traveler carried with him, too, an amateur's enthusiasm for one of the sciences. In a mountain ravine the landscape was small, the horizons close. But only here were the details of wild nature undisturbed by farmer and woodcutter. True enough, the details of the farm dwelling were picturesque, but the mountain chasm was natural, free, and picturesque too. Seen close at hand, New England's stony soil is not smooth. The rocky outcrops and the textures of rocks as well as tree trunks were rough and interesting. A score of American painters produced hundreds of canvases of New England's brooks and mountain ravines before the Civil War. John Kensett's *Bash-Bish Falls* is an example of the most extraordinary preoccupation with the surfaces of crystalline and granite rocks—perhaps in the history of painting. His work centers on these rocks under the impact of relentless mountain streams, the wedging of time, and sometimes the implacable beat of the sea.

No science prospered more than geology in the period we have considered. Though it was not formally related to painting the enthusiasm which it engendered enlivened the discovery of the indigenous landscape. The artist found there some scenes which were academically beautiful, some in which nature resembled the great architectural ornaments of civilization, and some which simply provided a spatial situation in which a heightened, even ecstatic experience was possible. The painter's demands were then as now rigorous and, though he might have been the last to classify his preferences geologically, it is evident that he had them. The polarity of macrocosm and microcosm had not yet lost its meaning. A rock in its finest detail was fully as paintable as a glorious panorama; and the streams were ceaselessly at work on each.[6]

Paul Shepard, Jr., College Art Journal (1957).

NOTES
1. "Domestic Art Gossip," *The Crayon* 2 (July 1855), 57.
2. Richard V. Happel, "Notes and Footnotes," *The Berkshire Eagle*, April 24, 1980, 24.
3. *Ibid.*
4. Letter from Kensett to J.F.E. Prud[homme], 1850, National Academy of Design Artists Biographical Files.
5. "Hugh Miller's *Footprints of the Creator:* A Review," *The North British Review* 11, no. 24 (Feb. 1850), 239.
6. Paul Shepard, Jr., "Paintings of New England Landscapes: A Scientist Looks at their Geomorphology," *College Art Journal* 17 (Fall 1957) 37, 41, 42.

SGS

Go up to the top of the mountains, look over the long range of hills, observe the flow of the rivers and all the splendour that opens before your eyes, and what feeling touches you? It is one of quiet devotion within you; you lose yourself in boundless space; your whole being undergoes a quiet refining and cleansing, your ego vanishes; you are nothing; God is all.[1]

Carl Carus, *Neun Briefe über Landschaftsmalerei* (1831).

After seven years in Europe, John Frederick Kensett returned to New York in November 1847 primed for success. By 1849 he was a full member of the National Academy and the Century Association. From 1850 on he was active in the Council of the Academy and exhibited sixty-eight works there from 1848 to 1863. "He was a recognized master of landscape, and all his pictures are biographical, for they all reveal the fidelity, the tenderness, and the sweet serenity of his nature."[2]

Henry T. Tuckerman appreciated Kensett's quiescent artistic voice:

Never invoking the assistance of a great or sensational subject, but sedulously seeking for the simplest material, he has by his skill and feeling as a painter, taught us the beauty and poetry of subjects that have been called meagre and devoid of interest.[3]

Book of the Artists (1867).

Similarly, Daniel Huntington eulogized Kensett's "distinguished coloring, which, always harmonious and refined, includes the atmosphere and the true sentiment of the hour and the scene as he feelingly rendered them. He delighted in silvery gray, and could send the mists drifting along the hill sides,"[4] as indeed he does in *Study from Nature*.

Kensett often depicted woodland scenes, usually including a body of water. *Study from Nature* is thus somewhat atypical in its focus solely on mountainous forest. Such a painting derives from his travels in the Catskills and the Green Mountains during the summers of 1848 through 1851.[5] Benjamin Champney, Kensett's traveling companion in Europe, was also with him in New Hampshire during the summer of 1850. Champney's description of the North Conway area has similarities to the painting:

. . . the fields just ripening for the harvest, with the noble elms dotted about in pretty groups. Then beyond the Saco, the massive forms of the ledges rose up, their granite walls covered with forests. . . . We had seen grander, higher mountains in Switzerland, but not often so much beauty and artistic picturesqueness brought together in one valley.[6]

Memories of Art and Artists (1900).

Though here Kensett depicts birches among the mossy rocks in the foreground, he shares the appreciation of native scenery. Champney subsequently praised Kensett's

brilliant studies brought back from the Catskills and White Mountains. . . . No one seemed able to give the sparkle of sunlight through the depths of the forest, touching on mossy rocks and shaggy treetrunks so well as he. These silvery studies were painted with conscientious care, but also with a poetic free translation of what he felt.[7]

Memories of Art and Artists.

Study from Nature can probably be identified with a painting of the same dimensions entitled *Landscape*, sold by the American Art-Union in 1852. It was purchased for ninety dollars by James Suydam, who bequeathed it to the Academy in 1865. The Art-Union catalogue described it as "a foreround of trees, with well-wooded mountains in the distance."[8] Looking more closely, we can also see three houses in the middle distance and a man in a red vest at the far end of the foreground path. This surrogate viewer might recall the lines of Wordsworth:

> —Once again
> Do I behold these steep and lofty cliffs,
> Which on a wild secluded scene impress
> Thoughts of more deep seclusion; and connect
> The landscape with the quiet of the sky.[9]
>
> "Tintern Abbey" (1798).

And the woods are an image of refuge in Emerson:

In the woods too, a man casts off his years, as the snake his slough . . . Within these plantations of God, a decorum and sanctity reign, a perennial festival is dressed, and the guest sees not how he should tire of them in a thousand years. In the woods, we return to reason and faith.[10]

"Nature" (1836).

NOTES

1. In Elizabeth G. Holt, *From the Classicists to the Impressionists* (New York: Doubleday, 1966), 89-90. Carus' letter has an affinity with Emerson's famous "transparent eyeball" passage from his essay "Nature," as well as Kensett's painting.
2. George Curtis, "Editor's Easy Chair," *Harper's Magazine* 46 (March 1873), 611.
3. Henry T. Tuckerman, *Book of the Artists* (New York: G. P. Putnam's, 1867), 512.
4. "Proceedings at a Meeting of the Century Association held in memory of John F. Kensett," New York, December, 1872, p. 5. National Academy of Design Artists Biographical Files.
5. See, for example, John Paul Driscoll, *John F. Kensett Drawings* (Exhibition catalogue, University Park: Pennsylvania State University, 1978), plates 40, 45-48. This source indicates Kensett was with Durand and Casilear during the summers of 1848 and 1849, 54-55.
6. Benjamin Champney, *Sixty Years' Memories of Art and Artists* (Woburn, Mass.: Wallace & Andrews, 1900), 102-03.
7. *Ibid.*, 140.
8. Mary Bartlett Cowdrey, *American Academy of Fine Arts and American Art-Union, 1816-52* (New-York Historical Society, 1953), 214, lot 182. This source lists three Kensetts entitled *Study from Nature* sold in 1848, 1850, and 1852. That Kensett would publicly exhibit this painterly canvas indicates the rise of the sketch aesthetic.
9. "Lines composed a few miles above Tintern Abbey," *The Miscellaneous Poems of William Wordsworth* (London: Longman, 1820) 2:268. Dr. Samuel Osgood in "Proceedings," *op. cit.*, p. 21, said of Kensett,: "There was not a little of Wordsworth's temperament and gift in his work."
10. "Nature," in *Selected Writings of Ralph Waldo Emerson* (New York: New American Library, 1965), 189.

LK

STUDY FROM NATURE, c. 1850
Oil on canvas, 19½ x 16⅛"
Unsigned
Suydam Collection

Among the "Eulogies on John F. Kensett" given at the Century Club upon the artist's death in 1872 two were presented by clergymen. One of these, Reverend Samuel Osgood, was paraphrased as saying:

Mr. KENSETT may not have had the most exalted inspiration, nor ascended to the beatific vision of God in nature as some others had done, but he surely saw the rising stairway from earth to heaven, and all his landscapes invite us to live in the peace that is not of this world. So in this way he is a preacher.[1]

The words of Reverend Osgood make even more explicit the often overt moral function of landscape painting in the nineteenth century, such that the role of the painter could be seen as analogous to that of the parson. It was the consensus of everyone who knew him that Kensett possessed the personal qualities virtually to fulfill that role. At the same meeting Reverend Henry W. Bellows was pleased to recall that Kensett suffered from none of the "irritability or over-sensitiveness of his class," but had rather "calmness and equilibrium and sweetness of personal habits."[2] In his treatment of Kensett's work, the contemporary art critic Henry T. Tuckerman echoed Bellows' praise and defended his extended description of the painter's character by asserting that

The disposition or moral nature of an artist directly and absolutely influences his works. . . . The calm sweetness of Kensett's best efforts, the conscientiousness with which he preserves local identities—the evenness of manner, the patience in detail, the harmonious tone—all are traceable to the artist's feeling and innate disposition, as well as to his skill.[3]
Book of the Artists (1867).

Osgood was thinking primarily of Kensett's numerous images of the North Atlantic seaboard when he characterized him as "preacher."[4] Among these works can be counted the Academy's *On the Narragansett Coast*, painted while Kensett was at Newport, Rhode Island, in the summer of 1864. Newport by this time already enjoyed a reputation as a scenic resort and artists' colony, and was one of Kensett's favorite summer haunts. Interestingly, however, the beaches of Newport and environs also had something of a theological tradition because of the notables who lived or visited there. It was between the Hanging Rocks at Sachuset Beach that the future Bishop Berkeley is supposed to have written his *Alciphron, or the Minute Philosopher* (1732), "an apology for the Christian religion," in which he included a brief description of his hideway[5] (see also the entry for *Paradise Rocks, Newport* by James Suydam, p. 57). Later, William Ellery Channing, the teacher of Emerson and one of the fathers of American Transcendentalism, referred to "yonder beach" at Newport as a favorite place for his theological studies:

Seldom do I visit it now without thinking of the work, which there in the sight of that beauty, in the sound of those waves, was carried on in my soul. No spot on earth has helped to form me so much as that beach. There I lifted up my voice in praise amidst the tempest. There, softened by beauty, I poured out my thanksgiving and contrite confessions. There, in reverential sympathy with the mighty power around me, I became conscious of the power within. There struggling thoughts and emotions broke forth as if moved to utterance by nature's eloquence of the winds and waves. There began a happiness surpassing all worldly pleasure, all gifts of fortune,—the happiness of communing with the works of God.[6]
"Christian Worship" (1836).

Finally, in a poem published in 1851, Tuckerman adds his own pious meditation on the roar of the surf at Newport:

Thy breath, majestic sea, was native air,
And thy cool spray, like Nature's baptism, fell
Upon my brow, while thy hoarse summons called
My childhood's fancy into wonder's realm. . . .

Then here, enfranchised by the voice of God,
O, ponder not, with microscopic eye,
What is adjacent, limited and fixed;
But with high faith gaze forth, and let thy thought
With the illimitable scene expand,
Until the bond of circumstance is rent,
And personal griefs are lost in visions wide
Of an eternal future! . . .

And thus beyond thy present destiny,
Beyond the inlet where the waves of Time
Fret at their barren marge, there spreads a sea
More free and tranquil, where the isles of peace
Shall yield thy highest aspiration scope,
And every sympathy response divine.[7]
"Newport Beach" (1851).

The intimate, indeed indivisible connection popularly advanced in this period between the sensuous appeal of Nature and the presence of the Divine is underscored by the fact that the words of Channing and Tuckerman are quoted in a tour guide to Newport published in 1854. Only two years later Kensett seemed to acknowledge this connection in one of his early coast scenes, entitled *Berkeley Rocks, Newport*, 1856 (Vassar College Art Gallery) in which a figure apparently dressed in clerical garb stands on an escarpment overlooking a tumultuous sea. Such explicit iconography subsequently disappeared from the artist's work; nonetheless, the record of his personality, of a locality, and of an age presumes a Providential light even in this serene and unassuming view.

NOTES

1. Reverend Samuel Osgood, paraphrased in "Eulogies on John F. Kensett" (New York: The Century, December 1872), 21. Copy in National Academy of Design Artists Biographical Files.
2. Reverend Henry W. Bellows. In *ibid.*, 17.
3. Henry T. Tuckerman, *Book of the Artists* (New York: G. P. Putnam's, 1867), 514.
4. As Osgood noted in his eulogy, he and Kensett were neighbors in the summertime (Kensett had a summer home in Darien, Conn.; Osgood had one in nearby Fairfield). The churchman thus had a special affection for Kensett's views of their mutual surroundings on the Connecticut shoreline. Indeed, Osgood described one of his favorite Kensett's as "that which presents the sea under the sunlight, with nothing else to divide the interest— . . . pure light and water, a bridal of the sea and sky. Is it presumptuous in a poor novice like me, to say that this is a great picture?" See "Eulogies on Kensett," 22-23.
5. Benjamin Rand, *Berkeley's American Sojourn* (Cambridge, Mass.: Harvard University Press, 1932), 25-26.
6. William Ellery Channing, "Christian Worship: Discourse at the Dedication of the Unitarian Congregational Church, Newport, Rhode Island, July 27, 1836." In Editor of the *Newport Mercury* [George C. Mason], *Newport Illustrated in a Series of Pen and Pencil Sketches* (New York: D. Appleton, 1854), 50.
7. Henry T. Tuckerman, "Newport Beach" (1851). In *ibid*, 50-51.

KA

ON THE NARRAGANSETT COAST, 1864
Oil on canvas, mounted on masonite, 9¾ x 20½"
Signed lower right: *J.F.K. 1864*
Suydam Collection

_____

JASPER FRANCIS CROPSEY

(1823-1900)
ANA 1844; NA 1851

Coast Scene is part of the Suydam Collection, bequeathed to the National Academy of Design in 1865. The painting may be the work sold to James A. Suydam in 1856 for 208 dollars, as recorded in Cropsey's account book.[1] A *Coast Scene* by Cropsey, possibly this one, was exhibited at the Third Winter Exhibition at the Academy in 1869-1870.[2] Otherwise, it does not seem to have been exhibited during Cropsey's lifetime. William Talbot conjectures that the painting might correspond to *Coast of Genoa*, exhibited at the Pennsylvania Academy of the Fine Arts in 1855 (no. 84).[3] *Coast of Genoa*, however, was first exhibited in 1854 at the National Academy of Design (no. 35), and the reviews describe a different composition.[4] It is more likely, as Talbot also suggests, that this is a scene along the coast of New England, either near Newport, where Cropsey sketched in 1854, or near Plymouth Rock, which he visited in 1855.[5]

In James Fenimore Cooper's essay comparing American and European scenery, published in 1852 in *The Home Book of the Picturesque* (which also included an engraving by Cropsey), he found the American coast inferior to that of the Mediterranean:

There is one great charm, however, that it must be confessed is nearly wanting among us. We allude to the coast. Our own is, with scarcely an exception, low, monotonous, and tame. It wants Alpine rocks, bold promontories, visible heights inland, and all those other glorious accessories of the sort that render the coast of the Mediterranean the wonder of the world.[6]

In this painting, however, Cropsey has concentrated more on the emotional than on the physical aspects of the American coast, depicting a specific time of day and giving the sky a dramatic importance. Even as a child, Cropsey was aware of the constant changes of the sky. In his unfinished "Reminiscences of My Own Time" (1846), he wrote that, as a youth

. . . I began to observe nature more closely and can recollect well, my delight, in the effects of the clouds, when a shower would be coming. . . . Once I remember leaning on the fence, watching the shower, as it came nearer and nearer, considering its beauty, rather than my exposure to the rain.[7]

Nine years later, in his essay "Up Among the Clouds," published in *The Crayon* the same year he painted *Coast Scene* (1855), he wrote: "Of all the gifts of the Creator, few are more beautiful, and less heeded, than the sky." Part of the great mission of the artist, he continued, "should be to give the delicate and evanescent beauty, that every hour in the day presents itself in the sky. . . ." Cropsey went on to describe how the region of the rain cloud excited a particularly emotional effect on the observer, as

. . . in a higher region of it, parted and drifting, spraylike, over the blue, with the sunbeams flickering through it, there is often presented a sky more pictorial than all others. . . . It is perhaps in its grandest moods more impressive than all the other cloud regions—awakening the deepest emotions of gloom, dread, and fear; or sending thrilling sensations of joy and gladness through our being.[8]

Cropsey tried to capture the constant movement and transformation of the sea and sky; the clouds in *Coast Scene* break like the waves below. Other American artists at mid-century also frequently painted both the approach and the breaking of the storm. As Cropsey noted: " 'The heavens declare the glory of God.' "[9]; the storm experience on the coast powerfully revealed the Divine presence. One writer asked in 1847:

For who, however timid he may be from natural disposition, can look upon the ocean in a time of its rage, and hear the mad roar of the crested billows, without losing all thoughts but those awakened by the majesty of nature displayed above and beneath him? Lakes, rivers, forests and mountains are beautiful, and indeed sublime. But are they animated beings like the waves of the ocean, whose hoarse and hollow voices are ever speaking in the sailor's ear—not showing him, but *telling* him in tones louder and more distinct than all the homilies ever delivered, "The Lord God Omnipotent reigneth?"[10]

[Codman], *Sailors' Life* (1847).

In *Book of the Artists* (1867), Tuckerman mentions Cole's influence on Cropsey:

Besides a remarkable tact and truth in color and a true sense of the picturesque, a moral interest was frequently imparted to his landscapes by their historical or allegorical significance, in which as in other respects he reminded his countrymen of Cole.[11]

Those other respects seem to be Cole's expressive brushwork and his romantic style, as in *View across Frenchman's Bay from Mount Desert Island, Maine, After a Squall*, 1845 (Cincinnati Art Museum).[12] Cole's painting was exhibited at the National Academy of Design in 1845, and it is conceivable that Cropsey saw it then and was influenced by it in his own version of a stormy coast scene. It seems fitting that Cropsey remarked that as early as 1840 he attributed his interest in painting partly to "my annual visits to the Academy of Design. . . ."[13]

NOTES
1. William S. Talbot, *Jasper F. Cropsey 1823-1900* (Ph.D. dissertation, New York University 1972. Reprint Garland Series, 1977), 315.
2. *Catalogue of the Third Winter Exhibition of the National Academy of Design (1869-1870) including the Third Annual Collection of the American Society of Painters in Water Colors*, page 14, no. 175, *Coast Scene*, J.F. Cropsey.

COAST SCENE, 1855
Oil on canvas, 17 x 26¼″
Signed lower center: *J.F. Cropsey 1855*
Suydam Collection

3. William S. Talbot, *Jasper F. Cropsey 1823-1900* (Exhibition catalogue, The National Collection of Fine Arts, Washington, D.C., 1970), 78.

4. *New-York Daily Times*, March 31, 1854. In National Academy of Design Artists Biographical Files.

5. Talbot, *Cropsey*, Exhibition catalogue, 78.

6. James Fenimore Cooper, "American and European Scenery Compared." In *The Home Book of the Picturesque, or, American Scenery, Art and Literature* (1852) (New York: G.P. Putnam's, 1868), 5.

7. Jasper F. Cropsey, "Reminiscenses of My Own Time," unfinished memorandum, 1846. Newington-Cropsey Foundation, Archives of American Art, Smithsonian Institution, N.Y., microfilm roll no. 336.

8. Jasper F. Cropsey, "Up Among the Clouds." *The Crayon* 2 (August 8, 1855), 79.

9. *Ibid.*, 79-80.

10. [John Codman], *Sailors' Life and Sailors' Yarns* (New York, 1847), 117-18. In Thomas Philbrik, *James Fenimore Cooper and the Development of American Sea Fiction* (Cambridge, Mass.: Harvard University Press, 1961), 197.

11. Henry T. Tuckerman, *Book of the Artists* (New York: G.P. Putnam's, 1867), 532-33.

12. See National Academy of Design Biographical Files on Cropsey.

13. Cropsey, "Reminiscences of My Own Time."

SMS

CHARLES TEMPLE DIX

(1838-1873)
ANA Elect 1861

Born February 25, Albany, N. Y. 1858 graduated from Union College, Schenectady, N. Y. Shortly thereafter moved to New York City to study art. Specialized in marine painting. Worked at Tenth Street Studio Building 1860-1862. Although elected did not submit diploma painting necessary for qualification as Associate of the National Academy of Design. Exhibited at Academy 1858, 1861, 1870, 1871, 1872. During Civil War served as major in the Union Army with father, General John A. Dix. After war traveled to Europe. 1867 exhibited at the Royal Academy, London. Also visited Gibraltar, the Channel Islands, and Rome. January 6, 1873, joined other American artists in Rome in signing resolution of mourning on death of John F. Kensett. Died March 11, Rome.

REFERENCES: Algernon Graves, *A Dictionary of Artists* (London: Henry Graves, 1901). George C. Groce and David H. Wallace, *Dictionary of American Artists 1564-1860* (New-York Historical Society, 1957). *A Century and a Half of American Art* (Exhibition catalogue, National Academy of Design, N.Y., 1975). Henry T. Tuckerman, *Book of the Artists* (New York: G. P. Putman's, 1867). H. Wilson, ed., *New York City Directory*, 74 (New York: John F. Trow, 1861).

Perhaps if Dix had lived beyond the age of thirty-five, his name would be more familiar to the public today. Of the hundreds of artists who exhibited at the National Academy of Design, Dix was always among the relatively few mentioned in the journalistic reviews. *The Crayon*, for example, noted that "Dix paints marine subjects with good appreciation of the movement of water and the atmospheric peculiarities of the sea."[1] This compliment was not insignificant in an age dominated by Ruskinian criticism, for John Ruskin considered the rendering of the sea one of the most difficult artistic undertakings:

. . . the sea *must* be legitimately drawn; it cannot be given as utterly disorganized and confused, its weight and mass must be expressed, and the efforts at expression of it end in failure with all but the most powerful men; even with these few a partial success must be considered worthy of the highest praise.[2]

Modern Painters (1855).

Capturing the exact time of day and specific character of natural objects was often central to the nineteenth-century aesthetic. Although the artist was expected to depart from indiscriminate imitation of nature just enough to emphasize its more sublime aspects, he was not allowed to stray too far from precise representation. God revealed Himself in every fragment of nature; thus, painting the landscape took on a moral aspect. Indeed, the artist's response to nature measured his moral character. Ralph Waldo Emerson wrote: "Man is fallen; nature is erect and serves as a differential thermometer, detecting the presence or absence of the divine sentiment in man."[3]

The search for a more profound understanding of the manifestations of the Almighty often led artists to explore the natural sciences. Geology was of particular importance. In 1859, *The Crayon* published an article on the "Relation Between Geology and Landscape Painting," which suggested that by observing the diversity of rocks and the processes of creation evident in various rock formations, the artist might attain ". . . the delightful consciousness that his picture is a representation of moral principles and sentiment; not merely an imitation."[4]

Rock strata represented the piling up of ages:

The solid earth, with its stores of organic remains, which now rises above the surface of the sea, may be compared to a vast collection of authentic records, which will reveal to man, as soon as he is capable of rightly interpreting them, an unbroken narrative of events commencing from a period indefinitely remote, and which, in all probability, succeeded each other after intervals of vast duration.[5]

Geology and Its Teaching (1861).

The same source held that scientific study of the fossils discovered in the layers of strata lent strong support to Charles Darwin's theory of evolution. Although this theory might have initially shaken the nineteenth-century artists' transcendental faith in the absolute in nature, they took solace for a while longer from the continued belief that God's natural laws were constant.

Dix's rocks are rendered with the exactitude of a geologist's examining eye. Perhaps his choice of subject matter was influenced by Ruskin's evaluation of the different types of rocks, the jagged, dramatic ones being the finest:

. . . these slaty crystallines form the noblest hills that are easily accessible, and seem to be thus calculated especially to attract observation, and reward it.[6]

Modern Painters (1855).

Ruskin attributed moral properties to the several forms of rock. He reconciled the apparent polarities of the eternal and the changing in his description of crystalline mountains:

We yield ourselves to the impression of their eternal, unconquerable stubbornness of strength; their mass seems the least yielding, least to be softened, or anywise dealt with by external force, of all earthly substance. And, behold, as we look farther into it, it is all touched and troubled, like waves by a summer breeze; rippled, far more delicately than seas or lakes are rippled; *they* only undulate along their surfaces—this rock trembles

MARBLEHEAD ROCKS, 1868
Oil on canvas, mounted on pressed wood panel, 38 x 60″
Signed lower left: *DIX 68* (monogram with letters DIX
superimposed and flanked by 68)
Gift of Mr. W. F. Havemeyer, 1911

through its every fibre . . . They [the mountains], which at first seem strengthened beyond the dread of any violence or change, are yet also ordained to bear upon them the symbol of a perpetual Fear: the tremor which fades from the soft lake and gliding river is sealed, to all eternity, upon the rock; and while things that pass visibly from birth to death may sometimes forget their feebleness, the mountains are made to possess a perpetual memorial of their infancy . . .[7]

The rocks that are fixed on Dix's canvas suggest the eternal in their petrified solidity. Yet their very form embodies the elements of change. In light of the prevailing beliefs, a spiritual interpretation may be read into Dix's landscape, as it might into many nineteenth-century American landscapes. Once again, Ruskin provides the key:

We take our idea of fearfulness and sublimity alternately from the mountains and the sea; but we associate them unjustly. The sea wave, with all its beneficence, is yet devouring and terrible; but the silent wave of the blue mountain is lifted towards heaven in a stillness of perpetual mercy; and the one surge, unfathomable in its darkness, the other, unshaken in its faithfulness, forever bear the seal of their appointed symbol:

Thy *righteousness* is like the great mountains:
Thy *judgments* are a great deep.[8]

Marblehead Rocks is an example of one of the many paintings

that Dix executed of the desolate New England coast, an area whose rugged, primeval character attracted artists from John F. Kensett to Winslow Homer. Dix's painting, however, does not evoke Kensett's luminist stillness; his sea thrashes too wildly to reflect the divine light in a luminist mirror. The waves are massive, looking forward to a sensibility more like that of Homer, with its post-Darwinian positivism.

NOTES

1. Review of the National Academy of Design exhibition, *The Crayon* 5 (1858), 147.
2. John Ruskin, *Modern Painters* (New York: John Wiley, 1855), 1:367.*
3. Ralph Waldo Emerson, "Nature," *Essays* 4 (1836; Boston: James R. Osgood and Company, 1876,) 146.
4. "Relation Between Geology and Landscape Painting," *The Crayon* 6 (1859), 255.
5. *Geology and Its Teaching, Especially as it Relates to the Development Theory as Propounded in "Vestiges of Creation," and Darwin's "Origin`of the Species"* (London: Houlston and Wright, 1861), 11.
6. Ruskin, *Modern Painters*, 4:113.
7. *Ibid.*, 114.
8. *Ibid.*, 95.

*In Library of the National Academy of Design

HR

131

WILLIAM TROST RICHARDS

(1833-1905)
HM 1862; NA 1871

William Trost Richards has been called an "ideal realist,"[1] a direct heir of Thomas Cole and the earlier Hudson River School generation. Richards established a reputation during the 1850s with highly detailed New England landscapes and nature studies such as those he exhibited at the Academy's annual exhibitions of 1858, 1859, and 1860: *Moonrise, Blackberry Bush, Study from Nature, The Spring,* and *Golden Rod and Blackberry.*[2] Richards was generally believed to have turned to marine painting around 1867: "He was primarily a landscape painter until after 1867, when a great storm at sea on his return from Europe drew his attention to the ocean, and thereafter he devoted more and more time to painting its varied moods . . ."[3]

He actually began before then, however, and in 1862 he painted a small oil entitled *Coastal Scene,* also in the Academy's collection.[4] Many of his marine paintings from the 1860s and 1870s are now considered among his finest works.[5] By the end of the 1870s his marines had earned him the reputation which would last the rest of his life. As a writer of 1877 wrote, "Mr. Richards's greatest triumphs have been achieved in what is known in Art as marine-painting."[6] Three years later, S.G.W. Benjamin also commented on Richards' renown as a marine painter:

Still another aspect of our scenery has been reproduced with fidelity by W.T. Richards, of Philadelphia. We refer to the long reaches of silvery shore and the sand-dunes which are characteristic of many parts of our Atlantic coast. . . . in his beach effects Mr. Richards maintains an important position; and if slightly mannered, has yet developed a style of subject and treatment which very effectively represents certain distinguishing features of our solemn coasts.[7]

Art in America (1880).

Still another critic reviewed a painting much like *Breaking Wave* when he wrote:

A recent picture of his . . . represents a scene on the ocean-shore. There is a little stretch of the sandy beach shown in the right foreground, but all else is water to the horizon-line. There is a broad and masterly sweep given to the wave-forms; every movement of the waves . . . is drawn and painted with power and skill. . . . we see the same patient elaboration of detail which belongs to his forest-studies, but it has a broader feeling, and we are at once instinctively impressed with its fidelity to Nature. This picture of the boundless ocean is impressive in its very simplicity. It contains no picturesque elements in the eyes of the multitude; but it commands attention from the memories of the sea-shore which it recalls, its play of light and shade on the swelling waves, its marvellous perspective and the charming unity of its tone. Mr. Richards's sea-pictures are usually grey-toned, and to some lovers of Art their delicacy of colouring in respect to tone is their most enjoyable feature.[8]

The Art Journal (1877).

Richards was familiar with the writings of John Ruskin, whose aesthetic guidelines were so important to the Americans. Ruskin had written:

To suggest the ordinary appearance of calm water—to lay on canvass [*sic*] as much evidence of surface and reflection as may make us understand that water is meant—is, perhaps the easiest task of art. . . . But to paint the actual play of hue on the reflective surface, or to give the flashing and rocket-like velocity of a noble cataract, or the precision and grace of the sea wave, so exquisitely modelled, though so mockingly transient—so mountainous in its form, yet so cloud-like in its motion . . . to do this perfectly, is beyond the power of man; to do it even partially, has been granted to but one or two, even of those few who have dared to attempt it.[9]

Ruskin, *Modern Painters* (1846).

In taking up Ruskin's challenge, Richards frequently sketched out of doors, following Durand's advice in his 1855 "Letters on Landscape Painting": "Yes! go first to Nature to learn to paint landscape . . ."[10] Similar guidelines were offered almost a decade later by the Society for the Advancement of Truth in Art, to which Richards belonged:

The new path into which the best minds of the present day summon the young to enter, is the earnest loving study of God's work of nature . . . Therefore, . . . the right course for young Artists is faithful and loving representations of Nature, "selecting nothing and rejecting nothing," seeking only to express the greatest possible amount of fact. . . . for Nature is absolutely right; it makes no difference to her whether Durand looks on her, or W.T. Richards; an Elm leaf is still oval and pointed, and a Hickory leaf long and sharp . . .[11]

The New Path (1863).

Richards, in sympathy with these ideals, studied and sketched from nature in its various forms. "There is," he wrote, "such a sense of strangeness and unreality in everything one sees for the first time, that as a painter I somehow lose hold of the facts that help to produce the impressions, and I have dared to try to paint only those things which I have seen long enough in some way to study."[12] Richards developed a studiously scientific approach to painting. Describing his methods in 1879, he wrote:

I watch and watch it [the ocean], try to disentangle its push and leap and recoil, make myself ready to catch the tricks of the big breakers and am always started out of my self possession by the thunder and the rush, jump backward up the loose shingle of the beach, sure this time I will be washed away; get soaked with spray, and am ashamed that I had missed getting the real drawing of such a splendid one, and this happens 20 times in an hour and I have never yet got used to it.[13]

So detailed were the results of his scrutiny that in the same year

BREAKING WAVE, 1887
Oil on canvas, 20 x 40″
Signed lower right: *Wm T. Richards. 1887*
Brewster Bequest

George Sheldon remarked: "He is a pre-Raphaelist, and his studies proper were begun on his return from this trip in 1858 [to Europe], he having been moved to them, he modestly says, by a growing conviction of his need of a painstaking and protracted study of Nature."[14] Other writers also commented on the detailed realism of his work:

... the sun is breaking through rich rifts of cloud; beneath lies a sandy beach—real sand, here—and tired waves are creeping in, ... Standing there, gazing into the far distance, we almost feel the dampness strike through our shoes ... "Nature and Art," says Goethe, "are divided by an enormous chasm." So they are. But we may safely trust ourselves upon the bridges which such conscientious labor builds across.[15]

Scribner's Monthly (1871).

An important aspect of Richards' discipline was the emphasis he placed on drawing: "When asked by younger men how to learn to paint, he always said, 'Learn to draw.' And he obeyed his own precept."[16] The Society for the Advancement of Truth in Art also reminded beginning artists that it was "their duty to strive for the greatest attainable power of drawing ..."[17] In 1912, a critic who was obviously sympathetic to the "old school" made the following comment, revealing much about general trends as well as about Richards' techniques:

If the paintings of Richards—landscapes and marines—represent any "school," that school is unknown or ignored today by nearly all our painters. "Nature" and "conscientious study"—does a generation of aspirants for tricky "effects" and smart "impressions" think of these in connection with painting? One can almost fancy some of our contemporary exhibitors saying: "Draw? Oh, no, I don't *draw*; I *paint*"—and if they do not say it they think it, even if they realize what a mighty serious and important thing "drawing" was to the men of the old school.[18]

Richards' essentially linear point-of-departure is apparent in *Breaking Wave* and in similar paintings, such as *On the Coast of New Jersey*, 1883 (Corcoran Gallery of Art) and *Seascape*, 1871 (private collection). His depiction of "long, thin, curving sheets of water" is a type also found in coastal scenes by Martin Johnson Heade, John F. Kensett, and James Hamilton.[19] A contemporary critic commented on the popularity of this subject among artists:

A few years ago, Mr. W.T. Richards took to cutting the thinnest waves he could, and laying them on sand-beaches; he has been followed by Bricher, and now by William De Haas, and the point of the contest seems to be to find out who can "sling" the smoothest, widest-circled, and most uninteresting disks of this sort.[20]

Scribner's Monthly (1875).

No specific location is given for *Breaking Wave*, although its similarities to *On the Coast of New Jersey* suggest that it may represent a section of the long, sandy shore of that state. After 1859, Richards frequently sketched the coast of New Jersey—he traveled there repeatedly between 1868 and 1874[21]—and his pencil and watercolor studies provided material to which he could return at any time. Linda Ferber suggests that Richards' titles may indicate the degree to which he "interpreted" or rearranged nature; he was likely to title the more literal transcriptions of nature with the names of their specific locations, but he felt freer to bestow poetic or general titles on landscapes that he rearranged or altered, however slightly.[22] Thus, *Breaking Wave* may indeed be a section of the New Jersey shore which the artist changed in some way.

Richards, who admired Thomas Cole and Frederic Church,[23] tried to infuse his landscapes with religious feeling in his own search for "a higher purpose than to make a good picture."[24] Like his poet wife, he felt that "To lucid minds the thoughts of Nature are the thoughts of God . . ."[25] and in 1876 he wrote to his friend George Whitney, "Every day I feel more deeply the strong influence of inanimate nature over heart and brain . . ."[26] Similar thoughts were expressed by Walt Whitman in an essay which seems especially appropriate:

Even as a boy, I had the fancy, the wish, to write a piece, perhaps a poem, about the sea-shore—that suggesting, dividing line, contact, junction, the solid marrying the liquid—that curious, lurking something, . . . which means far more than its mere first sight, grand as that is—blending the real and ideal, and each made portion of the other. . . . There is a dream, a picture, that for years at intervals, . . . has come noiselessly up before me . . . It is nothing more or less than a stretch of interminable white-brown sand, hard and smooth and broad, with the ocean perpetually, grandly, rolling in upon it, . . . This scene, this picture, I say, has risen before me at times for years.[27]

Whitman, "Sea-Shore Fancies" (1881).

Notes

1. Linda S. Ferber, *William T. Richards (1833-1905): American Landscape and Marine Painter* (Ph.D. dissertation, Columbia University, 1978. Reprint, Garland Series, N.Y., 1980), 201.
2. Mary Bartlett Cowdrey, ed., *National Academy of Design Exhibition Record, 1826-1860* (New York: J.J. Little & Ives, 1943), 2:96.
3. "Mr. Richards's Works Pencil Drawings and Small Watercolors by Him, on View at the Fogg Art Museum, Cambridge," *Boston Evening Transcript*, March 11, 1918, 11.
4. Card catalogue of paintings, National Academy of Design.
5. Ferber, *Richards* (1980), 239.
6. "American Painters.—William T. Richards," *The Art Journal* 3 (new series, 1877), 243.
7. S.G.W. Benjamin, *Art in America, A Critical and Historical Sketch* (New York: Harper & Bros., 1880), 74-75. Also published in "Fifty Years of American Art, 1828-1878," *Harper's New Monthly Magazine* 59, no. 352 (September 1879), 484.
8. "American Painters," 244.
9. John Ruskin, *Modern Painters* (1846; New York: E.P. Dutton, 1929), 2:55-56.
10. A.B. Durand, "Letters on Landscape Painting. Letter 1.," *The Crayon*, 1 (January 3, 1855), 2.
11. "Introductory," *The New Path*, no. 1 (May), 3; "Association for the Advancement of the Truth in Art," no. 1 (May), 11; "A Few Questions Answered," no. 2 (June), 15 (New York; Society for the Advancement of Truth in Art, 1863).
12. Letter from Richards to William Willcox. In Linda Ferber, *William Trost Richards, American Landscape and Marine Painter, 1833-1905* (Exhibition catalogue, The Brooklyn Museum, N.Y., June 20-July 29, 1973), 34.
13. Letter from Richards to George Whitney, July 14, 1879, from Wyke Regis, Dorset, England. In Ferber, *Richards*, (1980) 382-83.
14. George W. Sheldon, *American Painters* (New York: D. Appleton, 1879), 60.
15. "The National Academy Exhibition," *Scribner's Monthly* 2, no. 3 (July 1871), 330.
16. "Mr. Richards' Works," 11.
17. "Association for the Advancement of the Truth in Art," *The New Path* (New York: Society for the Advancement of Truth in Art, 1863), no. 1 (May), 11.
18. "*Richards: Masterpieces of the Sea*," book review, *International Studio* (New York, December 1912), xlvii-xlviii.
19. Ferber, *Richards* (1973), 31.
20. "The Academy of Design," *Scribner's Monthly* 10, no. 2 (June 1875), 251.
21. Ferber, *Richards* (1980) 228.
22. *Ibid.*, 325. An example of a "literal transcription of nature" is *Cove on Conanicut Island* (c. 1877, Cooper-Hewitt Museum, Smithsonian Institution). An example of an "interpreted" or "rearranged" landscape is *The League Long Breakers Thundering on the Reef* (1887, The Brooklyn Museum).
23. *Ibid.*, 15.
24. Letter from Richards to T.W. Richards, August 29, 1855, from Paris. In Ferber, *Richards* (1980), 66. In another letter written to an unknown addressee, September 18, 1855, from Florence, Richards complained that the paintings of Claude-Joseph Vernet that they had "no spark of refinement, no earnest motive, no noble purpose." In Ferber, *Richards* (1980) 65.
25. Anna Matlack Richards, "Sonnet—xvi," *Letter and Spirit* (Boston: J.G. Cupples, 1891), 31. An 1898 edition of this book of sonnets was illustrated by Anna Richards, their daughter.
26. Letter from Richards to George Whitney, 1876. In Ferber, *Richards* (1973), 32.
27. Walt Whitman, "Sea-Shore Fancies" (c. 1881), Floyd Stovall, ed., *Prose Works 1892 (2 vols.), vol. 1, Specimen Days* (New York: New York University Press, 1963), 138-139.

KN

Twelve untitled sketches
Oil: seven on wood panel, five on academy board,
3½ x 6″ each.
Unsigned
Brewster Bequest

Thomas Creighton, in his "Reminiscences" of William Trost Richards (1924), recalled meeting the artist:

I never met him but once, and that was in Carl Weber's studio over Mr. Earle's store [in Frankford, Pennsylvania]. He had made an oil sketch box, a thumb box he called it, from a flat cigar box, and he told us with great enthusiasm how handy it was to sketch near the surf. Mr. Weber told me at that time that he knew Mr. Richards very well, and that Mr. Richards had received instruction and advice from Mr. Weber's father [Paul Weber].[1]

The sketch box described by Creighton evidently served as an easel for small panels like the ones exhibited here and, simultaneously, as a supply case. Presumably, it would have allowed the artist greater mobility and a wider selection of vantage points from which to do plein-air oil sketches. According to Edith Ballinger Price, Richards' granddaughter, "WTR had three sizes of oil sketchboxes—this was the smallest, to be taken handily on short trips or brief walking excursions."[2] Wood and academy-board panels were cut in varying sizes, depending upon the sketch box to be used—the smallest was 3 ½ x 6 inches, the size exhibited here—and the panels were then "slipped into the slotted lid" of the box, which supported them while the artist painted.[3]

This image of Richards, standing at the water's edge with his sketch box, is one which he embellished himself in a letter to his friend and patron George Whitney in 1872: "I and my umbrelly, and a weather-beaten nose go up and down the shore together and take the sunshine and the pictures."[4]

Still another account tells us:

. . . he stood for hours in the early days of Atlantic City or Cape May, with folded arms, studying the motion of the sea,—until people thought him insane. After days of gazing, he made pencil notes of the action of the water. He even stood for hours in a bathing suit among the waves, trying to analyse the motion.[5]

Morris, *William T. Richards* (1912).

Studies such as these, brushed in with a quick and painterly stroke, were generally intended as references for larger, more detailed paintings to be done later. A critic of 1879 noted:

The Society of American Artists, composed chiefly of those young gentlemen, did not invite Mr. Richards to contribute to their first and celebrated exhibition in the spring of 1878. . . . The fact is, that most of these young gentlemen are exhibiting as finished pictures what to Mr. Richards are simply studio-studies, or out-of-door sketches—works the excellence of which Mr. Richards, doubtless, would be the first to see and acknowledge, but the incompleteness of which would be, in his eyes, positively painful and certainly inexcusable, except on the ground of juvenile incapacity.[6]

Sheldon, *American Painters* (1879).

In a letter to George Whitney, Richards voiced his own awareness of this difference in style. Referring to a large gouache of a Newport subject, which was shown at the Grosvenor Gallery in 1879, he said: "My drawing is hung between two Whistlers (oil)— 'a harmony in blue and green' and 'a harmony in blue and gold.' . . . The effect is peculiar an[d] looks like a joke; for my picture is by contrast so exceedingly realistic."[7]

There are many small panels by Richards in existence. He seems to have dashed off sketches like these, almost compusively, wherever he was.[8] This abundance indicates the artist's scientific interest in recording the infinite variations of wave action, lighting, and rock formations.

Richards became profoundly impressed with the sea, with the endless, ever-changing action of waves, and with the superb possibilities of cloud formations and atmospheric effects. To the sea he addressed the same patient and profound study which he had given to the details of landscape, and found a limitless opportunity to exercise his remarkable accuracy of draughtsmanship in the most difficult of problems.[9]

C. Matlack Price, "Ideal of Sincerity in Art" (1918).

The sketches were given to the Academy framed as they are now, in two composite frames holding six sketches each. According to Edith Ballinger Price, they were framed by the donors, Anna and William Brewster, and not by the artist: "All sketches, of whatever size, were just his file of notes—never intended to be exhibited or sold. He would be surprised . . . WTR most certainly did *not* frame the little panels. Aunt Anna doubtless did, thinking it would be nice to display them . . ."[10]

Although it would be difficult, if not impossible, to verify the exact location of each scene represented, a number have been labeled in pencil on the back of the panels. Edith Ballinger Price has noted in a letter:

In the autumn of 1905 my mother said to WTR (I was present) "Father, YOU know where all your sketches were made, but we don't. Let us mark them—we can do it bit by bit on Sunday afternoons." Though WTR didn't see why anyone would want to know the locality of his notes, he agreed. Mother began with the *smallest* size, and as she held them up, WTR identified them and she wrote on the back (I even marked some, in a childish hand.) I have a dozen or so of the same panels—all Mentone, Amalfi, or Bude Haven and Newquay. This marking was a good start (no *dates* were added, alas.) By the following Sunday, Grandfather was dead.[11]

Of the set which includes mainly flat beach scenes, only the first and second from the left were labeled: the first as "New Jersey," the second as "Bude Haven," a site in Cornwall, England. The other sketches, with their simple views of water and sky, could represent almost any ocean view.

The second set of sketches, studies of rocky cliffs, was more thoroughly labeled. From left to right, they were identified as "Foundations of Nero's Palace Near [?]," "Bude Haven," "Bude Haven," "Mentone, 1868," "Near Newquay [?]," and "Near Newquay" (another Cornish site). The date listed on the back of the fourth sketch ("Mentone, 1868") is problematic. The location probably refers to Menton, France (Italian spelling is Mentone), but Richards does not seem to have traveled abroad that year. Linda Ferber suggests a general 1890s dating for the sketches as a group because they are similar to many Richards painted during the final years of his life.[12] His European travels during this period included an 1892 visit to Italy (Venice, Capri, and Naples) and trips to Cornwall in 1892, 1896, and 1897.[13]

Richards studied and painted along the Atlantic coast from the rocks of Maine to the sands of New Jersey. Rocks, cliffs, shoals, beaches—these were not enough, and his eager interest in the sea in all its moods and manners took him painting in England, Scotland, Ireland, Wales, Cornwall—from John O'Groat's House to Land's End, and all about the Channel Islands, the Orkneys, Shetland and Guernsey.[14]

C. Matlack Price, "Ideal of Sincerity in Art" (1918).

Contemporary travel and guidebooks describe scenes which resemble those Richards sketched:

From Penzance, along the coast to Land's End, are wonderful formations in granite,—caverns, Druidic monuments, and ever the grand ocean views which give such majesty to the scene. . . . Two miles west of the point [Lizard Point] is the famous Kynance Cove. . . . one of the wonders of the Cornish coast. A steep descent leads down to the shore, among wild rocks that are grouped as if by a painter's hand, and with their dark and varied colors contrast exquisitely with the light tints of the sandy beach and the changeful azure of the sea.[15]

Leo de Colange, *The Picturesque World* (1879).

Such descriptions could have appealed to Richards not only through their potential as paintings; the references to various rock formations might have piqued his scientific curiosity about nature, and the passages concerning "Druidic monuments" could have attracted his romantic sensibility. So, too, could references to ruins and Roman villas have appealed to him:

The environs of Naples present a singular variety of views and objects; on the Pozzuoli shore we have seen remains of the convulsions of nature and of the prodigious works of man, remains which added to their present solitude give a venerable aspect to these regions where nature and man lie buried under the works produced by their efforts. . . . These shores were [in Roman times] covered with splendid villas and such sumptuous edifices both public and private . . .[16]

L. Piale, *Guide to Naples and Sicily* (1847).

Notes

1. Thomas Creighton, "Some Reminiscences of William T. Richards (The Artist)," *Paper Read before the Historical Society of Frankford [Pennsylvania]*, 3, no. 1 (Philadelphia: Walther Printing House, 1924), 13.
2. Edith Ballinger Price, in a letter to the author, May 8, 1980, from Virginia Beach, Virginia. I am indebted to Ms. Price for her generous assistance.
3. Linda S. Ferber, *William T. Richards (1833-1905): American Landscape and Marine Painter* (Ph.D. dissertation, Columbia University. 1978. Reprint, Garland Series, New York, 1980), 384.
4. Letter from Richards to George Whitney, July 2, 1872, from Good Harbor Beach, Gloucester. In Ferber, *Richards* (1980), 232.
5. Harrison S. Morris, *William T. Richards, Masterpieces of the Sea* (Philadelphia: J.B. Lippincott, 1912), 10. In this statement Morris quotes Richards' son.
6. George W. Sheldon, *American Painters* (New York: D. Appleton, 1879), 64.
7. Letter from Richards to George Whitney, 1879. In Linda S. Ferber, *William Trost Richards, American Landscape and Marine Painter, 1833-1905* (Exhibition catalogue, The Brooklyn Museum, New York, June 20-July 29, 1973), 34.
8. Linda Ferber, in conversation, April 22, 1980.
9. C. Matlack Price, "The Ideal of Sincerity in Art. Some Notes on the Work of William T. Richards," *The Art World and Arts & Decoration* 9 (September 1918), 259.
10. Edith B. Price, Letter, May 8, 1980.
11. *Ibid.*
12. Linda Ferber, in conversation, April 22, 1980.
13. Ferber, *Richards*, (1980), unpaginated chronology.
14. C. Matlack Price, "Ideal of Sincerity in Art," 259.
15. Leo de Colange, *The Picturesque World or, Scenes in Many Lands*, (Boston: Estes and Lauriat, 1878), 2:471, 465.
16. L. Piale, *Guide to Naples and Sicily* (Rome: L. Piale, Bookseller, 1847), 137, 119.

KN

Last summer I met a gentleman who . . . had just received a letter from a brother in Switzerland, an artist by profession, in which he said, that, "having travelled over all Switzerland, and the Rhine and Rhone region, he had not met with scenery, which, judged from a purely artistic point of view, combined so many beauties in connection with such grandeur as the lakes, mountains, and forest of the Adirondack region presented to the gazer's eye."[1]
                    William H. H. Murray, *Adventures in the Wilderness* (1869).

. . . in the Lake Belt the mountains are more scattered and broken, and are arranged in vast groups or clusters around some high peak that overlooks the wilderness of the lakes. . . . Another group lies around Mount Whiteface, whose Indian name is *Wa-ho-par-ten-ie*, and at whose base sleeps Lake Placid. . . . Upon its bare, storm-beaten summit some enthusiastic lover of the grand in nature has cut with reverent chisel, deep and clear into its everlasting rock, these words: THANKS BE TO GOD FOR THE MOUNTAINS.[2]
           Nathaniel Bartlett Sylvester, *Northern New York and Adirondack Wilderness* (1877).

Adventurers, vacationers, and artists alike were captivated by the beauty of New York's Adirondack Mountains, described in an 1894 guidebook as "far superior in variety and sublimity to the famous Catskills."[3] The mountains of the Northeast, with their lofty peaks surrounded by dense forests and quiet lakes, offered American artists "a union of the picturesque, the sublime, and magnificent."[4] It is not surprising, then, that Essex County, a region of the Adirondacks that includes Schroon Lake and Lake Placid, became a favorite sketching haunt of the artists. Richards was particularly fond of the Adirondacks, as evidenced by his many trips there. He first visited the mountains in 1855 and returned two years later. He may have traveled there again in 1859, and then made at least three, possibly five, trips back to the mountains during the 1860s.[5]

   This small oil sketch, showing Whiteface Mountain reflected in the mirrorlike waters of Lake Placid, was probably painted as late as the summer of 1904, when Richards again returned to the Adirondacks.[6] He was seventy-one years old at the time, but despite his age and the effects of a mild stroke, he was still very active as an artist.[7] Drawing and painting incessantly, Richards sometimes completed small paintings simply for his own pleasure. Thus Linda Ferber suggests that this painting, though conceived in broad areas of color and seemingly hastily painted in the manner of a sketch, may have been considered by Richards to be complete in and of itself.[8]

The broad strokes that record the essentials of the Adirondack scene produce a composition that is strikingly modern in its directness and simplicity of form. The work, in fact, shows a striking resemblance to certain works by the twentieth-century landscapist Georgia O'Keeffe. Her lyrical forms, though derived from nature, have, in their simplicity, an abstract quality, as do the images of the mountain and its bold reflection in this work by Richards.[9]

From the late 1880s to his death in 1905, Richards produced numerous oil sketches of a similar economy of form (see framed sketches, p. 135). Many served as studies for larger, more finished works. In general, Richards judged the sketches to be "lacking in charm"—merely the "bare bones." As Ferber states, Richards "either could not—or would not sustain" so bold and direct a style "on a larger scale."[10] However, he might have been concerned about the stylistic differences between his sketches and the finished works, since his wife remarked to his biographer, Harrison Morris, that she threw "tables and chairs at William to make him paint broadly."[11]

The "bare bones" of this painting, the lone peak of Whiteface Mountain and the still lake, viewed in the absence of any human presence, communicate a sense of solitude and silence—a silence characteristic of the Adirondack wilderness.

An 1864 guidebook describes the region:

The solitary summits in the distance, the cedars and firs which clothe the rocks and shores must be seen; the solitude must be felt; or if it is broken by the scream of the panther, the shrill cry of the northern diver, or the shout of the hunter, the echo from the thousand hills must be heard before all the truth in the scene can be realised.[12]

Joel Tyler Headley, *The Adirondack* (1864).

The "still, small voice" of nature—which Barbara Novak has identified as the "new sublime"—spoke with as much authority as the awesome, terrible, and magnificent in the nineteenth century.[13] As early as 1835, Thomas Cole spoke of the experience of silence and solitude as a sublime emotion in his "Essay on American Scenery." He described two lakes he had visited at Franconia Notch in the White Mountains:

. . . they have such an aspect of deep seclusion, of utter and unbroken solitude, that when standing on their brink a lonely traveler, I was overwhelmed with an emotion of the sublime . . . over all, rocks, wood, and water, brooded the spirit of repose, and the silent energy of nature stirred the soul to its inmost depths.

I would not be understood that these lakes are always tranquil; but that tranquility is their great characteristic. . . . in scenes like these the richest chords are struck by the gentler hand of nature.[14]

Richards himself often sought out solitude. In an essay of 1850

or 1851, he wrote that he was "fond of solitary walks . . . mid wild tangled woods . . . where one might with some choice companion, some spirit stirring poem or some modest sketch book, while away a lifetime . . ."[15] Certainly he must have been sensitive to the silence that reigned in the wilderness of the Adirondacks, and in this sparse painting he gives expression to its poetry.

Although he explored various approaches—from the extremes of a detailed Ruskinian realism to a simplicity of conception that approaches abstraction—Richards remained grounded in the mid nineteenth-century landscape tradition. Though he studied nature incessantly and refused to "lose hold of the facts,"[16] his vision was that of a romantic "who divined a spiritual significance behind the appearance of reality."[17] Thus in 1876 he wrote to his patron, George Whitney:

Every day I feel more deeply the strong influence of inanimate nature over heart and brain; I go to Wordsworth with a fresher sense of all that he meant, and find in him that which is "as true as the Bible"—How much I wish I could say to others, some little of what he says to me.[18]

Notes

1. William H.H. Murray, *Adventures in the Wilderness* (Boston: Fields, Osgood & Co., 1869), 10-11.
2. Nathaniel Bartlett Sylvester, *Historical Sketches of Northern New York and the Adirondack Wilderness* (Troy, N.Y.: William H. Young, 1877), 54.
3. E.R. Wallace, *Descriptive Guide to the Adirondacks* (Syracuse: Watson Gill, 1894), xvi.
4. Thomas Cole, "Essay on American Scenery" (1835). In "On Divers Themes from Nature," edited and introduced by Barbara Novak. In Kynaston McShine, ed., *The Natural Paradise: Painting in America, 1800-1950* (Exhibition catalogue, Museum of Modern Art, N.Y., 1976), 95.
5. Linda S. Ferber, *William Trost Richards (1833-1905): American Landscape and Marine Painter* (Ph.D. dissertation, Columbia University, 1978. Reprint, Garland Series, N.Y., 1980), 45, 104.
6. *Ibid.*, unpaginated chronology. This same subject appears in an 1885 photography by Louise Deshong Woodbridge, *The "Carry," Lake Placid to Whiteface*, private collection. For illustration, see John Wilmerding *et al.*, *American Light: The Luminist Movement, 1850-1875* (Exhibition catalogue, National Gallery of Art, Washington, D.C., 1980), 144.
7. Linda S. Ferber, *William Trost Richards, American Landscape and Marine Painter 1833-1905* (Exhibition catalogue, The Brooklyn Museum, New York, June 20-July 29, 1973), 102.
8. Conversation with Linda Ferber, Curator of Nineteenth Century American Art, The Brooklyn Museum, April 22, 1980.
9. See Lloyd Goodrich and Doris Bry, *Georgia O'Keeffe* (Exhibition catalogue, Whitney Museum of American Art, N.Y., 1970).
10. Ferber, *Richards* (1980), 373.
11. Harrison S. Morris, *Masterpieces of the Sea: William Trost Richards* (Philadelphia: J.B. Lippincott, 1912), 43.
12. Joel Tyler Headley, *The Adirondack; or Life in the Woods* (London: Clarke, Beeton, 1864), iv.
13. See Barbara Novak, *Nature and Culture: American Landscape and Painting, 1825-1875* (New York: Oxford University Press, 1980), 18-33.
14. Thomas Cole, "Essay on American Scenery" (1835). In John W. McCoubrey, ed., *American Art 1700-1960, Sources and Documents* (Englewood Cliffs, N.J.: Prentice-Hall, 1965), 104-105.
15. William Trost Richards, "Lansdowne" (1850 or 1851). In Ferber, *Richards* (1980), 10.
16. Ferber, *Richards* (1980), 374.
17. Ferber, *Richards* (1973), 32.
18. *Ibid.*, 32, Letter from Richards to George Whitney, 1876.

CC

Untitled (moonlight scene)
Watercolor on blue-gray paper, 6⅞ x 13⅜″
Unsigned
Brewster Bequest

Anna and William Brewster suggested that this moonlit water-color sketch was probably painted "in Germany about 1867."[1] It would be difficult to verify this, although we know that Richards made two trips to Germany—in 1856 and 1867.[2] During his second trip he visited Darmstadt, and in a letter to his patron, George Whitney, mentioned scenes such as this: "There is good nature to be enjoyed about Darmstadt. The fine forest of the Odenwald and the quaint villages give me endless pleasure, and I find great interest every where in the surrounding country."[3]

The painting does suggest an affinity with such German romantic artists as Caspar David Friedrich, whose interest in moonlit landscapes is well known. It is possible that this similarity indicates a more definite influence; Richards' painting instructor, Paul Weber, was also from Germany. This interconnection of Germany, romanticism, and moonlight was noted by critics such as Richard Muther, who wrote in 1907 that "for a time German Romanticism, with its lyrical temper and its sickly passion for moonshine, became the determining influence [on American painting]."[4] Other writers also commented on the impact of German art in America:

Down to the time of the Philadelphia Exposition, in 1876, . . . we slumbered inert and dumb under the German fog, through which we heard, while half protesting, half believing, the droning professors and lumbering critics proclaiming Cornelius and Overbeck the successors of Michael Angelo and Raphael, and calling us to the new cult of the Lessings, the Pilotys, the Müllers, the Schnorrs, and the Kaulbachs—"terrible Muses." . . . German pictures filled the dealers' shops, German artists monopolized the market, and for several years a public gallery for the exclusive exhibition of German pictures was a favorite showplace in New York.[5]

Cook, "Some Present Aspects of Art in America" (1896).

Linda Ferber suggests that a more likely location for the scene is the countryside near Frankford or Germantown, Pennsylvania, or some other small town in the Philadelphia vicinity.[6] Both Richards and his wife grew up in this area, and in 1859 or 1860 they made Germantown their home.[7] The scene depicted has marked similarities to a larger oil of 1870, *On Frankfort [sic] Creek Near Philadelphia* (private collection).[8] Although seen from different points of view, both include a cluster of rooftops dominated by a single pointed church spire. Both are nocturnes painted in muted tonalities, and in each the moon, placed somewhat off-

139

center and reflected in water below, is a dominant feature. An additional shared motif is the rail fence, which seems to be of identical construction in the two paintings. The paper Richards used for the watercolor is the blue-gray variety he favored from around 1868 to 1870, although he used it at other times as well.[9]

With its Gothic tracery of trees silhouetted against the moon, the painting adds to the American iconology of moonlight, which includes works by Washington Allston in the first half of the century and those of Ralph Albert Blakelock and Albert Pinkham Ryder in the second half. Birge Harrison's *The Hidden Moon* (c. 1910), in the present exhibition (p. 156), is another such addition.

Though pantheistic overtones are frequently present in Richards' paintings, here we find a suggestion as well of the late nineteenth-century mysticism even more apparent in works by Blakelock and Ryder. A statement made in 1914 by Walter Pach, in an attempt to define overall trends in American painting, seems applicable to paintings by these artists:

As Romanticism tinged the mind and the art of the early nineteenth century, and Realism, or the scientific spirit, its later years, so every indication to-day points to a deepening interest in the matters which go beyond self-conscious reasoning, and are dealt with by the power of intuition.[10]

"Point of View of the 'Moderns.'"

Richards' paintings actually combine all three elements cited here; although romanticism and realism are generally more prevalent in his work, this small watercolor is one of relatively few which verge on the mystical. Appropriate to Richards' work is the idea that "Fidelity to nature is a characteristic trait of American landscape art . . . a fidelity not inconsistent with the widest display of imagination and fancy, nor with freedom of individual expression."[11]

The moon frequently served as the subject for literary as well as visual explorations of mystic themes. Emerson wrote in his *Journal* of 1838:

Last night the moon rose behind four distinct pine-tree tops in the distant woods and the night at ten was so bright that I walked abroad. But the sublime light of night is unsatisfying, provoking; it astonishes but explains not. Its charm floats, dances, disappears, comes and goes, but palls in five minutes after you have left the house. Come out of your warm, angular house, resounding with few voices, into the chill, grand, instantaneous night, with such a Presence as a full moon in the clouds, and you are struck with poetic wonder . . . I sow the sun and moon for seeds.[12]

Richards and a number of contemporary writers also shared a general love of antiquity, which the moon certainly nourished:

Great restorer of antiquity, great enchanter! In a mild night, when the harvest or hunter's moon shines unobstructedly, . . . The village street is then as wild as the forest. New and old things are confounded. I know not whether I am sitting on the ruins of a wall, or on the material which is to compose a new one. . . . Consider the moonlight, so civil, yet so savage![13]
Thoreau, "Night and Moonlight" (1863).

A more quietly poetic treatment of the subject is Walt Whitman's essay of the same year, "The White House by Moonlight." It, too, recalls elements of Richards' small watercolor:

I wander about a good deal, sometimes at night under the moon. . . . everywhere a soft transparent hazy, thin, blue moon-lace, hanging in the air . . . under the lustrous flooding moon, full of reality, full of illusion—the forms of the trees, leafless, silent, in trunk and myriad angles of branches, under the stars and sky . . .[14]

Another passage by Thoreau indicates that he was impressed as well by certain visual effects which inspired Richards' painting: "I suddenly saw the moon with her attendant stars reflected full from a puddle in the road, and for a moment the earth dissolved under my feet."[15]

NOTES
1. Label, clipped to painting, in William T. Brewster's handwriting. It is difficult to determine whether such identifications were made by both the Brewsters or by Mr. Brewster alone, as Anna Richards Brewster died before the bequest was completed.
2. Linda Ferber, *William T. Richards (1833-1905): American Landscape and Marine Painter* (Ph.D. dissertation, Columbia University, 1978. Reprint, Garland series, New York, 1980), unpaginated chronology.
3. Letter from Richards to George Whitney, February 4, 1867, from Darmstadt. In *ibid.*, 199.
4. Richard Muther, *The History of Modern Painting*, 4 vols. (New York: E.P. Dutton, 1907), iv, 290. Muther continues with a discussion of Bierstadt's introduction of the "Düsseldorfian manner" to American painting.
5. Clarence Cook, "Some Present Aspects of Art in America," *The Chautauquan* 23, no. 5 (August 1896), 593-94.
6. In conversation with Linda Ferber, April 22, 1980.
7. Ferber, *Richards*, 1980, unpaginated chronology.
8. *On Frankfort Creek Near Philadelphia*, 1870, oil on canvas, signed and dated, 13 x 24", collection of Ellicott Wright, Jamestown, R.I. I am grateful to Linda Ferber for bringing this painting to my attention.
9. In conversation with Linda Ferber, April 22, 1980.
10. Walter Pach, "The Point of View of the 'Moderns,' " part IV of a series of five essays entitled "This Transitional Age in Art," *The Century Magazine* 87, no. 6 (April 1914), 864.
11. "Progress in the Fine Arts," unidentified article in National Academy of Design clipping files, labeled "1876," 412.
12. Ralph Waldo Emerson, *Journal*, May 11, 1838. In Bliss Perry, ed., *The Heart of Emerson's Journals* (Boston: Houghton Mifflin, 1926), 128-29.
13. Henry David Thoreau, "Night and Moonlight," *The Atlantic Monthly* 12, no. 73 (November 1863), 582.
14. Walt Whitman, "The White House by Moonlight" (February 24, 1863). In Floyd Stovall, ed., *Prose Works 1892*, (2 vols.), vol. 1, *Specimen Days* (New York: New York University Press, 1963), 40-41.
15. Henry David Thoreau, *The Moon* (Boston: Houghton Mifflin, 1927), 24.

KN

Untitled, 1901 (garden scene)
Watercolor, 5 x 8″
Signed lower left: *Wm T. Richards, 1901*
Brewster Bequest

In labeling Richards' watercolors at the time of the Brewster Bequest, Anna and William Brewster identified this scene as Fidelia Bridges' garden in Canaan, Connecticut.[1] Bridges was one of Richards' students around 1860, and remained a friend long afterwards.[2]

The painting is unique among those given to the Academy by the Brewsters; most of the Richards paintings are coastal scenes. The size, date, and subject of this painting suggest it may belong to a group of sixteen watercolors listed in the Academy's records as "'Birthday' pictures to his daughter Anna, painted between 1890 and 1901, 8 x 5[″] in size, in folder, very choice."[3]

The composition is a variation of the picturesque Claudian format used so frequently by artists earlier in the century. It includes a calm body of water mirroring objects near it, trees partially framing the scene, and mountains in the distance. Water was an important element of the picturesque ideal, whether represented in painting or gardening:

Water may be considered among the most pleasing objects of any scene. . . . Where a brook runs through the grounds [of an estate] it is a happy circumstance; and the greatest care should be taken that its character be not injured by the misapplied interference of art.[4]
    Bartell, *Picturesque Improvements in Ornamented Cottages* (1904).

There is nothing . . . that gives more ease, and has so fine an effect in the ornamental and flower garden department, as ornamental water, in any form it can be introduced; it gives a relief to the eye, from too much sameness of the living part of the created world . . . Independent of this, the cooling aspect it assumes, forms a fine feature in rural scenery.[5]
    Sayers, *American Flower Garden Companion* (1839).

This small watercolor adds to a tradition of flower iconology in painting, although individual flowers are less prominent here than in closer views by artists such as Martin Johnson Heade and John La Farge. The rustic floral garden, too, had a place in the picturesque view; as late as 1909, British writer Stewart Dick declared that

. . . when we reach the cottage garden we come to the dearest and most familiar garden of all. . . . In its small space it contains so much. Flowers in profusion everywhere . . . perhaps its greatest charm is its informality and lack of arrangement. The flowers cluster together in a companionable sort of way.[6]

Dick, *The Cottage Homes of England.*

Ruskin's advice to artists is similar:

In drawing villages, take great pains with the gardens; a rustic garden is in every way beautiful. If you have time, draw all the rows of cabbages, and hollyhocks, and broken fences, and wandering eglantines, and bossy roses: you cannot have better practice, nor be kept by anything in purer thoughts.[7]

Ruskin, "Sketching from Nature" (1865).

The moral and symbolic power of flowers suggested by Ruskin has long been a part of European iconology, and found expression in nineteenth-century America:

The culture of ornamental plants, is the most conclusive evidence of an advanced state of civilization. So unerring is it, that in passing through the country, I should have no hesitation in pointing out the relative moral condition of each family, from the plants which surround the house, or appear in its windows. They are the sure indications of intellectual cultivation and exemplary deportment. Vice and a love of plants are incompatible, for flowers are the emblem of virtue and the dearly cherished companions of pure hearts and polished minds. Where they are most fostered, the best faculties of the intellect and heart are most appreciated and developed.[8]

H.A.S. Dearborn, Letter, in *American Flower Garden Companion* (1839).

The nineteenth-century taste for the picturesque had, as yet another element, a corresponding preference for the old and worn:

The old gardens, although now gone to decay, are filled with a glory which is lacking in new gardens. The ancient trellises and ruined hedges have about them a glamour of the sunshine of olden days which are only to be lived over again in books or within their own boundaries. One feels the presence of the old worthies in the gardens as it is not felt in the houses . . . perhaps the greatest proof that the old appealed to them more than the new is found in the fact that they cared for their old gardens. Time could not tarnish their flowers. . . . When poverty pressed hard, the flower garden was the last thing to give evidence of it . . .[9]

Shurtleff, "Some Old New England Flower Gardens" (1899).

This yearning for things ancient, for objects or places with histori-

cal or cultural associations, was noted by an Englishwoman visiting America:

The Americans . . . would give anything if they could appropriate a Kenilworth Castle, or a Melrose or a Tintern Abbey, with its covering of ivy, and make it sustain some episode of their history. But though they can make railways, ivy is beyond them, and the purple heather disdains the soil of the New World.[10]

Isabella Lucy Bird, *Englishwoman in America* (1856).

Richards himself, in an undated essay, expressed similar thoughts:

I turned into a wood, where, after some little wandering I unexpectedly came upon the ruins of the Lansdowne baths . . . as I stood before them, strange mingled thoughts came crowding on the mind,—the sweet, wild flowers springing 'mong the scattered and forgotten stones whispered as with spirit-voices of both hope and love, while the old grey ruined walls, seemed all telling of the death of beauty. But they formed a glorious picture . . .[11]

Richards, "Lansdowne."

NOTES

1. Inscription on back of painting in William T. Brewster's handwriting. It is difficult to determine whether such identifications were made by both Brewsters or by Mr. Brewster alone, as Anna Richards Brewster died before the Bequest was completed.
2. Linda Ferber, *William T. Richards (1833-1905): American Landscape and Marine Painter* (Ph.D. dissertation, Columbia University, 1978. Reprint, Garland Series, New York, 1980), unpaginated chronology.
3. List entitled "William T. Richards, 1833-1905; Pictures and sketches bequeathed by his daughter, the late Anna R. Brewster, to the National Academy of Design," in Academy's file on the Brewster Bequest, included under subheading "Mounted Water Colors." The painting was mounted when given to the Academy at the time of the bequest.
4. Edmund Bartell, *Hints for Picturesque Improvements in Ornamented Cottages and their Scenery* (London: J. Taylor, Architectural Library, High Holborn, 1804. Published Westmead, England: Gregg International Publishers, 1971), 72-73.
5. Edward Sayers, *The American Flower Garden Companion, Adapted to the Northern and Middle States*, 2nd ed. (Boston: Weeks, Jordan, 1839), 21.
6. Steward Dick, *The Cottage Homes of England* (London: Edward Arnold, 1909), 228, 229, 232.
7. John Ruskin, "Sketching from Nature," *The Elements of Drawing*, originally published in 1857; this edition published in one volume with *The Ethics of the Dust* and *Fiction Fair and Foul*, 2nd ed. (1865, New York: Merrill and Baker, 1877), 311.
8. H.A.S. Dearborn, letter to Joseph Breck, from Hawthorn Cottage, Roxbury, March 28, 1838; in Sayers, *The American Flower Garden Companion*, vi.
9. Arthur A. Shurtleff, "Some Old New England Flower Gardens," *New England Magazine* 21, no. 4 (December 1899), 426, 423.
10. Isabella Lucy Bird, *The Englishwoman in America* (1856; reprint Madison, Wis.: University of Wisconsin Press, 1966), 135.
11. Linda Ferber, *William Trost Richards, American Landscape and Marine Painter 1833-1905* (Exhibition catalogue, The Brooklyn Museum, New York, June 20-July 29, 1973), 13.

KN

Untitled (marine with sailboats)
Watercolor, 8¼ x 14″
Unsigned
Brewster Bequest

Richards' watercolors from the late 1860s and 1870s—the height of his production in the medium—are generally considered among his best work. Of the two seascapes exhibited here, it is likely that the marine with sailboats was painted in the late 1860s or around 1870, and the marine, sunset slightly later, around the mid-1870s.[1]

Richards' contemporaries generally reacted favorably to his watercolors:

We have no artist so prolific, and at the same time so popular in the delineation of grey-toned coast scenes, as William T. Richards, of Philadelphia; but this year, unfortunately, he sent only two of this class of pictures to the exhibition—"High Tide, Brigantine Beach, New Jersey," and "Old Cedars" . . . Under this phase of Nature, Mr. Richards has no superior as a painter of water, and the precision of his drawing is shown in every wave-form, and is fully as interesting a study for the connoisseur as are the delicate gradations of colour with which they are brought out.

Art Journal (1875).

Another critic, writing a year earlier, was more reserved in his comments:

The European water-color painters, as a rule, are content with effects; the American water-color painters, as a rule, are anxious about details. The most remembable water-colors there were painted by A.F. Bellows, W.T. Richards, S.R. Gifford, L.C. Tiffany, J.D. Smillie, A.T. Bricher, and Miss F. Bridges. Mr. Richards always reminds us of himself: Mr. Bricher generally reminds us of Mr. Richards: Messrs. Gifford and Tiffany remind us of each other, with differences: Miss Bridges reminds us of no one. Mr. Richards's work is always good, but his range is limited, and his manner a little monotonous.[3]

Scribner's Magazine (1874).

Both writers were impressed with the high degree of detail in the paintings exhibited, a characteristic evident in the two shown here.[4]

A contemporary discussion of ten of Richards' watercolors of 1870, done near Atlantic City, New Jersey, indicates that his watercolors, too, were more than sketches:

Although supposedly painted on the spot as "notes for oil paintings," these watercolors are fully realized little compositions, with fore, middle, and background, in contrast to the rock studies of the summer before . . . It is highly likely that some of the foreground business in the 1870 series such as the anchor at the lower left in *Thoroughfare Absecon* . . . was added later in the studio in order to finish them more completely before sale . . .[5]

Metropolitan Museum of Art Handbook (1881).

That Richards intended such pieces for sale is also indicated by a catalogue of the sale of George Whitney's collection in 1885, which listed approximately sixty "water-colours, by Wm. T. Richards . . . painted to the order of or selected by Mr. Whitney."[6]

The marine with sailboats exemplifies Richards' most simplified marine format, utilizing the ruled, luminist horizon line he favored so often. The simple, tripartite composition of *Breaking Wave* (p. 133)—organized in three zones of shore, sea, and sky—has been reduced here to only two zones, sea and sky. William Gerdts has called Richards "probably the first of those 19th-century 'minimalists' who reduce the components of scenes to the barest elements—coast, sea, sky."[7] Another painting in this exhibition, Albert Pinkham Ryder's 1907 *Marine* (see p. 151) uses the same organization, although its mood is very different.

Unlike marine painters earlier in the century (such as the English-born artists Thomas Birch and Robert Salmon), Richards seldom placed ships in the foreground of his paintings. Those which do appear in his works were frequently reduced to small vertical accents in the distance, reminiscent of the tiny, far-off craft of the luminists Fitz Hugh Lane and Martin Johnson Heade. The boats in marine with sailboats were depicted in this fashion, brushed in simply with opaque gouache over the more transparent background. The schooner on the left, however, is more detailed in rendering and suggests that like Lane, Richards, when he wished, carefully studied its construction. In one of Richards' sketchbooks, given to the Academy as part of the Brewster Bequest, are a number of detailed pencil sketches of ships such as this one.

Anna and William Brewster tentatively identified both scenes exhibited here as unspecified sites along the New Jersey coast.[8] Richards first spent a summer on the New Jersey shore in 1859, and between that year and 1874 he returned frequently.[9] During the latter half of the century, the New Jersey shore was quite a popular vacation spot. Guidebooks of the 1870s and 1880s were lavish in their praise, stating in favorable comparisons that "Long Branch is the acknowledged Brighton of America . . ." and that "Atlantic City has been called the Long Branch of the Quaker City [Philadelphia] . . ."[10]

Richards frequented the Atlantic City area during many of his visits to the New Jersey shore. The marine with sailboats resembles contemporary descriptions of the area: "A series of buoys [as in

Untitled (marine, sunset)
Watercolor, 9⅞ x 15⅝″
Unsigned
Brewster Bequest

the foreground of the painting] marks the channel between the beach at Atlantic City and Brigantine Shoals. This is a favorite cruising-ground for pleasure boats."[11] "Barnegat Bay is all sport. In summer, hundreds of little vessels scud over its waters . . ."[12]

Richards' interest in the sky, displayed here in his fresh handling of clouds, brings to mind Frederic Church's cloud studies a bit earlier, as well as Ruskin's advice to beginning artists:

Now clouds are not as solid as flour-sacks; but, on the other hand, they are neither spongy nor flat. They are definite and very beautiful forms of sculptured mist; sculptured is a perfectly accurate word; they are not more *drifted* into form than they are *carved* into form . . . And the worst of all is . . . that if we put shade enough to express their form as positively as it is expressed in reality, we must make them painfully too dark on the dark sides. Nevertheless, they are so beautiful, if you in the least succeed with them, that you will hardly, I think, lose courage.[13]

Ruskin, *Elements of Drawing* (1857).

Just as Emerson made the comment, "What sculpture in these hard clouds," and described them as "boundless, cheerful, strong,"[14] Thoreau too had much to say on the subject. Like Emerson he added a moral tone to his discussion, with which Richards might readily have sympathized:

As the skies appear to a man, so is his mind. Some see only clouds there, some prodigies and portents; some scarce look up at all, their heads, like those of the brutes, are directed towards earth. Some behold there serenity, purity, beauty ineffable.—The world run [sic] to see the panorama, while there is a panorama in the sky which few go out to see.[15]

Journal (1852).

In the sunset of the marine, sunset, Richards indicates even more vividly his ability to invest natural phenomena with spiritual feeling. Again, Thoreau in his journal:

I go forth each afternoon and look into the west a quarter of an hour before sunset with fresh curiosity to see what new picture will be painted there, what new phenomenon exhibited, what new dissolving views. . . . Every day a new picture is painted and framed, held up for half an hour in such lights as the great artist chooses, and then withdrawn and the curtain falls.

This evening there are many clouds in the west into which the sun goes down, so that we have our visible or apparent sunset and red evening sky as much as fifteen minutes before the real sunset . . . After the sun has gone behind a cloud, there appears to be a gathering of clouds around his setting, and for a few moments his light in the amber sky seems more intense, brighter, and purer than at noonday, . . . like the ecstasy which we are told sometimes lights up the face of a dying man. . . . Then at last through all the grossness which has accumulated in the atmosphere of day is seen a patch of serene sky, fairer by contrast with the surrounding dark than midday, and even the gross atmosphere of the day is gilded and made pure as amber by the setting sun, as if the day's sins were forgiven it.[16]

Although Richards visited such popular resorts as Newport and Atlantic City, he seems to have preferred the "very lonely, rarely visited" places because, as he wrote to George Whitney in 1871, "there you seem to get a little closer to the heart of the sea than elsewhere."[17]

Alone in this dim summer light,—the air
Of ocean in the long sea-grass, and Flight
Of shining mist above me, what delight
To seem a part of Nature's self . . .[18]

Anna Matlack Richards, *Letter and Spirit* (1891).

This desire to be close to nature frequently had at its source a desire to be close to God, and to some degree views of the ocean seem to have satisfied both urges. In the words of Walt Whitman:

The attractions, fascinations there are in sea and shore! . . . That spread of waves and gray-white beach, salt, monotonous, senseless—such an entire absence of art, books, talk, elegance— so indescribably comforting, even this winter day—grim, yet so delicate-looking, so spiritual—striking emotional, impalpable depths, subtler than all the poems, paintings, music, I have ever read, seen, heard.[19]

"A Winter Day on the Beach" (1881).

Emerson, too, found more to admire in the ocean than its immediate appearance:

And behold the sea, the opaline, plentiful and strong, yet beautiful as the rose or the rainbow, full of food, nourisher of men, purger of the world, creating a sweet climate, and, in its unchangeable ebb and flow, and in its beauty at a few furlongs, giving a hint of that which changes not, and is perfect.[20]

Journal (1857).

NOTES

1. Dates suggested by Linda Ferber in conversation on April 22, 1980.
2. "American Society of Painters in Water-Colours," *The Art Journal* 1 (new series, 1875), 92.
3. "American Water Colors," *Scribner's Magazine* (1874), 761.
4. "American Society of Painters in Water-Colours," 91-92.
5. *Metropolitan Museum of Art Handbook* (1881). In Linda Ferber, *William T. Richards (1833-1905): American Landscape and Marine Painter* (Ph.D. dissertation, Columbia University, 1978. Reprint, Garland Series, N.Y., 1980), 274.
6. *Catalogue of the Collection of Modern Paintings Etc., formed by the late Mr. George Whitney of Philadelphia, And to Be Sold, By the Order of His Executors, On Wednesday, Thursday and Friday, December 16th, 17th and 18th, at Chickering Hall at the American Art Galleries* (New York, 1885), 29.
7. William H. Gerdts, "W.T. Richards: 'optimistic pantheism,' " *Art News* 72, no. 8 (October 1973), 64.
8. Labels attached to the paintings, in William T. Brewster's handwriting. It is difficult to decide whether such identifications were made by both Brewsters or by Mr. Brewster alone, as Anna Richards Brewster died before the bequest to the Academy was complete.
9. Ferber, *Richards* (1980), unpaginated chronology.
10. George L. Catlin, *Homes on the Sea-Shore On the Line of the New Jersey Southern Railway, for New York Business Men* (New York: New Jersey Southern Railway Co., 1873), 2. Gustav Kobbé, *The New Jersey Coast and Pines* (Short Hills, N.J.: G. Kobbé, 1889), 72.
11. William T. Richards, Commentary on Paintings (*Catalogue of the Collection of . . . George Whitney . . .*), 29.
12. Kobbé, *New Jersey Coast*, 64.
13. John Ruskin, *The Elements of Drawing*, originally published in 1857; this edition published in one volume with *The Ethics of the Dust* and *Fiction Fair and Foul*, 2nd ed. (1865, New York: Merrill and Baker, 1877), 329.
14. Ralph Waldo Emerson, *Journal*, May 25, 1843. In Bliss Perry, ed., *The Heart of Emerson's Journals* (Boston: Houghton Mifflin, 1926), 199.
15. Henry David Thoreau, *Journal*, January 17, 1852. In H.G.O. Blake, ed., *Winter: From the Journal of Henry David Thoreau* (Boston: Houghton, Mifflin, 1888), 193.
16. *Ibid.*, 128, 38.
17. Letter from Richards to George Whitney, June 10, 1871, from Gloucester. In Ferber, *William T. Richards* (1980), 257.
18. Anna Matlack Richards, *Letter and Spirit* (Boston: J.G. Cupples, 1891), viii.
19. Walt Whitman, "A Winter Day on the Beach" (1881). In Floyd Stovall, ed., *Walt Whitman, Prose Works 1892*, (2 vols.), vol. 1, *Specimen Days* (New York: New York University Press, 1963), 138.
20. Ralph Waldo Emerson, *Journal*, July 23, 1857. In Perry, *Heart of Emerson's Journals*, 277.

KN

NEW ENGLAND SHORE (probably near Newport), 1875
Watercolor and gouache on paper, 8⅞ x 13⅞"
Signed lower right: *Wm. T. Richards, 1875*
Brewster Bequest

YACHTS OFF NEWPORT, 1877
Watercolor and gouache on paper, 9⅛ x 14⅑"
Signed lower right: *Wm. T. Richards, 1877*
Brewster Bequest

Richards' interest in the effects of outdoor light and color found its fullest expression in the Newport watercolors of the 1870s. The subject of these magnificent watercolors, ostensibly the Newport shore—is actually, in Richards' words, the "sea with [the] effect of light."[1] Linda Ferber writes:

Light and atmosphere were of such prime importance in his [Richards'] marines that he could describe a watercolor to Whitney [his patron] as "A sea with effect of light, with Kyance Gull Rock and ledges of serpentine for objects." "A sea with effect of light" is the actual subject; "objects" are secondary.[2]

The special qualities of the light at Newport intrigued a number of artists in the second half of the nineteenth century. Richards is among the lesser known of these artists, as were Alfred T. Bricher and Francis A. Silva. John Wilmerding states that these three artists, though "often not as original or varied as the major figures of the later Hudson River School or the luminist movement . . . nonetheless produced a number of memorable and strong images."[3]

Certainly these two watercolors by Richards are among the memorable images produced by the artist. In *Yachts Off Newport*, the carefully controlled washes, combined with the crisply defined bright white accents of the sails and surf, convey the essence of the Newport coast under a breaking sun. Samuel A. Drake, in an 1875 guidebook to the New England coast, described his experience of such a Newport scene:

The air, after the sun had swept aside the vapors arising from the ocean, was intoxicating; it was so light and crystal . . . the sea glittered like silvery scales on fine armor.[4]

Drake, *Nooks and Corners of the New England Coast.*

Almost two decades earlier, the author and journalist George W. Curtis described the climate that contributed to the magic of Newport—the so-called "Italy of America"—and lured artists such as Richards:

This island was originally called Rhode Island from some fancied resemblance in its climate to that of the Isle of Rhodes. I do not wonder at the suggestion, for Newport is washed by a southern sea and the air that breathes over it is soft and warm. Its climate is an Italian air. These are Mediterranean days. . . . Only the monotonous and melancholy coast reminds you that you are not gazing upon Homer's sea . . .[5]

Curtis, *Lotus-Eating* (1856).

Of all seashore subjects, Richards found the Newport coast most congenial to his tastes. George W. Sheldon wrote in 1877:

Mr. Richards in the early years of his professional career showed a decided preference for the sea-shore as a field of study, and paid considerable attention to it whenever an opportunity offered. In 1865 he passed the summer at Nantucket, where his old love for the sea asserted itself . . . In 1870 he passed the summer at Atlantic City, on the southeasterly coast of New Jersey where he entered upon the study of coast scenery with great zeal, since then his summers have been passed at the seaside. Latterly he has made Newport his home, where, he says, the atmosphere, sea, and shore, are unsurpassed in artistic qualities.[6]

Sheldon, *Art Journal* (1877).

The geology of Newport, as well as its light and climate, attracted Richards and his contemporaries. Drake described the rocky coast:

There is a walk of singular beauty along the seabluffs that terminate the reverse of the hills on which Newport is built. It is known as the Cliff Walk. Everybody walks there. A broken wall of rock overhanging or retreating from its base, but always rising high above the water, is bordered by a foot-path with pleasant windings and elastic turf. The face of the cliff is studded with stony pimples; its formation being the conglomerate, or the pudding-stone, intermingled with schists. Color excepted, these rocks really look like the artifical cement used in laying the foundations of ponderous structures. They appear to resist the action of the sea with less power than the granite of the north coast. Masses of fallen rock are grouped along the beach underneath the cliff, around which the rising waves seethe and foam and hiss.[7]

Drake, *Nooks and Corners of the New England Coast.*

These "masses of fallen rock," evident in the foreground of both of these watercolors, provided Richards with the opportunity to pursue his continuing study of the action of the surf. In 1876 he wrote from Newport:

The early part of last week we had another tremendous surf, of which I got some record. But it is a little too much for me, perhaps for anybody for I do not remember any picture which gives any idea of the awful power of the breaking of a big wave against the rocks, much less of the tumult of the back action as it meets the incoming wave.[8]

Richards to George Whitney (1876).

In *New England Shore*, the surf pounds against the rocks. The billowing clouds seem to be breaking, perhaps signaling the end of a passing storm. Curtis could have had such a scene in mind when he wrote of Newport:

It is not a friendly coast; for at a little distance in the sea the waves break and foam over hidden rocks . . . after southerly storms the sea dashes itself in magnificent surfs that set the shore in flashing foam.[9]

Curtis, *Lotus-Eating* (1856).

The action of the surf at Newport provided a certain quality of picturesque drama. Offshore, yet another aspect of the Newport coastal scene attracted Richards' perceptive eye. Vessels, their sails full-blown in the summer breezes, sail in *Yachts Off the Newport Coast* and often appear in detailed pencil sketches in Richards' sketchbooks. (See Richards' sketchbooks at the National Academy of Design.) Richards may have been assisted in these drawings by a fellow native Philadelphian, Thomas Eakins. Ferber states that Eakins shared some practical advice regarding the technique of "draw[ing] a yacht sailing" in an 1877 letter probably addressed to Richards.[10] The yachts are given unusual prominence in this painting; perhaps they were inspired by Richards' observation of a race off the Newport coast.

Richards' use of gouache enabled him to "draw" in watercolor. Thus he was able to render the yachts with some precision, and high-light, with opaque white, the fine spray of the surf on the shore. As Linda Ferber states, "Richards' delicate and precise works were very much in keeping with contemporary taste in watercolor which still preferred a high degree of finish and detail at a time when taste in oil painting was beginning to turn to painterly suggestiveness."[11] In 1875, a reviewer of an American watercolor exhibit wrote that the artists who had taken up water-color

have done so with great earnestness, and more with the intention of using it for the production of pictures than as a mere diversion or adjunct for sketching. The fact is apparent, in the works of many artists who have shown that, while water-colors are delightful for sketching purposes, they are also capable of producing all the effects which are so attractive in oil-paintings.[12]

Art Journal.

As Richards' use of gouache for detail and highlighting brought him critical praise for the "precision of his drawing," his use of broad washes brought him praise for his "delicate gradations of colour."[13] The watercolor medium with its fresh transparency and fluidity, was particularly well suited for the depiction of the Newport coast. Richards used it in a masterly fashion to convey the luminosity of the vast expanses of sky and sea at Newport. He may have developed his technique in wash after the manner of J.M.W. Turner, whom he admired. He had seen Turner's watercolors in London in 1866 or 1867.[14] On a later trip to London he wrote:

Indeed there is a great deal to be learned about water colour drawing in London, and I wish I had the time to copy some of the Turners which after all are the most consummate pieces of art which have ever been produced in that material.[15]

Richards to Charles Matlack (1879).

Richards' success at producing varied effects in watercolor brought him contemporary recognition. By 1873 he was counted as "one of the best known water-color painters of America."[16] Certainly the high quality of these Newport works attests to his achievement in that medium.

Notes

1. William T. Richards to George Whitney, London, Nov. 4, 1879. In Linda Ferber, *William Trost Richards (1833-1905): American Landscape and Marine Painter* (Ph.D. dissertation, Columbia University, 1978. Reprint, Garland Series, New York, 1980), 373.

2. *Ibid.*, 373.

3. John Wilmerding, "The Luminist Movement: Some Reflections," in *American Light: The Luminist Movement, 1850-1875* (Exhibition catalogue, National Gallery of Art, Washington, D.C., 1980), 131.

4. Samuel Adams Drake, *Nooks and Corners of the New England Coast* (New York: Harper & Brothers, 1875), 374.

5. George William Curtis, *Lotus-Eating: A Summer Book* (New York: Dix, Edwards, 1856), 179.

6. George William Sheldon, "American Painters—William Trost Richards," *The Art Journal* 3, new series (1877), 242-43.

7. Drake, *Nooks and Corners*, 373.

8. Letter from William T. Richards to George Whitney, Newport, August 20, 1876. In Ferber, *Richards* (1980), 368.

9. Curtis, *Lotus-Eating*, 181, 182.

10. Letter from Thomas Eakins to "My dear friend," Philadelphia, June 19 (?), 1877. In Ferber, *Richards* (1980), 274, note. 49. Ferber states that "While Richards is not named as the addressee, the text of the letter makes it clear that the two were acquainted as fellow professionals and fellow Philadelphians" (295).

11. Anonymous, "American Society of Painters in Water-Colours," *The Art Journal* (1875), new series, 92. In Ferber *Richards* (1980), 274.

12. *Ibid.*

13. *Ibid.*, 91; quoted in Ferber, 275.

14. Ferber, *Richards* (1980), 329.

15. Letter from William T. Richards to Charles Matlack, London, November 26, 1879. In Ferber, *Richards* (1980), 329.

16. "Art: The Exhibition of Water Colours," *The Aldine* (April 1873), 87. In Linda S. Ferber, *William Trost Richards, American Landscape and Marine Painter, 1833-1905* (Exhibition catalogue, Brooklyn Museum, 1973), 32.

CC

MAURITZ FREDERICK HENDRICK DE HAAS

(1832-1895)
ANA 1862; NA 1867

Born Rotterdam, 1832; received early artistic training in native city. Studied at Rotterdam Academy of Fine Arts with figure painter Jacob Spoel and landscape painter Nicolaas J. Roosenboon. Later studied at the Hague under Louis Meyer, one of the most eminent marine painters; became official artist of the Dutch navy before emigrating to United States in 1859. Like his fellow Dutchman Kruseman Van Elten, he worked in Tenth Street Studio building (entered in 1865). Taught marine painting. 1867 elected member of American Water Color Society. During Civil War painted several coastal scenes for Admiral Farragut. Brother, William Frederick de Haas, also a marine painter, who came to United States in 1854. Exhibited at Boston Athenaeum, National Academy of Design, and Maryland Historical Society. Died November 23, New York City.

REFERENCES: Samuel G.W. Benjamin, "Fifty Years of American Art, 1828-1878," *Harper's New Monthly Magazine* 59 (Oct. 1879). George W. Sheldon, *American Painters* (New York: D. Appleton & Co., 1879).

Dutch-born Mauritz F.H. De Haas painted seascapes almost exclusively. In this sense, he may be seen as a product of the specialization which dominated Dutch painting from the seventeenth century.

The marine in the collection of the National Academy of Design is suffused with roseate light; no doubt the sun has just set. Two sailboats occupy the middleground. The activities of the figures on the boats are indistinguishable, but as one contemporary of De Haas observed about a similar painting by the artist (*Off the New England Coast*, exhibited NAD, 1893): "The picture is replete with life and snap and vigor. This does not come from the human element in it, for there is only a suggestion of men's figures in the nearest boat; but it comes from the carefully-studied, truthfully-rendered effects of nature . . ."[1]

During his lifetime, De Haas received ample critical recognition:

Of the peculiarities of Mr. de Haas' style we have not space to speak, if it were desirable or necessary so to do. If he can not actually control the winds and the waves, he has succeeded in being controlled by them to that degree that the very genii of ocean and sky seem to move on his canvas.[2]

The Aldine(1878).

An 1878 interview gives some insight into De Haas's work:

"Waves," said Mr. M.F.H. De Haas, the marine painter, as we were talking one afternoon in his studio, "never exactly repeat themselves; but a similar wave always comes back, so that, in making studies of them, I watch the appearance of just such a wave as I wish to represent, draw it at once and take its colour from a second wave. Only after long experience will the drawing be successful, and even then the correct aspect of a wave is hard to get. Waves in deep water have one distinctive aspect, waves in soundings another, waves along the shore another. In mid-ocean, for instance, they are rounder and hill-like; near the land they become sharp and broken up. As for colour, in deep water they are a dark, inky blue, difficult to describe because it varies with the appearance of the sky; while towards soundings they become greenish, and nearer the shore greener, where the coast is rocky, and yellowish where it is sandy. Waves in deep water are always the most difficult for me to paint; the motions of those on the coast are much more distinct and regular.

"The great charm of marine painting," continued Mr. De Haas, "consists in the fact that every cloud of any size affects the colour of the water, so much so that what you see is rather sky-reflection than the real colour of the water, except, of course, in the immediate foreground. Wind also comes in and changes the colour; the less wind there is the more nearly perfect is the reflection of the sky. On the surface of a lake, when there are [*sic*] no wind and no motion, the sky is perfectly mirrored. I have seen instances," he exclaimed, "when you could hardly tell which was sky and which was lake . . ."

The walls of this artist's studio are almost entirely covered with studies of sea-scenes. His process of making these studies is simple, and I was glad to get hold of it, because what an artist says about himself to a friend is always more interesting than what a critic says about him to the public. Each study was a foot and a half long by one foot wide, and took two hours in the making. "You can't work much longer than that," he said, "the light and almost everything else change so. As for the sky in the scene, sometimes you have scarcely fifteen minutes in which to paint it. In such cases I begin from Nature and finish from memory. For most things my memory is poor, but I never forget a sky. First of all, in making a study out-doors on the sea-coast, I paint the sky, then the horizon, and then the waves in the foreground. The colours of the sky I put on with a palette-knife, because this is the quickest way of doing it."

The most difficult part of his work is the rendering of the sky, although most marine painters find the water the most troublesome; and the most pleasant part of his work is the finishing after the canvas has been entirely covered, and all the parts have been roughly put together. The older he grows the harder he finds it to paint a picture. "Nothing is easier," he remarked, "than to make water look thin, transparent, and glassy-thin and transparent, so that any object would drop through it to the bottom; glassy, so that the waves would cut right into the object on it. The artist, however, gives you water on which a vessel can safely float—wet water, water with movement and body to it. I like nothing better than to paint a storm."[3]

The Art Journal (1878).

NOTES

1. New York Public Library Artists Clipping File. (Caption under reproduction *Off the New England Coast*), unidentified clipping, p. 269.

2. *The Aldine*, 8, no. 9 (1878), 286, New York Public Library Artists Clipping File.

3. "The Methods of a Marine Painter," *The Art Journal* 4 (1878), 168-69.

SGS

MARINE, c. 1867
Oil on canvas, mounted on board
18 x 30″
Signed lower right: *M.F.H. de Haas*

———————————————

ALBERT PINKHAM RYDER

(1847-1917)
ANA 1902; NA 1906

Born New Bedford, Mass., March 19. 1870 moved to New York. Entered National Academy of Design School for four seasons. 1873 exhibited at National Academy. 1875 in group show at Cottier & Co. 1877 founding member of Society of American Artists; spent a month in London. Around 1880 moved to Benedick Building, Washington Square, New York City, and began mature literary subjects. 1882 European tour with Daniel Cottier and Olin Warner. In mid-1890s moved to 308 West 15 Street, output declining. After 1900 painted few new works, but restored earlier works. Became reclusive. Died in Elmhurst, Long Island, March 28.

REFERENCE: Lloyd Goodrich, *Albert Pinkham Ryder* (Exhibition catalogue, Corcoran Gallery, Washington, D.C., 1961).

Two of Ryder's three older brothers were sailors, as was Albert in his way, for the sea was his primary motif. As Lloyd Goodrich explains, "the sea haunted him all his life—its vastness and loneliness, the rhythmic flow of its waters, the majesty of its storms, its profound peace. His frequent image of a lone boat sailing moonlit seas might be a symbol of man's lonely journey through infinity and eternity."[1] The sea is also a motif of Emily Dickinson's, whose poems are often similar in spirit to Ryder's pictures:

> Whether my bark went down at sea,
> Whether she met with gales,
> Whether to isles enchanted
> She bent her docile sails;
>
> By what mystic mooring
> She is held to-day,—
> This is the errand of the eye
> Out upon the bay.[2]

Untitled (copyright 1890).

Ryder did not date his paintings, and he often worked on them over a number of years. *Marine* was not among the pictures Ryder showed up through 1888, when he stopped exhibiting publicly. We only know from an old inscription on the reverse that *Marine* is Ryder's diploma painting of 1907, and the only one of his relatively rare works in the Academy's collection. Ryder made each one count, as Marsden Hartley attests:

I still retain the vivid impression that afflicted me when I saw my first

Ryder, a marine of rarest grandeur and sublimity, incredibly small in size, incredibly large in emotion—just a sky and a single vessel in sail across a conquering sea.[3]

Hartley, "Albert P. Ryder" (1917).

The absence of a boat in *Marine* makes it unusual, perhaps unique, among Ryder's sea pieces. The vast, open-ended expanse of water suggests the limitless ocean. The implied point of view is from a vessel. Indeed, in 1887 and 1896 Ryder traveled by ship to London and back to paint the Atlantic. *Marine* is probably the result of one of these voyages.

Though thickly and freely handled, it is not overpainted as much as many of Ryder's later works. Thus it is in better condition now than most. The coloration has not muddied; the white highlights amidst a pervasive blue tonality can only be compared to *Moonlight* (National Collection of Fine Arts) or *The Waste of Waters is Their Field* (Brooklyn Museum). Ryder had declared:

The artist should fear to become the slave of detail. He should strive to express his thought and not the surface of it. What avails a storm cloud accurate in form and color if the storm is not therein?[4]

"Paragraphs from the Studio of a Recluse" (1905).

That Ryder was successful is fortified by Walter Pach's observation: "To such a painter, a picture is not at all a thing external, but a part of his mind, a part of his life."[5]

Curiously, *Marine* is inscribed in French at the lower left corner: "[à] mon ami Capt. Robinson." In 1883 Captain John Robinson met Ryder through Ryder's dealer Daniel Cottier. Ryder later made his trans-Atlantic voyages on Robinson's vessels, as the Captain recalled:

Many evenings he would sit with me alone on board, and on moonlight nights he would go on to the bridge and watch the numerous craft passing up and down the Hudson, getting "moonlight effects." . . . In the year 1887 my old friend crossed the Atlantic with me on the S.S. *Canada*. He was a good sailor—I mean he was never seasick. When not studying cloud effects and the movements of the waves in all their various moods, he passed the time working on a panel picture, the *Temple of the Mind*.[6]

"Personal Reminiscenes of Albert Pinkham Ryder" (1925).

Thus did Ryder gather natural "effects" for paintings like *Marine*. Robinson also notes that the 1896 crossing was made to cure the "low nervous condition" Ryder developed, and did benefit his health.[7] The captain does not mention any painting done on this trip, nor that he had acquired any works by Ryder.

Finally, Robinson recounts, "In 1907, through failing eyesight,

MARINE, c. 1890
Oil on panel, 8¾ x 17¾″
Signed and inscribed lower left: *Mon Ami Capt. Robinson.*
Ryder
Diploma painting

I could no longer follow my profession, so I retired from the sea after forty-eight years of service."[8] That same year Ryder was elected Academician and submitted this picture inscribed to the captain. In his modest way Ryder thus rendered homage to the shared sea travels that Captain Robinson afforded him, which were, appropriately, the genesis of *Marine*.

NOTES
1. Lloyd Goodrich, *Albert Pinkham Ryder* (Exhibition catalogue, Corcoran Gallery, Washington, 1961), 12.
2. "Whether my bark went down at sea," *Poems of Emily Dickinson* (Boston: Roberts, 1892), 38.
3. Marsden Hartley, "Albert P. Ryder," *The Seven Arts* 2 (May 1917), 94.
4. "Paragraphs from the Studio of a Recluse," *Broadway Magazine* (September 1905). In Walter Teller, ed., *Twelve Works of Naive Genius* (New York: Harcourt, 1972), 301.
5. Walter Pach, "On Albert P. Ryder," *Scribner's Magazine* 49 (January 1911), 128.
6. John Robinson, "Personal Reminiscences of Albert Pinkham Ryder," *Art in America* 13 (June 1925), 180. Ryder also painted *Moonlight* (National Collection of Fine Arts) on the back of the panel with *The Temple of the Mind*.
7. *Ibid.*, 184.
8. *Ibid.*, 187.

LK

RALPH ALBERT BLAKELOCK

(1847-1919)
ANA 1913; NA 1916

Born New York City, October 15. Attended public schools. Two years at City College. Largely self-taught as an artist. First exhibited at National Academy of Design at age twenty. 1869 and 1872 traveled to Far West, including Wyoming, Utah, California, and Mexico; also Panama and West Indies. Made many studies of lives of Indians. Exhibited intermittently at Academy 1867-1873. Landscapes not well received and eked out poor existence. Moved briefly to New Jersey. Painted plaques and decorative panels for Newark art factory. Often painted up to two dozen small canvases a day, peddling them for rarely more than five to seven dollars to Third Avenue junk dealers and auction houses. Moved frequently in Manhattan and Brooklyn during these years. By 1891, depressed by failure and extreme poverty, his mind began to fail. Began to dress in fantastic costumes and became obsessed with the idea he was a millionaire. 1899, after several violent incidents, committed to Middletown (N.Y.) State Hospital for the Insane. There until 1916, when for a brief period his mind cleared. Released into guardianship of Mrs. Van Rensselaer Adams and returned to New York. Health did not improve, and 1918 returned to private sanitorium. Died of arteriosclerosis, August 9, on month's visit to Mrs. Adams' Catskill cottage, Elizabethtown, N.Y.

REFERENCES: Elliott Daingerfield, *The Life of Ralph Albert Blakelock* (New York: Frederic Fairchild Sherman, 1914). Norman Geske, *Ralph Albert Blakelock, 1847-1919.* (Exhibition catalogue, Sheldon Memorial Art Gallery, Nebraska Art Association, Lincoln, 1974). Lloyd Goodrich, *Ralph Albert Blakelock Centenary Exhibition In Celebration of the Centennial of the City College of New York* (Exhibition catalogue, Whitney Museum of American Art, New York, 1947). National Academy of Design Artists Biographical Files. New York Public Library Clipping File. "Of Moonlight and Forgery: 'The Blakelock Problem,' " *Humanities* 11, no. 2, (March 1972). W. Adelson, Blakelock, Blakelock and J. Tanzer, *Ralph Albert Blakelock, 1849 [sic]-1919* (Exhibition catalogue, M. Knoedler and Co., N.Y., 1973). "Ralph Blakelock, Mad Artist Dies," *The New York Times* August 11, 1919. Vernon Young. "Out of Deepening Shadows: The Art of Ralph Albert Blakelock," *Arts* (October 1957).

*L*andscape *(Sunset)*, although a small work, represents the artist at a critical moment in his career, working in autograph fashion. It is also a document attesting to the Academy's role as mentor and guardian for member artists.

Blakelock's history with the National Academy of Design was a singular association. He had first exhibited at the Academy in 1867, and his lifelong friendship with the artist and later secretary of the Academy Harry W. Watrous dates to about this time.

Watrous was clearly impressed by the young artist. In 1885, he stated that Blakelock ranked with Alexander Wyant and George Inness as one of the three greatest landscape painters working in America.[1] It was Watrous who often provided the artist with critical psychological and financial support throughout his career. After Blakelock's 1899 commitment and the subsequent attention and higher prices accorded his work (along with the wholesale forging of his characteristic moonlit scenes), Watrous' involvement became more public. A year later, a benefit exhibition of Blakelock's paintings was held at the Lotos Club. Among the sponsors were noted artists and collectors of the day, including William Macbeth, George A. Hearn, Henry Ranger, William T. Evans, Clarkson Cowl, and Watrous.[2] In 1903, *Hyde's Weekly Art News* announced the formation of a funding campaign to aid Blakelock and provide for his family, summing up with the observation: "Mr. Blakelock has done much for American art and the fund should be raised speedily."[3]

The popular appeal of the destitute, mad artist, removed from society and cut off from his family, his achievement diluted by the widespread forging of his paintings and exploitation of his situation, was, judging by the tenor of the newspaper response, substantial. As the *Evening Post* editorialized:

Now that he is confined in an asylum for the insane, we are hearing much of Ralph A. Blakelock and his art. Every exhibition or sale has one or more examples of his work, and no collection, however small, is thought to be complete without a canvas or two by him . . . With the painter in a madhouse, and his family [a wife and nine children] in distress, one can but wonder who has profited by it all.[4]

Paradoxically, Blakelock's paintings during his confinement constitute an important genre in themselves and may be viewed as representing a significant new direction in his art. After an initial settling-in period, during which he accustomed himself to asylum life, Blakelock resumed painting with an unexpected verve. The freedom to paint on an uncommissioned basis, without the enormous economic pressures of his earlier years, allowed the artist to experiment in a way that he could not have done during his peddling days. As one critic described the artist's work at about this time:[7]

Blakelock was by nature a dreamer with a desire to record his dream. To call him a landscape painter is incorrect. No artist has used the landscape as a means to an end more than he. The landscape merely provided forms with which he expressed his moods, inspirations, and eccentricities . . .

LANDSCAPE (SUNSET), 1916
Oil on cardboard, 3⅝ x 5½″
Unsigned
Inscribed in ink on reverse of support:
Painted by Ralph Albert Blakelock-Oct 1916
Diploma painting

Yet, in spite of the exuberance, the capriciousness, the phantasies, the trees that seem to dance and sing, there is mystery and dignity.[5]

Raymond Wyer, *International Studio* (1916).

According to his grandson, Blakelock's existence at Middletown was not altogether unpleasant.[6] He often sketched in the countryside surrounding the sanitorium. Families of hospital employees would invite him to dinner, and in return, Blakelock would play the piano or present his hosts with one of his sketches or paintings.

Many of the confinement works are small in scale, as is this example, and since painting supplies were scarce, executed on any available material. Although Blakelock had always utilized anything that came to hand, including fragments of paper, cigar box lids, pieces of wood and sections of wallpanels, reportedly even his own shirttails, the asylum paintings were executed on scraps salvaged from the trash bin.[7] Many were painted on cheap, commercial-grade cardboard, as *Landscape (Sunset)* illustrates. Pigments were similarly limited and Blakelock sought methods to increase the range of colors, for example, by letting the ground or support show through. He used ink washes or pen and ink, when paints were unavailable. Other examples during these years, such as this work, were packed full of color. The artist's grandson suggests that after a period of deprivation, Blakelock may have been so thrilled with the many pigments suddenly available to him, he could not resist splashing the entire range of the spectrum over these surfaces.[8]

Blakelock had always been aware of the expressive qualities of paint. His early biographer, Elliott Daingerfield, a fellow Academy member, noted about this time:

It was not unusual with him when some interesting mingling of color chanced upon his palette, to develop it there into whatever theme was suggested, and cut out the chosen piece of wood as expressive of artistic value. We find many of these little panels, unimportant so far as subject is concerned, but very beautiful in quality both of color and of surface.[9]

Ralph Albert Blakelock (1914).

A decade after the initial fundraising effort, the artist's financial position remained unimproved, despite his election to the Academy and the greater attention accorded his painting. Although a substantial amount of money had purportedly been raised to assist the artist and his wife, none of it was ever received by the family. The earlier spate of newspaper articles and sensational publicity, very little of which focused on Blakelock's paintings, had resulted in a number of benefactors stepping forth to "aid" the artist, usually by buying his paintings at cut-rate prices and later realizing a tidy profit on their sale. As one periodical wrote: "Drifting, dreamy and broke—and crazy—and honors being showered upon him who knows it not. Where can one match all this for pathos?"[10]

In 1916 another fundraising campaign was undertaken, headlined in the *Evening Post*, "Academy Would Take Advantage of Present Interest in Asylum Inmate to Make Permanent Aid for Future Blakelocks."[11] It seems fitting and not a little poignant that at this time, when the artist's mind had briefly cleared and he had been released to try to resume a life in the outside world, *Landscape (Sunset)* entered the Academy's collection as a suitable testament to the association between the artist, his friend Harry Watrous, and the Academy.

NOTES

1. "Belated Honors Come to Ralph Blakelock, Painter, 16 Years Insane" (May 4, 1913), New York Public Library Clipping File.
2. "Exhibition of Paintings by R.A. Blakelock . . ." (gallery leaflet, The Lotos Club, N.Y., Dec. 8, 1900), New York Public Library Clipping File.
3. *Hyde's Weekly Art News* (March 7, 1903), New York Public Library Clipping File.
4. "Art News: Ralph A. Blakelock and His Art," *The New York Evening Post*, February 21, 1903, n.p., New York Public Library Clipping File.
5. Raymond Wyer, "Art and the Man: Blakelock," *International Studio* (July 1916), xix.
6. W. Adelson, *et. al.*, *Ralph Albert Blakelock, 1849[sic]-1919* (Exhibition catalogue, M. Knoedler and Co., N.Y., 1973), essay by David Blakelock, 22.
7. *Ibid.*, 25. See also Norman Geske, *Ralph Albert Blakelock, 1847-1919* (Exhibition catalogue, Sheldon Memorial Art Gallery, Nebraska Art Association, Lincoln, 1974), 23.
8. Knoedler, 25.
9. Elliott Daingerfield, *The Life of Ralph Albert Blakelock* (New York: Frederic Fairchild Sherman, 1914), 13.
10. "Belated Honors," New York Public Library Clipping File.
11. *The New York Evening Post* April 21, 1916, n.p., New York Public Library Clipping File. For further information regarding Blakelock and his benefactors, see the essay by David Blakelock, "The Confinement Period" in M. Knoedler and Co., *Ralph Albert Blakelock, 1849[sic]-1919* (Exhibition catalogue, M. Knoedler, N.Y.; 1973) 20-26.

CB

(LOWELL) BIRGE HARRISON

(1854-1929)
ANA 1902; NA 1910

Born Philadelphia, October 28. Brother Thomas Alexander a leading marine painter and brother Butler a figure painter. Entered Pennsylvania Academy of the Fine Arts 1874. Convinced by John Singer Sargent to move to Paris. There, in 1876, entered the atelier of Carolus-Duran. Fellow students included Abbott Thayer and Theodore Robinson. Spent summers at Grez, on one occasion with Robert Louis Stevenson. Also studied at the École des Beaux-Arts with Alexandre Cabanel. In mid-1880s voyaged around world, producing illustrated travel articles for American magazines. Visited India, Australia, and the South Seas. Lived in California and among the Moquis and Navajo Indians in the Southwest. Moved to Plymouth, Mass., 1896. 1904-1906 director of Byrdcliffe Summer School of Arts and Crafts in Woodstock, N.Y. Experimented there with new kind of woodblock print. Founder and head instructor of the Art Students' League Summer School in Woodstock 1906-1911. Published *Landscape Painting* (1909), based on his Woodstock lectures. Spent some winters in Quebec, also traveled to Charleston, S.C., the Massachusetts coast, and back to Paris. Died May 12, Woodstock.

REFERENCES: Charles Louis Borgmeyer, "Birge Harrison—Poet Painter," *Fine Arts Journal* 29 (1913). Karal Ann Marling, *Woodstock, An American Art Colony 1902-1977* (Exhibition catalogue, Vassar College Art Gallery, Poughkeepsie, N.Y., 1977).

Birge Harrison painted *The Hidden Moon* at the beginning of 1907 or possibly earlier, since it was shown at the Century Association in April, 1907.[1] On October 5, 1907, Harrison wrote William Macbeth at Macbeth Galleries that he was sending him six paintings so that Macbeth could choose two for display. Harrison fixed the price of *The Hidden Moon*, one of the six, at 600 dollars.[2] Apparently the picture was not sold, since Harrison presented it to the National Academy of Design in 1910.

Harrison began his artistic career as a figure painter but turned to landscape painting in Paris. John E. D. Trask noted that

... Harrison, seriously studying figure-painting under Cabanel, in the late seventies, one day took his model out of doors and quite casually turned the whole trend of his career. Gradually in his work the figure dwindled in importance until finally it ceased to appear, so that, though his first large recognition came to him through the purchase by the French Government in 1882 of his "November," which is an out-of-door figure painting, his real reputation rests upon his landscape work alone.[3]
Scribner's Magazine (1907).

By 1911 Harrison was considered "one of the leading landscape men of this country."[4]

Harrison elucidated his theories on landscape in his book *Landscape Painting* (1909). The business of the artist, he wrote, is "... to transmit to picture-lovers through the medium of our pictures the emotions, and the impressions of strength and power, or of poetic beauty, which have come to us direct from nature ..."[5]

In a spirit similar to that of James McNeill Whistler, George Inness, and Dwight Tryon, Harrison aimed to capture the "moods" of nature, rather than the details of the scene, through limited color tones and the use of a delicate, diffused light:

For my landscape has a soul as well as a body. ... Its soul is the spirit of light—of sunlight, of moonlight, of starlight—which plays ceaselessly across the face of the landscape, veiling it at night in mystery and shadow, painting it at dawn with the colors of the pearl-shell, and bathing it at mid-day in a luminous glory. To this and to the ambient and all-enveloping atmosphere, with its clouds and its mists, its rain and its veiling haze, are due the infinite and ever-shifting *moods* of nature.[6]
Landscape Painting.

Many of Harrison's paintings concentrate on the lyrical qualities of the sky. He agreed with Francis Murphy who, when asked what it was in any potential picture motive that made him decide to paint the picture, replied: "The sky of course; always the sky. If I have my sky I have my picture, and I am willing to look about for months in order to find just the proper landscape to fit it."[7] Harrison advised his students to concentrate on the sky as he did, lowering the horizon as far as possible:

A vast sky always lends nobility to a picture. ... The low horizon line is peculiarly essential when the principal motive of the picture is found in the sky itself—some vast composition of rolling clouds, some gorgeous sunburst radiating its luminous streamers athwart the canvas, some castle in the air towering up and up to the zenith. In this case, a mere line of land is often sufficient—enough to give the dark and solid value that lends light and air to the upper reaches of the sky.[8]

He was particularly drawn to representing the moonlit sky. Of the thirty-seven paintings and fourteen pastels shown at the Century Association in 1907, ten had the word "moon" or "moonrise" in the titles. Besides longing to evoke the "brooding mystery of night,"[9] Harrison felt that concentration on the moonlit sky could give a painting a powerful simplicity lacking in landscapes full of nature's details:

THE HIDDEN MOON, c. 1907
Oil on canvas, 25¼ x 30⅛"
Signed lower left: *Birge Harrison*
Diploma painting

An out-door picture-motive is complicated indeed if it cannot be divided into four or five dominant values. If these are understood, and painted with sympathetic truth, it is astonishing how little detail it requires to complete the picture. . . . There is probably no better way of training the eye to simplicity of vision, than studying moonlight, for in moonlight effects, the broad masses alone are visible, and the shadows lie all over the picture in one big soft value.[10]

Unlike a sunlit scene full of sharp contrasts, the moonlight results in what Harrison called a "lost-edge" effect, "a general diffusion of tone,"[11] which envelopes the scene in an atmospheric veil. The moon hidden behind clouds in this painting allows only the faintest discernment of buildings or towers on the left and perhaps a river at the center where a tiny reflection of the moon appears. One critic found that this vagueness gave Harrison's landscapes their "completness," adding: "As a rule they are low-toned and run a short gamut, there are no intense contrasts of light and shade, no blatant notes, but the harmonies are perfect and suggest not accidental achievements but well-considered purpose. . . ."[12]

To another writer of the time:

It is no belittlement of Harrison's present work to say that had he not become a painter he would have been a poet. In all of his recent work one finds bigness of theme, combined with simplicity of presentation, and through it all runs a deep current of sentiment. . . . Less emotional than music, more sensual than verse, painting combines and harmonizes something of both; and in the blending of realism and idealism, Harrison is very happy.[13]

Trask, *Scribner's Magazine* (1907).

Charles Borgmeyer, who, in a 1913 article in *Fine Arts Journal*, called him "Birge Harrison—Poet Painter," believed that Harrison was drawn

. . . to the tender and poetic side of nature, rather than the dramatic. He loves her best in her gentler moods, and he chooses, by preference, that time of day which is fullest of the poetry of the outdoor world.[14]

Harrison would make only a drawing of his subject from nature, trusting

. . . to a well-trained memory for the color and effect of his pictures. He holds that only thus can the soul, the essential beauty of any subject be seized by the artist and fixed upon the canvas.[15]

He advised his students to do the same in order to capture the evanescent effect of nature:

But even where the effect is more lasting, and where a painter might have two or three hours to work direct from nature, I believe that the final picture must *always* be painted from memory; and I seriously question if any really great landscape was ever wholly painted in the open. A picture painted direct from nature must necessarily be hasty, ill-considered, somewhat raw, and lacking in the synthetic and personal quality which is the distinguishing mark of all great art. . . .[16]

Landscape Painting (1909).

NOTES

1. *Exhibition of Landscape Paintings by Birge Harrison* (Exhibition catalogue, The Century Association, 1907), no. 29, *The Hidden Moon.*
2. Letter to Macbeth from Birge Harrison, October 5, 1907, Macbeth Gallery Papers, Archives of American Art, Smithsonian Institution, N.Y., microfilm roll NMc 7.
3. John E.D. Trask, "Birge Harrison," *Scribner's Magazine* 42 (November 1907), 576.
4. Arthur Hoeber, "Birge Harrison, N.A., Landscape Painter," *The International Studio* 44 (July 1911), iii.
5. Birge Harrison, *Landscape Painting* (New York: Charles Scribner's Sons, 1909), 56.*
6. *Ibid.*, 155-56.
7. Birge Harrison, "Painting at Woodstock," *Arts and Decoration* 2 (May 1912), 248.
8. Harrison, *Landscape Painting*, 93-94.
9. *Ibid.*, 248.
10. *Ibid.*, 74.
11. *Ibid.*, 48.
12. L.M., "Birge Harrison's Paintings," *Art and Progress* 3 (November 1911), 379.
13. Trask, "Birge Harrison," 579.
14. Charles Louis Borgmeyer, "Birge Harrison—Poet Painter," *Fine Arts Journal* 29 (1913), 603.
15. *Ibid.*, 604.
16. Harrison, *Landscape Painting*, 171.
*In National Academy of Design Library.

SMS

DWIGHT WILLIAM TRYON

(1849-1925)
ANA 1890; NA 1891

Born Hartford, Connecticut, August 13. 1864-1873 worked as bookkeeper and clerk at Hartford's largest bookstore, painting, often from memory, in spare time. Taught class in calligraphy in business school. In 1873 abandoned business and opened studio in Hartford, giving instruction in painting and drawing. Visited Mount Desert Island, White Mountains, and Block Island. Autumn 1876 auctioned unsold work and moved to Paris. Studied drawing in atelier of Jacquesson de la Chevreuse, former pupil of Ingres, and at the École des Beaux-Arts. Worked for short time with J.B.A. Guillemet, pupil of Corot, with Henri Harpignies, and with Charles Daubigny, about whom he wrote a short monograph. Summer of 1877 in Guernsey with Abbott Thayer, beginning their long friendship. Subsequent summers in Brittany and Normandy, Venice, and Dordrecht, Holland. 1881 returned to New York. In 1883 built home and studio in South Dartmouth, on the Massachusetts coast, where he spent summers until his death. Winters taught classes in New York, and 1885-1923 was professor of art at Smith College. In 1889 met Charles L. Freer, who began to collect Tryon's work, along with that of James McNeill Whistler, Thomas Dewing, and Abbott Thayer. Invited with Dewing to make decorative murals for central hall of Freer's home in Detroit. Established Tryon Art Gallery at Smith College year of his death. Died July 1, South Dartmouth.

REFERENCE: Henry C. White, *The Life and Art of Dwight William Tryon* (Boston: Houghton Mifflin Company, 1930).

On his return in 1881 from four years of study in France, Tryon found a winter studio in New York in the Rembrandt Building and spent two summers in East Chester (now Eastchester), New York. At that time East Chester was a small village, remote from New York City. Henry C. White, Tryon's student, friend, and biographer, wrote of those summers:

He made sketches there and painted a few pictures, not particularly characteristic or significant, perhaps, though in one or two he struck an interesting note not often repeated. . . . Tryon did not find the character of East Chester very inspiring, and soon cast about for a summer home in more congenial surroundings.[1]

Life of Tryon (1930).

In 1883, on the suggestion of R. Swain Gifford, Tryon visited South Dartmouth, Massachusetts, and found he preferred it to East Chester as a permanent summer home.

The few paintings Tryon did at or from his studies of East Chester (he exhibited one of them in the 1883 National Academy of Design exhibition) reveal the influence, in subject matter and brushwork, of Corot and the Barbizon artists he had seen in Europe.[2] This influence became less and less apparent in his later work, and ultimately he declined to acknowledge it. Nonetheless, Tryon had the highest opinion of the Barbizon school's importance, writing:

The period which culminated in the so-called Fontainebleau-Barbizon school is unquestionably the most important epoch in the history of landscape painting which the world has yet known.[3]

"Charles-François Daubigny" (1889).

Tryon also admitted: "I was an admirer of [Corot's] work and had studied it deeply." And, according to White, Tryon "found something wholesome and vigorous about [the sturdy peasants of Millet], and the fact that they reeked of the soil was to him an attraction."[4] But he said he had little help with his work from Barbizon School artists Harpignies and Daubigny, although he formed a friendship with them, and later wrote a monograph on Daubigny.[5]

A frequent Barbizon subject was that of the farmer at work in the field. Tryon followed this example in his European paintings. He had noted that on his trip from America to Europe in 1876, he ". . . left New York in a mantle of snow, and I remember being impressed by seeing, all the way from Liverpool to London, green fields with farmers at work, some ploughing and others engaged in various agricultural tasks."[6] Tryon continued for a short time to be interested in this subject matter when he returned to America.

White notes, however, that during most of his career, Tryon was primarily preoccupied with pure landscape, without a trace of man. Still, ". . . scattered along the years are charming little studies of flowers, a bit of garden, children picking daisies in a meadow, haying scenes with figures of men and horses, cows at pasture, and other variations of landscape." In Tryon's late works, especially, figures seldom appear. "He used to say that the worse the painting of figures was, in landscape, the better the effect, and I think he ended by feeling them, or anything but a faint suggestion of them, to be an intrusion, at least in his own landscapes."[7]

Works such as this, done directly after his return to America, appeared to one writer to combine Tryon's intimate knowledge of New England with the still-retained French influence:

Even in one of his earliest landscapes painted about 1881, after his return from Paris, from studies made abroad, there is a decisively individual

LANDSCAPE, c. 1882
Oil on canvas, 24 x 36″
Signed lower left: *D.W. Tryon/East Chester, N.Y.*
Diploma painting

———————

note. It is a scene of ploughing, owned by Mr. Montross—a stretch of dark rich soil, with man and horses pushing the furrow toward a clear, cool horizon. There is a larger feeling than Daubigny would have portrayed; a sterner one, if you will, certainly one more bracing in its suggestion of vigorous earth and breezy sky, and more distinctly inspired than Harpignies could have made it, with the sentiment of the soil and sky in their relation to the life of man. Still, the motive of the picture is so far a borrowed one that, although it has the feeling of a New England scene, it has not its local characteristics of atmosphere or of soil colour, lacking the more sensitive quality of the one, and the tenderer hues of the other. . . . [Tryon] seems to have grown up with the smell of the soil in his nostrils as Millet did, though without the latter's saddened associations; to have been nourished with the brisk New England air, and to have gathered muscle over its ploughed and grassy uplands.[8]

Caffin, *American Masters of Painting* (1903).

Although the countryside depicted in Tryon's *Landscape* is not New England but East Chester, it is close enough for the influence of the region of his childhood to be felt. In a letter to White on February 14, 1897, Tryon claimed that only the landscape painter could understand the importance of his native soil:

. . . the faint reminiscences of childhood days, the memories of many a day afield, and who shall not say that even pre-natal memories come in the form of intuitions too subtle to define and, often unconsciously transferred to the picture. . . .[9]

The specific site of this painting may be more recognizable than in his later tonal paintings, which are concerned with season, time of day, and mood rather than with description of locale. Frederick Fairchild Sherman wrote in *American Painters of Yesterday and Today* (1919) that Tryon's early paintings showed the "fact" not the "significance of nature." That phase

. . . ends practically as soon as he has mastered his forms and settled upon his composition. . . . In the sense, however, that these earlier works are a more literal transcript of familiar rather than unfamiliar aspects of nature, more direct in their construction and less calculated in their elaboration, they correspond more closely to historic standards and satisfy more generally that large portion of the public which remains conservative in its appraisal of artistic merit.[10]

Tryon's later works retain the simple composition that he used in the East Chester landscape. The basic structure of the horizon-tals and verticals of *Landscape*, formed by the horizon, the long barn, and the square hay wagon, were to crystallize in those works consisting only of ground, trees, and sky. Charles Caffin's 1909 description of Tryon's paintings refers to both this rural scene as well as to paintings done more than twenty years later:

. . . the skies are usually cloudless; the foregrounds, for the most part, uncharacterized by conspicuous features. They are, in fact, to use a studio term, "empty spaces" in the composition, which serve to set off the middle distance, in which he places the objects of peculiarly local significance. Yet in the usual acceptance of the term, they are the reverse of empty. These cloudless skies are filled with light; wells of luminous fluidity, into which one gazes to find no hindrance or limit to the onward sweep of one's imagination. Similarly, the foregrounds have a depth of structural reality that makes them seem a part of the foundation of the earth itself.[11]

Art of Tryon.

NOTES

1. Henry C. White, *The Life and Art of Dwight William Tryon* (Boston: Houghton Mifflin, 1930), 58.
2. *Dwight W. Tryon: A Retrospective Exhibition* (Exhibition catalogue, Museum of Art, the University of Connecticut, Storrs, Conn., 1971), lists two paintings done at East Chester in 1882: no. 20, *Early Spring, East Chester*, and no. 21, *Haying*. Maria Naylor, *The National Academy of Design Exhibition Record 1861-1906* (New York: Kennedy Galleries, 1973), 1: 947, lists no. 674, *A Sketch—Springtime, East Chester N.Y.*
3. Dwight W. Tryon, "Charles-François Daubigny," *Modern French Masters*, John C. Van Dyke, ed. (New York: The Century Co., 1889), 157.
4. White, *Life and Art of Dwight William Tryon*, 56, 85.
5. Tryon, "Charles-François Daubigny," 155.
6. In White, *Life and Art of Dwight William Tryon*, 35.
7. *Ibid.*, 170, 76.
8. Charles H. Caffin, *American Masters of Painting* (New York: Doubleday, Page & Company, 1903), 159-60.*
9. In White, *Life and Art of Dwight William Tryon*, 50.
10. Frederic Fairchild Sherman, *American Painters of Yesterday and Today* (New York: privately printed, 1919), 16.
11. Charles H. Caffin, *The Art of Dwight W. Tryon: An Appreciation* (privately printed, 1909), 19.

*In National Academy of Design Library.

SMS

LOUIS PAUL DESSAR

(1867-1952)
ANA 1899; NA 1906

Born Indianapolis, Indiana, January 11. Moved to New York City 1873. Attended City College 1881-1883. Excelled in drawing, tried illustration. Studied at National Academy of Design under Lemuel Wilmarth and John Q.A. Ward until 1886. 1883-1886 maintained studio in New York City. 1886 to Paris; entered Académie Julian and studied under Adolphe William Bouguereau and Joseph Nicolas Robert-Fleury for three years. Additional courses at the École des Beaux-Arts 1889 and 1890. Summers between 1887 and 1891 sketched in London and on Island of Jersey, in Brittany, Madrid, Toledo, the Forest of Fontainebleau, Brolle, and Étaples. 1891 married; eight-month stay in Giverny, where Monet lived. 1892 built home at Étaples. Returned to New York City winters of 1894-1897 to paint portraits. Around 1900 bought home on Becket Hill in Lyme, Conn., where lived remainder of life. Died Preston, Conn., February 14.

REFERENCES: Helen L. Earle, *Biographical Sketches of American Artists* (1912), 5th ed. (Charleston, N.C.: Garnier, 1972). Mantle Fielding, *Dictionary of American Painters, Sculptors, and Engravers* (1926; reprint New York: James F. Carr, 1965). De-Witt McClellan Lockman interview with Louis Dessar, Sherwood Studio, 1927, microfilm, Archives of American Art, Smithsonian Institution. William Young, *Dictionary of American Artists, Sculptors, and Engravers* (Cambridge, Mass.: Arno Press, 1968). Peter Bermingham, *American Art in the Barbizon Mood* (Exhibition catalogue, National Collection of Fine Arts, Washington, D.C., 1975).

I n both subject matter and mood, this painting is reminiscent of the work of the French artist Jean-François Millet, who had written:

The gayest thing I know is this calm, this silence which one enjoys so deliciously . . . in the tilled fields . . . You'll admit that this is always dream-like, and of sad reverie, although delicious. You're seated under some trees . . . you see coming out of a little path a poor figure laden with faggots. The always unexpected and striking manner in which this figure appears to you carries you away involuntarily toward the sad human condition, fatigue . . . Is that the gay, jolly work which certain people would have you to believe? It is nonetheless there that I find true humanity, the great poetry.[1]

Robert L. Herbert, *Barbizon Revisited* (1962).

Millet was a popular figure in the United States in the nineteenth century. In 1908 Kenyon Cox noted that

Jean François Millet . . . is now perhaps the most famous artist of the 19th century . . . His slightest work is fought for by dealers and collectors . . . If any painter of the immediate past is definitely numbered with the great masters, it is he.[2]

Cox, "The Art of Millet" (1908).

It is not surprising that Americans, who held the work ethic dear, should respond so enthusiastically to Millet's images of the worker. In fact, however, in the third quarter of the nineteenth century, the works of all the Barbizon painters were popular, probably because the bucolic beauty of the Forest of Fontainebleau struck a sensitive chord in this country. The artist Henry Ward Ranger described the situation he found in New York in 1878:

Looking back it seems as though the galleries then were flooded with fine Barbizon pictures. It was no uncommon thing for a dealer, returning from his annual trip abroad, to bring back from fifty to a hundred examples of this school.[3]

Ralcy Husted Bell, *Art-Talks With Ranger* (1914).

Allegedly, Dessar decided to give up portrait painting and concentrate on landscape after seeing some Barbizon paintings in a private New York collection. According to William McCormick:

. . . Dessar's resolution to shift his ground was formed while painting the portrait of a New York society woman in her own drawing-room in which were hung some . . . paintings. As Dessar stood in that room at work on the canvas . . . surrounded by some of the most beautiful landscapes of the Barbizon school, these stirred him as he rarely had been by either portraiture or the figure.

As he worked there . . . with those calm and exquisite visions of the French countryside . . . there came to him the conviction that in such paintings there were preserved sounder traditions of the uttermost beauty in art . . . than can be found in the two *genres* he knew best. . . . By the time he had finished the portrait he had determined that he must justify his conviction through landscape humanized by workers in the fields and woods and the farm animals with which their toil is associated.[4]

McCormick, "Louis Dessar, Tonalist" (1924).

Dessar had painted landscapes previously, both in this country and in France—in Brittany and the Fontainebleau region where he built a home at Étaples in 1892. It was not until 1897, however, that he decided to concentrate on the genre.[5] Certainly his Barbizon experience was a prime motivating factor in his decision.

It was probably in 1900, at the time Dessar moved to Old Lyme, Connecticut, that he began to paint the Millet-like subjects that became his specialty—the "dimly lit view of farmyards and pastures populated only by farm workers with oxen or small flocks of sheep."[6] He must have been encouraged in his choice of subject matter by his "master and friend" Henry Ward Ranger, whom he had met at Étaples.[7] Ranger, whose sensibilities matched Dessar's, founded the Lyme Art Colony and it was he who urged Dessar to join him there.[8]

Lyme became the American counterpart to Barbizon, developing into a year-round artists' colony. Grace Slocum noted that

THE OX-CART, 1907
Oil on canvas, 18 x 24″
Signed lower right: *Dessar 1907*

. . . in Old Lyme, Connecticut . . . the artists, many of them National Academicians, have become an integral part of the community in the lovely Connecticut River Valley. They have bought and remodelled century-old homes and barns into homes of beauty and charm.[9]

Slocum, "Old Lyme" (1925).

Dessar himself bought a 600-acre farm near Lyme. He renovated the buildings, acquired a flock of sheep, and planted a large apple orchard.[10] He then painted the subjects at hand. In 1924, McCormick wrote that Dessar,

Exhibiting less often than the average American landscape painter . . . works steadily . . . in his isolated home crowning Becket Hill near Lyme, Connecticut, from spring to late autumn, and in a studio in New York in the harshest winter months. His sheep wander slowly along tree-embowered lanes beneath a softly brilliant sky, his oxen and horses haul loads of wood through the same rustic thoroughfares, his woodcutters ply their long saws through felled trees, each one of these motives being found on his estate that spreads its six hundred acres near farm and pasture and woodland.[11]

McCormick, "Louis Dessar, Tonalist" (1924).

Dessar clearly sought to capture the charm of rural Connecticut while including what he and Ranger termed the "humanizing" element in landscape—the farm worker. Ranger could have been speaking for Dessar when he commented:

I feel that my little bit of New England, which I know and love so well, is reeking with poetic suggestion. I often say to my foreign friends in a spirit of paradox: It is the oldest pastoral-landscape-country in the Western world. Our farms which were thoroughly tilled for a century or more have, for the past hundred years, been slipping back into picturesque neglect; while Europe has been forced to improve and utilise every agricultural resource, with the result that every lane has become a macadam road . . . The pond at Corot's *Ville d'Avray* has lost its charm . . . so it goes. But in New England, the country lanes are full of brush and grass . . . with the little-used waggon [sic] track zigzagging between tumbled-down stone walls . . .

He continued:

I am sorry for any one who knows this country and does not feel its romantic charm. I would like to get into my pictures of this region a little of the love I feel for those who made it. As for me, a landscape . . . must be *humanised*. All landscapes that have been well painted are those in which the painter feels the influence of the hand of man and generations of labour. . . . Sometimes I feel that I, a poor descendant of these men, mark a decadence by merely painting amidst the scenes of their heroic labours instead of doing more virile work.[12]

Bell, *Art-Talks with Ranger* (1914).

This last comment suggests a criticism that may be directed to Dessar's work. He did not paint "amidst scenes of [workers'] heroic labours," as did Millet, whose work he obviously paraphrased. As a result, the workers in his paintings lack the authenticity of Millet's peasants. Speaking of Dessar and his colleagues at Old Lyme, Peter Bermingham offered this criticism:

The holiday atmosphere within the group and the lovely, storybook appearance of Old Lyme and its environs were hardly conducive to the intensely serious search for nature's mystery that motivated the first artists in Barbizon. Yet, divested of the retrospective considerations and critical clockwork that force us to check to see if our American artists are on the proper historical schedule, we can still appreciate the low-keyed joy, sincerity, and occasional hypnotic charm of these modest canvases from the Old Lyme group.[13]

The "hynoptic charm" of Dessar's *Ox-Cart* resides in the reverie evoked by its warm, golden tonality. The predominance of this golden brown tonality effectively evokes a mood similar to that found in the works of the other Tonalists. But bright dashes of pure pigment, applied in an Impressionist manner, are also evident. Perhaps Dessar's use of these daubs of color can be attributed to the influence of the American Impressionist Childe Hassam, who took over the leadership of the Lyme community in 1903. These strokes may also show the influence of Monet, whose works Dessar must have studied during his eight-month stay at Giverny from 1891 to 1892. But clearly it was Ranger who had the greatest influence on Dessar. It was he who advocated an emphasis on "positive line, subtlety of colour, and sonority of tone," qualities evident in this painting.[14]

NOTES

1. Jean-François Millet. In Robert L. Herbert, *Barbizon Revisited* (Exhibition catalogue, California Palace of the Legion of Honor, *et al.*, San Francisco, 1962), 45.
2. Kenyon Cox, "The Art of Millet," *Scribner's Magazine* 43, no. 3 (March 1908), 328.
3. Ralcy Husted Bell, *Art-Talks With Ranger* (New York: G.P. Putnam's, 1914), 31.
4. William B. McCormick, "Louis Dessar, Tonalist," *International Studio* 79, no. 326 (July 1924), 296.
5. Peter Bermingham, *American Art in the Barbizon Mood* (Exhibition catalogue, National Collection of Fine Arts, Washington, D.C., 1975), 136.
6. *Ibid.*, 136.
7. Clara Ruge, "The Tonal School of America," *International Studio* 27, no. 107 (January 1906), lxvi.
8. Bermingham, *Barbizon Mood*, 136, 165-66.
9. Grace Slocum, "Old Lyme," *American Magazine of Art* 15, no. 12 (December 1925), 635.
10. DeWitt McClellan Lockman interview with Louis Dessar, Sherwood Studio, Archives of American Art, Smithsonian Institution, N.Y., microfilm roll 502, frames 815-45. By permission of New-York Historical Society.
11. McCormick, "Louis Dessar," 297.
12. Bell, *Art-Talks*, 79-80, 81-82.
13. Bermingham, *Barbizon Mood*, 89.
14. Bell, *Art-Talks*, 73.

CC

ABBOTT HANDERSON THAYER

(1849-1921)
ANA 1898; NA 1901

Born in Boston, August 12; raised in Keene, New Hampshire. As a boy, sold own paintings of dogs and horses. 1867 moved to Brooklyn and studied at Brooklyn Art School. By 1869 opened studio in Brooklyn. Early 1870s attended classes at National Academy of Design. Friends at Academy included Maria Oakey [Dewing], Daniel Chester French, John La Farge. Took studio in New York City about this time. 1875 left for Paris. Studied there with Charles Lehmann and Jean Gérôme. Circle of friends included Dwight W. Tryon and George de Forest Brush. 1879 returned to New York and in 1880s and 1890s lived in various Hudson River towns. Maintained New York studio part of this time. 1888 first of many summers spent in Dublin, New Hampshire. 1897 briefly joined group of painters who seceded from Society of American Artists; group became known as The Ten after he left. 1900 actively campaigned to save sea birds from extinction. 1901 moved to Dublin, N.H.; pupils there included Rockwell Kent and Thayer's cousin Barry Faulkner. 1909 illustrated book, *Concealing Coloration in the Animal Kingdom*, written by his son Gerald Thayer to explain Abbott's theories. 1910 or 1911 became involved in campaign to save Mount Monadnock from commercial development. 1909, 1911, 1918 published articles on concealing coloration of birds and animals. Died May 29, Dublin, N.H.

REFERENCES: Nelson C. White, *Abbott H. Thayer, Painter and Naturalist* (Hartford, Conn.: Connecticut Printers, Inc., 1951). *Dictionary of American Biography* (New York: Scribner's, 1943). Mantle Fielding, *Dictionary of American Painters, Sculptors and Engravers* (1926; reprint Greensfarms, Conn.: Modern Books and Crafts, 1974).

*W*inter Landscape represents a part of Abbott Thayer's oeuvre which has received relatively little attention; his portraits and figure studies were more celebrated during his lifetime. In 1899, Nancy D'Anvers Bell included him as one of "the four great portrait painters, James McNeill Whistler, John Singer Sargent, Cecilia Beaux, and Abbott Thayer,"[1] and nine years later Sidney Allen referred to him as "one of, if not the most, distinguished of our American figure-painters."[2] Although Thayer specialized in images of "ideal maidenhood"[3] and "pseudo-Renaissance angels,"[4] painting the American landscape was probably more important to him than many of his contemporary critics realized.

The landscape exhibited here may well represent a scene in the hills surrounding Mount Monadnock, in southern New Hampshire. In 1902, the year it was painted, Thayer was a resident of nearby Dublin. The painting seems to be similar in style and subject to others which depict the mountain itself, such as *Monadnock in Winter*, 1904. (Freer Gallery of Art), *Monadnock*, c. 1911 (Corcoran Gallery of Art), and *Winter Sunrise, Monadnock*, n.d. (Metropolitan Museum of Art). *Winter Landscape*, however, represents a more intimate hillside view than these slightly more dramatic images.

Thayer lived in nearby Keene as a boy. Later, he returned with his wife and children to spend the summer of 1888 in Dublin, where they continued to spend frequent summer vacations until settling there permanently in 1901.[5] Allen notes that "Never having been overfond of city life, he retired as soon as he could afford it to the country . . . where he could live entirely for his art and ideas."[6]

Mount Monadnock received its share of attention in the late nineteenth and early twentieth centuries. Artists who painted it include George de Forest Brush, William Preston Phelps, Joseph Lindon Smith, Edmund C. Tarbell, Hermann Dudley Murphy, Frank W. Benson, Birge Harrison, Charles Curtis Allen, and Charles Herbert Woodbury.[7] Ralph Waldo Emerson paid tribute to the mountain in 1847, in his first book of poetry,[8] and Henry David Thoreau described in his journal a visit to the area in 1860. Mark Twain, whose portrait Thayer painted in 1881, spent the summer of 1905 in Dublin[9] and wrote to a friend at the end of the summer: "I remembered that Abbott Thayer had said three years before that the New Hampshire highlands was a good place. He was right—it was a good place. Any place that is good for an artist in paint is good for an artist in morals and ink."[10]

Thayer's career brings to mind that of Winslow Homer. While Homer spent his final years in Prout's Neck, Maine, painting the stormy New England coast, Thayer chose a rugged, outdoor life in rural New Hampshire, and in his occasional landscapes depicted the surrounding mountains. The two artists were compared by a contemporary writer:

It is difficult to think of affectation in connection with Mr. Thayer's work; it is, in its own way, as simple and straightfoward as that of Mr. Winslow Homer. . . . His delicacy seems quite foreign to what we ordinarily understand by daintiness; his fastidiousness is so far from being finical [sic] that it is almost austere, apparently. We know of no better way in which to characterize his art than to say that it is the poetry of simplicity; for it is as poetic as it is simple . . .[11]

Anonymous, *Scribner's Monthly* (1880).

Other writers expressed similar thoughts. Helen M. Beatty noted

WINTER LANDSCAPE, 1902
Oil on canvas, 29⅜ x 34⅞"
Signed lower right: *Abbott H. Thayer/Jan. 1902*

———————

that "He painted a few landscapes, and in these his ability and sensitive feeling for the poetic beauty of nature are evident."[12] And Catherine Beach Ely wrote: "Thayer loved the grandeur of mountains, the loneliness of their transfigured peaks, the terror of their sombre shadows, the mysterious depths of forests . . ."[13]

Although landscape was not Thayer's usual subject, a majority of those he painted—especially as a mature artist—depict snowy New England winters. His love for this rugged season found expression in some of his miscellaneous writings, as well as in his paintings:

Winter here in our northern lands is the reign of the interstellar austerities. Earth is in the grip of the pitiless martial law of solar systems, and must stand dumb, . . . But just as one finds the night full of beauty after the eyes are accustomed to the lessened light, let us dare to visit winter in his own shrine. Let us climb laboriously to the dark spruces that form in places a mat almost impenetrable on some high shoulder of a northern New England mountain. The short day is near its end as we stand at last in the deep blue shade among the spruce spires.[14]

Undated written fragment.

Among American writers, Henry David Thoreau seems closest to Thayer in attitude and sensibility, expressing a similar admiration for winter:

The wonderful purity of nature at this season is a most pleasing fact. Every decayed stump and moss-grown stone and rail, and the dead leaves of autumn, are concealed by a clean napkin of snow. In the bare fields and tinkling woods, see what virtue survives. . . . A cold and searching wind drives away all contagion, and nothing can withstand it but what has a virtue in it, and accordingly, whatever we meet with in cold and bleak places, as the tops of mountains, we respect for a sort of sturdy innocence, a Puritan toughness. All things beside seem to be called in for shelter, and what stays out must be part of the original frame of the universe, and of such valor as God himself.[15]

Thoreau, "A Winter Walk" (1843).

Writing in 1908, Sidney Allen commented on Thayer's sense of design:

Abbott H. Thayer . . . ranks to-day among modern painters as a particularly sensitive exponent of the decorative side of nature, and as a close student of the subtleties of pictorial design; he has an exceptional power of seizing upon just those aspects of life which lend themselves best to rhythmical arrangement and carefully balanced composition. He is, too, a colorist of much distinction, . . . He never cared for so-called brilliant and startling effects, but rather shunned them in order not to disturb the quiet harmony of his work. Even in his backgrounds he avoided all naturalistic detail, confining himself to simple and impressive lines.[16]

Allen, Smith's Magazine (1908).

Others, with the scientifically detailed paintings of the later Hudson River men in mind, emphasized this decorative element. An anonymous writer commented that "In comparison with Mr. [Frederic E.] Church's 'gorgeousness,' we confess it has an almost decorative look."[17]

For Thayer, art was "the presenting alone of any one of nature's jumbled impressions."[18] His technique of leaving large portions of his landscapes relatively empty may be related to his knowledge of Japanese art. We know that he was a friend of Charles Lang Freer, whose taste in Oriental art is displayed at the Freer Gallery in Washington, D.C. Although Thayer studied at the École des Beaux-Arts with Lehmann and Gérôme during the mid to late 1870s,[19] his looser, more painterly brushstroke has more in common with that of the Post-Impressionists. His landscapes, espe-

cially those of Monadnock, frequently utilize a high horizon reminiscent of Cézanne.

American landscape-paintings at the present time divide themselves into those where great detail appears and those which convey through large and simple treatment the sentiment as well as the general character of the scene they portray. Of the former class are Whittredge, McEntee, Hubbard, Kensett, and the older landscapists, such as Durand. Another set of men, conceiving landscape art rather as a combination of impressions than in its photographic detail, however beautiful the latter may be, render it through great masses of light and shade, rich colour, with here and there, in significant positions, firm and precise outline, or solid, definite drawing.[20]

Anonymous, The Art Journal (1878).

In one of Thayer's "philosophic fragments" he shows his affinity with the second set of landscapists described above: "if art were only what popular praise assumes—the mere feat of photography—it would *lag superfluous*, because it would always pay us better to *do our own looking*. Since there is everywhere we turn our eyes a scene—actual things to see, why look at the *apparently* actual?"[21] And, of a landscape done at Capri in 1901, he comments: "It is . . . a *study* of it rather than an idealization of it. I somehow lean that way in my preference as to my use of landscape."[22]

Thayer's technique, however, was not universally admired. Writing in 1896, Clarence Cook noted: "Photography, that relentless betrayer of the faults in an artist's technique, has done its best to accuse Mr. Thayer's apparently too hasty brush and his now-and-then seemingly uncertain drawing . . ."[23] Because Thayer's landscapes received relatively little critical attention during his lifetime, it is likely that many such comments refer primarily to his figure studies. His painting technique remained much the same whatever his subject, however, so criticism such as this can probably be applied to the landscapes as well.

Thayer, who "scrutinized nature with the curiosity of a naturalist,"[24] was the philosophical descendant of those earlier American artists who combined interests in art and science. He played an active role in preservation of the country's natural resources, and one of several issues that involved him was a campaign to save Mount Monadnock from possible development:

Because the evolution of all modern institutions inevitably overwhelms and obliterates even the most beautiful and representative forms of primitive nature, museums gather into their collections all possible examples and tokens of this vanishing period. The primeval forest in general doomed [sic], like the rest, . . . This northern slope of Monadnock is perhaps the only wild forest in New England that has ever *come near* being saved, in this way, from the swelling tide of inevitable vulgarization. Oh if it could be saved! . . . Emerson says ("Forbearance")

"Hast thou named all the birds without a gun
Loved the woodrose, and left it on its stalk?"

It is not that we may ever lack the infinite. The firmament of stars is safe and is enough. What the world *needs* is what Emerson in that poem reminds us of—some proof that man can *see* without *taking*. . . .[25]

Thayer, Draft of a letter (c. 1911).

That Thayer quoted Emerson was natural; his admiration for the poet was so profound that he named one of his sons Ralph Waldo.[26] In this letter, he also shows his affinity with Thoreau, who had expressed concern about preserving the American landscape fifty years earlier:

What are the natural features which make a township handsome? A river, . . . a lake, a hill, a cliff or individual rocks, a forest, and ancient trees standing singly. Such things are beautiful; they have a high use which dollars and cents never represent. If the inhabitants of a town were wise, they would seek to preserve these things, though at a considerable expense; for such things educate far more than any hired teachers, . . . Most men, it seems to me, do not care for Nature, and would sell their share in all her beauty, as long as they may live, for a stated sum. Thank God, men cannot as yet fly, and lay waste the sky as well as the earth. We are safe on that side for the present.[27]

Thoreau, *Journal* (1861).

NOTES

1. Nancy D'Anvers Bell, *Representative Painters of the Nineteenth Century* (New York: E.P. Hutton, 1899), 53.

2. Sidney Allen (Sadakichi Hartmann), "Abbott Handerson Thayer: An Appreciation of His Work," *Smith's Magazine* (March 1908), 903.

3. Bell, *Representative Painters*, 55.

4. Donelson F. Hoopes, *The American Impressionists* (New York: Watson-Guptill Publications), 1972, 16.

5. Allen, "Abbott Handerson Thayer," 903. Nelson C. White, *Abbott H. Thayer, Painter and Naturalist* (Hartford, Conn.: Connecticut Printers, 1951), 53, 99.

6. Allen, "Abbott Handerson Thayer," 903.

7. Allen Chamberlain, *The Annals of the Grand Monadnock* (Concord, N.H.: Society for the Protection of New Hampshire Forests, 1936), 175. Dorothy W. Phillips, *A Catalogue of the Collection of American Paintings in the Corcoran Gallery of Art* (Washington, D.C.: The Corcoran Gallery of Art, 1973), 2:61.

8. Chamberlain, *Annals*, 1, 175.

9. White, *Abbott H. Thayer*, 40, 113, 114.

10. Samuel Clemens to Frederick A. Duneka, 1905. In *ibid.*, 114.

11. "The Younger Painters of America," *Scribner's Monthly* 20, no. 3 (July 1880), 326-27.

12. Helen M. Beatty, "Abbott H. Thayer," *The American Magazine of Art* 12, no. 10 (Oct. 1921), 331.

13. Catherine Beach Ely, "J. Alden Weir," *Art in America* 12, no. 111 (April 1924), 118.

14. White, *Abbott H. Thayer*, 200.

15. Henry David Thoreau, "A Winter Walk," (1843), *The Writings of Henry David Thoreau*, vol. 5, *Excursions and Poems* (New York: Houghton Mifflin, 1906), 167.

16. Allen, "Abbott Handerson Thayer," 903, 913.

17. "Younger Painters of America," 328.

18. White, *Abbott H. Thayer*, 201.

19. *Ibid.*, 195, 23.

20. "American Painters—J. Appleton Brown," *The Art Journal* 4, no. 43 (July 1878), 198.

21. White, *Abbott H. Thayer*, 233.

22. Abbott H. Thayer to Charles Lang Freer, regarding a painting of Monte Solaro at Capri, later purchased by Freer. In *ibid.*, 91.

23. Clarence Cook, "Some Present Aspects of Art in America," *The Chautauquan* 23, no. 5 (Aug. 1896), 601.

24. Nathaniel Pousette-Dart, *Abbott H. Thayer* (New York: Frederick A. Stokes, 1923), vii.

25. White, *Abbott H. Thayer*, 142-43.

26. *Ibid.*, 38.

27. Henry David Thoreau, *Journal*, January 3, 1861. In H.G.O. Blake, ed., *Winter: From the Journal of Henry D. Thoreau* (New York: Houghton, Mifflin, 1888), 108, 110.

KN

ROBERT WILLIAM VONNOH

(1858-1933)
ANA 1900; NA 1906

Born Hartford, Conn., September 17. At fourteen entered a lithographic house and worked cleaning press. Studied at Massachusetts Normal Art School in Boston 1875-1879. 1879-1881 taught at the Massachusetts Normal Art School, Roxbury Evening Drawing School, and Thayer Academy in South Braintree, Mass. 1881-1883 studied at the Académie Julian in Paris, under Gustave Boulanger and Jules Joseph Lefebvre. Returned from Paris 1883 and began career as portrait painter. Became principal of East Boston Drawing School 1883-1885 and instructor at Cowles Art School 1884-1885. 1885-1887 principal instructor in portrait and figure painting at Boston Museum of Fine Arts. Went abroad 1887-1891. 1891-1896 principal instructor in portrait and figure painting at Pennsylvania Academy of the Fine Arts. Married sculptress Bessie O. Potter in 1899. 1907-1911 abroad again. 1918-1920 instructor in composition and life figure painting at Pennsylvania Academy of the Fine Arts. Pupils included Robert Henri, John Sloan, and William Glackens. 1920 until death divided time between Lyme, Conn., and Gréz-sur-Loing, France, near the Forest of Fontainebleau. Was a member of Lyme Art Colony. Did little painting from 1923-1933 because of poor eyesight. Reportedly interested in real estate; active in promoting the building of cooperative artists' studios at West 57th Street, New York, and elsewhere. Died December 28, at Nice.

REFERENCES: Harold Donaldson Eberlein, "Robert W. Vonnoh, Painter of Men," *Arts and Decoration* 2, no. 11 (September 1912). Helen L. Earle, *Biographical Sketches of American Artists* (1912), 5th ed. (Charleston, N.C.: Garnier, 1972). Mantle Fielding, *Dictionary of American Painters, Sculptors, and Engravers* (1926) (New York: James I. Carr, 1965). Eliot Clark, "The Art of Robert Vonnoh," *Art in America* 16, no. 5 (August 1928). *New York Times*, obituary, December 29, 1933. William Young, *Dictionary of American Painters, Sculptors, and Engravers* (Cambridge, Mass.: William Young, 1968). William H. Gerdts, *American Impressionism* (Exhibition catalogue, Henry Art Gallery, University of Washington, Seattle, 1980).

Robert Vonnoh must be considered historically one of the pioneer impressionists of America. When the low tones of the Barbizon school were in the ascendent, this innovator was experimenting in pure color. A scientific turn of mind and receptive nature made Vonnoh doubly susceptible to the new discoveries of light and air. He was probably the first American painter to grasp the significance of the scientific color relations of the impressionists. At a time when Twachtman was still absorbed in tonal grays Vonnoh was applying paint almost directly from the tube in a system of vibratory complementary relations.[1]

Eliot Clark, "Art of Robert Vonnoh" (1928).

Vonnoh began working in an Impressionist manner around 1887. Only six years earlier he had been in Paris studying French academic painting with Boulanger and Lefebvre. In 1883 he returned to the United States to begin his career as a portrait painter.[2] During the following years he developed an interest in Impressionism. As Clark wrote:

His work out of doors, and perhaps also study of pastels, led him to the consideration of light and color. Impressionism was in the air. It was like letting the sunlight into a sombre room. The second trip to France in '87 brought the painter in direct contact with the work of the Impressionists. This was the decisive period of Vonnoh's art as a colorist. His own nature seemed perfectly attuned to the new conception.[3]

Vonnoh, as one of America's "pioneer Impressionists," was considered something of a revolutionary:

Mr. Vonnoh stirred up, and thoroughly startled the art world of the period. Many of the leading artists considered his method and technique revolutionary and not to be trusted. They regarded him as extremely radical and his work created a great furore [sic].[4]

Eberlein, "Robert W. Vonnoh, Painter of Men" (1912).

Though some American critics, like Richard Riordan, defended the Impressionist cause and tried to clarify the objectives of the movement, others, more conservative, vehemently criticized the Impressionists.[5] In 1891, one critic went so far as to describe Monet's paintings, exhibited at New York's Union League Club, as "defiant and commonly brutal in their exaggerations."[6]

As late as 1907, Richard Muther, in his *History of Modern Painting*, criticized Vonnoh for "the barbaric means" and "hazardous schemes of colour" he employed to attain the effect of light in his work.[7]

In his desire to explore the subject and technique of the Impressionists, Vonnoh traveled to Giverny where Monet had taken up residence in 1883.[8] Monet was the most popular of the Impressionists among the American converts to the movement, and his presence at Giverny attracted many of these artists to the hamlet. A writer in the 1887 edition of *Art Amateur* reported:

Quite an American colony has gathered, I am told, at Givernay [sic], seventy miles from Paris on the Seine, the home of Claude Monet, including our Louis Ritter, W. L. Metcalf, Theodore Wendell, John Breck, and Theodore Robinson of New York. A few pictures just received from these men show that they have all got the blue-green color of Monet's impressionism and "got it bad."[9]

According to Eliot Clark, Vonnoh painted *A Sunlit Hillside* at Giverny.[10] The painting shows several of the red-roofed houses

A SUNLIT HILLSIDE, 1890
Oil on canvas, 25 x 20¾″
Signed lower left: *Vonnoh, 1890*

that dotted the landscape of the village. The simple houses and the wide slope of lawn in the foreground are enveloped in the bright light of a noonday sun. Characteristically,

It is a painting of fine color, typical of the carefully considered treatment which distinguishes Vonnoh's work. There is vibration in the light . . . and the painting takes on the transparent, luminous quality of sunny atmosphere itself.[11]

Anonymous, "Vonnoh's Half Century" (1923).

Giverny was a region particularly suited for Impressionist studies, as Clark reported in 1921:

The surrounding country [of Giverny] is happily related to the predilections of the modern painter. It has a peculiarly delightful and intimate charm. The river reflects the opposite shore and its banks are grown with picturesque poplars; the fields are cultivated with varicolored products; the hillsides, only so high as to define the valley, are mapped out in interesting patterns, and the little hamlet of Giverny, with red-roofed houses and simple facades, belongs to the intimacy of the landscape. It is a decidedly friendly country and has nothing of the forbidding, the austere, or the solemn grandeur of uncultivated nature.[12]

Clark, "Theodore Robinson" (1921).

In his conception of this scene at Giverny, Vonnoh probably owes a debt to another American artist who painted in the village—Theodore H. Robinson. Robinson first went to Giverny in 1887; he returned there in the summer of 1888 and settled next door to Monet.[13] He and Monet became close friends, and the French master offered advice and encouragement regarding his career. None of the other Americans at Giverny (Vonnoh included) enjoyed that good fortune. Monet refused to teach, and evidently met only infrequently with American visitors.[14] It must be concluded, then, that most of the American artists in Giverny learned primarily from the example of Monet's work and had to look to one another for support and encouragement. Certainly Robinson, because of his close relationship to Monet, could have been an influential figure in this community.

Robinson's *Winter Landscape* of 1889 (Daniel J. Terra Collection), also a Giverny landscape, is similar in subject and composition to Vonnoh's *Sunlit Hillside*.[15] In both paintings there are Cézannesque elements. William Gerdts discusses the elements of similarity between Robinson's and Cézanne's work in words that may be applied to Vonnoh's *Sunlit Hillside*:

Many of Robinson's landscape compositions have an obvious geometric structuring, based on a series of dominant, parallel diagonals which are determined by the viewpoint selected, and the placement of forms of buildings, and other elements in the landscape, and echoed by the repeated diagonal direction of the broken brushwork. A kinship with the work of Cézanne is suggested here, but a connection between the two artists is so far unrecorded.[16]

There is no recorded connection between Vonnoh and Cézanne. It is probable that Vonnoh was influenced in his structuring of this painting by the example of Robinson's work, completed a year earlier than his. Robinson, in turn, was probably introduced to Cézanne through Monet, who was quite an admirer of Cézanne's work. As Lilla Cabot Perry wrote:

Monet was most appreciative of the work of his contemporaries. . . . In his bedroom, a large room over the studio, he had quite a gallery of the works of such Impressionists as Renoir, Camille Pissarro . . . [and] a charming hillside with little houses on it by Cézanne, about whom Monet had many interesting things to say.[17]

Perry, "Reminiscences of Claude Monet" (1927).

It is interesting to speculate that Robinson may have seen this painting and used it as a model for his painting of 1889. This is only a conjecture that demands further investigation. At the very least, though, it seems likely that Monet shared his enthusiasm for Cézanne with his friend Robinson, who could have passed this influence on to Vonnoh. Such an enthusiasm also would have coincided with a long American tradition of respect for planar and geometric relationships within the painting.

Although Vonnoh was primarily influenced by Monet and shared his interest in expressing the effects of outdoor light and color, he did not go nearly as far as the European master in exploring these concerns. He remained basically a "realistic Impressionist."[18] By the end of the first decade of the twentieth century, critics judged this artist—who was still termed a "bold colorist" as late as 1907—a conservative figure. Just a year before the 1913 Armory Show in America, Eberlein wrote:

[Vonnoh] was the arch-impressionist of the day. So accustomed are we now to having all our sensibilities jolted afresh each year by the screaming vagaries of extremists that, looking back calmly at this distance of time, it seems almost impossible to realize what could possibly have stirred up all the disturbance regarding him. Since then others have gone far beyond his most radical ventures. In fact, it would be perfectly correct to describe Mr. Vonnoh as a conservative impressionist. . .[19]

Eberlein, "Robert W. Vonnoh" (1912).

NOTES

1. Eliot Clark, "The Art of Robert Vonnoh," *Art in America* 16, no. 5 (August, 1928), 229-30.
2. *Ibid.*, 232. Vonnoh may have been painting in an Impressionist manner earlier, but it was in 1887 that he went to France, where he came in direct contact with the work of the Impressionists. Further research is needed to more precisely record Vonnoh's stylistic development.
3. *Ibid.*
4. Harold Donaldson Eberlein, "Robert W. Vonnoh, Painter of Men," *Arts and Decoration* 2, no. 11, (September 1912), 383.
5. See "From Another Point of View" by R.R. (probably Richard Riordan) and W.H.W., "What is Impressionism? II." In *The Art Amateur* 28, no. 7 (December 1892), 5.
6. Anonymous, "Claude Monet," *Collector* 2, no. 8, (Feb. 15, 1891), 91.
7. Richard Muther, *History of Modern Painting* (London: Henry and Co., 1907), 3:490-91.
8. John Rewald, *History of Impressionism*, 4th rev. ed. (New York: New York Graphic Society, 1973), 489. No publication makes mention of Vonnoh being in Giverny. We do know that he was in Grez-sur-Loing, near the Forest of Fontainebleau, where he painted *November*, 1890 (Eberlein, 383). However, the card on file at the National Academy of Design on *A Sunlit Hillside* reads "Painting done at Giverny, France per EC [probably Eliot Clark]." Clark's determination of the location of the subject can probably be verified fairly certainly visually by the comparison of Vonnoh's work with two paintings, definitely painted at Giverny, by Theodore H. Robinson. See William Gerdts, *American Impressionism* (Exhibition catalogue, Henry Art Gallery, University of Washington, Seattle, 1980), 52, for a reproduction of Robinson's *Winter Landscape*, 1889 (Daniel J. Terra Collection); and Florence Lewison, "Theodore Robinson and Claude Monet," *Apollo* 78, no. 19 (September 1963), 209, for a reproduction of Robinson's *Bird's Eye View: Giverny, France*, 1889 (Metropolitan Museum of Art). Both paintings show houses with simple facades similar to those that appear in Vonnoh's work, and the hilly terrain of Giverny. All of the paintings were probably executed in the same locale, thus placing Vonnoh in Giverny sometime in 1890.

170

9. "Greta," "Boston Art and Artists," *The Art Amateur* 17, no. 5 (October 1887), 93. In Gerdts, *American Impressionism*, 30.

10. See note 8.

11. Anonymous, "Vonnoh's Half Century," *International Studio* 77, no. 313 (June 1923), 232.

12. Eliot Clark, "Theodore Robinson," *Scribner's Magazine* 70, no. 6 (December 1921), 766.

13. Gerdts, *American Impressionism*, 51-52.

14. Walter Pach, "At the Studio of Claude Monet," *Scribner's Magazine* 43, no. 6 (June 1908), 765-66.

15. For a reproduction of Robinson's painting, see Gerdts, *American Impressionism*, 52, note 10.

16. *Ibid.*, 53.

17. Lilla Cabot Perry, "Reminiscences of Claude Monet from 1889 to 1909," *American Magazine of Art* 18, no. 3, (March 1927), 125.

18. See Eliot Clark, "The Art of Robert Vonnoh," 231.

19. Eberlein, "Robert W. Vonnoh," 383.

CC

(Frederick) Childe Hassam

(1859-1935)
ANA 1902; NA 1906

Born October 17, Dorchester, Mass. 1876 apprenticed to Boston wood engraver. Did freelance illustration for books and magazines. Around 1879 first studied painting under I.M. Gaugengigl in Boston. 1883 first trip to Europe; visited Great Britain, Holland, France, Italy, Spain. Took studio in Boston on return. 1886 second trip to Europe. Took studio in Paris; attended Académie Julian, studying under Gustave Boulanger and Jules Lefebvre. 1887 exhibited at Paris Salon; began painting in Impressionist style. 1889 won Bronze Medal at Exposition Universelle, first of many awards. Returned to New York; maintained studio on Fifth Avenue. 1897 third European trip; visited Italy, France, England. Resigned from Society of American Artists and formed "Ten American Painters" with J. Alden Weir, John Twachtman, and others. 1898 first exhibition of "Ten" at Galerie Durand-Ruel, N.Y. 1903 first summer at Old Lyme, Conn. 1905 first one-man show at Montross Galleries, N.Y. 1908 to San Francisco and Oregon. 1910 last trip to Europe; visited France and Spain. 1914 to California. 1919 major retrospective of works at Montross Galleries. 1920 elected to American Academy of Arts and Letters. 1927 to California. Besides Old Lyme, summered at Isles of Shoals, Me.; Provincetown and Gloucester, Mass.; New Canaan and Cos Cob, Conn.; East Hampton, L.I. Died August 27, East Hampton.

REFERENCE; Donelson F. Hoopes, *Childe Hassam* (New York: Watson-Guptill, 1979).

C hilde Hassam painted *The Jewel Box, Old Lyme* in the summer of 1906 while staying at the home of Miss Florence Griswold in Old Lyme, Connecticut. Through the hospitality of "Miss Florence" and the village community, the increasing numbers of artists who assembled at Old Lyme each summer formed for a time the largest summer art colony in the East, superseding older havens such as Newport and Lake George.[1] In the category of rural landscape painting, Old Lyme was a major center of American Impressionism, at its height in the opening years of the present century. Among the other artists painting there in this period were Louis Paul Dessar and Gifford Beal, both represented in the present exhibition.

When Hassam first visited Old Lyme in 1903 he wrote to his friend and fellow Impressionist J. Alden Weir in Branchville, Connecticut:

We are up here in another old corner of Connecticut and it is very much like your country. There are some very large oaks and chestnuts and many fine hedges. Lyme, or Old Lyme as it is usually called, is at the mouth of the Connecticut River and it really is a pretty fine old town.[2]

Letter, July 17, 1903.

It seems significant that Hassam should refer not to broad prospects or hilly horizons but to near-at-hand components of the local landscape. This limited perspective best suited the Impressionist mode he had learned in France, which concerned itself primarily with the play of light on objects and a pictorial scheme oriented toward the picture plane. Hence, as one can see in Hassam's picture, all the painter now really required for his model, and often preferred, was a few square feet of space. For this modest scope of interest, the critic J. Walker McSpadden in 1923 called Hassam, oddly enough, "typically American, and a painter who never finds it necessary to leave New York in winter, or certain spots of New England in summer, to make a grand tour in search of the picturesque."[3] In a related vein, Donelson F. Hoopes has likened Hassam's summer haunts on the Connecticut shore (Old Lyme and Cos Cob) to Monet's retreat at Giverny.[4] He thus implies that such oft-repeated motifs as the Congregationalist Church and the woodland interiors at Old Lyme are similar in interest to the Frenchman's famous series of water lilies.

The "grand tour" referred to by McSpadden was, of course, a fashion chiefly among landscape painters of the preceding century. Certainly, the panoramic impulse of that era had, at least temporarily, abated. So too had the age of exploration and development that had inspired it. By 1890 the American continent had been contained by its people. By the turn of the century a few alert individuals had begun to recognize the environmental implications of this occupation and to consider preserving the natural splendors that had survived the territorial hunger of Manifest Destiny. The new restricted breadth of the American landscape painter's vision was in some measure echoed by a national sentiment, indeed policy, of restricting the unscrupulous consumption of the land. Although in his conduct of foreign affairs President Theodore Roosevelt remained an adherent of the doctrine of Manifest Destiny, he repeatedly warned of its domestic consequences. In 1907, for example, he observed:

Optimism is a good characteristic, but if carried to an excess it becomes foolishness. We are prone to speak of the natural resources of this country as inexhaustible; this is not so. The mineral wealth of the country . . . does not reproduce itself, and therefore is certain to be exhausted ultimately; and wastefulness in dealing with it to-day means that our descendants will feel the exhaustion a generation or two before they otherwise would. But there are certain other forms of waste which could be entirely

THE JEWEL BOX, OLD LYME, 1906
Oil on canvas, 20 x 24″
Signed lower left: *Childe Hassam 1906*
Diploma painting

stopped—the waste of soil by washing, for instance . . . is easily preventable, so that this present enormous loss of fertility is entirely unnecessary. The preservation or replacement of the forests is one of the most important means of preventing this loss.[5]

"Seventh Annual Message" (1907).

In response to his own call Roosevelt set aside hundreds of millions of acres of forest land for preservation or controlled use, and created numerous national parks and refuges.[6] The public acts circumscribing these natural areas can be seen in one sense as analogous to the artistic impulse of the American Impressionists in fashioning their own more intimate preserves on canvas. Both acknowledged—one officially, one tacitly—the limits of the previous century's boundless horizons, and regarded the remaining landscape with a less sweeping eye. This is especially true of the American Impressionists, who often maintained a respect for the integrity of the object which distinguished their art from the more amorphous vision of their exemplars in France.[7]

Mineral, soil, and trees: these mundane elements that Roosevelt sought to protect are all that comprise Hassam's picture—adding, of course, the broken sunlight that transfigures their surfaces. This is one of the happier instances in which the artist did not fancifully insert an idle nymph into his forest interior, creating, in critic Royal Cortissoz' words, "a somewhat specious effect."[8] As if in place of the nude figure Hassam has embedded a huge stone in the center of the composition. One must imagine that the scintillating character the painter has lent to the boulder and its surroundings suggested the title for this picture, since there does not presently exist in Old Lyme a site called "The Jewel Box." In any case Hassam occasionally titled his works metaphorically,[9] an understandable tendency in that Impressionist vision can vividly reveal the poetic potential of matter, even that of inanimate stone.

In the year that Hassam painted this picture the New England farmer Robert Frost abandoned his ill-fitting career for a temporary one as a teacher, even as he was struggling for recognition as a poet.[10] Though Frost the poet ultimately achieved enduring fame, he never relinquished the illusion of himself as an ordinary agrarian: his themes, imagery, even his poetic voice were cultivated from a provincial ambience. In these excerpts from a poem of 1921, Frost's narrator finds refuge and inspiration in an astral rock as plain and precious as that in Hassam's *Jewel Box*:

> Never tell me that not one star of all
> That slip from heaven at night and softly fall
> Has been picked up with stones to build a wall.
>
> Some laborer found one faded and stone cold,
> And saving that its weight suggested gold,
> And tugged it from his first too certain hold,
>
> He noticed nothing in it to remark. . . .
>
> He did not recognize in that smooth coal
> The one thing palpable besides the soul
> To penetrate the air in which we roll. . . .
>
> Nor know that he might move it from the spot,
> The harm was done; from having been star-shot
> The very nature of the soil was hot
>
> And burning to yield flowers instead of grain,
> Flowers fanned and not put out by all the rain
> Poured on them by his prayers prayed in vain. . . .

> It went for building stone, and I, as though
> Commanded in a dream, forever go
> To right the wrong that this should have been so.
>
> Yet ask where else it could have gone as well,
> I do not know—I cannot stop to tell:
> He might have left it lying where it fell. . . .
>
> Though not, I say, a star of death and sin,
> It yet has poles, and only needs a spin
> To show its worldly nature and begin
>
> To chafe and shuffle in my calloused palm
> And run off in strange tangents with my arm
> As fish do with the line in first alarm.
>
> Such as it is, it promises the prize
> Of the one world complete in any size
> That I am like to compass, fool or wise.[11]

"A Star in a Stone-Boat" (1921).

NOTES

1. The Old Lyme art colony enjoyed preeminence from 1906 to 1914, and survives to the present in the form of the Lyme Art Association. See the introduction by Robin Richman in *The Art Colony at Old Lyme* (Exhibition catalogue, Lyman Allen Art Museum, New London, Conn., 1966), 7-21.

2. Childe Hassam, Letter to J. Alden Weir, July 17, 1903, Hassam Papers, American Academy of Arts and Letters; microfilm in the Archives of American Art, Smithsonian Institution, N.Y., roll NAA 2, frame 67.

3. J. Walker McSpadden, *Famous Painters of America* (New York: Dodd, Mead, 1923), 403. Hassam actually traveled more widely than McSpadden suggests in his characterization of him. However, he is accurate in distinguishing the artist from the picturesque painter who wandered in search of remote wilderness landmarks to represent for a travel-hungry public. On the whole, Hassam's affections were regional, as were those of many other American Impressionists. For a discussion of this regional focus in American landscape of the early twentieth century see Charles Eldredge, "Connecticut Impressionists: The Spirit of Place," *Art in America* 62 (Sept.-Oct. 1974), 85-89.

4. Hoopes observes: "Under Hassam, the shoreline of Connecticut became a kind of Giverny of America." See Donelson F. Hoopes, *The American Impressionists* (New York: Watson-Guptill, 1972), 16.

5. Theodore Roosevelt, "Seventh Annual Message," December 30, 1907. In *Theodore Roosevelt Cyclopedia*, Albert Bushnell Hart and Ronald Ferleger, eds. (New York: Roosevelt Memorial Association, 1941), 102.

6. For a chronology of Roosevelt's accomplishments in the field of conservation, see *Theodore Roosevelt's America*, Farida A. Wiley, ed. (New York: Devin-Adair Company, 1955), 400-02.

7. For a discussion of "form integrity" in American Impressionism, with reference to Hassam in particular, see Barbara Novak, *American Painting of the Nineteenth Century* (New York: Praeger, 1969), 59-60, 244-45.

8. Royal Cortissoz, *American Artists* (New York: Scribner's, 1923), 140.

9. One of Hassam's biographers reports, for example, that he painted a picture at Old Lyme which he named *The Dragon Cloud* for its sky effects. See Adeline Adams, *Childe Hassam* (New York: American Academy of Arts and Letters, 1938), 89.

10. For an account of Frost's life in the years 1905-1907, see Lawrance Thompson, *Robert Frost* (New York: Holt, Rinehart and Winston, 1966), vol. 1, *The Early Years*, 313-34.

11. Robert Frost, "A Star in a Stone-Boat." In *Collected Poems of Robert Frost* (New York: Henry Holt, 1930), 213-15. Frost first published this poem in the Yale *Review*, January, 1921. See Thompson, *Robert Frost*, vol. 2, "The Years of Triumph," 154, 569, n. 19.

KA

LEONARD OCHTMAN

(1854-1934)
ANA 1898; NA 1904

Born in Zonnemaire, Holland. Emigrated to America in 1866. Lived with family in Albany, N.Y. and painted landscapes of the surrounding area. Self-taught. At age sixteen, began ten-year stint as draftsman in wood engraving office (c.1870-1880). Mid-1880s moved to New York, acquired studio near Union Square. About this time, attended one winter session at the Art Students' League of New York. 1882 exhibited at the National Academy of Design for the first time. 1885 or 1886 traveled to England, France, Holland. 1891 built studio in Riverside (Greenwich), Conn., where he held classes for five years. 1892 birth of daughter, Dorothy, also a painter. 1896 built home/studio, Grayledge, in Mianus, Conn., overlooking Mianus River. Moved there in 1897. 1899 participated in first exhibition of Society of Landscape Painters, in Chicago. Sometime around 1900 moved to Cos Cob, Conn., where he remained the rest of his life. 1927 trip to England. Died October.

REFERENCES: Mantle Fielding, *Dictionary of American Painters, Sculptors and Engravers* (1926; reprint Greensfarms, Conn.: Modern Books and Crafts, 1974). "The Society of Landscape Painters," *Brush and Pencil* 4, no. 2 (May 1899). "Ochtman Paintings Now Being Shown at NYC Gallery" [Old Greenwich, Conn.] *Village Gazette*, January 10, 1963. Alfred Trumble, "A Painter's Progress," *The Year's Art as Recorded in the Quarterly Illustrator* 2, no. 5 (Jan.-March 1894). Helen L. Earle, *Biographical Sketches of American Artists* (Lansing, Mich.: Michigan State Library, 1924).

*W*oodland was probably exhibited for the first time in the spring of 1899, at the Chicago exhibition of works by the Society of Landscape Painters. A reproduction of the painting, entitled *In the Woods*, appeared in the May issue of *Brush and Pencil* that year, illustrating a review of the exhibit.[1] The writer was favorably impressed with Ochtman's contributions:

On the opposite walls are some really fine and poetic landscapes by Leonard Ochtman, who would be preferred by many to any of the other artists represented. His color is very charming and delicate, his compositions are always pleasing and as a whole attractive, and show an intimacy with nature and poetic sentiment which is rare,—particularly so in this group of painters.[2]

In expressing his preference for Ochtman's work, the critic stressed the importance of outdoor or plein-air painting:

The members are well-known painters and all but two have their studios in New York City. They are . . . Leonard Ochtman, Connecticut, Charles H. Davis, Connecticut, . . . One might make the remark, after studying the exhibition, that if there were more studios in Connecticut, instead of in New York City, the collection would be none the worse for it. This idea

crowds one at first sight,—the number of good things in this display of landscapes which are studio pictures that never saw the benign light of an out-door sky. . . . the exhibition forces the moral that Davis, Ochtman, [Walter] Palmer, and [Walter] Clark demonstrate that it is important to live in nature, study it, and paint it personally.[3]

Ochtman is a relatively little-known member of the group loosely defined as American Impressionists. In 1905, Samuel Isham wrote:

This complete adaptation and assimilation of the new theories and methods [of Impressionism], developed in Paris during the seventies, so that they might be applied to the rendering of the spirit of American scenery naturally and without trace of their foreign derivation, culminated in a group of men like [Dwight W.] Tryon, Ochtman, J. Appleton Brown, who stand somewhat in the place that [George] Inness and Homer D. Martin occupied twenty years or so before. They are not as yet such commanding or such isolated figures and it is not possible to tell what consecration time may bring.[4]

History of American Painting.

Other contemporaries reviewed Ochtman's work favorably, although after his death, according to Richard Boyle, "his reputation dimmed and his work was stored away in attics":[5]

Among the artists of this country who have taken the lead in studying nature in the light of the open air, Ochtman has won a foremost position. He is keenly sensitive to the quiet moods of nature and to the manifestations of subtlest quality. Few canvases equal his in refinement of observation and delicate tonality.[6]

Caffin, *Story of American Painting* (1907).

George Inness and Alexander Wyant were among those who reportedly admired his work and "predicted a future" for him. Negative criticism, on the other hand, suggested that his paintings were "sometimes inclined to sensationalism," that his landscapes "lack warmth of feeling, and, at times, look rather empty."[7] One critic wrote: "Some might desire a little stronger dramatic quality, and technically, more solidity in the foregrounds . . ."[8]

Ochtman moved from New York City to Mianus, Connecticut, in 1897,[9] and was probably living in that area when he painted *Woodland*. He remained in the Greenwich area the rest of his life, and many of his paintings depict the surrounding countryside. Early in this century Ochtman began to list his residence as Cos Cob, Connecticut.[10] The importance of this little town was indicated by Lincoln Steffens, writing in 1931:

Cos Cob, Conn., is a little old fishing-village strung along one side of one long street facing Cos Cob harbor in the town of Greenwich, . . . Within commuting distance of New York, many people who could not lose touch

WOODLAND
Oil on canvas, 16 x 20"
Signed lower left: *Leonard Ochtman*
Diploma painting

with the great city went there for their country homes or board, the rich to parklike Greenwich, the others to picturesque Cos Cob. . . . Quiet, almost dead, it was a paintable spot frequented by artists who worked, painters who actually painted: [John] Twachtman and the Murphys, Childe Hassam and Elmer MacRae . . . It was an "art colony"; the painters there were sometimes called "the Cos Cob school". . .[11]

Steffens, *Autobiography.*

J. Alden Weir settled in nearby Branchville as early as 1883; John Twachtman moved to Cos Cob in 1886. Other artists who visited the area included Theodore Robinson, Albert Ryder, Ernest Lawson, and Childe Hassam.[12] Hassam, more of a city man himself, dubbed Twatchman and the others the "Cos Cob Clapboard School" to indicate the rural nature of their painting, and a more recent writer has referred to that portion of the Connecticut shore as "a kind of Giverny of America," emphasizing its importance to the development of American Impressionism.[13]

Of Ochtman's exact relationship with the other artists, very little seems to be known. One writer said that "His specialty— landscape—was entirely self-taught." The Academy's records confirm this, although both sources indicate that Ochtman studied at the New York Art Students' League for about three months.[14] Alfred Trumble suggested that:

From the time he settled in New York, Mr. Ochtman's progress was rapid. To the slender, reserved young man, . . . every gallery among whose treasures he wandered, silently observant and studious, was a school. He had already, by a natural process of development, learned to think and paint for himself. Now, learning how others thought and painted, he unconsciously gathered strength.[15]

"A Painter's Progress" (1894).

Although concerned with plein-air realism, in *Woodland* Ochtman displays an American conceptual bias toward the local color of objects, rather than the perceptual bias of the French Impressionists:

Though living under skies as radiant as those of Spain or Greece, we as a nation are strangely unresponsive to the appeal of color. Whether it be due to the rigorous mental cast of our pioneer settlers, to drab Puritan and gray Quaker, or to more deeply rooted circumstances, the fact remains that the typical American looks askance upon any degree of chromatic license.[16]

Brinton, "Conquest of Color" (1917).

The titles of many of Ochtman's paintings indicate an interest in time of day, season, and weather. The Academy's annual exhibition catalogues provide such descriptive titles as *Autumn Glory, Gray Morning, Frosty Acres, Evening Light,* and *Morning in Early Summer.*[17] Rather than the optical concerns of some of the French Impressionists, Ochtman's emphasis seems to have been closer to that of the American Impressionists as a whole— one of sentiment and poetry.[18]

In his decision to portray the quieter moods of nature, Ochtman was artistic successor to such intimate luminist painters as Fitz Hugh Lane and Martin Johnson Heade. Unlike their open-ended compositions, however, *Woodland* depicts a more enclosed site, one of the "quiet, sylvan moods of the Impressionists."[19]

It is very possible that the decline of panoramic art is due to the fact that mere breadth, extent, physical bigness, yields no such mental elation as does the contemplation of a corner of the world viewed by an artist of

distinguished temperament, lyrical in his emotions, and possessed of all those sanctities of sight that a loving study of, and living with, nature has endowed him.[20]

Fowler, "New Heritage of Painting of the Nineteenth Century" (1901).

At night I went out into the dark and saw a glimmering star and heard a frog, and Nature seemed to say, Well do not these suffice? Here is a new scene, a new experience. Ponder it, Emerson, and not like the foolish world, hanker after thunders and multitudes and vast landscapes, the sea or Niagara.[21]

Ralph Waldo Emerson, *Journal* (1838).

There is an emphasis on modest and local subjects in these comments, reiterated, for example, by Catherine Beach Ely, in an article on J. Alden Weir in 1924: "He preferred the ordinary (though not repellant [sic]) aspects of his own country to the more convenient picturesqueness of foreign lands; he did not feel obliged to expatriate himself in order to find inspiration."[22] In 1894, Hamlin Garland had expressed similar thoughts:

. . . art, to be vital, must be local in its subject; its universal appeal must be in its working out,—in the way it is done . . . The impressionist is not only a local painter, in choice of subject he deals with the present. The impressionist is not an historical painter, he takes little interest in the monks and brigands of the Middle Ages. He does not feel that America is without subjects to paint because she has no castles and donjon keeps. He loves nature, not history. His attitude toward nature is a personal one.

"Impressionism."

In the intimate setting of Ochtman's landscape, even the tree stump—sometimes used as symbol of "Nature in her freaks" or destructive moods—seems quiet and natural. Whether it is the result of man's activity or of natural decay, it is far removed from the ominous, twisted white trees called "bleached bones" or "bucks' horns" that Thomas Cole depicted in his sublime landscapes.[24] In Ochtman's *Woodland,* nature is peaceful and man's influence felt only slightly. Henry David Thoreau described this sense of harmony in his journal:

It seems as if Nature did for a long time gently overlook the profanity of man. The wood still kindly echoes the strokes of the axe, and when the strokes are few and seldom, they add a new charm to a walk. All the elements strive to *naturalize* the sound.[25]

The virgin forests of America received attention from writers of the period as well as from painters. The transcendental writers, for example, found in such woodland scenes an element of pantheism not inappropriate to Ochtman's painting. Emerson wrote that "In the wood, God was manifest, as he was not in the sermon."[26] And Thoreau too dealt with such themes:

A forest is in all mythologies a sacred place; as the oaks among the Druids, and the grove of Egeria, and even in more familiar and common life, as "Barnsdale wood" and "Sherwood." Had Robin Hood no Sherwood to resort to, it would be difficult to invest his story with the charms it has got.[27]

Going up the hill through Stow's young oak wood-land, I listen to the sharp, dry rustle of the withered oak leaves. This is the voice of the wood now. It would be comparatively still and more dreary here in other respects, if it were not for these leaves that hold on. . . . It is remarkable how universal these grand murmurs are, these backgrounds of sound,— the surf, the wind in the forest, waterfalls, etc.,—which yet to the ear and in their origin are essentially one voice, the earth voice, . . .[28]

NOTES

1. "The Society of Landscape Painters," *Brush and Pencil*, 4, no. 2 (May 1899), 114.* The painting reproduced in black and white on page 124, labeled *In the Woods*, appears to be identical to *Woodland* in every detail except one. *In the Woods* is dated 1898 or 1899 in the lower left corner, just under Ochtman's signature, while *Woodland* does not have a date. Although it is possible that *Woodland*, which was given to the Academy in 1904, is a replica of an earlier painting, their otherwise identical appearance suggests that the artist may have touched up *In the Woods*—possibly painting out the date—to serve as his diploma painting when he became an Academician.

2. *Ibid.*, 125.

3. *Ibid.*, 117, 126.

4. Samuel Isham, *The History of American Painting* (New York: Macmillan, 1905), 454.

5. Richard J. Boyle, *American Impressionism* (Boston: New York Graphic Society, 1974), 139.

6. Charles H. Caffin, *The Story of American Painting* (New York: Frederick A. Stokes, 1907), 345.

7. Sadakichi Hartmann, *A History of American Art*, rev. ed. (Boston: L.C. Page, 1901), 1:115. Alfred Trumble, "A Painter's Progress," *The Year's Art as Recorded in the Quarterly Illustrator* 2, no. 5 (Jan.-March 1894), 48.

8. "The Society of Landscape Painters," 125.

9. Maria Naylor, *The National Academy of Design Exhibition Record, 1861-1900*, (New York: Kennedy Galleries, 1973), 2:699.*

10. One example: a letter from Ochtman to Harry W. Watrous, from Cos Cob, May 14, 1904. National Academy of Design Artists Biographical Files.

11. Lincoln Steffens, *The Autobiography of Lincoln Steffens* (New York: Harcourt, Brace, 1931), 436.

12. Charles Eldredge, "Connecticut Impressionists: The Spirit of Place," *Art in America* 62, no. 5 (Sept.-Oct. 1974), 85. William H. Gerdts, *American Impressionism* (Exhibition catalogue, The Henry Art Gallery, University of Washington, Seattle, January 3-March 2, 1980), 14, 112.

13. Donelson F. Hoopes, *The American Impressionists* (New York: Watson-Guptill, 1972), 16. Eldredge, "Connecticut Impressionists," 85.

14. Helen L. Earle, *Biographical Sketches of American Artists*, 5th ed. (Lansing, Michigan: Michigan State Library, 1924), 235. Questionnaire, n.d., in National Academy of Design Artists Biographical Files.

15. Trumble, "A Painter's Progress," 49.

16. Christian Brinton, "The Conquest of Color," *Scribner's Magazine* 62, no. 4 (October 1917), 513.

17. National Academy of Design annual exhibition catalogues of 1902, 1903, 1904, 1908, and winter exhibition, 1910.*

18. Van Deren Coke, "Impressionism in America," *French Impressionists Influence American Artists* (Exhibition catalogue, Lowe Art Museum, University of Miami, Coral Gables, Fla., March 19-April 25, 1971), 14.

19. Florence Lewison, *The Landscapes of Leonard Ochtman, American Impressionist, 1854-1934* (Exhibition catalogue, Florence Lewison Gallery, N.Y., Jan. 8-Feb. 2, 1963), unpaginated.

20. Frank Fowler, "The New Heritage of Painting of the Nineteenth Century," *Scribner's Magazine* 30, no. 2 (August 1901), 256.

21. Ralph Waldo Emerson, *Journal*, April 26, 1838. In Bliss Perry, ed., *The Heart of Emerson's Journals* (New York: Houghton Mifflin, 1926), 127.

22. Catherine Beach Ely, "J. Alden Weir," *Art in America* 12, no. 3 (April 1924), 118.

23. Hamlin Garland, "Impressionism," *Crumbling Idols* (1894; reprint Cambridge, Mass.: Belknap Press of Harvard University, 1960), 104.

24. John E. Bradlee, *Bradlee's Pocket Guide to the White Mountains, Lake Winnipiseogee, and Lake Memphremagog* (Boston: John E. Bradlee, 1862), 13, 14.

25. Henry David Thoreau, *Journal*, Dec. 25, 1841. In H.G.O. Blake, ed., *Winter: From the Journal of Henry D. Thoreau* (New York: Houghton-Mifflin, 1888), 18.

26. Emerson, *Journal*, May 26, 1838, 130.

27. Thoreau, *Journal*, Dec. 23, 1841, 8-9.

28. Thoreau, *Journal*, Jan. 2, 1859, 102-03.

*In Library of National Academy of Design.

KN

FREDERICK CARL FRIESEKE

(1874-1939)
ANA 1912; NA 1914

Born April 7, Owosso, Mich. Studied at Art Institute of Chicago, 1894; Art Students' League, N.Y. 1895. 1898 studied at Académie Julian with Benjamin Constant and Jean Paul Laurens. Also briefly at Whistler School. 1899 painted mural decorations for patron Rodman Wanamaker's store and Shelbourne Hotel, Atlantic City. Early 1900s exhibited at Paris Salon. Associate, Société Nationale des Beaux-Arts 1901. Received many honors during following years. Paintings bought by major collectors in Europe and United States. 1906 bought summer house and studio in Giverny, previously owned by American Impressionist Theodore Robinson and next door to Monet's home. Painted at Giverny from April through December, working out-of-doors as much as possible. Remained in France from 1906 on. From 1912 with Macbeth Galleries in United States. Visited America infrequently. After World War I at Mesnil-sur-Blangy in Normandy. Died there August 28.

REFERENCES: National Academy of Design Artists Biographical Files. Moussa M. Domit, introduction to *Frederick Frieseke, 1874-1939* (Exhibition catalogue, Telfair Academy of Arts and Sciences, Savannah, Ga., Nov. 5-Dec. 5, 1974). Allen S. Weller, "Frederick Carl Frieseke: The Opinions of an American Impressionist," *The Art Journal* 28, no. 2 (Winter 1968).

Frieseke's impressionist canvases were at the height of their popularity and critical acclaim during the second decade of the century. He won the Grand Prize for Painting at the Panama-Pacific International Exposition held in San Francisco in 1915. *Hollyhocks* dates from this period of recognition, a time when Impressionism had not yet begun to seem outdated in the face of more radical formal idioms:

Though it cannot be held that America has taken conspicuous part in the creation of these turbulent artistic currents we have not been oblivious to their existence. . . . Impressionism having attained its final accent in the delectable outdoor confections of Frieseke, our less timid men have already turned to fresher fields.
. . . Mr. Frieseke proved the official as well as popular success of the exhibition. By no means profound, or divulging any disquieting depth of feeling, his canvases are nevertheless captivating in their sheer, bright-toned beauty, their luminous iridescence, whether of boudoir or sun-flected river bank.[1]
Brinton, *Impressions of the Art at the Panama-Pacific Exposition* (1916).

The Academy's canvas is representative of the predominant theme in Frieseke's *oeuvre*: women, out-of-doors in sun-filled gardens. The garden was often his own at Giverny and here he was interviewed in 1914:

There is nothing like a long, faithful study of nature to lead one away from the artificial, is there? . . .
No, it is sunshine, flowers in sunshine; girls in sunshine; the nude in sunshine, which I have been principally interested in for eight years, and if I could only reproduce it exactly as I see it I would be satisfied . . . No, I know nothing about the different kinds of gardens, nor do I ever make studies of flowers. My one idea is to reproduce flowers in sunlight . . .
If one realizes the effect of sunlight in a room, and by studying finds out how many changes there are in sun and shadow in the course of a day, think how much there must be out of doors with the myriads of scintillating lights, their reflections, and shadows, and the interplay, too, of each on the other. It is impossible to paint everything one sees, but one must give the effect of having done so.
If you are looking at a mass of flowers in the sunlight of out of doors, you see a sparkle of spots of different colors; then paint them in that way. I do not believe in touching up a picture inside after beginning it outdoors, nor do I believe in continuing a study from memory in the studio. No one has a good enough memory, and often one obtains accidental notes out of doors which really construct the picture . . .
In making an impression of nature, one should never consider time or method, but only the result. This may be obtained in ten minutes . . .
Nor do I believe in constructing a picture from manifold studies which have been made in "plein air." One is in a nervous tension then, and falls into no studied methods or mannerisms. One's work is more naive and spontaneous, and one is not in danger of becoming too theoretical. One should never forget that seeing and producing an effect of nature is not a matter of intellect, but of feeling.[2]
New York Times.

Years later, Frieseke still received favorable reviews: *Art Digest*, in 1932, called him, . . . "Perhaps America's best known contemporary painter."[3] Yet, sales of his paintings were greatly diminished even in the 1920s, in part because of a conflict between Frieseke's choice in subject matter—the female figure, often nude, out-of-doors, and the taste of the buying public in the United States, which tended toward domestic scenes.[4] Of his extended stay in France, the artist had commented:

I stay here because I am more free and there are not the Puritanical restrictions which prevail in America. Not only can I paint a nude here out of doors, but I can have a greater choice of subjects. As there are so few conventionalities in France, an artist can paint what he wishes. I can paint a nude in my garden or down by the fish pond and not be run out of town.[5]
New York Times.

Despite the fall in sales, Frieseke kept to his personal idiom, though modernist developments in France and social realism in America had begun to make his lovely gardens seem dated.[6] A

HOLLYHOCKS, c. 1914
Oil on canvas, 25½ x 32″
Signed lower right: *F.C. Frieseke*
Diploma painting

shift in his work occurred around 1932, when he had his first show of pure landscape paintings at the Macbeth Galleries.

It is a pleasure to salute Frederick C. Frieseke in the role of experimentalist. For years we have known him only as a painter of pretty women in an atmosphere of frou-frou. Now, at the Macbeth Gallery, he turns to landscape, and as though to put himself to the severest test he devotes himself entirely to winter scenes. He paints them with the objectivity that has always characterized his work, and his impressions are to be valued in the first place for their truth. He gives us in a picture the unmistakable portrait of a place, and sometimes, as in *Melting Snow* or the *Winter In Sun*, he invests his landscape and his buildings with something like charm.[7]

New York Herald-Tribune.

NOTES

1. Christian Brinton, *Impressions of the Art at the Panama-Pacific Exposition* (New York: John Lane Co., 1916), 25, 97.

2. Frieseke, interview with Clara T. MacCheseney, *New York Times* (June 7, 1914), section 6, 1.

3. "Frieseke, at 68, Turns to Landscape," *The Art Digest* 6, no. 12 (March 15, 1932), 12.

4. Moussa M. Domit, Introduction to *Frederick Frieseke, 1874-1939* (Exhibition catalogue, Telfair Academy of Arts and Sciences, Savannah, Ga., Nov. 5-Dec. 5, 1974), 10-11.

5. Frieseke, MacCheseney interview.

6. Domit, *Frieseke*, 12. See Domit's introduction for a detailed discussion of Frieseke's art in relation to American taste and later art movements.

7. Review, *New York Herald-Tribune*, March 27, 1932, National Academy of Design Artists Biographical Files.

JR

GIFFORD BEAL

(1879-1956)
ANA 1908; NA 1914

Born February 4, New York City. 1891-1900 studied with William Merritt Chase. Spent two additional years at the Art Students' League under George Bridgeman and Frank V. Du Mond. Meanwhile attended Princeton: graduated 1900. 1899 first painting exhibited at National Academy of Design. Exhibited regularly thereafter. First studio in Y.M.C.A. building, 57th Street and Eighth Avenue. 1901 to 1908 painted throughout Hudson River Valley from Newburgh to Poughkeepsie. 1901 painted in Cuba. 1903 received first medal, from Worcester Museum, Mass. Later received awards from more than ten art groups, including 1937 Paris Exposition; Palmer Memorial Prize at 130th Annual Exhibition of National Academy. 1908 married and traveled in Great Britain and Norway. Represented in 1913 Armory Show. Taught at National Academy of Design. 1916 toured Puerto Rico with artist Paul Dougherty. 1919 visited Bahamas. Also traveled to Bermuda, Guatemala, Honduras, and Nicaragua. 1914-1929 president of Art Students' League. Painted in Woodstock, N.Y., Lyme, Conn., Provincetown, Marblehead, and Gloucester. Settled for a time on Cape Ann in Rockport, Mass. Died February 5, New York City.

REFERENCES: Richard Beer, "As They Are," *Art News* (May 19, 1934). Obituary, *New York Times*, February 7, 1956. Obituary, *New York Herald Tribune*, February 6, 1956 (clippings in National Academy of Design Artists Biographical Files).

A t the turn of the century, many academic artists in America viewed Impressionism with hostility. To eyes accustomed to the established aesthetic, the Impressionist color seemed untrue, its subjects too casual. Two American artists, William Merritt Chase and Robert Henri, studied in Europe and played major roles in bringing various aspects of the Impressionist aesthetic to the United States. Chase taught during the summer at Shinnecock, Long Island, from 1891 to 1902. In 1896 he founded the Chase School (eventually the New York School of Art) which was maintained until 1907.[1] Robert Henri also taught there.[2] Gifford Beal attended Chase's school for ten years.[3] Among his classmates were Glenn O. Coleman, Edward Hopper, George Bellows, Rockwell Kent, and Leon Kroll.[4]

Impressionism had gained widespread acceptance by the time Beal reached artistic maturity. Though he visited many of the popular haunts of contemporary landscape artists, he did not formally ally himself with any artists' colony:

They're like clubs. At first they're made up of a few good men. Then the floaters and hangers-on come in and spoil everything. It's the social life that keeps those places going, and that saps your energy so that you can't work. Some of the artists may accomplish something, but they're the ones that would get ahead anywhere.[5]

Beal, quoted in *Art News* (1934).

As a contemporary critic observed:

. . . a characteristic of Mr. Beal is, paradoxically speaking, to have no characteristics—more exactly, perhaps, no mannerisms. He has kept himself untrammeled by any expected allegiance to any group of painters, and has resolutely avoided allying himself with any so-called "school." He paints things as he sees them, strongly and vividly. . .[6]

Ralph W. Carey, *International Studio* (1911).

Perhaps the best description of Beal's approach to art is Howard Russell Butler's characterization of Chase:

It has always seemed to me that artists fall naturally into two classes . . . the evolutionists and the technicians. In the former class we are apt to find the idealists, in the latter the realists. Chase belonged to the latter class. . . . He was not subjective in expression, not a mystic, and very little of a poet, and he was never transported by passion. . . . he was a lover of nature, a master with wonderful control of his means of expression . . . He knew his method far too well to be tempted into any lines of experimental revolution.[7]

Scribner's Magazine (1917).

Beal, in turn, remembered Chase with respect and affection:

When a student was somewhat timid about painting he would say: "Never be sparing in the use of paint; always paint with a full brush"; or if a student was prone to work the life out of a canvas, his comment would be: "It takes two to paint a picture, one to do the painting and the other to stand by with an axe to stop it at the right moment."[8]

Scribner's Magazine (1917).

A vivid sense of time and place is created by Beal's description of Chase's studio:

Chase had one peculiarity. He would never allow anything above the level of the floor in the studio to be dusted, but the floor was painted nearly black and polished so that you could see your face in it. It gave a very curious effect. All the walls and the hangings gray with dust and the floor shining in between. There was a Turkish corner down in one end of the place made out of a big man of war's flag draped over a couple of crossed spears. It was a regular old-time studio.[9]

Art News (1934).

As a teacher himself, and as a juror for exhibitions, Beal was known for keeping an open mind and for encouraging young artists to develop their individual styles. His deliberative manner and discerning eye were invaluable assets when he served as a juror for one Academy show in particular:

THE MALL—CENTRAL PARK, 1913
Oil on canvas, 30 x 40″
Signed lower right: *Gifford Beal 13*

They put up one that looked just like an advertisement you saw everywhere at the time. I don't remember now what the ad was for, some sort of soap, I think. You saw it in the street-cars and on billboards, a couple of men in oilskins standing on a beach with their backs turned toward you. Well, this picture was exactly like that ad, two men in oilskins standing on a beach, and when it was put up three or four of the jury began to call out "Soap! Take it away!" But I slid along and had a closer look at the picture and down in the left hand corner I saw H-O-M-E-R in red letters.

'Gentlemen,' I said, 'it's a Homer.' And that was one picture they didn't send to the 'morgue.'[10]

Perhaps Beal was especially partial to Homer's works. There is some feeling of Homer's weight in the figures that inhabit Beal's *The Mall—Central Park*. The assertive flat slabs of color in the women's dresses also give the otherwise ethereal figures a density more reminiscent of Manet than of Chase. Known for his sensitivity to light and color, Beal captures the atmospheric clarity of a cool summer morning. The colors are fresh without becoming sweet. Even in the shadows we find unexpected and enlivening highlights of blue or orange. An air of festivity animates this painting, calling to mind Theodore Dreiser's first impression of New York in the early 1900s:

It had the feeling of gross and blissful and parading self-indulgence. It was as if self-indulgence whispered to you that here was its true home; as if, for the most part, it was here secure.[11]

A Book About Myself (1922).

Central Park was a popular subject for the "realist" artists. Chase, William Glackens, Hopper, and Maurice B. Prendergast are just a few of those who painted there. Indeed, the park was itself considered a work of art:

Very few of those who gladly enjoy the gracious restfulness of Central Park ever stop to think that it is unique among the parks of the great cities of the world in that it was not an inheritance but a creation. . . . Its beauty was called into being by the genius of its designer, Frederick Law Olmsted; it is intentionally a work of art and not casually a work of nature.[12]

Scribner's Magazine (1917).

A guide book of the period lured visitors to the Mall with an enticing description:

The Mall, a broad pathway, a quarter of a mile long, and with a total width of 208 feet. The main central walk, is 35 feet wide, lined on each side with magnificent shade-trees, the rest of the plateau being covered with greensward. Seats are numerous and are placed as close together as comfort will allow. Near the head of the Mall, on the west side, is the music pavilion, an exceedingly ornate structure of the pagoda fashion. Music is provided here during the summer season by first-class bands, generally on Saturday or Sunday afternoons. The goat-carriages, for hire to infant visitors, are located to the east of the Mall. The statues to be found here embrace the most artistic to be found anywhere in the park.[13]

Guide to Central and Riverside Parks . . . (c. 1900).

In Beal's art, especially, Central Park was a recurrent theme, and *The Mall—Central Park* displays Beal's strongest qualities:

There was warmth in the vision, sheer love of living, that transcended literalness and gave his work at best robust sparkle and vitality . . . to the last there was a quality of youthful enthusiasm.[14]

New York Times (1956).

_____

NOTES

1. Ronald G. Pisano, *William Merritt Chase* (New York: Watson Guptill, 1979), 8.
2. Milton W. Brown, *American Painting From the Armory Show to the Depression* (Princeton, N.J.: Princeton University Press, 1955), 12.
3. Richard Beer, "As They Are," *Art News* 32 (May 1934), 11.
4. Brown, *American Painting*, 12.
5. Beer, "As They Are," 11.
6. Ralph W. Carey, "Some Paintings by Gifford Beal," *International Studio*, 1911.
7. Howard Russell Butler, "Chase—The Artist," *Scribner's Magazine* 61, no. 2 (Feb. 1917), 256.
8. Gifford Beal, "Chase—The Teacher," *Scribner's Magazine* 61, no. 2 (Feb. 1917), 257.
9. Beer, "As They Are," 11.
10. *Ibid.*
11. Theodore Dreiser, *A Book About Myself* (New York: Boni and Liveright, 1922), 452.
12. "The Point of View," *Scribner's Magazine* 61, no. 2 (Feb. 1917), 253.
13. *Guide to Central and Riverside Parks, General Grant's Tomb* (New York: Caxton Book Concern, c. 1900), 22.
14. "Memorial Tribute: Exhibition at the American Academy Pays Hommage to Gifford Beal," *New York Times*, Dec. 16, 1956. National Academy of Design Artists Biographical Files.

HR

LILIAN WESCOTT HALE

(1881-1963)
ANA 1927; NA 1931

Born December 7, Hartford, Conn. Studied at Hartford Art School; with William Merritt Chase, and at Boston Museum School with Edmund Charles Tarbell and Philip Leslie Hale. 1902 married Philip Leslie Hale, painter and art critic. Permanent address until 1953, Dedham, Mass. Studio in home in Dedham; frequently used views from studio for charcoal drawings. Daughter Nancy also frequent model for paintings. Concentrated primarily on portraiture, earning honors at national exhibitions, including Panama-Pacific Exposition in San Francisco, 1915, and First Altman Prize for Portraiture, National Academy of Design, 1927. Exhibited frequently at Academy from 1924 through 1949, then occasionally until her death. 1953 moved to Charlottesville, Va. Continued to paint portraits. 1963 traveled for first time to Italy, visiting Venice, Florence, and Rome. Died shortly after return to United States, in St. Paul, Minn., November 7.

REFERENCES: National Academy of Design Artists Biographical Files. Exhibition records for Hale, 1900 to present, National Academy of Design. William Gerdts, *American Impressionism* (Exhibition catalogue, Henry Art Gallery, University of Washington, Seattle, January 3-March 2, 1980). Nancy Hale, *The Life in the Studio* (Boston: Little, Brown, 1969).

Lilian Wescott Hale earned her reputation as a portrait painter: paintings exhibited over a forty-year span at the National Academy of Design reflect the domination of figural compositions in her *oeuvre*. Hale, however, did not limit herself strictly to indoor portraiture. She produced some pure landscapes, such as *An Old Cherry Tree*, possibly shown at the Arlington Galleries in New York in early 1922. The titles of several other works in that exhibition indicate paintings with landscape backgrounds or perhaps even pure landscapes: *Rocky Hillside* and *Spring by the Wayside*.[1] Of *Celia's Arbor* (Metropolitan Museum of Art), also shown at that time, a contemporary critic wrote:

Mrs. Hale does not confine her work to indoor problems, she has to her credit some difficult out-of-door pictures. *Celia's Arbor*, a painting recently purchased by the Metropolitan Art Museum, is one of these, and its excellence is proof that Mrs. Hale could go very far in the out-of-door problem, if she might wish to follow it up. . . .[2]

Berry, "Lilian Wescott Hale," *The American Magazine of Art* (1927).

Hale's style indicates special sensitivity to plein-air problems of light and color. Her teachers, William Merritt Chase and Edmund C. Tarbell, were both important American Impressionists and members of "The Ten," and Philip Leslie Hale had studied, as Tarbell had earlier, at the Académie Julian in Paris in the 1890s. After their marriage and move to Dedham, Lilian Hale successfully combined the domestic and professional elements of her life:

. . . The subjects of her pictures lie all about her. . . . There is a garden which she has planned and planted so beautifully, that one is fascinated by its color, its beauty, and its spell. There are old trees, untrimmed bushes, tall scraggy plants concealing paths that wind and twist. There is an old God-Terminus in one shaded nook: there's a sun dial marking the "happy hours," and all around the hallowed spot, an old, old chain, festooned with lavender wisteria and pink roses, *shuts in* the glory of the garden, and *shuts out* only that which is less beautiful. Small wonder that the canvases which come from her studio are calm, restrained, breathe loveliness, and carry peace; elements not always found in beauty.[3]

Berry, "Lilian Westcott Hale" (1927).

Hale even listed gardening and farming as outside interests on the biographical data sheet sent out by the Academy to its members. In the years after her husband's death. Lilian Hale spent her summers at Cape Ann and here too she tended to her garden. Years later, Nancy Hale recalls her mother working "unsparingly" at this favorite task:

"Come and help me!" she used to cry, though not so often after years of my making it plain that I did not want to.
I had in mind more sybaritic summers, like the pictures in *Vogue*. "Why don't we let it all run to lovely field grass?" I said.
A look of passionate distress twisted her features—stained with sweat, streaked with dirt where she'd slapped a mosquito, but still, like an old statue's, beautiful.
"It wouldn't be the way you imagine," she said. "Nature can't just be left, like that."
The standard for her gardening afternoons was the same as for painting mornings—quite simply, perfection.[4]

Nancy Hale, "Inheriting a Garden" (1968).

In *An Old Cherry Tree* Lilian Hale is also concerned with order. The fence and plantings mark a clear border to the yard, beyond which nature is less strictly controlled. The grass has even been clipped neatly away from stones leading up to the gate. Hale's decorative awareness is indicated by the moonlike cut out in the gate and the play of delicate branches against the sky. The cherry tree itself is carefully delineated, a dark silhouette posed against a lighter and more loosely worked background. There is a sense of "restraint" in the coloring, and of balance in the play of silhouette forms. At moments, the clarity, almost starkness, of the cherry tree against the more complex tangle of smaller trees suggests that this is indeed a portrait of one element of the garden. Hale has taken her portrait painter's sense of close observation and combined it with the influences of Impressionism in capturing details of light

An Old Cherry Tree, c. 1922
Oil on canvas, 30 x 25″
Signed lower left: *Lilian Westcott Hale*
Diploma painting

and atmosphere. Nancy Hale wrote that neither her mother nor her father could tolerate painters who "painted things out of their heads": "They wanted to 'render the object'—an immensely subtle process involving the interplay of the painter's subjective view with the way the light actually fell upon the object. The conflict—rather, the marriage—of objectivity and subjectivity was what made art such a wildly exciting and magical thing to my parents that they cared about literally nothing else, except maybe me."[5]

This concentrated effort to render effects of light as it actually moved across an object, or scene, is an essential element found also in Lilian Hale's drawings. These drawings, often of the winter landscape in Dedham received special attention when shown in 1936:

... In fact, her drawings have long evoked appreciation through a singular distinction and charm. They are mostly of New England landscape, with the old buildings of Dedham showing dimly through the snowy air, wrapped in a kind of atmospheric film and bare tree forms entering felicitously into the foreground. . . .

The hour is changed and the light of day replaces the light of the moon, but the white stillness is there, the silence, and the simple poetry which belongs to icebound New England. . . . Her touch is delicate, precise and never hard. It is marked, too, by a most engaging originality. These are fresh, new-minted impressions, redolent of an artistic personality. They have the hall-mark of truth, and over them hangs a cool, distinctively American beauty. . . .[6]

Herald Tribune.

Earlier, Rose Berry had remarked:

... in her drawing it is safe to say that she is without a rival. The delicacy of her black and white is indescribable; the whiteness of the white, and the paleness of the gray are notable always, but the subtlety of the two as they become one, tests the eye of the average observer. . . . Mrs. Hale's drawings disclose a sensitive beauty, which, fine as her painting is, it can't do, because color will not, and paint cannot express such delicacy. Her shading is obtained by an exquisite mingling of the dark and light masses . . . There is something astonishing in the way she works: the accomplished drawing is but a series of straight lines. . . . Then there comes the modelling *which is not modelling:* the white areas in the drawing that take on a curved or an oval contour, shaping themselves into the lovely cheek of a young girl, or the delicate petal of a flower. . . .[7]

Berry, "Lilian Westcott Hale" (1927).

One might quarrel a bit with this critic. In *An Old Cherry Tree* Lilian Hale has indeed managed with paint and color to express "such delicacy," and offers as well some of the "pure line" that distinguished her drawings.

NOTES
1. *Paintings and Drawings by Lilian Westcott Hale* (Exhibition pamphlet, Arlington Galleries, New York, Feb. 23-March 16, 1922).
2. Rose V.S. Berry, "Lilian Westcott Hale—Her Art," *The American Magazine of Art* 18, no. 2 (February 1927), 67.
3. *Ibid.*, 63-64.
4. Nancy Hale, "Inheriting a Garden," *The New Yorker* (May 18, 1968), 112.
5. Nancy Hale, "Eyes and No Eyes, or the Art of Seeing," *The Life in the Studio* (Boston: Little, Brown, 1969), 20.
6. "Drawings by Lilian Westcott Hale," Exhibition at Grand Central Galleries, *The Herald-Tribune* (Feb. 2, 1936), New York Public Library Clipping File.
7. Berry, "Lilian Westcott Hale," 67-69.

JR

CHARLES EPHRAIM BURCHFIELD

(1893-1967)
ANA 1952; NA 1954

Born Ashtabula Harbor, Ohio, April 9. Youth spent in neighboring Salem. Often lonely, spent hours drawing and exploring the nearby woods. 1912-1916 studied art at the Cleveland School (now Institute) of Art. 1916 won scholarship to National Academy of Design; left after one day. Returned to Salem, worked at W.H. Mullins Co., metal fabricating plant, until 1921. (Spent seven months in army at Camp Jackson, S.C., July 1918-January 1919.) Moved to Buffalo to work as wallpaper designer for M.H. Birge and Sons. 1925 moved to suburb of Gardenville. Four years later resigned job to devote himself full time to painting. Switched dealers from Montross Gallery to Frank M. Rehn Gallery, both in New York City. Taught occasionally after 1949 at neighboring colleges and art schools, as well as at Ohio University and University of Minnesota. Died January 10, West Seneca, N.Y.

REFERENCES: Matthew Baigell, *Charles Burchfield* (New York: Watson-Guptill, 1976). John I.H. Baur, research by Rosalind Irvine, *Charles Burchfield* (Exhibition catalogue, Whitney Museum of American Art, N.Y., 1956). Edith H. Jones, ed., *The Drawings of Charles Burchfield* (Exhibition catalogue, The Drawing Society, N.Y., 1968). National Academy of Design Artists Biographical Files.

Goldenrod in November, suggestive in its title of the passing of seasons, is representative of Burchfield's continuing fascination with the changing landscape and is a typical work of his late period.[1] In its depiction of multiple elements of nature, alive with movement, and in its sense of foreboding, suggested by murky clouds and twin black trees, the painting is an example of what might be termed Burchfield's "gothic landscape."[2]

Burchfield often ascribed anthropomorphic qualities to elements in nature. Here the stark, twisted trees spiral upward; disembodied branches hover above and at the sides, suggesting the rustling of the wind or the flight of birds. Grasses and wildflowers agitate in the foreground. These forces could easily become malevolent. As he had written in his journal, quite early in his career, "I do not wander the woods free of superstition any more. Something seems to be lurking behind stumps or writhing logs—flowers have faces, but they are not always pleasant."[3] *Goldenrod in November* seems descriptive of the bleaker side of nature, an impulse which perhaps had found its equivalent expression earlier in the artist's stark portrayals of Midwestern towns and factories.[4] As Burchfield commented in his diary:

You cannot experience a landscape until you have known all its discomforts. You have to curse, fight mosquitoes, be slapped by stinging branches, fall over rocks and skin your knees, be stung by nettles, scratched by grasshopper grass and pricked by brambles . . . before you have experienced nature.[5]

John I.H. Baur, "Burchfield's Intimate Diaries," *Art News* (1956).

Burchfield's investigations of the changing seasons amounts to a virtual leitmotif in his *oeuvre*, and his interest about this time in the active quality of that transition, the cycle of bud, bloom, and decay, is characteristic. By the late 1940s, Burchfield's interaction with nature, never that of a passive observer, had become even more intense. The paintings of this period have been referred to as "apocalyptic landscapes"[6] and Burchfield's comments at about this time give an indication why:

. . . he wrote that he would stare at the sun for a few moments and then paint the effects this had on the images he saw. At times, he might lie down on the ground, then jump up quickly to see the earth quivering in a trembling white light.[7]

Matthew Baigell, *Charles Burchfield* (1976).

The depiction of a transforming nature, almost kinetic in its multiplicity of movement, characterizes this landscape. Burchfield had begun during his students years to portray nature's changing aspects, and through an interest in Chinese scroll painting, sought to unite these elements in a single composition. At one point he devised a plan, never completed, to paint the changing seasons in a series of paintings that could be viewed as separate compositions or could be hung sequentially.[8]

Burchfield always relied on his sketching notebooks and what he called his "idea notes" (written suggestions of a mood or a specific site). They were carefully filed and labeled according to month and season (he noted that March, April, and August always piled up),[9] and accessible for easy reference when painting.

I keep the notes, handy, classified, and then, sometimes years after the first conception, the idea is fully incubated, and comes forth full-blown in a finished water-color—I cannot choose the time.[10]

Letter to John I.H. Baur (1955).

His interest in weather encompassed all of nature's moods. As he wrote:

My love of all kinds of weather provides the keynote to a good part of my art—for me there is no such thing as bad weather or good weather—all weather is fascinating and therefore potentially beautiful. The moment when rain is changing to snow is most enchanting and exciting; when people say to me "Isn't the weather awful today?" I agree, but in my heart I know it is otherwise; it is beautiful . . . My absorption in trying to record rugged weather, of course, is one reason why so much of my work

GOLDENROD IN NOVEMBER, 1952
Watercolor with charcoal, 37 x 29¾"
Signed lower left: *CEB*
Diploma painting

fails to arouse a response in the public appreciation. Fortunately I also love the milder aspects of nature![11]

Letter to John I.H. Baur (1955).

Burchfield's election to the National Academy of Design, perhaps characteristically, was not a straightforward process.[12] After being elected an Associate in 1944, he declined because as a landscapist he felt he could not fulfill the Academy's entrance requirement of a self-portrait. By 1952, however, submission of a portrait photograph had become a more common means of filling the membership requirement and Burchfield was again invited to become a member, and he accepted.[13]

Shortly before, in 1945, Burchfield made a statement about his art, which, for all its modernist emphasis on form, joins him to an American tradition that extends back to Cole and Durand:

Stating it as simply as I can, I may say that I am one who finds himself in an incredibly interesting world, and my chief concern is to record as many of my impressions as possible, in the simplest and most forthright manner. In short, life, with all that the word implies, is of first importance. No idea, however, can stand by itself, but must be re-created thru the medium of design and organization. A picture must have a sound structure, with all parts co-ordinated. The inner structure must be the result of the close study of nature's laws, and not of human invention. The artist must come to nature, not with a ready-made formula, but in humble reverence to learn. The work of an artist is superior to the surface appearance of nature, but not its basic laws.[14]

"Artist's Statement" (1945).

NOTES
1. Burchfield himself viewed his work in a periodic fashion, beginning with the early romantic fantasy landscapes, 1917-1919, through the Midwestern scene paintings of 1919-1942 to his later period, 1943-1967—a return to and continuation of the fantastic landscapes of his youth. See John I.H. Baur. Research by Rosalind Irvine. *Charles Burchfield* (Exhibition catalogue, Whitney Museum of American Art, N.Y., 1956), Matthew Baigell, *Charles Burchfield* (New York: Watson-Guptill, 1976). Samuel Golden Correspondence, Archives of American Art, Smithsonian Institution, N.Y.
2. Baigell has used this designation in referring to these works. *Charles Burchfield*, 191.
3. John I.H. Baur, "Charles Burchfield—His Early Years." In *Interpretations of Nature, an Exhibition and Sale of Early Watercolors by Charles Burchfield* (Exhibition catalogue, Bernard Danenberg Galleries, N.Y., 1970), 16.
4. Baigell, *Charles Burchfield*, 195.
5. John I.H. Baur, "Burchfield's Intimate Diaries," *Art News* (January 1956), 66.
6. Baigell, *Charles Burchfield*, 191.
7. *Ibid.*, 191.
8. Baur, "Early Years," 17.
9. Belle Krasne, "A Charles Burchfield Profile," *Time* (Dec. 15, 1952), 21.
10. Charles E. Burchfield, Letter to John I.H. Baur, March 15, 1955, Library, Whitney Museum of American Art, N.Y.
11. *Ibid.*, March 28, 1955.
12. One recalls Burchfield's initial reaction to the Academy in 1916 when he received a scholarship to study at the National Academy of Design only to walk out on the Life Drawing class after one day, having had enough of formal studio instruction.
13. Burchfield wrote at this time: "In regard to the presentation of one of my water-colors to the Academy I do not know just the procedure, but I wish to comply with one of my best things. I have sent to the current show . . . my "GOLDENROD IN NOVEMBER," 37″ x 30″ painted in 1952 would the committee wish to consider this as my contribution?" (Letter to Eliot Clark, March 15, 1954, National Academy of Design Artists Biographical Files).
14 Burchfield, "Artist's Statement," 1945, for American Artists Group, Inc. Samuel Golden Correspondence, Archives of American Art, Smithsonian Institution, N.Y., microfilm roll NAG 1.

CB

HENRY WOODBRIDGE PARTON

(1858-1933)
ANA 1921; NA 1929

Born November 28, Hudson, New York. Attended public school and Hudson Academy. No formal art instruction. Influenced by two elder brothers, Arthur and Ernest Parton, both landscape artists. Worked in rug-designing department of Alexander Smith and Sons Carpet Company for 37 years. Retired and devoted approximately last twenty years of life to oil painting. Began with flower paintings, exhibited *Roses* at Royal Academy 1885. Several trips to Europe, visited London and Paris. During early career some design work under French designer Eugène Petit. Later turned to figure painting, some portraits, finally landscapes. Began exhibiting at National Academy of Design in 1881. Listed studio address at 51 West 10 Street for annual exhibitions from 1881 to 1892. Exhibited at Academy through 1932. Was member of Salmagundi Club, Century Association, Painters and Sculptors Gallery Association. 1921 elected Life Member of National Arts Club (NAC), N.Y. Apartment and studio in NAC building at 119 East 19 Street. Died March 1, New York City.

REFERENCES: Parton Family Papers, Archives of American Art, Smithsonian Institution, N.Y., microfilm roll #723, frames 1086-1182. Mantle Fielding, *Dictionary of Painters, Sculptors, and Engravers*, rev. ed., (1926; reprint Conn.: Modern Books and crafts, Inc., 1974). Algernon Graves, F.S.A., *The Royal Academy of Arts: A Complete Dictionary of Contributors and their Work from its Foundation in 1769 to 1904*, vol. 6 (London: Henry Graves and George Bell & Sons, 1905). Henry Parton, New York Public Library Clipping File, Sunday, March 2, 1933. *Who Was Who in America*, vol. 1, 1897-1942 (Chicago: The A.N. Marquis Co., 1943). Catalogues of annual exhibitions at National Academy of Design, 1875-1932.

Parton was best known for his landscapes, often termed "rugged" by critics. At the time of his death, several notices described his paintings as "bold panoramas of mountains against the sky."[1] Biographical facts offer some insight into his connection with landscape tradition. Both elder brothers were landscapists and Parton spent his youth in Hudson, New York, near the homes of Thomas Cole, Asher B. Durand, Sanford R. Gifford, and Frederic E. Church. According to an undated note, possibly in Parton's hand, the artist did in fact meet Gifford and Church,[2] and we know that Parton was a tenant at the Tenth Street Studio Building at the same time as Church.

Berkshire Hills was given to the Academy in 1929 as Parton's diploma painting; several other canvases of scenes in the Berkshires were exhibited at the Academy's annual exhibitions. Along with this region of Massachusetts, the area near Beaverkill in the Catskills, where the artist's brother Arthur had a cottage, also appears as a frequent subject.[3]

Parton summered in the Berkshires during the 1920s, and exhibited at the annual exhibitions of the Stockbridge Art Association held from late August through early September. The first exhibition of the Art Association was held in 1909, and over the years the circle of contributing artists widened, attracting painters from all over the region.[4] Numerous financiers as well as artists, summered in Stockbridge and the cultural life of the community flourished. As Frederic Crowninshield, an artist and Stockbridge resident who contributed to the exhibitions, commented:

You ask me to write a few words concerning art in Stockbridge and the recent exhibitions. . . . Judging from the many pictures I have seen, painted long before my advent, Stockbridge must have been a favorite sketching ground for what—in default of a better name—is called "the Hudson River School". . . .
Why do artists come here, you may ask? Primarily because it is a good land wherein to dwell, and secondarily because it offers a goodly number of lures for the exercise of their profession.[5]
Crowninshield, "Art in Stockbridge" (1914).

Among the more prominent exhibitors at Stockbridge was the sculptor Daniel Chester French, who had a summer home and studio in the town. French's studio, Chesterwood, is now a museum. Three of Parton's paintings of the Berkshire countryside, landscapes in oil, are currently part of the Chesterwood Collection: *Berkshire Storm*, a mountain landscape, *Summer Clouds*, and *Palm Ball Mountain—Berkshires*. The latter bears the inscription on the reverse: "View from the west porch of Chesterwood, Stockbridge, Mass., presented by Henry W. Parton to Margaret French Cresson, 1925" (daughter of Daniel C. French).[6]

Parton's involvement with the Stockbridge artistic community lasted through the late 1920s. A review of the annual Stockbridge art exhibition in 1929 noted:

Henry W. Parton has a host of Berkshire friends who always admire his beautiful landscapes. This year he has two typical scenes of this highland country. One is of late afternoon, with overhanging shadows. The other shows the light coming up from the horizon after a storm.[7]
New York Times.

Berkshire Hills, too, reveals not only Parton's concern with the "highland country," but an eye aware of the changing qualities of 92light, the movement of clouds, time, and the moods suggested by light, the movement of clouds, time, and the moods suggested by weather. Though the painting is faithful to a realistic vision of the scene, the sloping ridges and hills seem to be compressed, as if the distance between points had been shortened. Perhaps we can conjecture tentatively that this quality of compression or flatness

191

BERKSHIRE HILLS, c. 1929
Oil on canvas, 24 x 30″
Signed lower right: *Henry W. Parton*
Diploma painting

is an outgrowth of Parton's long years as a rug designer, as well as an indication of the artist's awareness of modernist planarism.

As Crowninshield indicated, the Berkshires had long been a frequent retreat for artists, inspiring nineteenth-century writers as well. The spirit of several earlier texts still applies to Parton's landscape:

As mountains are the most conspicuous objects in landscape, they will take the precedence in what I may say on the elements of American scenery. . . .

American mountains are generally clothed to the summit by dense forests, while those of Europe are mostly bare, or merely tinted by grass or heath. It may be that the mountains of Europe are on this account more picturesque in form, and there is a grandeur in their nakedness; but in the gorgeous garb of the American mountains there is more than an equivalent; and when the woods "have put their glory on," as an American poet has beautifully said, the purple heath and yellow furze of Europe's mountains are in comparison but as the faint secondary rainbow to the primal one. . . .[8]

Thomas Cole, *Essay on American Scenery* (1835).

The truth is that, for six or seven weeks after the mid-September, among the mountains of Massachusetts and Connecticut, the mere *fusion* of earth and air and water, of light and shade and colour, the almost shameless tolerance of nature for the poor human experiment, are so happily effective that you lose all reckoning of the items of the sum, that you in short find in your draught, contentedly, a single strong savour. . . . So I throw myself back upon the fusion, as I have called it—with the rich light hanging on but half-a-dozen spots. This renews the vision of the Massachusetts Berkshires—land beyond any other, in America, to-day, as one was much reminded, of leisure on the way to legitimation, of the social idyll, of the workable, the expensively workable, American form of country life; and, in especial, of a perfect consistency of surrender to the argument of the verdurous vista. This is practically the last word of such communities as Stockbridge, Pittsfield, Lenox. . .[9]

Henry James, *The American Scene* (1907).

NOTES

1. Obituary notice, *Art Digest* 5 (March 15, 1933), 10.
2. Undated note on National Arts Club stationary, Parton Family Papers, Archives of American Art, Smithsonian Institution, N.Y., microfilm roll 723, frame 1126.
3. New York Public Library Clipping File, March 2, 1933.
4. Walter Pichard Eaton, ed., *Stockbridge* 1, no. 9 (September 1, 1914), 3.
5. Frederic Crowninshield, Letter to the editor, "Art in Stockbridge," *Stockbridge* 1, no. 9 (September 1, 1914), 6.
6. Listing of Parton's paintings from the Artist Index of the Inventory of American Painting, National Collection of Fine Arts, Smithsonian Institution, pp. 14239-14240. Information about the individual works, including previous ownership and inscriptions, is from a telephone conversation with Susan Frisch, Program Assistant at Chesterwood, April 16, 1980.
7. Review of Stockbridge's 21st Annual Exhibition, *New York Times*, Sept. 8, 1929, Section 1, 29.
8. Thomas Cole, "Essay on American Scenery" (1835; reprint in John Conron, *The American Landscape: A Critical Anthology of Prose and Poetry*, New York: Oxford University Press, 1973), 571-72.
9. Henry James, *The American Scene* (1907; reprint Bloomington: Indiana University Press, 1968), 40.

JR

PETER HURD

(1904—)
ANA 1941; NA 1942

Born Roswell, N.M., February 22. Attended New Mexico Military Institute; 1921 entered U.S. Military Academy at West Point. Sold first painting there, *West Point Moon*, for ten dollars. 1923 resigned to study painting. Attended Haverford College 1923-1924; in summer of 1924 began studying under N.C. Wyeth at Chadd's Ford, Penn. While there worked on landscape, illustration, still life, and portrait painting, and aided Wyeth with his commissions. Studied at Pennsylvania Academy of the Fine Arts during the academic year. Married Henriette Wyeth, also an artist, 1929. Moved back to New Mexico in mid 1930s; bought ranch at San Patricio. War correspondent for *Life* magazine 1942-1945. Commissioned to paint murals in post offices and colleges in Texas and New Mexico. Painted official portrait of President Lyndon B. Johnson. Author and illustrator of several books.

REFERENCES: Paul Horgan, *Peter Hurd: A Portrait Sketch from Life* (Austin, The University of Texas Press, 1964). Peter Hurd, "Painter of New Mexico," *Magazine of Art*, 32 (July 1939).

*E*vening in the Sierras was probably painted in 1938 or early 1939, since it was shown at the gallery of Mrs. Cornelius J. Sullivan in April 1939.[1] On notification of his election as Academician in 1942, Hurd promised to send "one of my best landscapes" when he returned from an assignment as war correspondent for *Life*.[2] The arrival of the painting was delayed until early 1947, however, when *Evening in the Sierras* was submitted following a Carnegie Institute exhibition.[3]

In the introduction to the catalogue of the 1939 exhibition at Mrs. Sullivan's gallery, the writer Paul Horgan, a neighbor and childhood friend of Hurd's, described the landscape of New Mexico that has concerned Hurd since the 1930s, earning him the title of Regionalist:

The New Mexico painted by Peter Hurd has many faces, most familiar of which are mountains and plains; and many tempers, most constant of which is daylight of golden, illimitable clarity. It is a place where the eye triumphs over distance, and enters upon the color of the world with a curious exhilaration. Towns are few, and small. Comparative solitude is the law for living things there. The land is the hero of life in the Southwest, and also the villain. The mountains are vast, and they wall off empires of arid plain. The lot of man is a hard one when he must take from such terrain the stuff of his needs.[4]

Even in childhood his native scenery affected Hurd:

One of my earliest memories as a youngster is of standing under a cottonwood tree on my father's farm in New Mexico one morning in winter and looking west across the prairies to the blue sierras beyond. In the clear, winter sky the waning moon was setting over the Sierra Capitán. Our small, irrigated farm lay on the outskirts of the town of Roswell and beyond the cottonwood was the unbroken plain extending to the foothills of the mountains sixty miles away. At wide intervals were cattle ranches which were like tiny islands on a vast, calm sea. There is something about my memory of that moment—the color and the light and the remoteness of it in space that makes me believe it was one of the things that influenced me to become a painter.[5]

Magazine of Art (1939).

In the early 1930s, when Hurd went back to New Mexico after studying in the East, he remembers realizing

. . . that for me my native land was much the most exciting of any I knew. I saw again the level plains under the infinite sky-dome; I saw the march of distant rain storms and smelt the fragrant prairie grass and the rain-moist earth. And I remembered when, as a child, I had first known the beneficence of rainfall, feeling its mystery and sacredness as I suppose only people can who live in arid lands. An engulfing emotion overtook me; I decided that I must contrive somehow to re-establish myself there.[6]

Magazine of Art (1939).

Hurd found a small ranch fifty miles west of Roswell:

At San Patricio, a village of a few families . . . in an irrigated valley with overgrazed hills of classic form and a thread of shallow river—the Ruidoso—he found a section or so of land with an ancient L-shaped house, half of which was filled with apples stored out of the orchards between house and river.[7]

Paul Horgan, *Peter Hurd: A Portrait Sketch from Life* (1964).

Since then he has primarily painted New Mexico, although people have suggested to him that he

. . . travel afar to record the beauty of such places as Lake Tahoe, the French Riviera, and the Swiss Alps. I have always patiently explained why I prefer this part of the world. My preoccupation with this area has nothing to do with political boundaries, but rather with this quality of light and air; this, and the very colors of the earth itself as it exists here. Nor is it based on any chauvinism relating to the fact that this is the land of my birth. . . . [In] this region the air, usually dry and thin, combines with the sun of our latitude to form an ever changing succession of atmospheric effects. These effects, the product of lens-clear air and full sun, seem infinite in the variety of their combinations.[8]

Hurd, *Sketch Book* (1971).

Hurd defines his motive in painting a landscape:

What is it that motivates me in the first place and brings on these frenzied races against time and light? If the effort is destined to have any success, it must be triggered by an inner elation, an excited reaction to some color or light effect which by its inevitable evanescence is always productive of delight and despair—despair in that it is so quickly changing, so difficult to record.[9]

Sketch Book (1971).

EVENING IN THE SIERRAS, c. 1938
Egg tempera on gessoed panel, 24¼ x 42″
Signed lower left: *Hurd*
Diploma painting

He seems almost to be describing *Evening in the Sierras* when he writes of the drama of twilight:

Any time and any place can exhibit this transience of color and light. Perhaps the most dramatic is here in San Patricio itself where light effects at dusk have so often caused an exciting race with time; the figures of my neighbors involved in a lost-and-found pattern created by the dust haze of evening, the orange-ochre light from a window in a house in our village instantly evoking for the beholder the warm security that dwells within earthen walls. . . . I have also wished in vain for some way in which to suggest the lowing of cattle or the tinkle of goat bells as the goatherds bring in their flocks at dusk, for some way in which to capture my reverie—and sometimes tears—for the changing earth, an earth weary of man: man the pillager, man the super vandal.[10]

Sketch Book (1971).

The truck returning home in the evening sends up in its wake a cloud of dust, the result of the day's unrelieved dryness:

Sometimes I'm asked by people who notice my preoccupation with late afternoon and early morning light if there is a visible difference in dawn and sunset. My answer is yes. In general there is an increased dust effect at sunset due to the activities of man and of his machines and animals.[11]

Sketch Book (1971).

After working for several years in oil, Hurd taught himself the technique of tempera painting on gessoed panel, which suits the incandescent quality of the New Mexico landscape. Hurd prefers the tempera since, unlike oil paint, it

. . . dries almost instantly, so I can work out a passage over and over without having to wait for the pigment to dry. . . . While the surface is glassy smooth, the depth and richness of many layers are ever-present.[12]

American Artist (1979).

NOTES
1. *Exhibition of Paintings and Drawings by Peter Hurd, Gallery of Mrs. Cornelius J. Sullivan, April 11-29, 1939* (Exhibition catalogue), no. 5 *Evening in the Sierras*.
2. Letter from Peter Hurd to Charles C. Curran, June 14, 1942. National Academy of Design Artists Biographical Files.
3. Letter from Peter Hurd to Mr. Lober, December 18, 1946, *ibid*.
4. Paul Horgan, introduction, *Exhibition of Paintings and Drawings by Peter Hurd*.
5. Peter Hurd, "Painter of New Mexico," *Magazine of Art* 32 (July 1939), 390.
6. *Ibid.*, 432.
7. Paul Horgan, *Peter Hurd, A Portrait Sketch from Life* (Austin: The University of Texas Press, 1964), 40.
8. Peter Hurd, *Sketch Book* (Chicago: The Swallow Press Inc., 1971), 21.
9. *Ibid.*, 11.
10. *Ibid.*, 11-12.
11. *Ibid.*, note to no. 88, *Return at Dusk*.
12. "Peter Hurd/Egg Tempera," *American Artist* 43 (Feb. 1979), 82.

SMS

NEWELL CONVERS WYETH

(1882-1945)
ANA 1940; NA 1941

Born October 22, Needham, Mass. Studied at Mechanic Arts High School; Massachusetts Normal Arts School; Eric Pape School of Art, and with Charles W. Reed. Attended illustrator Howard Pyle's school in Wilmington, Del., 1902-1904. Maintained close ties with teacher. Later returned to live in Brandywine countryside. Received magazine commissions from 1903 on. Trip West in autumn of 1904 provided material for years to come. Executed numerous illustrations of western scenes for *Scribner's Magazine*, *Saturday Evening Post*, *Collier's Weekly*, and *McClure's Magazine*. After return East, set up studio in Wilmington. Spring 1908 to rural Chadd's Ford, Penn. Spent summers at Port Clyde, on Maine coast. Both rural locations furnished material for magazine illustrations and easel paintings. Created book illustrations for Scribner's series of juvenile classics including *Treasure Island* (1911) and *Kidnapped* (1913), and for other publishers as well. Murals for Missouri State Capital, New York Public Library, and New First National Bank in Boston, among others. Member of Society of Illustrators and other groups. Died October 19 at Chadd's Ford.

REFERENCES: Douglas Allen and Douglas Allen, Jr., *N.C. Wyeth, The Collected Paintings, Illustrations and Murals* (New York: Crown Publishers, 1972). *The Brandywine Heritage: Howard Pyle, N.C. Wyeth, Andrew Wyeth, James Wyeth* (Exhibition catalogue, Brandywine River Museum, Chadd's Ford, Penn., 1971). *Exhibition of Paintings by N.C. Wyeth, N.A., 1882-1945* (Exhibition catalogue, Knoedler's Gallery, N.Y., Oct. 29-Nov. 23, 1957). National Academy of Design Artists Biographical Files.

*B*lubber Island, Maine became part of the Academy's collection in 1942.[1] Wyeth had long used full size canvases when making the original designs for illustrations, and in the 1930s he turned increasingly to easel painting. Wyeth felt that the illustrator was no less a professional than the painter and recommended that

The training course for the illustrator should not be one whit different, or less thorough than that of the painter.[3]
    N.C. Wyeth, "The Illustrator and his Development" (1917).

As a painter, Wyeth was best known for works meticulously done in tempera on gessoed panel. The use of oil paint on a gessoed surface, as in *Blubber Island*, is a less common technique. Wyeth's first one-man exhibition of paintings was held in December 1939 at the Macbeth Galleries in New York City. Wyeth asked his son-in-law, the artist Peter Hurd (see illus. p. 195), to write the preface to the exhibition catalogue:[4]

These works introduce for the first time publicly a new aspect of the art of N.C. Wyeth. They are the product of revolt against the inevitable limitations of that art of illustration which Mr. Wyeth has long served with sincerity and grace. . . . In his mind he lives on a heroic plane, the humble familiar, as all men may be, of the poet Homer, of Beethoven and of Thoreau. Without trying to measure a near man against far titans, you feel that he is of their kind; and, secured in his spirit by their common honesty of creative life; he is free to acknowledge any means to his painter's purpose. Of the illustrator's heritage he takes freely and consciously those components which may relate to painting: a strongly dramatic presentation but one freed from the paraphernalia of archaeology; an ability to establish vividly the quality of a certain moment in which he enfolds the observer and causes him to see, to hear, and, above all; to feel. . . . It seems to me that in these works is implicit the essential character of the man, the gauge of truth which confirms victoriously Robert Henri's remark that "A work of art is the trace of a magnificent struggle."[5]

Hurd, *Maine Paintings by N.C. Wyeth* (1939).

Wyeth spent many summers at his studio on the Maine coast, and his letters as well as his paintings attest to his affinity for the coastal region, including such small islands as "Blubber Island." In easel painting, Wyeth found the means to break away from the constraints of illustration and forward his search for greater personal expression. Years before this latest phase of his career, the artist had written to his father:

I realize definitely now the penalty one pays in one's effort to discover one's true identity, that is, what it is that makes one sense and feel things differently than any other mortal ever *did* or ever *will*. It is only when we reveal this individual reaction to life that art becomes creative. . .
    It has become (what I have yearned for for years) an obsession with me now, to uncover *something* of the vast amount of accumulated emotional experience which it has been my keen pleasure and ecstatic anguish to have gathered. . . .
    And so it is that I have felt the necessity of cracking open a new and progressive phase of development. And I am convinced that I am on the trail! Two recent canvases prove to me beyond the shadow of a doubt that I have gained a footing, and that it is only a matter of good health and perserverance to achieve something. . . .[6]

Wyeth, Letter (1927).

Wyeth was still at Chadd's Ford, when his son Andrew and daughter-in-law Betsy went to Port Clyde; he wrote to them of his strong feelings for the sea:

One of my great and blessed relaxations is to concentrate upon any chance detail associated with remote Port Clyde and the sublime sea that bathes its shores—even the imagined sight and sound of a small ordinary wave, glass-clear and jewel-green, gliding over the smoothed surface of a gently shelving ledge, laving its surface as with a magical and luminous lacquer, then finally cresting into the delicate complications of incredible

Blubber Island, Maine, 1940
Oil on gessoed panel, 25 x 39⅝"
Signed lower left: *N.C. WYETH*
Dated on reverse: *1940*
Diploma painting

silver lace. I feel desperate at times to be there with it and with you both, and to feel the air moan in the hollows of my face. . . .[7]

Wyeth, Letter (1940).

that that captivates us! All great painting is something that enriches and enhances life, something that makes it higher, wider, and deeper.[8]

Wyeth, Letter (1944).

Several years later, Wyeth wrote to his son expressing his thoughts about an artist's inspiration and expectations:

The week has been, to me, a singular mixture of ineffable sadness and inspiration—two moods that often happen together. But there is a persistent melancholy which I seem unable to shake off.

To circumvent these feelings I have devoted most of my spare time to reading, especially at night when sleep eludes me.—Thoreau, Goethe, Emerson, Tolstoy—all have struck me, as always, with incisive vitality and freshness. My ruminations have again been vividly stirred.

These great men forever radiate a sharp sense of that profound requirement of the artist, to fully understand that consequences of what he creates are unimportant. "Let the motive for action be in the action itself and not in the event. . . ."

The greats in all the arts have been primarily romanticists and realists (the two cannot be separated). They interpreted life as they saw it, but, "through every line's being" soaked in the consciousness of an object, one is bound to feel, beside life as it is, the life that ought to be, and it is

Notes

1. See Wyeth's letter of February 5, 1942, to the Academy. National Academy of Design Artists Biographical Files.
2. Douglas Allen and Douglas Allen, Jr., *N.C. Wyeth, The Collected Paintings, Illustrations and Murals* (New York: Crown Publishers, 1972), 116.
3. N.C. Wyeth, "The Illustrator and His Development," *The American Art Student* 4 (1917), New York Public Library Clipping File.
4. N.C. Wyeth, *The Wyeths: The Letters of N.C. Wyeth, 1901-1945*, Betsy James Wyeth, ed. (Boston: Gambit, 1971), letter no. 622, October 30, 1939, 798-99.
5. Peter Hurd, introduction (Exhibition catalogue, *In the George Islands, Maine, Paintings by N.C. Wyeth*, Macbeth Galleries, New York, December 5-30, 1939).
6. Wyeth, *The Wyeths*, letter no. 580, March 25, 1927, 733-34.
7. *Ibid.*, letter no. 626, June 10, 1940, 802.
8. *Ibid.*, letter no. 657, February 16, 1944, 833-34.

JR

GEORGE WESLEY BELLOWS

(1882-1925)
ANA 1909; NA 1913

Born Columbus, Ohio, August 19. Entered Ohio State University 1901. Left three years later to study painting with Robert Henri and Kenneth Hayes Miller at New York School of Art. 1906 rented studio at 1947 Broadway. 1910 married; taught at Art Students' League and helped arrange Independent Artists' Exhibition. 1911 spent part of summer with Robert Henri at Monhegan Island, Maine. Following two summers at Monhegan. 1913 exhibited at Armory Show. Continued to spend summers in Maine, visiting Ogunquit in 1915, and Camden in 1916. 1916 began lithography. Summer 1917 to artists' colony, Carmel, California; fall, taught at Art Students' League. 1918 and 1919 spent summers in Middletown, Rhode Island. Fall 1919 taught at Art Institute of Chicago. 1920 rented summer home in Woodstock, New York, where built home and studio in 1922 and spent following two summers. January 8, at age forty-two, died of appendicitis in New York. Memorial exhibition held at Metropolitan Museum of Art 1925.

REFERENCES: Frank Crowinshield, Introduction, *Memorial Exhibition of Works of George Bellows* (Exhibition catalogue, Metropolitan Museum of Art, 1925). Frederick A. Sweet, Carl O. Schniewind, and Eugene Speicher, *George Bellows* (Exhibition catalogue, The Art Institute of Chicago, 1946). Charles Morgan, *George Bellows, Painter of America* (New York: Reynal & Co., 1965). Mahonri Sharp Young, *The Paintings of George Bellows* (New York: Watson-Guptill Publications, 1973). National Academy of Design Artists Biographical Files. National Academy of Design Exhibition Records.

Monhegan Island, an approximately two-mile-square island about ten miles from the nearest mainland and twenty miles from Boothbay Harbor, Maine, is the subject of this striking, broadly painted landscape by George Bellows. It was one of four paintings Bellows completed in the fall of 1911 from more than thirty oil sketches done the previous summer while visiting the island with his fellow artist Robert Henri.[1] Rockwell Kent, who studied with Bellows under Henri's instruction at the New York School of Art, began painting on the island several years earlier.[2] He spoke of its appeal to the artists:

Monhegan: its rock-bound shores, its towering headlands, the thundering surf with gleaming crests and emerald eddies, its forest and its flowering meadowlands; the village, quaint and picturesque; the fish-houses, evoking in their delapidation those sad thoughts on the passage of time and the transitoriness of all things so dear to the artistic soul . . . shall I go on? No, that's enough. It was enough for me, enough for all my fellow artists, for all of us who sought "material" for art. It was enough to start me off to such feverish activity in painting as I had never known.[3]

Kent, *It's Me O Lord* (1955).

Letters from Bellows to his wife document his activity that summer and his own seemingly boundless enthusiasm for the Maine landscape:[4]

This is the most wonderful country ever modelled by the hand of the master architect. . . .
Well, if the trunks come we're [Bellows, Henri, and Davey] hard at it tomorrow, and believe me you'll see some pictures. We've got the best tools in the world, the best place, and the best company that any artist ever had to create masterpieces. . . .
I have my sketch box outfit and I've painted seven little beauts all of which will make beautiful big canvases if I succeed in enlarging the idea in size. The Island is only a mile wide and two miles long, but it looks as large as the Rocky Mountains. It's three times as high as Montauk and all black and gray rock. Beautiful pine forests and wonderful varieties of all kinds. . . .
I painted two more canvases today. It was the most wonderful day we have had, yet it changed so rapidly I did not get a great picture. I really don't know how good they are, but they are fair, I guess. They make 23 pictures. . . .
Everything going fine. Paint rags arrived. . . . I have 24 panels painted, only six more blank ones and have written for some more. The moon has left us but the stars do just as well. Great wonderful clouds in the starlight tonight. My head is full of millions of great pictures which I will never have time to paint.
The island is endless in its wonderful variety. We painted today in what is called Cathedral Forest, and it is a majestic place. Gothic spires everywhere. Tomorrow a storm is predicted. The surf has started tonight and [I] will probably be down on the rocks tomorrow morning.[5]

George Bellows to his wife, summer of 1911.

Bellows' response to nature is reminiscent of nineteenth-century attitudes. As did American landscapists a half century before, he expressed a deep-felt love of nature and an awe, perhaps even reverence, for its infinite variety and constantly changing appearance. He also acknowleged God—"the master architect"—in nature. But he speaks with the boldness and directness of the twentieth century. Contemporary critics responded to his direct, vigorous handling of the subject on canvas with mixed feelings. As Charles L. Buchanan wrote in a 1914 review:

Strength—a great, broad, bulging, muscular strength, a strength with all its imperfections and crudities, its advantages and its disadvantages largely thrown at you in the raw, so to speak, by an apparent sincerity of purpose. There, so I rightly or wrongly take it, you have George Bellows . . .
So far as I grasp his intentions he merely wishes to reproduce what he sees, never bothering his head to discriminate, sympathize with or rearrange, intruding the merest casualty upon you with the drums and tramplings of the epic. He suggests to me the alertness of American journalism turned painter, the reportorial spirit armed with palette and brush. Art is a free country and Bellows riots in the liberties of free speech.

THREE ROLLERS, 1911
Oil on canvas, 39⅝ x 41¾"
Signed lower right: *Bellows*

Here, at least you bid farewell to the still, small voice of beauty, become, instead, a raucous and very vehement slang.[6]

      Buchanan, "George Bellows, Painter of Democracy" (1914).

Though Bellows was perceived as being revolutionary, in some respects he was just continuing a style practiced by Manet in Europe a half century earlier. As Bellows' colleague, Guy Pène du Bois wrote in *Arts and Decoration* in 1914:

. . . Manet painted with big, fat heavily laden brushes the truth as he saw it, the truth about light and air, about form, about line, about nature . . . he did bring back to artists the love of paint, of color, of quality of those painter virtues to which they pay so much heed and to which the layman pays so little. With Hals, Manet shall be remembered as one of the greatest painters in the history of art, as an inventor, the creator of a style, the starting point of a very important trend in painting.

      Du Bois, "French Impressionists and their Place in Art."

As to the charge that he had exchanged "the still, small voice of beauty" for "raucous and vehement slang" Bellows replied:

I am a patriot for beauty. . . . I have been called a revolutionist—if I am, I don't know it. First of all I am a painter, and a painter gets hold of life—gets hold of something real, of many real things. That makes him think, and if he thinks out loud he is called a revolutionist. I guess that is about the size of it.[8]

      Bellows, as quoted in "The Big Idea" (1917).

Almost a decade later, at the time of his sudden death, Bellows' work found favorable review:

When all is said, the genius of George Bellows resides in this: his power to evoke on canvas a world stirring with a mysterious energy. The life that palpitates in the pigment stings us into a startling awareness of itself. It is as though we were observing life with an entirely new set of faculties and participating in some magical process of creation.[9]

      Roberts, "George Bellows—An Appreciation" (1925).

In his depiction of the Maine island isolated against the stormy sky, Bellows shows concerns similar to his nineteenth-century predecessors (see J.F. Cropsey, *Coast Scene*, p. 129) and his twentieth-century successors (see N.C. Wyeth, *Blubber Island*, p. 197). Today his art may be considered in the mainstream of American landscape painting.

NOTES

1. Identification of the subject of this painting and the dating are from Charles Morgan, *George Bellows, Painter of America* (New York: Raynal & Co., 1965), 145-46. According to Morgan, Bellows worked on four canvases, based on his summer sketches at Monhegan, during September and October of 1911: *Three Rollers, Evening Swell, The Sea,* and *The Rich Woods.* (The National Academy of Design had dated the painting c. 1913.) Regarding Henri's invitation to Bellows to join him for the trip to Monhegan, Morgan (133) states that Henri "craved competent, congenial junior companionship, a group sympathetic to his point of view and respectful of his personality. This clannishness . . . was typical of Henri's method of working." Henri's pupil Randall Davey also joined the group.

2. Frederick A. Sweet, Carl O. Schniewind, and Eugene Speicher, *George Bellows* (Exhibition catalogue, The Art Institute of Chicago, 1946), 19. According to Sweet, Kent, who was the same age as Bellows but had begun his training earlier, was the envy of the newer students at the New York School of Art. Bellows was a great admirer of Kent and was influenced by him in his early work. "This was especially apparent," states Sweet, "in Monhegan scenes where identical subject matter is treated in much the same way." For examples of Kent's Monhegan scenes, see Rockwell Kent, *Rockwellkentiana, Few Words and Many Pictures* (New York: Harcourt, Brace, 1933). Unpaginated plates: *Monhegan Coast, Maine* 1909 (Ralph Pulitzer Collection), and *Back Head, Monhegan,* 1910 (George P. Putnam Collection)

3. Rockwell Kent, *It's Me O Lord, The Autobiography of Rockwell Kent* (New York: Dodd, Mead, 1955), 120. Edward Hopper also worked at Monhegan after 1910. See Lloyd Goodrich, *Edward Hopper* (New York: Abrams, 1976), 18.

4. See Morgan, 133. Emma Bellows stayed in New Jersey with her family since she was pregnant with the Bellow's first child. She and her husband wrote to each other almost every day for the four weeks (mid-July to mid-August) that Bellows was away.

5. *Ibid.,* 135-36, 137, 139, 141. Bellows refers to Montauk, Long Island, where he and his wife had gone the previous year. Bellows probably developed a love for the shore as a boy when he spent summers on Long Island with his family.

6. Charles L. Buchanan, "George Bellows, Painter of Democracy," *Arts and Decoration* 4, no. 10 (August 1914), 370-71.

7. Guy Pène du Bois, "The French Impressionists and their Place in Art," *Arts and Decoration* 4, no. 3 (January 1914), 103. Du Bois and Bellows were fellow students at the New York School of Art under Henri's tutelage. Henri encouraged his students to take Manet, as well as Hals, Velazquez, Courbet, and Rembrandt as examples. See Sweet, Schniewind, and Speicher (13) and Barbara Rose, *American Art Since 1900* (New York: Praeger, 1973), 25. Rose states that Henri often took his students to the Metropolitan Museum of Art to study the Manets in the collection.

8. Anonymous, "The Big Idea: George Bellows Talks About Patriotism for Beauty," *Touchstone* 1, no. 3 (July 1917), 269.

9. Anonymous, quote from *The Nation,* in Mary Fanton Roberts, "George Bellows—An Appreciation," *Arts and Decorations* 23, no. 6 (October 1925), 40, 76.

      CC

PAUL RESIKA

(1928-)
ANA 1976; NA 1978

Born August 15, New York City. 1940-1944 private study with Sol Wilson. 1942-1946 attended High School of Music and Art. 1945-1947 studied painting at Hans Hofmann School. 1948 first one-man show at George Dix Gallery, New York. 1950-1953 independent study in Venice; 1954 studied in Rome. 1958 emphasis shifted primarily to landscape painting. Employed as instructor of art, 1965, University of Oregon at Eugene; 1966 at Parsons School of Design; 1966-1976 Cooper Union; 1968-1969 Art Students' League of New York; 1973 and 1976 Skowhegan School of Painting and Sculpture; 1974 and 1979 University of Pennslyvania, Graduate School; 1977 State University of New York at Purchase; 1978-1980 Parsons School of Design, MFA Program. Maintains studio and continues to reside in New York City. Dealer, Graham Gallery.

REFERENCES: Interview with the artist, May 15, 1980. The Artist's File, Graham Gallery, New York. National Academy of Design Artists Biographical Files. Claire Nicolas White, "Resika's Delectable Mountains," Art News 66, no. 2 (April 1967).

Painted in September of 1979 at Horseleech Pond, Wellfleet, Cape Cod, *The End of the Hurricane* represents a theme that has interested Paul Resika for years. The artist and his wife own a summer house on Horseleech Pond, and since the late 1960s Resika has frequently visited Cape Cod to paint.[1] Certain landscape motifs, such as the one in this painting, appear repeatedly in his work:

The sense of place is very strong in all of his pictures. He keeps returning to these places—that stretch of dunes on the Cape, that fallen tree in the Ramapos—painting them over and over, . . . The painter returns to them year after year, spring and autumn, to capture their mystery and meaning. Color and light play on them, change with the seasons . . . enter into and expand their meaning, giving a history to the place.[2]

Campbell, *Art/World* (1979).

Of *The End of the Hurricane* and an earlier painting of Horseleech Pond Resika says: "The newer painting has more atmosphere, it's bolder; I painted the scene a hundred times in between."

The End of the Hurricane was completed rapidly: "I painted it as if in a trance, so quickly you can't think . . . it took less than a few hours." Other paintings by Resika have taken years, however; years during which the artist set the painting aside, returned to the location, and made changes and additions at the site and in his studio.

Resika has always lived in New York City, but, as Mimi Shorr writes:

. . . he has no interest in painting the city. "It's dead, it's flat," he says. "It doesn't have the vibration of nature, of life. It isn't resonant." For the same reason he only paints in oil, never in acrylics. He wants the depth, texture, interaction with light—"vibrancy"—that he finds only in *natural* substances. In his New York studio he works on paintings begun in other places, . . . In New Jersey, about an hour away from the city, he has a shack [on the Ramapo River] where he also goes to paint. It's in the woods where no people or houses can be seen. He paints either outdoors or in the natural light of his studio and wishes that his paintings would be seen in such light.[3]

American Artist (1972).

Resika's love for nature is obvious in his work, although he is primarily concerned with painting. In the article, "Must an Artist Know Landscape in Order to Paint It?", he wrote:

The main beneficiaries of the fashion of outdoor painting—and I think it is a fashion—are the manufacturers of French landscape easels [sic]. I'm all for the love of fields and streams, but it is painting—composition, form, color, drawing, painting quality—that I am concerned with. . . . For myself, I don't go to nature to express its inner forces—whatever they may be—but to avoid regularity, poverty of form. In short, to be inspired. . . . Ryder, Rubens, and Ruisdael, all of whom were every bit as conscious of elemental forces [as Cézanne], never painted outdoors at all. The point is that all these painters were making images that pleased them, or as people used to say, that "expressed" them. That is what is important.[4]

Resika in *American Artist* (1976).

Like the Hudson River School painters of the last century, Resika maintains a New York studio while traveling to neighboring states to paint outdoor scenery. It seems that many of his landscapes are completed "on location," except for finishing touches which are added later in the studio.[5] He feels that "The landscape artist can work in a studio, from memory, from other art as well as outdoors in nature."[6]

The End of the Hurricane, with its wide, sweeping brushwork, brings to mind *The Three Rollers* by George Bellows (see p. 199). Resika agrees with this comparison, adding, "I love the painting of Bellows—the butteriness of it." It is precisely in his handling of paint, along with color and light, that Resika excels. Called a "painter's painter,"[7] he follows the tradition established in America by William Merritt Chase and continued by Bellows:

The term "painter's painting" was invented to designate a kind of art so rich in the elements of technical virtuosity as to make an especially strong appeal to a member of the craft. It was Chase's distinction to practice "painter's painting," to inculcate it in the American school, and to rouse an interest in it outside the studios.[8]

Cortissoz, *Paintings by William Merritt Chase* (1927).

THE END OF THE HURRICANE, 1979
Oil on canvas, 23¾ x 29″
Signed lower right: *Resika*

The influence of Hans Hofmann, with whom Resika studied, is also evident in his handling of paint:

Resika has developed a highly refined, consciously pondered, and at times nearly ritualized vocabulary of marks, some of which are simply marks, others of which are also shapes, and they are assembled in different combinations in each picture. If this sounds quite regular and deliberate, it is, but there also are many subtle variations within each category of mark; the marks are not put down mechanically, but with much emphatic, robust, even exuberant flourishing of brush and knife. . [9]

Turner, *Arts Magazine* (1979).

The pictures, which were almost all landscapes, displayed some of the most disarmingly voluptuous paint handling I've seen in a realist painter's work in a while; the whole repertory has been called into play, from palette-knife passages and loaded brushstrokes to scribbles and scratches with the wooden end of the brush.[10]

Perl, *Art in America* (1976).

He is obviously in love with paint and painting and extravagant in his expenditure of painterly ideas.[11]

Mainardi, *Art News* (1975).

Gulley Jimson, the fictitious artist created by Joyce Cary, expressed it well:

"But what I do like," I said, "is starting new [paintings]." And the very notion made me feel full of smiles. The vision of the nice smooth canvas in front of me, . . . newly primed in white, and then the first strokes of the brush. How lovely the stuff is when you've just put it down. While it's still all alive and before it dies and sinks and fades. Paint. Lovely paint. Why, I could rub my nose in it or lick it up for breakfast.[12]

The Horse's Mouth (1944).

Resika, who is, himself, deeply involved with the craft of painting, says: "I don't do it to communicate something to you; I do it to make the thing. . . . Whereas painting is a craft, it's also an art. That's the glory of it—it has all the elements."

Although he says it is not in the nature of an artist to teach, Resika is quite knowledgeable in the history of art, claiming that "all artists know art history." Like artists of the nineteenth century, he believes in the instructional value of "nature and classical art." Among his favorites are Renoir, Cézanne, Degas, Delacroix, Titian, and Watteau. The American artists he most admires are Albert Pinkham Ryder, Ralph Albert Blakelock, and Robert Loftin Newman. His similarity with them seems primarily one of loose, painterly technique and expressive power. His paintings seldom express the sense of mysticism for which these other artists are known, although some of Resika's—including *The End of the Hurricane*—do evoke strong moods and associations.

Again, there are similarities with the work of Bellows, as described by Charles Morgan: "At times [Bellows] seemed almost to model in paint the contours of the ocean and of the rocks repelling it. The forms sometimes became so broad as almost to shed their immediate identities and stand as symbols . . ."[13] Mimi Shorr has described Resika's work in similar terms:

The paintings, moody and haunting, hover between offering a momentary glimpse of a scene and making a statement beyond temporal change. For despite the fact that Resika is concerned with specifics—the shadows cast at a certain time of day, the way one body of water looks as opposed to another—it is the *essence* of cloud he wants to convey, a truth more fundamental than merely reproducing a given cloud could express.[14]

American Artist (1972).

The simple forms, thick pigment, and loose brushwork of *The End of the Hurricane* also recall the work of Ryder (see *Marine* p. 151), who said:

In my desire to be accurate I became lost in a maze of detail. Try as I would, my colors were not those of nature. The old scene presented itself one day before my eyes framed in an opening between two trees. It stood out like a painted canvas—the deep blue of a midday sky—a solitary tree, brilliant with the green of early summer, a foundation of brown earth and gnarled roots. There was no detail to vex the eye. Three solid masses of form and color—sky, foliage and earth—the whole bathed in an atmosphere of golden luminosity. I threw my brushes aside; they were too small for the work in hand. I squeezed out big chunks of pure, moist color and taking my palette knife, I laid on blue, green, white and brown in great sweeping strokes.[15]

Broadway Magazine (1905).

And Robert Loftin Newman, another nineteenth-century visionary, concurred; "Beauty of outline, beauty of masses as beauty of color, require an incessant sacrifice of detail."[16]

A final similarity Resika shares with Ryder is the desire to create something new and original. At the beginning of the twentieth century, Ryder stated that he "saw nature springing into life upon [his] dead canvas. It was better than nature, for it was vibrating with the thrill of a new creation."[17] Like such works by Ryder,

Resika's paintings are . . . *of* nature, but they are *about* the transformation of a "natural" scene into the man-made reality of art. In that sense, as he says, all painting is abstract: "Yes, you use nature, but you make it yourself, make it over."[18]

Shorr, *American Artist* (1972).

To repeat Resika's words, "It's all in the spiritualization—not the copying—of nature."

NOTES

1. Interview with Paul Resika, May 15, 1980. Unless otherwise indicated, all statements attributed to the artist were made at this time or during subsequent conversations with the author.
2. Ronald J.B. Campbell, "A Strong Sense Of Space," *Art/World* (March/April 1979), 1, 14.
3. Mimi Shorr, "Paul Resika: Passions in Balance," *American Artist* 36, no. 365 (December 1972), 27.
4. Paul Resika, "Must an Artist Know Landscape in Order to Paint It?" *American Artist* 40, no. 410 (September 1976), 13.
5. Norman Turner, "Paul Resika," *Arts Magazine* 53, no. 9 (May 1979), 20.
6. Resika, "Must an Artist Know Landscape," 13.
7. Alan Gussow, *A Sense of Place, The Artist and the American Land* (San Francisco: The McCall Publishing Co., 1972), 46.
8. Royal Cortissoz, *Paintings by William Merritt Chase, N.A., LL.D.* (Exhibition catalogue, Newhouse Galleries, St. Louis, 1927), unpaginated.
9. Turner, "Paul Resika," 20.
10. Jed Perl, "Paul Resika at Graham," *Art in America* 64, no. 4 (July/August 1976), 106.
11. Patricia Mainardi, "Paul Resika," *Art News* 74, no. 6 (Summer 1975), 149.
12. Joyce Cary, *The Horse's Mouth* (1944; reprint New York: Harper and Row, 1958), 192.
13. Charles H. Morgan, *George Bellows, Painter of America* (New York: Reynal, 1965), 171.
14. Shorr, "Paul Resika," 24.
15. Albert Pinkham Ryder, "Paragraphs from the Studio of a Recluse," *Broadway Magazine* 14 (September 1905). In John W. McCoubrey, *American Art 1700-1900, Sources and Documents* (Englewood Cliffs, N.J.: Prentice-Hall, 1965), 187-88.
16. Robert Loftin Newman, 1867. In Marchal E. Landgren, *Robert Loftin Newman, 1827-1912* (Exhibition catalogue, National Collection of Fine Arts, Washington, D.C., Oct. 26, 1973-Jan. 6, 1974), 22.
17. Ryder, "Paragraphs from the Studio of a Recluse," In McCoubrey, *American Art*, 188.
18. Shorr, "Paul Resika," 24.

KN

ANNE POOR

(1918-   )
ANA 1972; NA 1975

Born January 2, New York City. Studied at Art Students' League, with Alexander Brook, William Zorach, and Yasuo Kuniyoshi. Bennington College 1935-1938. 1937 in Paris at Académie Julian, ateliers of Jean Lurçat and Abraham Rattner, and École Fernand Léger. Assisted father, Henry Varnum Poor, with murals in true fresco for Justice and Interior departments, Washington, D.C., c. 1935-1938. Mural commissions from Public Works Administration for post offices in Gleason, Tenn., and Depew, N.Y., 1937. In Women's Army Corps 1943. Artist-correspondent for Air Force through 1945. One year in Pacific theater of Operations. Exhibited illustrations and paintings of war years. Member of permanent faculty and a director of Skowhegan School of Painting and Sculpture, Maine, 1947-1961. Murals and frescos at Skowhegan School, 1948 and 1954 and also at Wellfleet, Mass., 1951-52; at South Solon Free Meeting House, Maine, 1957; and for Mr. & Mrs. Robert Graham, Stamford, Conn., 1958. Taught course in fresco, Skowhegan School, 1978. To Europe several times from 1937 on; Japan and China 1943-45; Soviet Union 1965; West Indies 1979. Currently resides in New City, N.Y. Dealer Graham Gallery.

REFERENCES: National Academy of Design Artists Biographical Files. *Who's Who in American Art* (New York: R.R. Bowker, 1978).

*D*erricks on the Horizon, Haverstraw was probably painted during the winter of 1974, near Anne Poor's home just west of the Hudson River. Poor includes elements of the industrial plants lining the river banks: derricks and factory buildings surface out of an atmosphere primarily of whites and grays. Exhibitions of the artist's work from the 1970s were held at the Graham Gallery in New York and at the Rockland Center for the Arts in Nyack, New York, in 1980. Included were oils and pastels of the Haverstraw region.[1]

At the Skowhegan School in Maine, Anne Poor produced paintings of the northern landscape. A review of her show at the Graham Gallery in 1971, referring to "small-town landscapes," also serves to comment on the essentials of her paintings done near Haverstraw:

Anne Poor is an artist who has a winsome way with nature. She possesses an understanding and feeling for her subject matter and a fluid, stenographic touch to interpret it. Her small-town landscapes are more intimation than explicit fact. Although they show a countryside of mood and atmosphere in the full presence of winter, they glow with a warm lyricism. Miss Poor's landscapes lack human figures but they certainly don't lack humanity. . . .[2]

Shirey, *New York Times*.

Poor collaborated with writer Henry Miller in creating *Greece*, a book of her drawings published in 1964. The artist's drawings of the landscape made Miller feel as if he were reliving his own trip to Greece; and more specifically:

The very size of them is in itself a delight: through it the artist has succeeded in re-creating the never to be forgotten impression which every visitor is sure to retain—of immensity in littleness. . . .

I come back to the drawings again and again, to marvel over their simplicity and exactitude. What intrigues one is their suggestive quality. What has been left out—with purpose, to be sure—remains like some mysterious X quantity, or effluvium rather. Ambiance is all. One does not have to be an archaeologist to mentally reconstruct the beauty and the splendor of a bygone time. . . .[3]

Miller, *Greece* (1964).

In a recent telephone interview (April 1980) Anne Poor responded to general questions from which the following commentary has been composed:

The area around Haverstraw is very close to me. I've lived near the river all my life. It's always magic to go down there, by the river, particularly during the winter or the fall, when the Hudson is buried in snow. At Haverstraw there is something special in the light and the way it lies out in the middle of the river. . . .

I'm not really interested in realistic particulars of a scene, I'm trying to do something more . . . not just rely on objects. I'm trying to get at a sense of big spaces and the larger whole. I prefer working on a large scale. . . . I like to work on a painting until the subject has been annihilated, until only the substantial parts are left. I don't want to be too dependent on the actual objects in it. . . .

Derricks on the Horizon, that was probably done in the dead of winter, probably 1974, if it was in the annual exhibition of 1975. The flat river land down there at Haverstraw, that was where bricks were made, now it's a huge gravel pit . . . they put the gravel up in piles and it's moved back and forth. It's spectacular in winter when the gravel forms dark shapes with tops of snow. The dun gray of the gravel pit is really something. The derricks are poised down there in space. There's one in particular with a castle of red and green that fascinates me. . . .

*N*OTES
1. Exhibition catalogues from 1971, 1979, press releases, courtesy Graham Gallery, New York. I wish to thank the Graham Gallery for information about the recent show of Poor's work at the Rockland Center for the Arts in Nyack.
2. David L. Shirey, review of Poor's 1971 exhibition at Graham Gallery, *The New York Times*, Nov. 20, 1971. Xerox clipping courtesy Graham Gallery.
3. Henry Miller, *Greece* (New York: Viking Press, 1964), 8-10.

JR

DERRICKS ON THE HORIZON, HAVERSTRAW, c. 1974
Oil on canvas, 30 x 45″
Signed lower left: *Anne Poor*
Diploma painting

JANE WILSON

(1924-   )
ANA 1975; NA 1979

Born April 29, Seymour, Iowa. Phi Beta Kappa at University of Iowa. Received B.A. in 1945 and M.A. in painting 1947. Taught art history at University of Iowa, including Renaissance, ancient, and Oriental art. To New York City in 1949. Experimented briefly with abstract painting. By mid-1950s was painting landscapes from memory. 1952-1957 associated with Hansa Gallery; 1958-1959 with Stutman Gallery; then until 1966 with Tibor de Nagy Gallery, all in New York. 1965 turned to cityscape. Series of trips to Europe beginning in Summer 1965. 1967-1969 taught art history at Pratt Institute. Began painting still life about 1969. Taught painting privately. Represented by Graham Gallery 1968-1977. Beginning in 1973 taught studio art at Parsons School of Design. A year later returned to teach for semester at University of Iowa. After 1975 affiliated also with Columbia University School of the Arts. Latest work: drawings and figure studies in pastel and conte crayon. Currently represented by Fischbach Gallery, N.Y.

REFERENCE: Interviews with the artist, spring 1980.

*V*illa and Vineyards was painted in August 1967, in Porto Ercole, Italy, "the place where Caravaggio died," says the artist, "and I could never get it out of my mind."[1] Although Wilson had arrived in Porto Ercole in July,

it wasn't until mid-August that I began to paint [that] landscape. I was up on the roof, in the incredible Italian heat, and I was painting what was there. It was all very different in that light.

She recalls the "mesmerizing, 4 o'clock light," the mountains and water, and the winding road.

It was all I could ever want in life. . . When I was young I sort of had a fantasy of going there and painting, and it completed the fantasy.

After her student years in Iowa, Wilson moved to New York in August 1949:

[I] arrived in the full throb of Abstract Expressionism, a terrific time to have arrived. There were very important women working, and working in so many different ways. When I came to New York I was hit between the eyes by what was really going on here. I kept painting as I had been painting—and then came to a halt. I tried painting expressionistically, abstractly. . . . I was trying to find out where I was in that movement. I didn't want to be a Second Generation anything. I felt the only chance I had to do anything was to take a chance on something of my own.

After about five years, Wilson found herself painting landscapes, not of specific sites, but out of her head, from memory.

Her interest in landscape was more an unconscious response to remembered experience than a deliberate decision to paint landscapes. She would recall in her mind a place or event and "what would come out would be a landscape. It wasn't like I said I'm going to sit down and paint a landscape." She also painted still lifes during this period. "Also made up. They came out of my head and were about objects that were lost or broken. After they had disappeared, they became images in my mind." In both the still life and landscape painting, "there was something about that departure . . ." that triggered an image and produced those paintings:

At first I thought I was influenced by French Impressionists or Dutch landscapists and was painting light and air I hadn't seen. But a conversation with a painter from Minnesota [Jon Schuller] who had similar feelings to mine about a vast sky with a low band of clouds on the horizon changed my mind. He told me that at one point in his life he felt he had to find that particular landscape and live in it. So he spent a whole year searching for it in Scotland, where he was sure it was, only to find it back in Minnesota. The same thing happened to me. I went to the Midwest, and there was that particular sky I was looking for, trying to get into my paintings.[2]

Of the experience of growing up in that setting, she has remarked, "Nobody painted landscape in Iowa. You went out in it."

The landscape was enormously meaningful to me. I used to roam around a lot by myself as a child, and when I think of a landscape, I think of the great weight of the sky and how it rests on the earth. And I remember the light. Light is specific to certain places, and what sort of light and landscape formation you grow up with is immensely influential to what you do later on.[3]

American Artist.

Wilson would begin these "remembered landscapes" by setting up the horizon division and the sky, "and then I could find out what the earth would be in relation to it."

By 1965, there began a shift from open, outdoor landscapes to painting cityscapes. She explains:

I changed because outdoorsness seemed to have run out for me. I found ways to question whether the world is blue and green . . . I had the distinct sensation of going from an open plane which extends beyond but needs to be dealt with by the picture plane [to a point where] landscape became this city. The park [Tompkins Square on the Lower East side of Manhattan, where Wilson was then living] and the city became like a landscape inset. It took me all that time, since 1949, to react to the city. It had been like a toy city to me. The idea of cityscape made me begin the fluid brushstroke. It might not be the best way of coping with the city. The city was not atmospheric space. The park was like an atmospheric quote in the middle of the city.

VILLA AND VINEYARDS, 1967
Oil on canvas, 16 x 20″
Signed lower left: *Jane Wilson*
Dated on reverse of stretcher: *1967*
Diploma painting

Initially, Wilson thought of the city as "like a box open from the top, extending from me to the horizon. I thought of the city in purely vertical terms, [and as] symmetrical, but it wasn't. The sidewalks and buildings weren't horizontal and vertical."

The recognition of the asymmetrical character of the city was an important one for Wilson and challenged her sense of landscape as geometric and symmetrical. As this realization evolved, she recalls, "everything had to be overhauled completely." Her feelings for landscape as a horizontal, weighty band of sky and air and light, and for the city as a vertical entity, were fundamentally altered by a trip to Europe in 1965, with subsequent return visits over the next few years. Wilson recalls being struck on her first trip to Europe by the buildings leaning back from the canals in Venice and over the canals in Amsterdam. "It gradually occurred to me that nothing is really vertical or horizontal, including things in New York: the streets arch, the buildings are set back."[4] *Villa and Vineyards*, painted two years after this initial recognition, incorporates that asymmetrical vision in describing a specific place and time of day.

It's almost as if there were kinds of modes of landscapes—blond landscapes, hazy landscapes—bleached out by light, deep, round landscapes, and windy landscapes.

The European trip affected her work in other ways. "It had a lot of effect on my color. It got me to work in a half-conscious way, spots and shapes..." Her brushstroke, too, was altered by the dictates of the landscape. "I thought of brushstroke as if I were writing the signature of the tree or the mountains. That was the way of responding."

By about 1969 Wilson had begun turning increasingly to painting still life, as an extension of her concerns in landscape painting. "I thought of still life as landscape," she says, and there is a lot that is similar in her still lifes of this period—often intricately arranged, richly textured asymmetrical juxtapositions of forms and volumes, with strong colors and tactile brushwork.

Although Wilson has a strong background in art history, she has not particularly drawn on that knowledge in her painting. She was not, for instance, conscious of the work of earlier American landscapists when she began her investigations of landscape. She does recall being "totally immersed in European painting," and says: "We were absolutely blind to American painting except for Abstract Expressionism. When I began to get involved with still life, I became very interested in American still life." She mentions especially late eighteenth-century still life artists, as well as Severin Roesen and John F. Peto, of whom she says, "He's top banana for me."

Not American landscape. I didn't go look at their landscapes. I liked Inness, not passionately, but I liked him. I liked Whistler. There is always an embarrassment about glimpsing the Americanness in yourself. You couldn't recognize it in painting and in people and could never identify its character in yourself. Except that everything you did was marked by it.

Wilson's feelings about being an American became clear, paradoxically, only after her travels in Europe:

What Europe does is make me feel intensely American. Traveling alone, putting yourself in a situation where people react to your alienness. I don't know why it's so important to keep coercing that experience, but I'm sure that I go because of a need to have this rawly defined . . . it's an awkward experience. It may be important in my case. I was third-generation, but a great deal was made of that. The German side, the French side, the Scotch-Irish . . . a kind of admiration for European culture. The reading that you do growing up, the music you play, the plays you see, are European. I married a European. Everything you see, except the movies, comes out of that European heritage. It's very persuasive. The big paintings are there. As the whole world knows, it's very persuasive painting. But the basic message is "work out of your own life." [Going to Europe] makes the problem somehow clearer. [The experience] takes you with it, but it puts you right back to being American.

NOTES

1. Unless otherwise specified, all quotations from Wilson are from conversations with the artist, spring, 1980.
2. Diane Cochrane, "Jane Wilson: Remembrances of Images Past and Present," *American Artist* 38 (December 1974), 26.
3. *Ibid.*, 26.
4. *Ibid.*, 29.
5. An example of Wilson's still life painting *Hammer and Tongs* (1975) is in the collection of the National Academy of Design.

CB

WOLF KAHN

(1927—   )
ANA 1979; NA 1980

Born October 4, Stuttgart, Germany. As a child, studied drawing and painting in Frankfurt. Moved to Cambridge, England, 1939. 1940 to the United States and settled in New York. Enrolled in New York High School of Music and Art. Graduated 1945. Studied briefly with Stuart Davis at New School for Social Research. 1947-1949 attended Hans Hofmann School. Served as class monitor. B.A. University of Chicago 1950. Returned to New York. With other artists, organized the cooperative Hansa Gallery 1951-1952. First one-man show there 1953. Traveled to Mexico 1955; Venice 1957 and 1958. Numerous awards, including a Fulbright Grant, 1963-1964, which enabled him to paint in Milan and Rome, and a Guggenheim Fellowship, 1966-1967. Spends summers in New England, most often on his farm in Vermont. 1960-1961 visiting associate professor of painting, University of California, Berkeley. Served as adjunct associate professor of painting, Cooper Union Art School, 1960-1977. Since then has taught on graduate level at Columbia University, Rhode Island School of Design, Queens College, and Hunter College. 1980 traveling exhibition organized by the Arts Club of Chicago. Has exhibited frequently in the United States and Europe. Currently represented by the Borgenicht Gallery.

REFERENCES: National Academy of Design Artists Biographical Files. Thomas B. Hess, "U.S. Painting: Some Recent Directions," *Art News Annual* 25 (1956). *Wolf Kahn* (Exhibition catalogue, Grace Borgenicht Gallery, N.Y., 1979).

While retaining an active appreciation for artists of the past—George Inness, Albert P. Ryder, and Ralph A. Blakelock are some of his favorites—Wolf Kahn bases his art on thoroughly twentieth-century precepts. The American landscapist's pantheistic approach to nature faded with the waning of the nineteenth century. Today, in Kahn's paintings, though something of this attitude lingers, the artist begins with a concern for formal problems. He claims not to have any "overt feelings about nature"; it is a pretext for painting.[1] Qualities of light, tonal relationships, structure, and flow of color are the issues about which he wishes to make a visual statement. Because of the changes in light and color effects caused by atmospheric conditions, "Some of my favorite days are when there's an inversion. I live for the visual." As for feeling in modern art, he quotes Seurat's saying: "There is no poetry in painting; I just follow my system."

Often the scene that Kahn paints does not rely directly on nature. Many paintings are begun outdoors—usually in the vicinity of his Vermont farm—and are finished in his New York studio where there are not the "distractions of nature." Some works, like *Pond in November*, are not of a particular place at all, but are "synthetic paintings" that bring together images Kahn has painted numerous times.

Pond in November is one of Kahn's favorite paintings: "What I like especially about it is its color, its austerity. It has very strong tonal and chromatic contrasts that I don't usually indulge in." An interest in color, and in light, plays a central role in his work:

Landscape painting has been the preferred vehicle for the representation of radiance, beginning with the Venetians and evolving through Lorrain, Hobbema, Turner, the American Luminists, Whistler, Ryder, Van Goch, [sic] Morandi. We easily associate radiance with events in the outdoors: a late winter afternoon, certain hazy days when the sun barely breaks through, dawn, dusk. This radiance may assume quasi-mystical qualities and become a living symbol for transcendence. Aldous Huxley in a famous essay ascribes the value we assign to the cut diamond to its rarity rather than to its emanation of an inner light, which to him was the nearest physical analogue to that light which resides at the centre of things, the divine light. My own mystical leanings are relatively undeveloped yet I often ask myself why certain kinds of light have such a satisfying, fulfilling quality—even when reflected on the sides of factories and oil tanks.[2]

In Borgenicht Gallery exhibition catalogue (1979).

When he painted *Pond in November*: "If I thought about anything, I thought about Rothko." There is significance to this, relating to the kind of presence he creates. He once told an interviewer of an experience he had when painting on a foggy day:

As I got up, I saw the silhouette of a town hall looming up in front of me, filling nearly my whole field of vision. I found the confrontation exciting and sat down again to make a pastel, using what for me was a whole new scale. In the process of working, I thought of a large, black sculpture by the minimalist Ronald Bladen I had recently seen. His work seemed much like that ungainly wooden building with its mansard roof that I was trying to put down on paper. Since then I've been on the lookout for similar moments of confrontation with barns, large boulders standing by themselves in the woods—anything that could be seen as a large volume in a simple surrounding. And once I found it, my drive is to express the kind of space which will explain its importance.[3]

American Artist (1974).

With *Pond in November*, the "confrontation" is with a wall of trees. Although the painting is not large, the simplified masses of the landscape take on a monumentality reminiscent of Rothko's simple blocks of color. Kahn says: "One of the reasons I like *Pond in November* is because it is not a very particular painting: it has

POND IN NOVEMBER, 1975-1978
Oil on canvas, 29 x 36″
Signed lower right: *W Kahn*

———————————

a certain generality." The generality he achieves is of the same sort as that found in minimalist works which communicate a fundamental sense of "thereness," of being. By dwelling on the stark, the simple, he aims for an eternal quality inherent in the forms:

To me the interest is the struggle to make the thing become a scheme rather than an illustration. Sometimes I don't know what the image will be until the end. I want spontaneity to dictate what happens.

Because he is not "deliberate" in his method, Kahn feels that a degree of "desperation" is conveyed through his painterly stroke: "Mistakes build up the surface." Yet this expressionism never becomes an end in itself. Kahn's sense of balance between the formal and the expressionistic reminds one that he was a student of Hofmann's. Hofmann stressed standards of formal quality. He gave his students "something to shoot for"; one could "go from one level to another." Expression was not discouraged, per se, but Hofmann warned against becoming too expressionistic or falling into the decorative. This caution is reflected in Kahn's belief that in contemporary society the artist is sometimes raised to too much importance. Self-revelation in itself is of no value. When a painter approaches the canvas he ought to "be neutral"—he should not impose himself. The artist, says Kahn, must try to become coherent about his experience. He should take the public by the hand and lead them through the chaos. Most important is the necessity to undertake a painting without preconceptions of what the final product should look like or what sentiment it should communicate: "Innocence: it's the key word." Feelings will creep into a work without the artist intending it to happen.

Despite his focus on formal matters, Kahn admits that in landscape painting, "What everyone is trying to do is to create a new picturesque. There are new feelings." He cites, for example, a landscape that he painted in 1978-1979 entitled *Unimproved Land*:

I like to approach landscape painting as though I were making a portrait. In portraiture the main preoccupation is to achieve a resemblance. This cannot be done without considering the overall colouration of the face, its texture, the scale of the features in relation to the size of the head. The greatest challenge for the portraitist is in trying to infuse an undistinguished physiognomy with uniqueness and personality.

The small corner of Vermont land I chose to paint here was neither picturesque nor special in any way. The foreground was criss-crossed with bulldozer tracks, the trees were stunted and broken and the pond, once the home of the beaver, was filled with the effluent from a nearby building site.

Yet when I found this spot I immediately knew that I wanted to paint there. Perhaps I liked the colouration of the fall vegetation against the hazy background ridge, a colour so much like the sediment of a rich Burgundy wine. Perhaps I simply liked the overall texture of the spot, a scheme in which even the bulldozer tracks gained importance, even charm.[4]

Borgenicht Gallery exhibition catalogue (1979).

The bulldozer tracks caused a feeling of forlornness—and transition—as if some one might give the place some thought one day. Similarly, in *Pond in November*, a view that would normally be overlooked, takes on significance. Unlike *Unimproved Land*, *Pond in November* does not depict a specific site, yet its generalities possess a sense of character as well as of presence. Somehow it is a scene everyone knows. Its damp chill envelopes the viewer in an intimate atmosphere of memory. Ultimately, underlying all of Wolf Kahn's landscapes: "The feeling is one of affection."

NOTES
1. In conversation with Wolf Kahn, April 15, 1980, New York City. Unless otherwise noted, all quotations by Kahn are from this interview.
2. *Wolf Kahn* (Exhibition catalogue, Grace Borgenicht Gallery, N.Y., 1979), unpaginated.
3. Diane Cochrane, "Wolf Kahn: Updating Landscape Painting," *American Artist*, 39 (Nov. 1974), 63.
4. Borgenicht Gallery Exhibition catalogue.

HR

INDEX